THE EVOLUTION OF A RURAL
FREE BLACK COMMUNITY

CARTER G. WOODSON INSTITUTE SERIES
Deborah E. McDowell, Shawn Leigh Alexander, and Robert T. Vinson, Editors

The Evolution of a Rural Free Black Community

Goochland County, Virginia, 1728–1832

REGINALD D. BUTLER

Edited by Peter S. Onuf

UNIVERSITY OF VIRGINIA PRESS

Charlottesville and London

Published in association with the University of Virginia's Carter G. Woodson Institute

The University of Virginia Press is situated on the traditional lands of the Monacan Nation, and the Commonwealth of Virginia was and is home to many other Indigenous people. We pay our respect to all of them, past and present. We also honor the enslaved African and African American people who built the University of Virginia, and we recognize their descendants. We commit to fostering voices from these communities through our publications and to deepening our collective understanding of their histories and contributions.

University of Virginia Press
© 2025 by the Rector and Visitors of the University of Virginia
All rights reserved
Printed in the United States of America on acid-free paper

First published 2025

9 8 7 6 5 4 3 2 1

LIBRARY OF CONGRESS CATALOGING-IN-PUBLICATION DATA
Names: Butler, Reginald D., author | Onuf, Peter S. editor
Title: The evolution of a rural free Black community : Goochland County, Virginia, 1728–1832 / Reginald D. Butler ; edited by Peter S. Onuf.
Other titles: Carter G. Woodson Institute series
Description: Charlottesville : University of Virginia Press : published in association with the University of Virginia's Carter G. Woodson Institute, 2025. | Series: Carter G. Woodson Institute series | Includes bibliographical references and index.
Identifiers: LCCN 2025005667 (print) | LCCN 2025005668 (ebook) | ISBN 9780813952598 hardback alkaline paper | ISBN 9780813952604 paperback alkaline paper | ISBN 9780813952611 ebook
Subjects: LCSH: Free African Americans—Virginia—Goochland County—History—18th century | Free African Americans—Virginia—Goochland County—History—19th century | Free African Americans—Virginia—Goochland County—Social conditions | Goochland County (Va.)—Race relations—History | BISAC: HISTORY / African American & Black | HISTORY / United States / State & Local / South (AL, AR, FL, GA, KY, LA, MS, NC, SC, TN, VA, WV)
Classification: LCC F232.G65 B87 2025 (print) | LCC F232.G65 (ebook) | DDC 305.896/075545509033—dc23/eng/20250326
LC record available at https://lccn.loc.gov/2025005667
LC ebook record available at https://lccn.loc.gov/2025005668

Cover art: Gooch Land County, John Wood, 1820. (Library of Virginia)
Cover design: Kelley Galbreath

· CONTENTS ·

Editor's Preface   vii
    Peter S. Onuf
Preface   xi
    Gertrude J. Fraser
Introduction: Race, Status, the Local, and the Personal   xv
    Joshua D. Rothman

Prologue   1

Introduction   9

1. Born into Freedom   27

2. Manumission and Planter Response   43

3. Securing Freedom   71

4. Youth and Bound Labor   90

5. Work and Freedom   105

6. Kin, Neighbors, and Community Consolidation   123

Courthouse Custom as an Archival Filter: Comparing Goochland
    Sources with Other Central Virginia Counties   147
    Robert Vernon

A "Forceful and Effective" Leader: Reginald D. Butler's Intellectual
    Legacy as Director of the Carter G. Woodson Institute, 1996–2005   189
    Scot A. French

Recollections 217
Shomer Zwelling and Kathleen Halley

Notes 223
Index 273

· EDITOR'S PREFACE ·
PETER S. ONUF

Reginald D. Butler (1944–2019) never published his pathbreaking and oft-cited doctoral dissertation, "Evolution of a Rural Free Black Community: Goochland County, Virginia, 1728–1832" (Johns Hopkins University, 1989). The present volume incorporates limited revisions Butler undertook as a research fellow at the Smithsonian Institution and in his first years at the University of Virginia, where he began a distinguished teaching career in 1991 and served as director of the Carter G. Woodson Institute for African-American and African Studies from 1996 until his retirement in 2005. Butler's colleagues and friends agree that his pioneering research and interpretation of the free Black experience in rural Virginia are of enduring value and warrant publication.

Butler's great achievement is to show how free Black Americans struggled to secure their vital interests and those of their families on the margins and in the interstices of a world dominated by white people. Keenly aware of the harsh realities of racial hierarchy, Butler never exaggerates the agency of the individual free Black Virginians he studies or romanticizes the autonomy of the community they forged. But he is remarkably successful in illuminating the lived experiences and restoring the humanity of his subjects. His success as a researcher mirrors the experiences of his subjects. Working with widely dispersed, poorly organized, inaccessible, and incomplete sources mostly generated by white elites, Butler's hard-won insights have been—and will be—a model and inspiration to social historians, genealogists, and general readers.

Joshua D. Rothman's introductory historiographical essay in this volume assesses the state of the field when Butler first visited the Goochland County Courthouse and shows how scholarship has subsequently evolved. When

Butler embarked on his pathbreaking project in the 1980s there was a rich and growing literature on the history of enslaved people in the antebellum South but relatively little on free Black Americans, particularly in the formative late colonial and early national decades. There were likewise few viable models for community-level social history in Virginia, and none centered on the lives of freed people. The young researcher thus faced daunting conceptual and methodological challenges as he defined the parameters of his study and assembled a wide array of often elusive documentary sources that could answer the questions he posed. Butler asked illuminating, generative questions that enable his readers to see something—the connections within and among free Black families that constituted a "community"—that previously had been invisible. Every monograph is, as Rothman's essay shows, a product of its own time, subject to revision and therefore incomplete. Butler's monograph is of course no exception. Yet the way he conceived his project remains compelling. We hope its belated publication will inspire future historians to take up his questions and follow his lead.

Robert Vernon's comprehensive essay on accessible sources in the digital age celebrates Butler's extraordinary achievement as a researcher but also emphasizes the limitations of the evidence he had to work with. By showing where new evidence might take us now, Vernon pays tribute to Butler, his friend, collaborator, and unofficial mentor. Vernon rightly emphasizes the provisional, ongoing, open-ended, and incomplete character of research in a field that is sure to yield future rich harvests. Butler's pioneering work in the archives helped set the stage for identifying new sources and making them accessible to a broad range of scholars, students, and interested readers. In a fitting memorial to Butler's vital contribution to the field, Vernon is making some of these sources available to researchers in the Reginald D. Butler Local History Archive at the University of Virginia (https://community.village.virginia.edu/cvhr/universalviewer/scans).

If we regret Butler's turn away from a project that we know—and he tells us—was profoundly, personally important to him, we celebrate his successful efforts as a scholar, teacher, and administrator to promote broader and deeper engagement with the history of race, locally and globally, and its enduring implications for our world. In his essay, Scot A. French, Butler's longtime friend and colleague at the Woodson Institute, focuses on the hard and crucially important work of a gifted administrator in fostering scholarship—and transforming a university. French situates Butler's scholarship in the context of his commitment as an educator and citizen to promote better understanding of race, place, and community in American and African American history.

Butler's monograph may have been ahead of its time—and this may be why it remains so timely. But his all-absorbing work at the Woodson responded to the extraordinary demands of momentous times at the institute, the University of Virginia, and the world beyond. As Virginia historian Kirt von Daacke, a specialist in the field, told me, Butler stood "at the nexus of social history, African American history, the micro-historical approach, and community-based research privileging community knowledge." "In his administrative leadership, scholarship, and mentoring," von Daacke concludes, "he in many ways created that nexus at Virginia and embodied their interconnectedness." Butler's career at the Woodson Institute should be seen as the continuation and culmination of his ongoing commitment to enlightened scholarship and civic engagement.

We hope *The Evolution of a Rural Free Black Community* will command a broad readership at a moment when the legacies of slavery and racial hierarchy have assumed such a prominent place in our historical consciousness. Free Black Virginians in Goochland struggled to sustain community ties and find a place for themselves in a polarized world where hierarchy was institutionalized and their very existence barely acknowledged. Their world is not ours, but their experiences still resonate. Butler's research and the research he inspired and promoted will enable readers to make connections—genealogical as well as social and cultural—across generations. May Butler's book contribute to our consciousness of—and connections to—the history we all share.

· PREFACE ·

GERTRUDE J. FRASER

In the 1980s, Reginald and I were graduate students at Johns Hopkins University. We were in different departments, me in anthropology and he in history, but we shared the common linkage created by the Atlantic History and Culture Program. That program had the grand, somewhat realized, ambition of training a new generation of scholars to examine the societal, economic, and cultural patterns developed through the almost six-hundred-year association of people, plants, animals, commodities, and destinies brought into contact and conflict across the worlds integrated by and bordering on the Atlantic Ocean. Memory, history, identity, money, power, enslavement and rebellion, sugar, blood. We were being offered a way to connect worlds and ideas that seemed so separate into a geography of interactions and influences. Imagine the enthusiasm and anxiety generated by being expected to deliver on that mission as graduate students. What were we going to contribute to the heated debates and theoretical frameworks being laid down by grand eminences such as Sidney Mintz, Philip Curtin, Jack Greene, David Cohen, Rolph-Michelle Trouillot, Ida Altman, and many others?

Reginald stood out because among our peers, he seemed so grounded. He had a son, owned a house in West Baltimore, desegregated labor unions, and had held serious jobs as an ironworker on the Baltimore docks; he put up huge structures and he took some down as well. Reginald grew up in Philadelphia in the 1950s and 1960s and spent summers with his grandparents in rural Virginia. As a young man he rode freight trains from Philadelphia to California and then to Hawaii on a cargo plane. He had logged old wood in the Pacific Northwest and contracted on a salmon fishing boat for multiple seasons. He knew how to build things and take them apart, and he had an indescribable capacity to connect to people from divergent walks of life. He knew the old guy on Lexington Street in Baltimore who was among the last door-to-door "arrabbers" selling produce on a horse-driven cart. He coached young inner-city basketball players and somehow managed to get merchants to buy uniforms for his team. His friends included Native American ironworkers whose high-style feats on iconic New York structures were legendary, and if you wanted to know more about African American musicians who created the famous Philadelphia Sound, you could ask Reginald about Kenny Gamble and Leon Huff, who grew up in his neighborhood, and the genius jazz trumpeter and composer Lee Morgan, who died so young. I could tell you more, but Reginald, who had an intense sense of cool, would say, "Gert why are you getting so excited?" And I know no one else who could wear a French-style beret or straw fedora on his head and Allen Edmonds leather shoes, look like a meticulously groomed Esquire model, and slide into the Atlantic History seminar room as if he was in khakis and loafers.

I hope you get the message I most want to give—that among us graduate students at Johns Hopkins in the early 1980s, Reginald had a tremendous breadth of experience, a polyglot knowledge of places and cultures and histories of working people, an appreciation for materials and tools well-made and enduring. More than most, he understood what it was to live across borders, to be shaped by hard work, to belong and yet constantly push against expectations. In a sense he had a deep well of experience that allowed him to access what for many of us were abstract concepts of world systems and cultural interchange. What it must have been like to be an eighteenth- or early nineteenth-century West African seaman pulling into the Liverpool docks or a young girl like Sally Hemings enslaved yet like-free in the diplomatic houses of Paris or the Irish worker digging trenches and catching malaria alongside free and enslaved African Americans on the Erie Canal project?

Reginald asked beautiful questions, the ones that brought you up short and had you reassess where you had so confidently begun to lay down the lines of your thinking. He had a gift for telling stories, the details so meticulously crafted, people so finely described, that you might swear you had indeed been there when the longshoremen strike went down on the Seattle docks in 1916. For Reginald, the goals of an Atlantic world perspective made sense, but in my opinion, it sat at some cross-purposes with the approach to social history he found most compelling. He always wanted to draw from the archives the details of the small interactions, to unravel the individual choices and dilemmas, how African American people lived in and used the landscape, the creeks and rivers, how their bodies marked out brutal punishments, the freezing rain, the low bend needed to pick cotton and lima. One of his favorite books was Theodore Rosengarten's *All God's Dangers: The Life of Nate Shaw* (also known as Ned Cobb).

Reginald's book is a masterpiece. It reflects his desire to mine the archives of a single place—Goochland County, Virginia—to give voice to people who could not have been interviewed—as Ned Cobb was—but who had lived meaningful though harsh lives in the eighteenth-century Piedmont plantation world. When Reginald originally conducted his research and wrote this manuscript in the 1980s, historians of African American life had only barely begun to interrogate the archives creatively, to look in the crevices of county records, papers of indenture, depositions by human beings not legally considered fit for giving evidence in courts of law, inquiries into crimes, wills and inventories of free Black people and those who witnessed for them. These papers intended to document legal transactions and procedures in Reginald's hands—I can see them now, holding the large, bounded will books in the Goochland County clerk's office—were transformed into intimately drawn profiles; kinship and friendship networks; the yards and fields abutting and behind formally mapped homesites; how people died, married, and gave birth; the children orphaned or taken into servitude; the repeated taxonomy of names—the Coopers, the Mealys. Reginald loved to work with the original documents, spending hours and days and months turning each page, learning the letterings of Ss and Fs in the eighteenth-century penmanship and the variable orthography of places and people.

Among the lawyers and realtors searching deeds in the small clerk's office, he would often be the object of curiosity, the strange historian who showed up early and did not leave until closing. Why did he cleave so closely to the archives? In part it was because Reginald knew that the evidence for a community of free African Americans, some, though not all, of African and European descent, and for families with enslaved and free members, had to be carefully traced though the hundreds of pages, almost like watermarks, which only became visible when you developed an eye for the telling clues. The archives documented the deep history of Reginald's family in Goochland County—his grandmother was a Cooper and his grandfather a Mealy. This connection of his scholarship to the particular lives of people who would have shared common ancestors meant a great deal. The hundred-years run of written records established a powerful material presence against the systemic erasure of African American history and ownership from rural places like Goochland County. Reginald's work on local history and his successes in collaborating with genealogists, amateur historians, teachers, and community organizers ruptured the reigning idea that only academics could produce and legitimize the intellectual rationale and infrastructure for the documentation of local knowledge. He was willing to invest the effort in making those connections and in building trust. It is my honor to contribute to the fruition of his dream to have this work published. It is done Reginald. Rest well, courageous friend.

· INTRODUCTION ·

Race, Status, the Local, and the Personal

JOSHUA D. ROTHMAN

In 1822, the Goochland County Court denied the petition of Moses Cross to remain in Virginia. Born enslaved, Cross was more than forty years old when he purchased his own freedom in 1820, and a state law designed to limit the growth of Virginia's free Black population meant exile or re-enslavement unless Cross received a legal exemption from its provisions. The local judges in Goochland told Cross that they rejected his petition on a technicality, so Cross tried again, appealing a few months later directly to the General Assembly in Richmond.[1]

Hiring a white attorney to draft his life story for the legislators, Cross described how he had been enslaved by the husband of Judith Peers, and how he came into her possession and effectively began managing her plantation after her husband died. Cross reported how he had once rescued Peers and her family from a house fire, and how he always listened for and reported any rumors he heard of discontent among the enslaved and free Black populations in the county. Cross mustered support for his petition from Peers's son, enclosing an affidavit from Thomas Peers, who swore that Cross was as sober, hardworking, responsible, and trustworthy as any white man, and that Judith Peers had even asked Cross to sleep in the same house as she did and stand guard when whisperings of a slave insurrection frightened her. Moses Cross, Thomas Peers assured Virginia lawmakers, was not like other free Black people.

Once Cross had adduced evidence of his industriousness and his loyalties to white Virginians, he also noted that were his appeal to be denied, he would be forced either to leave his still-enslaved wife and children behind in Virginia or to become a slave himself once again. Whether legislators sympathized with the agony of such a choice or were persuaded that Cross was a reliable Black person who accepted the fundamental order of the society he lived in is unknown. But they approved his appeal. Cross lived out the rest of his life as a free man in Goochland County.

The story of Moses Cross and his efforts to stay in Virginia exemplify many of the salient themes of Reginald Butler's work. They show the deep intertwining and reciprocities among enslaved, free Black, and white lives in early national Virginia. They reveal how profoundly the oppressive racial hierarchy of the state's legal order structured those lives but also how the letter of the law could give way to conditions on the ground. They evince the relentless insistence of free Black Virginians that they deserved their freedom and independence but also that their freedom and independence entailed at least the strategic pretenses of abasing themselves before white people and distancing themselves politically from enslaved people. The survival of free Black families and communities, on terrain designed to make their survival difficult and their very existence suspect, required constant negotiation and perseverance in the face of what sometimes seemed insurmountable obstacles.

Appearing almost exactly halfway through Butler's *Evolution of a Rural Free Black Community*, the story of Moses Cross also illustrates Butler's thorough and meticulous engagement with the archival record, as Butler pieces together what we can know about Cross not only from his petitions but from fleeting appearances he made in Goochland's deed books, court order books, and tax records. Yet at the same time, Butler is acutely aware of the silences and distortions of the archive, noting, for example, that while Cross's "claims to a high level of social and psychological distance from his peers and close identification with whites suited the requirements of his petition," they "seem highly unlikely given his long years as a slave." Finally, Butler's account bespeaks his ability to convey with understated yet powerful prose the poignancy and fragility of the position of free Black people in a slave society. When Thomas Peers estimated that Moses Cross was as good as a white man, Butler notes bitingly that it "must have been the greatest compliment that he could conceive of paying" him. Yet Cross had to embrace such condescension and avoid betraying even a hint of resentment toward slavery if he wished both to keep his family intact and retain the liberty he had labored so hard to achieve. To be free and Black in a slave society, Butler observes, Cross "walked a very thin edge."[2]

Although *Evolution of a Rural Free Black Community* has heretofore never been published, it is among those rare manuscripts that hold up well decades after being written. It sat on the leading edge of the historiography on free Black southerners when Butler began crafting it more than thirty years ago, and it contains arguments that make it an original and important contribution to the field even today. While the literature on free Black life in Virginia and elsewhere in the American South has expanded substantially and gone in new directions since Butler was last at work on this book, in fact, significant elements of what Butler achieves in it presaged where scholars would venture in the years to come.

Moreover, while we will never know precisely what a final version of *Evolution of a Rural Free Black Community* might have looked like, over the course of his career Butler helped build and inspire a research model that was itself ahead of its time and that points toward some of the directions he might have gone. Butler, for example, believed deeply in the revelatory power of immersion in the archives, and though he worked initially in an era when scholars collected whatever materials they could find with little but pen and paper, ongoing records processing at archival repositories and the innovations of computing and the internet have since radically changed evidentiary possibilities for historians. Nothing demonstrates some of these possibilities better than Robert Vernon's steadfast work in central Virginia courthouse records, conducted in regular consultation with Butler over several decades. Among other things, Vernon reveals how we have been increasingly able to compile something like a complete picture of the surviving archival record and make new connections across different pieces of that record, sometimes with means as simple as a keyword search. There is no doubt that today Butler would have been able to provide us with an even more fully realized portrait of Moses Cross and the communities of which he was a part.

Butler's work with Vernon and with scholars such as Scot French, meanwhile, shows the value he placed on collaborative scholarship and on communities of researchers sharing efforts and ideas to produce something greater than any one of them might be able to produce on their own. Whether as longtime director of the Carter G. Woodson Institute for African-American and African Studies at the University of Virginia, as cofounder of the Central Virginia Social History Project, or in innumerable other roles, Butler's belief in communal ties was not merely an artifact of his own research in Goochland County. They were something he understood as foundational to historical work at its finest. In that way, the contribution of *Evolution of a Rural Free Black Community* to the field and the discipline lies beyond even the penetrating insights it offers about free Black people and their lives in the early republic. The manuscript was at the same time a galvanizing force for other projects and investigations of the past whose outcomes have in some cases yet to be seen in their fullest.

Written originally as a dissertation in the second half of the 1980s at Johns Hopkins University under the direction of Jack P. Greene, *Evolution of a Rural Free Black Community* draws in part on the extensive historiography of slavery and the social evolution of colonial and early national Virginia. It is impossible to read the accounts of a pair of infanticide cases from the late eighteenth century with which Butler begins the book, for example, and not be reminded of some of the set pieces in Rhys Isaac's Pulitzer Prize–winning *The Transformation of Virginia, 1740–1790*. Butler, like Isaac, takes a practically ethnographic and dramaturgical approach to these stories, making a case for how specificities of landscape and geography shaped the cognitive horizons of historical actors, and how social realities and cultural norms were made on those stages through both everyday and uncommon behaviors and interactions.[3]

An accounting of other clear influences on Butler's work would include scholarship such as Mechal Sobel's *The World They Made Together*; Edmund S. Morgan's *American Slavery, American Freedom*; and T. H. Breen and Stephen Innes's *"Myne Owne Ground."* Individually and collectively, these books and others demonstrate the ways white and Black Virginians "made" one another in the seventeenth and eighteenth centuries. They show as well the ways race and slavery took shape imperfectly and gradually, leaving lasting legacies for Virginians and the legal and social orders of the state that were far more convoluted than we usually allow or that a superficial glimpse might suggest.[4]

But *Evolution of a Rural Free Black Community* is rooted most deeply in the historiography on free Black people in the slave South. Butler worked at the end of what was then nearly a century of scholarly literature on the subject. And most of that literature explored and tried to answer some of the same fundamental questions Butler himself attempted to answer about what it meant to be free and Black in a society that equated Blackness with slavery. Yet the methodologies, approaches, and suppositions scholars brought to those questions had changed measurably over time.

The earliest significant effort to delineate the basic contours of free Black life in Virginia specifically was John H. Russell's *The Free Negro in Virginia, 1619–1865*. Published in 1913, it was one of several state studies of free Black populations that appeared in the late nineteenth and early twentieth centuries, and like many of them, Russell's was pioneering in some important ways. As Russell pored through records of county courts and church parishes, minutes of Quaker meetings, laws and decisions of the colonial General Court and the state Supreme Court, newspapers, and proceedings of the House of Burgesses and the General Assembly, he crafted an elemental roadmap of primary materials that historians working on the subject have followed ever since. Moreover, Russell established many of the analytical and organizational categories within which nearly every other scholar of free Black people has operated, arranging his material into considerations of the numbers and distribution of the free Black population across the state, the origins of the free Black population in the colonial era and its growth thereafter, the various manumission mechanisms for enslaved people and the ebbs and flows of their uses over time, the status of free Black people in law, and their positions in the social order.[5]

Oddly, the subject of free Black people remained a sort of lacuna in historical scholarship on the slave South for more than sixty years after the publication of Russell's work. Historians obviously did not entirely neglect discussions of them in broader studies, but work focused specifically on the topic emerged only in fits and starts. From the 1920s through the 1940s, the study of free Black populations was largely the province of a small number of Black historians. In 1925, for example, Carter G. Woodson published *Free Negro Heads of Families in the United States in 1830*, which comprised a brief historical overview of the social, legal, and economic positions of free Black people in the United States, along with a list of free Black families, organized by state, drawn from the 1830 federal census. It would then be nearly twenty years before more studies appeared, most notably Luther Porter Jackson's *Free Negro Labor and Property Holding in Virginia, 1830–1860*; John Hope Franklin's *The Free Negro in North Carolina, 1790–1860*; and E. Horace Fitchett's series of articles, published over the span of seven years in the 1940s in the *Journal of Negro History,* on free Black people in Charleston. All brought new perspectives to bear on the demographic, legal, and social questions engaged by Russell. They particularly fleshed out the economic positions of free Black southerners, pushing back against some of the racist underpinnings of Russell's work that took Black inferiority as a given, demonstrating instead how hard free Black southerners labored to build sustainable communities and make their own lives and fortunes. Together these scholars showed how free Black Americans managed to accumulate property and capital despite slanderous racial prejudice, legal restrictions, and structural barriers that might not have consistently been brought to bear but were nonetheless always meant to marginalize them socially, politically, and economically.[6]

Following this small burst of published work, a smattering of doctoral dissertations written in the 1950s engaged in state-level examinations of free Black southerners, particularly looking at the antebellum period. But then the field again lay relatively dormant until the 1970s, at which point scholarship began proliferating considerably. Easily the most important book that both reflected and shaped this new generation was Ira Berlin's *Slaves without Masters: The Free Negro in the Antebellum South,* published in 1974.

Slaves without Masters is capacious in scope and extensively researched, and in it Berlin acknowledged that the situations of free Black southerners varied widely across the southern landscape. He particularly detailed social, legal, and cultural distinctions he saw between the upper South and lower South that shaped the racial demography of free Black populations and the contexts in which those populations had to maneuver if they wished to be successful. Moreover, Berlin described a slave South where free Black people might prosper economically, carve out positions of privilege and standing for themselves and their families, and build communities and institutions that could buffer them against white antagonism. Still, for Berlin, that antagonism was very real and ultimately the most salient fact of life for free Black people. It defined their existence nearly everywhere, forcing them to the economic margins of southern society, containing their aspirations with discriminatory laws at every turn, squeezing them into dependent relationships with white people for their own protection, and ultimately delimiting their freedom so appreciably that their status often barely rose above slavery itself.[7]

Berlin understood that his work was part of what he called a "modest renaissance" in scholarship on "the Southern free Negro caste." He attributed the revival in part to interest in the 1960s and 1970s in the field of comparative slavery and to burgeoning historical examinations of race, slavery, and freedom across the Americas. He knew that it also came from the broader concern of historians with Black history that was of a piece with and emerged from the civil rights movement in the 1950s and 1960s. And Berlin knew too that it came from the vogue in the historical profession for social history and especially for "history from the bottom up," as scholars began scouring local and state archives to find traces and stories of women, workers, poor persons, and other nonelites who often did not leave behind the written materials out of which historians most conventionally built their narratives.[8]

Ironically, even as Berlin deployed social history methods and recognized the importance of particularity and variability, his emphasis lay so heavily on how free Black people were hemmed in and restricted by white southerners that close examinations of how they actually lived their lives became subordinated in *Slaves without Masters*. Accordingly, many of the historians who followed in Berlin's wake sought to bring those subjective experiences to the fore, often in the form of community and county studies.

First made popular among scholars of colonial New England who published scads of town studies beginning in the early 1970s, methods and models of what came to be known as the "new social history" started to be brought to bear by historians of other areas of the country by the 1980s.[9] A non-exhaustive list of studies of southern places that appeared in the middle of that decade alone, for example, would include Darrett B. Rutman and Anita H. Rutman's work on Middlesex County, Virginia; Orville Vernon Burton's account of Edgefield, South Carolina; Richard R. Beeman's analysis of Lunenberg County, Virginia; and Robert C. Kenzer's examination of Orange County, North Carolina.[10] But the study of free Black people was especially ripe for this sort of treatment, and as works on the subject by Suzanne Lebsock, Barbara Jeanne Fields, Michael P. Johnson and James L. Roark, Michael L. Nicholls, Gary B. Mills, Adele Logan Alexander, and others were published, the arguments of scholars from John Russell to Ira Berlin were put to the test. What variability and particularity really meant could finally be seen, and the granularity of being free and Black in a slave society could finally come into focus.[11]

It is at precisely this juncture that Reginald Butler started his research, and it is in this scholarly milieu that *Evolution of a Rural Free Black Community* entered the picture. Butler had personal connections to Goochland County, having grown up there himself among relatives whose residence in the county went back to the colonial era. But Goochland was well-chosen terrain for historical consideration regardless of Butler's own associations with the place. Situated in the Virginia Piedmont and founded in 1727, Goochland's social and economic development was distinct from that of the Tidewater or the Eastern Shore. In those places, the presence of Europeans and Africans extended to the early seventeenth century, and historians had long looked at free Black populations there whose origins could be traced to a time before racial hierarchy had become thoroughly entrenched. By contrast, Goochland was a slave society practically from the beginning, and by the turn of the nineteenth century, roughly half of the county's population was enslaved. Moreover, the understandable attention paid by historians to slavery and enslaved people in overwhelmingly rural places like Goochland had led to relative scholarly neglect of the hundreds of free Black people who struggled to sustain themselves economically and build families and communities in a world defined by Black bondage.[12]

Goochland was a small place, but Butler argues that it was in such "'small places' that the main questions about the nature of slavery and freedom, race and class will ultimately be answered." And what Butler found when he looked at free Black life in the county suggests conclusions that add complexity and nuance to most previous scholarly assessments. For Butler, free Black Virginians in Goochland County were not Ira Berlin's "slaves without masters." Nor were they anomalies in southern society who existed in an atomized and paralyzing state of siege, their lives defined solely by restrictive laws and demeaning ideologies. Rather, Butler argues, free Black people in Goochland lived simultaneously in two worlds. One was limited by laws that targeted them and made them inherently suspicious, and one was rife with opportunities to cultivate multiracial social networks and shape their own destinies. The two, Butler asserts, were "in constant interplay, now affording free African Americans great latitude and at other times drastically circumscribing their lives." The peril of being free and Black was significant but so too was the determination of those facing it.[13]

Any number of facets of free Black life in Goochland might be brought to bear to illuminate Butler's argument. He describes laws designed to keep free Black and enslaved people disconnected and socioeconomic circumstances where free Black people might have power over the enslaved that sometimes extended as far as slave ownership itself. But he also describes conditions under which free Black Virginians had considerable family ties with the enslaved and provided crucial labor for white planters that made separating them from those in bondage effectively impossible. He highlights a clearly coercive system of youth apprenticeship that bound out free Black children for purposes of racial control and labor exploitation but one that also provided legal avenues for vigilant Black parents to insist in court that white masters abide by the conditions of the indentures. He demonstrates how free Black workers could almost never stand outside the system of plantation slavery altogether and often labored on the economic margins but also how they made themselves invaluable to white landowners by being flexible and commanding a variety of skilled and unskilled occupations. They often received competitive wages with white workers, and free Black rates of land ownership in Goochland tripled in the last decades before the Civil War.

Throughout *Evolution of a Rural Free Black Community*, Butler constantly draws the reader's attention to the push and pull among legal and institutional structures; social custom; and the personal, familial, and communal relationships of white, enslaved, and free Black people in Goochland County. He has a finely attuned sense for irony and paradox, and to pattern and the particularities of location and circumstance alike. He speaks to the quiet persistence of free Black people who made their way out of slavery and steadily built wealth, connections, and means to protect themselves and their families across generations. But he never yields to sentimentalism that might lead him to underplay the impact of racial oppression that kept some families irretrievably divided between slavery and freedom and kept even free Black people who managed to accumulate resources and security in a vise that could tighten at any time.

And Butler wrings countless stories from painstaking years in the archives. Anyone who has spent time with the deed books, court minute and order books, tax lists, free Black registers, marriage records, legislative petitions, and other materials fundamental to the work of a social historian knows they give up only scraps and fragments of information, snippets that may or may not ever fit together into something coherent. Yet a rich texture of free Black life suffuses Butler's work, and the reader gets a strong feeling for the experiences of the men, women, and children he found in the Goochland County Courthouse and the Library of Virginia but who left almost nothing behind written in their own hands. Particularly considered in light of technological advances since the 1980s that have considerably facilitated the abilities of historians to collate and sift through mountains of material, that texture and that feeling are testaments to Butler's diligence, rigor, and talents as a researcher and a writer.

In some ways, the field has moved in important different directions since Butler was last at work on *Evolution of a Rural Free Black Community*. Historians have produced and continue to produce an extensive body of literature centered on the experiences of free Black women, for example. Studies of the relationship of free Black people to the legal system have become more prevalent, as has scholarship considering their position relative to larger structural considerations of race and both free and unfree labor. Still other important work engages in comparative analyses, finding connections and contrasts among varying portions of the United States and even abroad, thus folding the American story of freedom and slavery into a hemispheric and global one.[14]

Yet studying local communities and even individual families remains a common approach to questions about being free and Black in a slave society. Moreover, while the answers to those questions vary, given how much exploring the particularities of time and place inheres to social history methods, some of the best work continues to come around to conclusions not unlike those Reginald Butler reached decades ago. This is especially the case for work on the upper South, which housed roughly 85 percent of the southern free Black population in 1860.[15] In his 2004 Bancroft Prize–winning study of a free Black community in Prince Edward County, Virginia, known as Israel Hill, for instance, Melvin Patrick Ely similarly finds that antagonistic laws and ideology did not at all close avenues for free Black economic independence. Like Butler, Ely makes a case for a lived reality where free Black southerners might use the law to their advantage, where they interacted routinely and on reasonable terms with white people, and where "ties of culture, faith, affection, and economic interest could span the barrier between black and white." Ely understands that Butler was on to something years before he was, noting in his book that he did not come across *Evolution of a Rural Free Black Community* until he was very far along in his research and writing process but that when he did, he was "deeply struck" by the "harmony" between what he and Butler saw in the archives.[16]

Along the same lines, Kirt von Daacke argues that "a relatively easygoing interracial social order" could be found in Albemarle County, Virginia, well into the nineteenth century. Von Daacke makes no pretenses that Albemarle was a "racial utopia," but it was one of those small places characterized by a deep "culture of personalism" where free Blacks "carved out lives for themselves that belie the slaves-without-masters model." Individual free Black people in Albemarle lived in a thoroughly hierarchical society, but it was nonetheless one where they could settle into a status that might have had no "formal name or any real legal backing." But it still had "social power, which turned out to be far more important to those who possessed it."[17]

Indeed, it is likely that local studies like *Evolution of a Rural Free Black Community* will always be central to our understanding of free Black people in the slave South. Warren Eugene Milteer Jr.'s excellent recent overview of the southern free Black experience, titled *Beyond Slavery's Shadow*, reveals why. Milteer argues that free Black people in the South were "both privileged and victimized, both celebrated and despised." White supremacy and legal and economic precarity did condition their lives. But there was also great variety in how those things manifested themselves and thus in the capacity of free Black people to fight discrimination and mistreatment, and to make spaces for themselves in which they might survive and even thrive. That variety came because different states had different legal regimes and because different histories lay behind the development of free Black populations in different parts of the South. But it came too because relationships among free Black, enslaved, and white people on the ground were complicated by family and community ties, and because "intersecting social hierarchies" of wealth, gender, occupation, and reputation could scramble the supposed imperatives of regimes rooted in slavery and white supremacy. Such inconsistencies, Milteer rightly observes, were not exceptions to how southern society worked. On the contrary, the inconsistencies *were* how southern society worked. Examining the interface of large power structures with small places shows how that was so. Arguably, it is the only way to show how that was so.[18]

It is lamentable that Butler never finished the transformation of his work from dissertation into a revised manuscript and published it as a book. In what was left behind, he gestures toward later chapters that were never written, and there are certainly pathways that he could have profitably explored. *Evolution of a Rural Free Black Community* might have benefited from greater attention paid to the working lives of free Black women or the religious and cultural experiences of free Black people in Goochland County. Much might also have been said about the impact of the domestic slave trade on free Black families and communities, and life in Goochland County might have been placed in a wider geographical context, providing a sense both of its porosity and its ties to other places and other communities. And it is surely no accident that the closing date for Butler's study is 1832, the year after the Southampton Rebellion led by Nat Turner set the state of Virginia down the road that would lead to the Civil War. Given the significant hardening of the socioeconomic and legal environment for free Black people in Virginia and throughout the South in the decades after the Southampton Rebellion, one wonders what Butler might have written about the likely dramatic reshaping of the landscape for free Black Virginians in Goochland.[19]

But *Evolution of a Rural Free Black Community* ends nevertheless on a thematically and methodologically appropriate note, with Butler discussing how even the success of some free Black people in Goochland County rarely meant a life without challenges or without an intense awareness of status. And it nearly always entailed linkages to both enslaved and white people, as the poles of slavery and freedom set the ever-present boundaries of existence. The pathos could be nearly overwhelming, as suggested by one of the final stories Butler tells, that of the Granthum family.

Catherine Granthum was born enslaved, and while she was manumitted in 1797, her two sons, Woodson and Gideon, and her husband, Phil, remained in slavery. She worked and earned enough to purchase two hundred acres of land and to manumit the rest of her family by 1802, and when she died just five years later, she left her property to Phil to use and to provide for their children during his lifetime. But she also had two white slaveholders serve as executors of her estate, act as trustees for the inheritances of her children, and, if it were to become necessary, apprentice them to tradesmen in the event that Phil died before the children reached adulthood. The archival record tells us nothing about the nature of the relationship between Catherine Granthum and these white men. We do not know whether they were patrons who genuinely cared for Granthum's well-being and that of her family or whether she thought the free status of her children insufficiently secure and best supplemented with connections to wealthy white people. As Butler notes, ambiguity was inescapable in the lives of free Black people in Goochland County, and achieving freedom was a triumph that meant everything and guaranteed nothing. Freedom was, rather, made through relationships forged every day on ground that was unpredictable and paradoxical; it nurtured roots of communities that both sunk deep and whose tendrils filled with ambivalence and uncertainty. It was ground that Reginald Butler knew would never tell all of its secrets.[20]

THE EVOLUTION OF A RURAL
FREE BLACK COMMUNITY

Prologue

The death and suspected murder of two newborn infants opens a window into the interior worlds of free African Americans and their white neighbors. Our senses become attuned to the experience of living Black and free in the seventeenth- and eighteenth-century slave South.

The Goochland County Court heard the first of these infanticide cases on May 7, 1787, and the second seven years later on January 15, 1794. Although we are primarily interested in everyday activities, the events resulting in a text that we are able to interpret are extraordinary occurrences in the lives of the participants. Indeed, only seven infanticide cases occurred in the county from 1730 to 1832.[1] A child dies under mysterious circumstances, charges are brought against the parents, and neighbors and kin are called to give testimony.

Virginia legislation required that any suspicious death be investigated. The first stage of inquiry involved a formal inquisition "taken on the body of the deceased." Based on the evidence gathered during the inquisition, the court could then decide whether to lodge formal charges. If charges were brought, the accused was jailed while awaiting their arraignment.

During the trial, the court heard testimony under oath from subpoenaed witnesses who were required to post security attesting to the veracity of their statements. Their testimony appeared in the records as depositions, transcribed by the county clerk or some other scribe. It is important to take into consideration the circumstances under which the texts were produced.

These texts have already undergone a set of contemporary interpretations. Between the time of the supposed crime and their appearance in court, for example, the witnesses had no doubt rehearsed their testimony, in the privacy of home and in talking to neighbors. In turn, the clerk translated the colloquial language of the speaker's oral recollections according to the conventions of eighteenth-century legal discourse. We cannot assume that the depositions either tell the full story or the story as it was spoken. But this shortcoming of the sources is mitigated to some extent because when they testified, men and women with varied stakes in the cases' outcome and of different social and racial groups provided their interpretations of causality, the sequence of events, and participants' motivations. These many perspectives allow for a multidimensional view of the same incidents.

Lilly Anne Craddock a white woman, and James Cooper, a free Black carpenter and farmer, stood accused of having murdered their infant son immediately after his birth in the early morning of April 27, 1787. By all accounts, the couple lived together with an older child in the county's upper district at a house owned by Lilly Anne. That morning, described by one witness as "early in the morning of the night of the same day" (which would suggest the predawn hours), Lilly Anne emerged from the house and went into the garden where, she later told a woman neighbor, she had gone because of a "straining lax." The terminology used here might well have been the clerk's, who chose a euphemism to refer to what must have been an urge to defecate. Lilly Anne misread her bodily signals. In the garden, her labor began in earnest. Unable to go for help, she delivered the child while leaning against the garden fence and then wrapped it in her coat.[2]

The subsequent actions of the main participants are less clear. During her travail, Lily appeared to have been alone. But not long after, she alerted James, who according to one witness was seen in the garden earlier than usual that morning. The child had been stillborn, died soon after birth, or was murdered. James would later report that he dug a shallow grave, laid some boards, and buried the infant in the garden.[3]

Something of the mythical emerges. The second investigation also involves a woman giving birth outside the social institution of marriage and literally out of doors, beyond the support of female kin and helping neighbors. But the details differ. Bridgett Cooper was a free Black woman in her mid-twenties who was manumitted along with other members of her family in 1782. She was charged with the death of her infant. Bridgett had been living away from her mother's household for some time. Evidence in the case describes her as residing in a house in the "forest," though in proximity to her family. It is possible that Bridgett was cohabiting with her baby's father, though he is never mentioned in the records. A few days before Christmas, she delivered her child while enroute to her home. The next day Bridgett's younger sister, Becca, arrived for an extended visit. Perhaps she intended to be with her in the last days of the pregnancy. When she arrived, however, Becca observed that Bridgett "had no appearance of being with child as she had sometime before." And she further testified that she had seen her sister "milk her breast on a hot iron." This action referred to the belief that by expelling breast milk on a hot iron there would be a similar effect of drying up the flow of milk. According to present-day older African American women in Virginia, when mothers wished to wean their toddlers, they "ironed they breast." Almost two centuries earlier, we see Bridgett Cooper relying on the same practices in order to hide the fact of her recent pregnancy.[4]

By these clues, therefore, the sister and the rest of the family suspected that Bridgett had had her baby without alerting them to its birth. Once alerted, they suspected that she had buried the child in the garden. The evidence neither confirmed nor denied whether the child was murdered. But in both instances, given the unusual and somewhat surreptitious circumstances surrounding the birth, death, and burial, family and neighbors investigated what they perceived as unorthodox behavior and eventually notified court officials. Neighbors and family were intimately aware of one another's daily routines. Neither Lilly Anne nor Bridgett could hide the fact of her infant's death for very long.

What meaning do these two traumatic episodes offer to our understanding of the eighteenth-century worldview of free Blacks, whites, and men and women in the county? The geographic location of household, garden, and the world beyond—the forest or woods—provided important cognitive categories. Becca, for example, recalled that her sister had gone into the garden and "there took out of the ground something of a brown color." She watched and followed "as far as the fence" but then lost sight of Bridgett. Becca remained within the confines of the yard and did not attempt to investigate her sister's behavior once she entered the "woods." The garden represented domestic space where behavior could be easily scrutinized. Outside of that domain—out of sight—in the forest or the woods, behavioral norms could not be monitored as closely.

Sophia Parrish's deposition elucidates these points. The wife of a white planter, she was the mistress of four slaves and lived in some proximity to the Craddock-Cooper household. Despite the seeming social distance, however, she offered womanly and moral support to the bereaved mother. In recreating the event for the court, Sophia Parrish used the house and the garden as the stage on which the drama of the birth and death of the child occurred. She remembered that the mother was in the house when she arrived. If it conformed to the architectural norm, this house would have been either a one- or two-room dwelling.[5] In the intimacy of this space, Lilly Anne unburdened herself to Sophia, who believed the new mother's version of events was true.

Later, Sophia went to the garden where her observations helped to corroborate the woman's story. She testified that "there was blood on the garden pails," and she believed it had come from the afterbirth. The deposition noted that the sign of "blood was seen by her [Parrish] near some artichokes by the side of the garden." George Tyler, a free Black carpenter and also a witness, recalled that in the "light of the morning" he had noticed James "on very urgent business near some artichokes by the side of the garden." Both Tyler and Parrish used these locational cues: the garden, the fence, and the artichokes.

In eighteenth-century Virginia, few areas of the domestic domain were hidden from public view. Neighbors took note of and participated in the everyday activities taking place within the fenced-in garden and house. Mechal Sobel has written of the close interaction among whites and Blacks within and outside the enclosed spaces of home, garden, and neighborhood in eighteenth-century Virginia.[6]

In both these cases, the parents buried the infants within the garden, suggesting that they fully expected their actions would be discovered and motivations publicly debated. James Cooper, for example, told his brother's wife that the child had been buried. Subsequently, neighbors entered the garden in his presence and located the grave. Among other observations, they noted that the grave was too shallow. Sophia Parrish challenged James directly: "How could you bury this child here? Why the dogs would scratch it up, it was so shallow." To which James replied, "I knowed it would be taken up again and I did not think it worthwhile to bury it any deeper."

The body was indeed taken up and brought into the house by Sophia, who thoroughly inspected it while the mother watched. Her unofficial inquisition would precede the formal one of the courts. In the case of Bridgett's child, the corpse was brought into the house, where the family along with the two white women noted that the infant's body was "very limber," that "blood [had] settled about its face and as low as the pit of the stomach," and that there were lumps of dirt in its hair.[7]

Debra Pleasants testified that "on our way home we stopt at the place where the prisoner [Bridgett] had lived to examine the place where Becca conjectured the child had been buried." Like James Cooper's neighbors, these women wanted to see the evidence in order to reach their own conclusions. With a seeming relish for the details of the story and for her own part in it, Debra told of taking Becca Cooper along to Bridgett's yard where Becca "with a fire shovel opened the hole being cautioned not to dig the hole any larger, but only to take out the loose dirt." Debra observed that there were "several rocks" near the suspicious hole that seemed to be "lately cut," and that "there were also several small holes near the long hole out of which these stones appeared to have been lately taken."[8]

Although the courts ultimately adjudicated these cases, we are already beginning to see that the neighbors and family members played important roles as inquisitors, counselors, adversaries, and arbiters of social behavior. Rhys Isaac has described eighteenth-century Anglo- and Afro-Virginians as sharing an "ethos of close neighborhood" in which the maneuvers of every person were known to a great many others—or could be guessed.[9]

A cross-section of the neighborhood's residents in our two cases involved themselves in the events that transpired. In the first case, James Cooper immediately went to his brother Daniel's house and broke the news of the child's death to his sister-in-law Polly Cooper. The reported conversation is revealing. "Lilly has got it," he cryptically informed her to which she replied "what?" and he further explained, "She's got a little one." Who was there, when did she bring it, and where is the child? Polly asked in short order. By this series of inquiries, she immediately established the expected etiquette of behavior that normally preceded the birth of a child. Birth was an event that activated the network of reciprocal relationships among family and neighbors, and women were at the center of these exchanges. Polly's usual response would most likely have been to alert the appropriate women of the impending birth. She may have performed this service at the birth of the couple's first child. But when James replied, "I buried it," another set of responses set in.

Instead of visiting with Lilly Anne, as was perhaps usual after a birth, Polly went directly to William Smith, Lilly Anne Craddock's brother, and told him the news. Subsequently, William stopped by Sophia Parrish's home and asked her to accompany him to his sister's house. In addition, Sophia's husband, Peter, together with Thomas Farmer and his wife, Fanny, all whites living in proximity to the household, congregated in the garden.[10]

None of the depositions remark on the moral or religious impropriety of the cohabitation of James and Lilly Anne, who did not hide the intimacy of their relationship. Yet Virginia's laws clearly prohibited fornication, legally defined as sexual interaction outside of marriage. In their discussion of the couple's behavior, the neighbors and relatives on both sides seemed to have taken their cohabitation for granted.

Relationships between free white women and free Black men were not confined to servant women in the seventeenth and early eighteenth centuries. This case also brings into question the widely held view that by the mid-eighteenth century, all white Virginians were intolerant of sexual intimacies between white women and Black men. Scholars write with unchallenged certainty about the dominant culture's repulsion for this form of sexuality. Recent historical research has begun to unravel white and Black attitudes toward miscegenation. They reveal that only after Reconstruction did actual or suspected transracial intimacies between African American men and white women draw the systematic violence and ire of white men and the application of legal sanctions.[11]

The conduct of the white women witnesses on arrival at James Cooper's household is best understood in terms of their shared experience as women and mothers, rather than as moral arbiters of Lilly Anne's interracial union with James. According to their testimony, they focused their attention on the parental behavior of James and Lilly Anne. Did they kill the child? Why was no one called to help when labor began? Was the child full term and why had Lilly Anne been unaware of the impending birth? Had she not known she was in labor? Perhaps in this group of interacting neighbors and kin, the fact of an interracial union may not have stirred the destructive passions that have been documented in other times and places in Virginia.[12]

The network involved in Bridgett Cooper's case included her mother, Chloe, and two younger sisters, Becca and Clarissa. In addition, Polly Younghusband Maddox and Debra Pleasants, two white women, visited the home during the crises. They were both members of a prominent Quaker family, most of whom had a decade earlier divested themselves of their slave property.[13]

After she was freed by Thomas Pleasants, Chloe settled and rented land on the plantation and raised her children there. The white women's depositions suggested that the Coopers and Pleasants had maintained patron-client links that may well have extended to more intimate interactions. In their testimony, Polly and Debra evoked a sense of compassion and long familiarity with Bridgett and her sisters. They might well have been the same age and grown up together.

Debra Pleasants was herself married to a slaveholder.[14] Informal reciprocal relationships between free Blacks and whites developed at the same time that structural constraints on free Black social and economic behavior oppressed and undermined the stability of the free Black community. These cases provide clear evidence of how this situation operated at the level of everyday behavior.

Although the two births occurred in extraordinary rather than normal circumstances, women nonetheless took center stage. Indeed, men were directly involved only in the earlier case. And in that instance, James, the accused father, and the men who proceeded to dig in the garden in search of evidence, stood on the periphery of the drama. They remained outside of the home and did not hear the women's conversation. Sophia Parrish consoled Lilly Anne and attempted to support her recitation of events. "How goes it," she asked on first entering the house. "What is the matter, I hear you have had a child." Despite the seeming social distance, she offered womanly and moral support to the bereaved mother, reserving commentary on her sexual behavior and racial indiscretions.[15]

Similarly, and perhaps more dramatically, the women who came to Chloe Cooper's house provided support and practical advice. The specter of the judicial system and the sanctions brought against women who committed infanticide guided their conversations. Besides assessing the condition of the infant's body, Polly Younghusband Maddox and Debra Pleasants sought to interpret and then to protect Bridgett from the consequences of her actions. They feared that her surreptitious burial of the infant would be easily interpreted as a criminal act by the courts. Thus, while gathered in Chloe's house, with Clarissa and Becca seated nearby, and with Bridgett in the backroom, Polly inquired of those present if any prebirth preparations had been made for the child.

Proof that the birth had been anticipated and welcomed would be useful in a court trial. "Did she have any baby clothes made?" she asked. Receiving no response, she persisted, informing the family that if Bridgett "had only a [baby's] cap [to show] it might save her life." Bridgett's sister Clarissa then brought out a "bundle of cloths," from which she extracted "part of a child's shirt . . . which was cut out but not made." In asking about the existence of the newborn's clothing, Debra focused on Bridgett's conduct as an expectant mother and ignored the fact that the child was conceived out of wedlock. Furthermore, she did not attempt to judge innocence or guilt but only to prepare Bridgett for the inevitable court trial. By indicating that the clothes had been started but not completed, she may have further implicated Bridgett in the death of the child.

The fates of the accused are unknown. The county justices were unable to reach a decision in either case and remanded them to the general and district courts, whose records for that period have been destroyed. It appears that James Cooper and probably Lilly Anne Craddock as well were exonerated. He is listed as a taxpayer in the 1791 tax list, four years after the baby's death.[16] Bridgett Cooper, however, completely disappeared from the records. But the outcome of either case is no more important than the lessons that may be learned from a close analysis of the cultural dynamics set into motion when the group determined that individuals had stepped beyond the limits of socially acceptable behavior.

The dominant institutional metaphors that undergirded the actions of the participants in these social encounters were those of the judicial system and the court of law. This should come as no surprise given the nature of the episodes. Yet the degree to which family and neighbors took on the responsibilities of investigating the specifics of the infants' deaths, before the intervention of the authorities, suggests that their conceptions of civic and communal duty characterized what Isaac has called a "great metaphor." This he defines as "shared meanings that influence the roles cultural actors take on, the modes of self-representation and interaction with others and their perceptions of what constitutes significant action or drama."[17]

Throughout the development of the free African American community, the struggles were fought and lost in defending the legitimacy of their presence in Virginia—on establishing that they shared in a common set of rights and values that should neither be abrogated nor denied. I intend these family stories of child death to stand as metaphors for the complex history of free African American life-worlds in the slave society of Goochland County.

Introduction

This book examines the history of free African Americans living in Goochland County, Virginia, from just after the General Assembly created the county's boundaries, in 1727, to 1832. It seeks to answer a seemingly simple question: what did it mean to be free and a person of color in a rural Virginia county during a century in which the Old Dominion defined itself as a society based on chattel slavery? Discussion of the nature and condition of free Black status in Goochland County leads to a broader concern with the system that brought free and enslaved Blacks and whites together and defined their structural and personal connections to one another.

I am in a long line of historians who have struggled to portray the lives and histories of free Blacks in the slave South. They have borrowed images from institutions and settings construed to be somehow like the world of the free Black person. They search for the right words to describe the contradictions of having free Black status in the plantation South. Caleb Perry Patterson, in a pioneering study, described a free Black Tennessean as "a sort of inmate on parole," evoking a notion of freedom as contingent on the free Black person's "good behavior." Later studies reiterate this theme. Leonard P. Curry refers to the "incompleteness" of freedom for free African Americans living in the "shadow of a dream." Others use the image of life on a tightrope—dimensionless, with the direction of movement rigidly circumscribed. Shifting legislative tides and the rise and fall of white hostility keep free people on a steady course or plunge them over the edge into economic and social despair.

"Freedom," in Michael P. Johnson and James L. Roark's characterization was "eggshell thin," requiring the tender ministrations of those African Americans with this special status. Historians elsewhere speak of the "tiny borderland" staked out by free people of color. There is even a turn to popular cultural referents in Philip D. Morgan's imagery of free Black communities inhabiting a "twilight zone" between the worlds of slavery (Black) and freedom (white). Free people of color led "ambiguous," "constricted," or "anomalous" lives—"neither slave nor free." In Ira Berlin's phrase, they were "slaves without masters," "straddling hell's boundaries." Joel Williamson, in his study of free African Americans of mixed racial heritage, discovers a species of "new people," embodying the middle ground of color and status between Blackness and whiteness, slavery and freedom. These metaphors—mixed and otherwise—represent the labor of historians to create a working analytical framework sufficient to comprehend the lives of people whose status was not simply ambiguous but for practical purposes invisible in a society bent on having only two classes of people—enslaved Blacks and free whites.[1]

Unlike many Caribbean and Latin America societies, southern plantation society never established a fixed middle tier status that separated free people of color from the enslaved and whites. Across time periods and in different parts of the American South, no matter their individual or collective initiative, or their efforts to place themselves apart, free African Americans were defined in terms of their supposed social and biological proximity to slaves, rather than by any distance from them. Assumptions about shared Black racial inferiority took their place alongside an equally potent fear that some free people of color looked—indeed were—so much like whites that, without strong policing measures, they would surreptitiously, and permanently pass into whiteness.

Anxieties about nearness and distance proved the hallmark of the interactions among free Blacks, slaves, and whites. In some circumstances, as a recent study has claimed, early eighteenth-century free Black Virginians might have found it economically and socially profitable to affiliate themselves with whites, and for Black free men to see economic advantage in choosing white mates.[2] Under similar conditions, other authors point to the mutually advantageous associations of enslaved and free families. Other paradoxes flourished. Local governments discouraged encounters among enslaved and free people of color, yet eighteenth- and nineteenth-century planters did not hesitate to use a combined force of free and enslaved laborers.

For whites, this often-inchoate set of beliefs and expectations could lead to radically opposed perspectives on how to protect status boundaries and interests while affirming clarity on the matter of the racial inferiority of Blacks as a group. Allan Kulikoff has written of eighteenth-century white Virginians' fear "that a class of freed blacks would grow in their midst, thereby tearing asunder the social contract between gentlemen and yeomen that protected the human property of slaveholders."[3] This fear did not in other circumstances prevent the formation of strong ties of service and reciprocity among groups of whites and free people of color. Indeed, in such a system, the benefits of being regarded by whites as exceptional, or special, may have well placed a brake on the free Black individual's or family's desires to see any general growth in the "class" of free African Americans. Thus, in a strange calculus, white and free Black sentiments could be conjoined. The turn to metaphor reflects one dimension of historians' efforts to explore the conflicted responses of whites, enslaved, and free Blacks to these complex sets of circumstances.

Scholarly interest in the history of free Blacks in the South began at the turn of the century. Following an initiative encouraged by the Departments of History at Johns Hopkins and Columbia Universities, young scholars set out to document state-by-state histories of free Blacks for their doctoral dissertations. Between 1888 and 1936, published monographs and articles appeared on Georgia, Virginia, Maryland, Mississippi, North Carolina, and Texas.[4] These descriptive state studies served most of all to herald the presence of a community that had been invisible to previous historical analysis but that had figured so dominantly in the imagination of white southerners. Their authors did not entirely avoid Ulrich B. Phillips's nostalgia for slavery, or his ideas about Black inferiority, yet they moved the scholarship considerably forward. Ralph B. Flanders, for example, dryly commented in his study of Georgia that the constant legislative and policing attention given to the state's free Black residents seemed in great disproportion to their small numbers in the state's population.[5] He was at pains to suggest the factors that contributed to these circumstances. But what he gave with one hand, identifying the injustice of white Georgians' attacks on free people of color, he took back with the other, blaming the natural docility and ignorance of free Blacks for their debased status.

The long-term legacy of the best of these works includes the strong push for serious primary research in state public records. Research in the trenches of federal, state, and local archives yielded new perspectives on free Black history, thus creating a comparative perspective, if not within then across the range of studies. Among the shared themes in this early output were the origins as well as the "numbers and condition" of each state's free Black population; their relations with whites and slaves; and how attitudes toward free Blacks changed through the seventeenth, eighteenth, and nineteenth centuries. Research in legislative collections and court cases delineated the course of the law with regards to manumission and civil and property rights, and with a prescient nod to social history, these studies also offered brief glimpses of the patterns of free Black family and community in their respective states, primarily through biographical sketches.

Published in 1913, John H. Russell's *The Free Negro in Virginia, 1619–1865* is the most widely acknowledged work in this first-generation scholarship, frequently cited by modern scholars of the Chesapeake as a significant contribution to the field. One defining characteristic of Russell's work is its investigation of the framework of laws and sanctions pertaining to the free Black presence in the state. Its success rested in a well-contextualized reading of the statutes. With this approach, Russell did more than most to avoid a strictly biological determinist explanation. He asked about the underlying material conditions and political climate that could, for example, lead to a loosening of manumission laws in the late eighteenth century, and to their repeal only a quarter of a century later, or that determined the rise and fall in Black property ownership.

Russell used the historical materials as a means of judging the merits of the case against free Blacks in the South. True, he pointed to the undue legal burdens placed on free Black Virginians. He set out to disprove the most serious of white charges against this social group, but then saw some justification in the supposed "propensity" of this population to steal or to collude with slaves in "roguish" behavior. "Free negroes," he judged, were "surpassed [by] no other inhabitants of the Commonwealth in the number and variety of their depredations."[6] The industry and achievement of the few had to be favorably judged against the "natural laziness" of the many. Russell's work reflects a moral drama played out between the white historian steeped in the racist ideology of his time and the preponderance of the evidence that directly challenged the intellectual foundation of those beliefs.

Among this group there was also the seriously flawed, but influential work of Ulrich B. Phillips, who devoted a chapter to free Blacks in his *American Negro Slavery*, published in 1918.[7] Phillips argued that slavery was a benevolent institution. White planters, in his view, provided not only the material necessities of life but also the moral and social restraints that would be otherwise absent in the biological makeup of an inferior race. His negative description of free Blacks rhetorically focused on their reputed moral, sexual, and economic debasement brought on by a natural inability to comprehend and act on the privileges of liberty. Without slavery's reins, Blacks ran amok. Free Blacks' pariah status proved the measure of slavery's beneficial role in preserving southern civilization. Phillips justified slavery on moral, biological, and philosophical grounds. His discussion of free Blacks served as further justification for his apologia on behalf of southern slavery. Nonetheless the work presaged an enduring historiographical effort to link the study of free Blacks to a broader analysis of the politics of race and slavery.

Where early white historians had only grudgingly pointed to the achievements of southern free Blacks and rationalized the hostility of whites, a small group of African American scholars working in the 1940s and 1950s, including the historians Luther Porter Jackson and John Hope Franklin, dismantled the presumption of free Blacks' inferiority, pointing instead to the enormous successes of this group against incredible odds. Jackson's *Free Negro Labor and Property Holding in Virginia, 1830–1860* and Franklin's *The Free Negro in North Carolina, 1790–1860* continued the tradition of working closely with state archival records, but they brought a new vision of coherent and self-sustaining free Black communities.

Along with a group including African American sociologist E. Horace Fitchett, this second generation of scholars revisited the terrain of free Black studies. Their work would establish that the knowledge of community building and capital accumulation developed by free Blacks in the nineteenth century helped to midwife the transition of the majority to free status after the war.

Writing of Virginia, for example, Jackson identified the antebellum period as the most brutal to the liberties of the free Black population because of the aggressive postures of proslavery forces. A series of harsh legislative restrictions, brought on in large part by white reaction to Nat Turner's insurrection, boxed free Black people in on all sides. Yet in a paradox that set the analytic paradigm for his argument, Jackson pointed to the counterintuitive evidence that strongly indicated the greatest free Black economic advancements during this same period, from 1830 to 1860. "Despite the avalanche of laws and abuses," he wrote, free Blacks "stayed in the state and they prospered."[8]

How was this possible? Political and legislative action took second place to the economic conditions that created a need for free Black labor and artisanal skills. Free Blacks, in turn, used this advantage to drive a wedge into the system that had previously kept them at the economic margins. In Jackson's world, free Blacks acted on the potential to be masters of their own fate. They acquired property, purchased and manumitted their enslaved friends and kin, and inserted themselves into every phase of Virginia's urban and rural economic revival. Property and capital mitigated the worst effects of antebellum legislation. This occurred, Jackson pointed out, not only for an exceptional few but for a significant proportion of Virginia's African American residents. Contrary to Phillips, then, Jackson demonstrated widespread Black achievement outside of slavery. Rather than a cast of inherently lazy characters, he pictured a community of strivers, limited only by the obstacles placed in their path. Another dimension of this work is that he identified the emergence of a free Black elite whose presence challenged the then-prevailing historical and popular view that "the Negro started his career in 1865 with nothing."[9]

These second-generation scholars sounded the modern themes that have occupied subsequent work. What was the impact of restrictive legislation and white hostility on the lives and actions of free Black southerners? Which kinds of evidence most reveal the nature of this impact on free Black property holding, rates of criminal activity, class differentiation in the free Black community, demographic patterns of growth, household formation and residential stability, the range of free Black and white interaction, and the creation of independent free Black social and religious institutions?[10] Ira Berlin's classic study *Slaves without Masters: The Free Negro in the Antebellum South* crystallized the scholarship around these questions. His title suggests that Berlin already knew the answers, thus leaving little room for deeper analysis. But this is deceiving. Ranging in breadth from the 1780s to the Civil War, and incorporating massive quantitative and qualitative material from the Upper and Lower South, Berlin offered a complex view of the fortunes and fates of free Black southerners. He pointed to the specific nature of free Black community life over time and space. Circumstances were nowhere exactly the same. Across the comparative reach of his work, he showed that the experiences of individuals varied from exceptional affluence to an abject poverty in which free and enslaved status were barely distinguishable.[11]

Building on Franklin's and Jackson's work, Berlin pointed to the range of factors that impinged on the lives of free Blacks. His commitment to a strong condemnation of southern slavery often seemed to make him reticent to make any definitive claims about free Black achievement. He provided an account that balanced the evidence of free Black agency against that which exposed the repressive forces of southern society. Overall, Berlin wrote with rare subtlety. His focus on statutory power, however, has left him open to the charge that he overly objectified free Black life, leaving his historical subjects little room for independent maneuver.

Clearly the politics of how best to depict free Black life has never been removed from the intellectual engagement in the arcana of dusty reading rooms and archives. Scholars have similarly debated such issues in the study of slavery.[12] Loren Schweninger takes up the matter full force in his study of slave and free Black property holding across the South through 1910. His is the most comprehensive analysis of local and regional patterns of African American economic development and class differentiation in the South.

For Schweninger the quest for economic security, more than any other factor, defines the history and character of free Blacks in the South: "Free blacks held the acquisition of land in the highest regard" and "exerted every effort to enter the property-holding class." Where historians like Franklin and Jackson emphasized the role of property in consolidating a distinctly African American community, Schweninger resolutely attends to the capitalist drives of individuals. Economic individualism provided the transformative catalyst that made Africans and their descendants into Americans. Free Blacks, he argues, consciously used property accumulation as a means of setting themselves apart and of gaining entry into the world without either hyphens of color, culture, or status. Even with the risk that white jealousy could occasionally flare up, Schweninger contends that for free Blacks to be propertied was to be truly free and American. If in this quest they created ties to one another, then these were the byproducts rather than the goals of self-interested accumulation. Further, property not only cushioned individuals from white depredation but also untethered them from any residual links to African culture—a tradition that privileged collective over individual welfare.[13]

The nineteenth-century free Black southerner as individualist is no more fully developed than in Michael P. Johnson and James L. Roark's description of William Ellison, a former South Carolina slave who by virtue of his skills as a gin-maker and planter amassed a considerable fortune in land and slaves. Johnson and Roark uncovered a wealth of family papers that had previously been unavailable to scholars of free Black life. They joined these sources to more traditional public records to craft a finely detailed history of William Ellison's family over three generations in Stateburg, South Carolina. As a study of family, household, and community in a place over time, *Black Masters* inspires a sense of the potential for new directions in free Black historiography. Its approach has greatly informed this book. As with any local study, however, we are confronted with the issue of where such a finely detailed study fits into a general depiction of the free Black southern experience. Johnson and Roark are ambiguous on this point, sometimes pointing to the special nature of Ellison's experience, sometimes suggesting its applicability to South Carolina or the Lower South, sometimes attending to the role of class as the significant variable, and in other instances arguing for some larger relevance to southern free Blacks as a whole. If not always clear on how the pieces fit, the authors remind us of the need to decipher the particularities as well as the commonalties among free Blacks in the South.

If nowhere else, it is in their discussion of how William Ellison strategically and consciously negotiated his privileged status as a free person that the authors lay claim to a larger interpretive model. Ellison's success, in his biographers' view, came because he was able to capitalize on his considerable skills as a machinist; just as importantly, he knew how to comport himself so as to build a broad base of approval among the whites of Stateburg and its environs. In their reading of the evidence, this approval governed Ellison's every action: where he lived, which church he attended, who his children married, and who his friends were.[14]

In the authors' depiction, a level of calculated self-consciousness imbued Ellison's worldview. Free status could never be taken fully for granted.

Accordingly, free Blacks succeeded to the extent that they avoided even the suspicion of association with the slave majority. Even their interactions with other free Blacks were carefully measured. In the case of William Ellison, the richer he became, the further he distanced himself from the local free Black populace. Johnson and Roark chronicle Ellison's progressive abandonment of Stateburg's small free Black community for an exposed, alienated life in a rural area dominated by white planters. Family is the cloak that Ellison drew around himself. Any tighter connections to the local free Black community was, in Johnson and Roark's view, filled with risk.

Ellison's ownership of upwards of sixty slaves, according to the authors, was not only a necessity to his agricultural and manufacturing enterprises but also a means of signaling his full acceptance of the racial and social order. They provocatively argue that a main motivation for free Black ownership of non-kin slaves was that it offered a form of self-protection. With capital invested in slaves, a free Black person demonstrated that his interests were aligned with those of white slaveowners. Paradoxically, according to this interpretation, the free status of some Blacks was erected on the backs of those they exploited for labor and symbolic value. Johnson and Roark argue that for free Blacks like Ellison, success was founded on the degree to which they could get whites to see them as exceptions to their race. But the authors go further. At the level of consciousness, they say, successful free Blacks believed themselves to be first of all free men and women, and "negroes second."[15] The negotiation of status led not only to a repertoire of strategic self-protecting behaviors but also to an internal psychology that subordinated any collective consciousness based on race or shared status as free people of color. Herein, these authors suggest, lay the foundation for free Black strategies of resistance and personhood.

Subjective materials available to Johnson and Roark put the free Black individual at the center of the stage. From that vantage point, it appears that they find free Blacks profoundly incapable of orchestrating the rhythm and tempo of their lives without being consumed by the hegemonic imperatives of Low Country slave society. Johnson and Roark argue that it was in attending to the everyday political and social consequences of their actions under white scrutiny that free Blacks gained self-mastery.

This new scholarship joins together two levels of questions. The first has to do with the structure of free Black communities and the nature of white response. The second concerns the subjective nature of the free Black experience. To the extent that we can track the direction of this new scholarship, less than a decade into its emergence, what is apparent is the view that the security of free Black status came at the expense of community formation and explicit political affinities to slaves. Southern free Blacks found salvation through an uncompromising attention to work, wealth accumulation, and reputation as it was defined by the planter class. The realities of southern slave society allowed few other avenues for free Black autonomy.

Virginia's laws, like those of South Carolina, could be brutal in their sanctions against the free Black population. Yet I find in Goochland County rather more flexibility in the range of options and strategies taken by free Black residents. At times they seem downright cavalier in testing the outer limits of white accommodation. How did free Black residents of Goochland County establish identity and negotiate status? How and under what circumstances did they create communities or circumvent them? What were their strategies in their interactions with the enslaved and whites? The goal of this book is to forcefully think through these issues for one county in the Upper South.

Even with the vigorous tradition of the historical study of free Blacks starting at the turn of this century, writing about them has often been perceived as a form of curiosa, an engagement with the burlesque or sideshow that in the end deflects attention away from the broad sweep of the tragedy and power of the institution of slavery. The obvious criticism, fairly stated, is that too narrow a focus on the flexibilities that allowed for a durable freedom for some Blacks leads us to underestimate the power and damage caused by the ideology of racism. A number of overlapping reasons may be cited for these responses to the scholarship.

Most apparent is the matter of demography. If demography alone provided an index of importance, then free African Americans would demand only a historical footnote. For example, at the end of the eighteenth century, free Blacks in the Upper South accounted for only 10 percent of the Black population and only 2.1 percent in the Lower South. And although in some states their numbers grew through the nineteenth century, with fully a half of Maryland's Black residents and an overwhelming majority of Black Delawareans (97%) free in 1860, the general pattern more closely mirrored the situation in nineteenth-century Virginia with about 10 percent of the African American population living in freedom. Many African Americans who were enslaved and most whites in the eighteenth and nineteenth centuries could have encountered very few free persons of color in their entire lives.

But what of the small numbers? Ira Berlin turns the problem on its head. It is the very anomalous nature of this social grouping that in his view justifies its close study. Social historians have always been drawn to the outsider. Careful investigation of those on the margins undermines the illusion of consensus while exposing the gap between the society's ideal and actual social identities. Other historians have focused not on the small numbers or exceptionalism of free Blacks as a group but pointed instead to the inordinate attention placed on free African Americans in the localities where they resided. Barbara Jeanne Fields notes on this score that the mere presence of a free Black populace, regardless of numbers, "lent slavery a defensive strain.... [It led] to suffering on the part of black people because slavery on the defensive could be especially overbearing.... But it also placed in the hands of both free blacks and slave a moral, ideological, and, upon occasion, practical weapon that the most determined effort of the slaveholders never managed to spike."[16]

A second reason for the ambivalence is that, save the above exceptions, the literature on free Blacks in the South has resolutely avoided comparative overviews.[17] The genre that seems most sympathetic to the subject hews either to the earliest models of local, state, and regional studies, or to closely textured family narratives. From outside the field, this approach, with all its merits, appears to have played second fiddle to more expansive slave studies. It has contributed to the view that the study of free Blacks is off the beaten path, or that the work has already been done and the sources offer nothing new to be discovered. To the contrary, the turn toward the social history of specific places is precisely where the study of free Blacks can add significantly to general scholarship on southern history. The body of work discussed above suggests that it is in these "small places" that the main questions about the nature of slavery and freedom, race and class will ultimately be answered.

On the consolidation of slavery in the Chesapeake, the works that most effectively convey the complex development of relations of race, gender, status, and class in the South are those like T. H. Breen and Stephen Innes's *"Myne Owne Ground"* and Joseph Douglas Deal III's "Race and Class in

Colonial Virginia" that decipher the dense social relations among individual and social groups as they define and are defined by strategies of power and authority.[18]

As the reader takes up our historical account, it will become apparent that free African Americans inhabited two status spheres—the one determined by administrative control through laws and prevailing systems of belief about race and society, and the other shaped by everyday customs and interactions in specific locales. These two spheres, which we may think of as statutory and customary status, were in constant interplay, now affording free African Americans great latitude and at other times drastically circumscribing their lives. Laws chipped away at the foundation of African American freedom. Occasionally they expanded or protected it. Whatever the outcome, in the absence of political power or participation in the most fundamental responsibilities and privileges of citizenship, free African Americans could scarcely affect the forces that determined their contractual status. As we will see, in the matter of their customary status, they could do much to influence its terms to their own advantage. The abiding difficulty for the historian, therefore, is to ascertain how these free people negotiated their status, imbued it with meaning, and fell victim to or rose above the pitfalls of a society created on a foundation of inhumanity to people of color.

I have kept these issues at the forefront of this work in order to sustain a sense of the very different world that free Blacks in Goochland County faced when compared to our own. They constituted a segment of society whose existence most forcefully emerged in laws that sought to render them invisible and whose sense of place and personhood depended in large part on local customs and conventions that may only be barely apprehended on the edges of the historical frame.

An example from Virginia secures the point. In 1793, the General Assembly created a system of registration to ensure that all free Black inhabitants would be fully identified and accounted for in the localities where they lived. Registers indicated how the person gained free status as well as the vital statistics of name, gender, and age. But even more tantalizing, county clerks described in some detail the skin and eye color, height, and visible physical features or scars of each free Black individual who appeared before them once every three years as required by law. John Brown, for example, was noted to be of dark complexion and to have a scar under his eye, and

Judith Howell, a "black" woman, bore a mole on the left side of her breast when both registered in 1804 at Goochland Courthouse. In this way the records signal the presence of free Blacks on the social landscape but give few insights into where or how people lived once they left the clerk's office. Many of them never again surfaced in any official records. Furthermore, what seems a crucial device to police the free Black residents of the county never fully accounted for a significant proportion of people who simply did not show up to be registered at any time. For those historians who would see African American free status as akin to "living on hell's boundaries," the free register was yet another form of punishment. Others, like myself, recognize the coercive intent of the registers but emphasize the interplay of law and custom in creating the experience of freedom.[19]

I explore in this book, therefore, the purposes to which free Blacks put the registration law and their certificates of registration, to affirm their status and to legitimate their presence in the county, or to avoid the entire process when it suited them. They also "lent," or had registrations stolen by enslaved persons, who then used these certificates of freedom on their own behalf. The point is that the historical project of reclaiming the history of free Blacks in the South is not an easy one. They, like other historical subjects, have as much to hide as to reveal about their motivations and experiences, nor was the course of legislation and white attitudes toward these people completely transparent, or purposeful.

My motive is to expose the relentless depredations visited on free African Americans while not giving way to the idea that they were totally and exclusively defined by them. I can think of no better way to accomplish this task than to take up the traditional tools of the social historian. I mine the details of state and local records to build a portrait of a people and place over time. By focusing on this specific place over a century and a half, and through remarkable changes in Virginia's broader economic and political history, we can honor the particularity of free African American individuals, and nowhere more forcefully than in acknowledging the structural limitations that shaped the general patterns of their lives and the histories of their communities.

The structural framework of laws and racial ideologies that locked most free Blacks into this social, political, and economic liminality also stimulated a high degree of ingenuity and strategic negotiation for places of security where they could ensure intergenerational transmission of free status, if nothing else. I have often been struck by the insistence of free people of color, under daunting circumstances and in the heat of white intolerance of their presence, to stand their ground in the places they considered home. I have been drawn equally to how such assertions, expressed in ways both subtle and direct, influenced local conventions about boundaries between whites and Blacks, slave and free. In such matters, patterns developed, tensions ebbed and flowed. Networks of friends and kin emerged over the long history of a specific place as people made meaning and gained a degree of mastery of the world around them. The social historian's attention to the details of situation, of the warp and woof of domestic and public life, of the mundane and the extraordinary, can best illuminate how free African Americans lived their lives in the "shadow" of slavery.

It is important to reveal my personal stake in this study. My maternal kin still call Goochland home. Family narratives, some with only the skeletal outlines remaining, trace connections both to Anglo and African American free people as well as to slave ancestors. Although I worked at the archives in Richmond and elsewhere during my research, I always preferred to use the original sources at the county clerk's office. Working in that space kept me constantly aware of the long and continued interrelationship of power, race, authority, and the law in rural Goochland County. I gained an ongoing feel for the subtleties of place that guided my incursions into the world of the past. Additionally, eighteenth-century references to my family linked personal biography to broader historical patterns. And at welcome moments, they enlivened the tedium that was a constant companion in the painstaking search of county records.

When I first entered the archival room at the Goochland County Courthouse, I was the object of much curious, perhaps anxious attention. Lawyers, real-estate agents, the county clerk and his assistants, the sheriff, and an occasional genealogist—all white—worked confidently with the historical and contemporary records housed there. On the other hand, the few African American residents who came on official business invariably stood politely in the outer office and requested a clerk's employee to find whatever pertinent legal document they needed—whether for land transactions, criminal cases, marriage licenses, or traffic violations. Whites mediated access to these public resources.

Although the county had been the home for generations of my maternal relatives extending back to the early eighteenth century, though I had lived there with my grandparents through adolescence, more than two decades later when I walked into that public space, I felt as if I had broken a taboo. My uncle, a lifelong resident, expressed some apprehension when he learned that I intended to do historical research "down at the courthouse." From his perspective, and that of many African Americans, these materials were simply outside the boundaries of the familiar—off-limits. African Americans rarely entered that somehow sanctified space without being "helped" by white employees. All clerks in the county's history have been white; at the courthouse, all but the custodial staff are white. African Americans tread the halls of the administrative buildings primarily as clients, litigants, or prisoners awaiting trial. Even in the instances when employees of the clerk's office gave considerate and respectful help, it is easy to see how African Americans viewed these public records and histories with trepidation and with the sense that they properly belonged to whites. Eventually, by virtue of academic credentials, I gained access and a certain privilege in the clerk's office that remained unavailable to most African American residents. The issue of a Black presence at the courthouse environs is of course not a new one. It proved sufficiently bothersome to nineteenth-century county administrators that they, in an 1836 order, empowered the sheriff to "keep all slaves and free negroes out of the courthouse while the court is sitting unless they have business before the court."[20] Black county residents in the nineteenth century were strongly invested in the activities taking place at the Goochland Courthouse.

By the late 1980s, however, an African American in the main archival room of the clerk's office was an oddity. What did I intend to do with the records? How had I become so familiar with the material housed within, and what gave me the authority to break traditional racial and social boundaries? How would I interpret the records? This book, I hope, answers some of these questions, and for others continues a dialogue about past and present in Goochland.

Goochland County lies in the center of the Virginia's Piedmont plateau. In 1727, it was the last county on the western periphery of the colonial frontier, stretching indefinitely beyond the Blue Ridge Mountains. The county's geographic history is convoluted. Separate political entities took shape and its borders contracted over time. Goochland originally included more than forty miles on either side of the James River and the length of Tuckahoe Creek on its eastern border with Henrico County. The James and its many tributaries still dominate the landscape and shaped, in large part, the county's agricultural, commercial, and social history. Eventually, the river would become its southern border separating it from Cumberland County.

Administrative apportionment of territories reflected a period of considerable population growth in the Piedmont as increasing numbers of white settlers and enslaved Africans and African Americans pressed the capacities of county seats either to serve their governmental needs or to command service in return. The shifting outlines of this frontier were permanently fixed in 1749 when Cumberland to the south and Albemarle to the west became separate counties. In turn, Powhatan, Fluvanna, Cumberland, Louisa, and Buckingham, all contiguous with present-day Goochland's borders, were created. When expedient in following individuals and families whose lives overlapped administrative demarcations, our narrative crosses these county lines. In general, however, this study is confined to the area politically designated as Goochland and served by its central county seat at Goochland Courthouse. That area is roughly thirty-two miles long and covers over three hundred square miles.

The single most relevant socio-geographic characteristic that shapes this study's exploration of free Black life is that Goochland lies in the Virginia Piedmont. In the early eighteenth century, the Piedmont was home to a society of immigrants. The swell of migration began in the 1720s with white settlers and planters from the Tidewater in search of arable, affordable land suitable for tobacco cultivation and available in sufficient quantity to meet the demands of a rising generation of Tidewater sons hungry for their own real property. The Tidewater contingent would later be augmented in the 1740s by white settlers from Pennsylvania. Enslaved African Americans experienced in the ways of Tidewater agriculture accompanied their owners. They no doubt had their own desires for—or apprehensions about—life in this new place but were subject to their white owners' sanctions and institutions. So too were the large numbers of Africans brought directly from Africa. Together, these enslaved people provided the minds and bodies that would not only develop the agricultural economy but also contribute greatly to the cultural transformation of the region.[21]

At times, the historiographical impulse to describe the Piedmont by comparison with the Tidewater proves frustrating for understanding the region on its own terms. The exercise has a certain utility, however, as a way of making sense of this region's emergence, its maturation, and its subsequent role in shifting the economic center away from the Tidewater. The Tidewater template, for want of a better phrase, is of an early dependence on white indentured servants and a handful of slaves for the production of tobacco through the third quarter of the seventeenth century, of a certain fluidity of racial and status boundaries that allowed for the provisional emergence of a recognized class of free people of color, which then dramatically shifted to the almost total reliance on enslaved labor after 1675.

By the 1720s, the opportunities for free communities of color had effectively closed down. Individual free people of color continued to live in the Tidewater alongside African and African American slaves, their destinies shaped as they had not been before by legal sanctions defining a severely restricted freedom and prohibiting manumission. Did the colonial Piedmont frontier follow the above template or did its settlers build on the by then familiar patterns of a mature Tidewater?

The jury is out on how best to answer this question, and where to look for appropriate evidence. The narrative is unwavering, however, with regards to the consolidation of slavery in the region by midcentury. Demographic evidence provides the most conclusive evidence that the combination of importations of enslaved Africans and the growth of a creole population led to a comparative leap in the Piedmont's portion of the Black population. Philip D. Morgan notes that by midcentury one-third of Virginia's enslaved population lived in the Piedmont and by the 1800s they constituted fully a half of the total. This pattern continued into the nineteenth century.[22] Goochland was typical in this respect. By 1790, it held a majority Black population.

Demography alone conveys the narrow wedge allowed free Blacks living in the Piedmont. While slave households and communities developed thick networks of kin, free Blacks scattered across the region had fewer opportunities to create similar ties based on a recognition of free status. It is at this point that the interpretation of slavery's impact on the status of a free Black community diverges. Was the glass half full or half empty?

Richard S. Dunn argues that the sheer numbers of slaves in the Piedmont and the entrenched nature of the institution forestalled the development of free Black communities, separate from slaves and independent of whites. Philip Morgan, in a final codicil to his larger work on slavery in the Piedmont, notes the opening demographic and political possibilities for vigorous, albeit small, communities of free Blacks in the region. Where

Dunn finds a hardening of attitudes toward all Blacks, both slave and free, Morgan discovers a greater recognition of slave humanity in the post-revolutionary period grounded in the spiritual awakening of a core group of white planters. This cushioning of attitudes, in his view, extended out to free Blacks and would encourage, if not provide a catalyst for, the free Black population growth of between 5 and 9 percent in ten rural counties and over 20 percent in Richmond and Petersburg. The current state of the scholarship allows for no firm conclusions. These opposed visions strongly suggest, however, the need for systematic work. Morgan's figures indicate a broad range of local variation in the level of tolerance for free Blacks' action in clearing a space for themselves within the system of slavery.[23]

As a result of the compelling work on the early Tidewater and Eastern Shore, many nonspecialist readers can claim intimate knowledge of Mary and Anthony Johnson or of Emanuel and Frances Drigus, free people of color who gained property and reputation in a seventeenth-century Virginia not yet fully committed to the repressions of a race-based social order.[24] The early hope and final tragedy of free African Americans such as these invoke the mystery and possibilities of a path not taken. By contrast, free people in the eighteenth- and early nineteenth-century Piedmont present no such hold on our hearts and imaginations. Slavery and its consolidation do. Historians of the region have for the most part devoted their concerns to this aspect of the Piedmont world. The narratives of free African Americans in Virginia only get fully taken up again in the nineteenth century on the eve of the Civil War. This work then is an initial foray into the field to give flesh to the history of free Black life in the Virginia Piedmont.

· 1 ·

Born into Freedom

As in the rest of Virginia, free status for African Americans in Goochland County came through birth to or descendance from a free woman and after 1782 through manumission. The free Black population between 1728 and 1782 was constituted by a small number of individuals scattered throughout the county living in close association with enslaved African Americans and free and indentured whites yet no doubt aware of their own separate social status and identity. Recognition of free status, however, did not, without the power of numbers, translate into a living, self-perpetuating free community of African Americans. Only with the demographic and social impact of manumission after 1782 did such a community evolve. Yet as early as the 1730s, freeborn individuals appeared in the county's historical record as "mulatto" children born to white indentured mothers. By the mid-1750s, marriages and baptisms signaled interfamilial alliances. Legal disputes revealed the complexity of personal relations and experiences, and tax records showed where people lived and labored and with whom. The life-worlds of these individuals and families in the first half-century of Goochland's history speak to the long, arduous duration of African American freedom on the county's social landscape.

One hundred and sixty-five individuals living in the county during the period between 1728 and 1782 have been identified as free people of color.[1] Evidence from Virginia as a whole also supports the conclusion that, though proportionately small compared to the white and slave population, free Blacks in Goochland County exceeded the numbers derived from the records. Historians have convincingly challenged previous estimates of the early free Black population, arguing that the figure has been too low. Where it has been previously accepted that only 2,800 free people of color resided throughout the state in 1782, estimates now suggest there were more than twice that many.[2]

Such numbers gain greater meaning when they are attached to the names and lives of individual men, women, and children. Certain surnames reoccur among the free Blacks living in the county in the period before 1782. Shared surnames reflect parental as well as sibling relationships. Of the forty-three children apprenticed by the county courts, for example, there were eleven sibling groups, ranging from two to six children. Thirty-four separate surnames appear in the records, and of these, eight names—Banks, Cochran, Coopers, Cousins, Granthum, Howel, Mealy, and Scott—predominate. These family names continued to appear with frequency through 1832. And for the most part, they did not mirror those of whites. This mark of difference suggests that free Blacks had separate patterns of family names. It is difficult, however, to know their origins.[3] Perhaps, they hearken back to seventeenth-century Tidewater free people of color whose progeny moved to the Piedmont and eventually to Goochland County.[4]

White women who gave birth to mixed-race children may have passed on their surnames along with free status. Especially if their fathers had been slaves without surnames, children of such unions would have naturally taken the names of their mothers. A search of early marriage and baptismal lists to identify the maiden names of white women found few correspondences between the maiden names of white women and the surnames of free people of color.

Naming patterns have been used as one means of deciphering slave and free Black consciousness. Historians have argued that for both slaves and free Blacks the ability to name oneself and one's children provided a mark of self-determination and personal autonomy. Scholars have documented, for example, the decision of recently freed slaves to abandon the names given to them by their former masters and to take on newly minted first and last names. Here, the act of naming represented a major rite of passage as newly freed persons discarded their old status for the new and, in this act of self-confirmation, challenged the slave system as a whole.[5]

In a similar fashion, surnames in Goochland's early free Black community may be seen as one means by which individuals gained a sense of autonomy and group connectedness. The very act of being able to name oneself and one's descendants signaled free status as well as the ties between affinal and blood relations. Christian names also provide insight into the early development of free Black consciousness in the county.[6] Adults as well as children were distinguished by the almost scrupulous attention given to names derived from English religious and secular traditions. Biblical names were restricted to the more common among them, such as James, John, David, Daniel, Mary, Judith, Agnes, and Hannah. English diminutives were similarly nondescript, including Betty, Aggy, Billy, Tom, Ben, Sall, and Dick. Full name counterparts appear with frequency, for example, Benjamin, Margaret, Elizabeth, Richard, and William. Fully half of all the first names appearing on the registration lists, to take one sample, were derived from the Bible, and the remainder may be classified as secular.

The baptismal records of six free Black children provide a measure of parents' use of English names. Ruth Mathews and Lucy Howel, free women of color, both baptized their daughters in 1756. They named their daughters, respectively, Elizabeth and Judah. Four other children with the names Richardson, Milly, Betsey, and Lucy were baptized between 1756 and 1779, presumably named by their parents, who accompanied them to their Episcopal baptisms. The naming of these children reflected another common pattern: most persons in the core sample carried only a first and last name.[7]

The nomenclatural system used by free Blacks, one that continued with little variation throughout the period, can be interpreted from a number of perspectives. Absence of African names signaled an attempt on the part of free people of color, most of whom had never been slaves, to create a symbolic distance between themselves and an enslaved status. If Africanized names belonged to those slaves born in Africa or the close kin of Africans, then by taking on English names, free Blacks affirmed that they were an English-speaking people, born in the New World and acculturated to New World traditions and culture. This symbolic distancing occurred at the same time that free people of color closely interacted with African as well as creolized slaves on a regular basis. Further, the explicit avoidance of Africanized names did not necessarily lead to the rejection of the underlying patterns of familial naming according to kinship ties—from child to grandparent, from aunts and uncles to nieces and nephews. It must be recognized that in putting aside African names, free Blacks were no different from their white counterparts, who also abandoned naming patterns and cultural traditions from their natal societies.[8] The historical process by which names fell into disuse reflected deeper patterns of cultural transformation as African and English immigrants and their descendants adapted to their New World experiences.

The presence of persons described as "mulattoes" indicate that interracial sex played a part in individual and group life histories. But what part? The early records verify the presence of individuals who were the offspring of free white women and Black men. Fathers remain invisible so we are unable to say whether they were enslaved or free. But whatever the status of the male partner, as early as 1691 the Virginia Assembly prohibited marriages between white women and Black men.[9]

This statute, together with one passed in 1705, imposed severe sanctions. All white women who married Black men or bore their children faced banishment, imprisonment, or heavy fines. A free white woman was to be indentured for five years if she was unable to pay a fifteen-pound fine on the birth of her mixed-race infant. A white servant woman in similar circumstances had to serve another five years beyond her original indenture or pay a fine of fifteen pounds.[10]

The same 1691 law that condemned such women imposed lengthy periods of indenture on their mixed-race children. Caught in the web of a white society's need to delimit the freedoms given to Blacks, mixed-race children were reduced to near slavery at birth, forced to serve until their thirtieth year, with an additional year added in 1705. This long period of indenture stood for sixty years until the assembly, in 1765, reduced the term to twenty-one years for males and eighteen for females.[11] In 1730, two years after the founding of Goochland County, the church wardens bound out Hannah, "a mullatto orphan," to learn "the arts of a sewer and spinner." One year later they bound out two African American children "born of the bodies" of free women. Tom, the son of Doll, "a mulatto," was apprenticed to James Cocke in August. No master was immediately available for Elinor, the "orphan" of Elizabeth Griffen, a white indentured servant, however, so the courts ordered that one be found. Sixteen years later in 1747, Elizabeth, who by then must have been released from her original indenture, again appears in the records. Yet another of her children, a mixed-race girl, also born out of wedlock, was to be bound out by the church wardens.[12] Enforcement of miscegenation laws appears to have been directed toward the status of juvenile offspring rather than the sexual activity of the white mother.

But even then, the laws seem not to have been consistently applied. Free white women entered into intimate relationships with Black men outside of the immediate context of a shared dependent status. At times, their children escaped the servitude imposed on the offspring of servant women. A baptismal record from 1760 documents the birth of a male child to James Mathews, a free Black, and Susannah Ford, a white woman. Richardson, their son, was born on April 17, 1760, and baptized two months later by an Episcopal minister, the Reverend William Douglas, who served in Northam Parish at the Dover church. Both parents' names appeared on the official baptismal register.[13]

These two individuals were sufficiently confident that the minister would recognize their informal union when they brought the child to church and had its birth consecrated. The child was probably given his father's surname. By baptizing Richardson, Douglas acknowledged the legitimacy of the couple's union and appeared to sanction the actions of a white woman who, in defiance of the 1705 statute, publicly displayed her sexual attachment to a Black man, albeit a free individual. Barred from legitimizing their union through the sacrament of marriage, Susannah and James took advantage of the opportunity for the church to formally, albeit indirectly, recognize their union.

Before bringing his son to be baptized in the church, James Mathews was acquainted with Reverend Douglas's church. In 1756, during the first decade of his residency in the county, Douglas recorded the baptism of eight-year-old Elizabeth, the daughter of one Ruth Mathews, and in 1775 conducted marriage services for Bristol Mathews and Nanny Lynch. These may have been James's relatives, all living in Northam Parish. The Mathewses had established a connection with the church that accounts for James's and Susannah's forthrightness in bringing their son to be baptized and Reverend Douglas's decision to perform the ritual.[14]

In his capacity as minister to the county's residents, Douglas baptized the children of slaves brought in by their owners. He also performed this sacrament for a number of the county's free Black residents. The Mathews-Ford case is the only one, however, in which he performed the sacrament of baptism on the child of an interracial couple. Yet Douglas was himself a substantial slaveholder, owning fourteen slaves in 1775. His action, therefore, cannot be read as an overt challenge to Goochland's racial and social norms. Indeed, as Mechal Sobel has effectively argued, there were "great inconsistencies" within planters' worldviews and in their subsequent behavior toward African Americans. Douglas's baptism of Richardson Mathews is exemplary of such inconsistencies. But as Sobel further points out, the existence of what appears to the historian as contradictory may well have had "an overall functional coherence."[15]

In Virginia, free African Americans, particularly those born of white mothers, were perceived as posing a threat to the social order. As a slaveowner and representative of the official church in the county, Douglas may well have shared this view. Yet, obviously, he allowed himself some flexibility in performing his duties, even if such actions went against law and custom. Intriguingly, Douglas employed William Cooper, a free Black man, as his overseer, a position of some authority.[16] Perhaps his willingness to baptize Richardson may also be best understood as precipitated by the minister's acquaintance with the individuals involved as well as by his ongoing interactions with specific free Black persons.

Throughout the period, whites of the upper as well as middling classes supported the ideology that represented free Blacks as a threat to the social order. They readily accepted limitations on the rights of free people of color as a group and viewed the growth in their numbers with considerable hostility. Yet, running parallel to this abhorrence of the group, many whites seemed relatively willing to make exceptions for free Black individuals with whom they had personal ties—whether based on economic, religious, or familial relationships. The interpersonal nature of these patronage relationships meant that disciplinary power rested squarely with whites, who could give and take according to their inclination. Free African Americans maneuvered to gain the most benefits from these relationships while mitigating the damage such dependence could incur. In this regard, pre- and postrevolutionary free Blacks faced the same dilemma and may have acted in similar ways to test the boundaries of their oppression.[17]

That James Mathews and Susannah Ford did not hide their relationship suggests they were sufficiently comfortable about the response of other residents. There is no indication that legal sanctions were enforced to punish Susannah or that there were any social recriminations against James or the child.

Historians have offered what may be termed a developmental-demographic model of the wax and wane of miscegenation in early Virginia. Discussion of sexual interactions between white women and slaves illustrates the underpinning of such interpretations. This model posits that in the early colonial period, the close interaction of white female servants and slaves resulted in sexual intimacies between the two groups. As Virginia's social hierarchy concretized, increasing sanctions against women participating in such unions and the reduction in the total numbers of indentured servant women coming into the colony all but eliminated these relationships.[18]

At the same time, miscegenation, particularly among white women and Black men, became socially repugnant. Scholars often cite the text of legislation referring to the "shame" and "disgrace" of such unions as well as to the "abominable mixture and spurious issue" of mixed-race children born of such unions in order to illustrate the society's growing intolerance of sexual relations between white women and Black men, especially with slaves. In this view, by the early eighteenth century, miscegenation was on the decline.[19]

In the seventeenth century and throughout the period of our study, some white women in Goochland County, not all of whom were servants, freely chose Black partners in spite of the specter of severe punishments for themselves and their children. Perhaps the demography of their own social milieu rather than any county or regional patterns defined the nature of these choices. As to the level of intolerance based on a distaste for white female/Black male intimacies, this too may have varied across time and space. In the end, local justices permitted wider latitude in regard to miscegenation than the colonial assembly had intended. The absence of presentments in the local courts against white women for intimacies with Black men can be taken to indicate the low level of such interactions. But alternatively, this evidence may be used to suggest that neither county residents nor the local authorities pressed charges in all the instances where such unions occurred. Taken by themselves, presentments do not tell the entire story.

Often ignored in recent discussions is that to a great extent miscegenation can neither be explained entirely by reference to demography, nor can its cultural meaning for the colony's residents be measured solely by reference to legislative acts. In the seventeenth century Chesapeake, white men outnumbered white women by a ratio between two and three to one.[20] Perhaps, then, the level of miscegenation among white men and free Black or slave women can be discussed as a consequence of the skewed sex ratio. Yet staying within the same terms of analysis, we would expect few if any incidents of miscegenation between white women and Black men, particularly in the early phases of the colony's formation. But, as Edmund S. Morgan points out, the nature and extent of sexual relations between white women and Black men ran counter to what would be predicted from demography alone: "Women were still scarce in Virginia in 1691 and doubtless continued to be for another twenty or thirty years. At the turn of the century, there were probably about three men for every two women. The laws against miscegenation were aimed at confining the affections of these rare white women to white men. And there seems to have been good reason for concern.... It would appear that black men were competing all too successfully for white women, even in the face of severe penalties."[21]

Unlike Morgan, some historians have found Black male/white female miscegenation in Virginia sufficiently anomalous that they have attempted to "explain" its existence. Joel Williamson suggests that miscegenation was characteristic of early Chesapeake settlers, most of whom were servants and for the most part unrepresentative of English society. Interracial sexuality, then, was restricted to the early period and to the human flotsam and jetsam that fled the social upheaval of seventeenth-century England. Joseph Douglas Deal, on the other hand, speculates that such liaisons may have involved some form of coercion on the part of slave men wishing to bear free children. In a more extreme hypothesis, Ira Berlin argues that white planters, in order to realize further service from servant women, possibly forced them to cohabit with slaves. None of these arguments holds up under closer examination. At least in Goochland County, evidence of either behavior pattern is not forthcoming.[22]

Miscegenation continued as an element of African American and white relations well into the postrevolutionary period. This does not mean that unions between free persons of color and whites were ever the norm. Indeed, any skepticism about the conclusions of these historians lies not with prevailing norms. Rather it is with the degree to which they ignore the unevenness and irregularity of individual experiences within overarching socio-structural patterns.

Marriage records for the prerevolutionary period yield a sample of solemnized marriages between free Black individuals. All of the eleven marriages that were officially recorded during the years from 1759 to 1778 were between mixed-race couples. Complexion and proximity may have played an important role in an individual's choice of a partner. With one exception, wives and husbands resided in the proximity of Dover Episcopal Church in the southeast corner of the county. They may well have been members of the church, for Reverend Douglas performed the rites. The earliest marriage dates from December 1759, when Francis Cousins was joined in wedlock with Mary Martin. Both were mixed-race living in Maniken Town, an early eighteenth-century Huguenot settlement bordering on the James River in the county's lower district. Francis subsequently moved to the county's upper district where he was listed in 1806 as a cooper. Apparently he had remarried, for he was listed as residing with Chloe, "his wife," also a mixed-race woman. In 1761, William Lansford from Dover Parish married Elizabeth Scott, who was originally from Hanover, a county on Goochland's northeastern border.[23]

Besides giving information on the possible criteria that may have directed the choice of a spouse, the marriage records also reveal that free Blacks lived in residential clusters with closely related kin. Drury Ferrar married an unnamed woman in 1769. Four years later, in September and November 1773, respectively, Joseph Ferrar and Molly Gantlet and Stephen Scott and Molly Ferrar, all described as mulattoes, were legally married at the Dover Church. The close dates of the marriages between Molly and Joseph and the shared surnames among the three couples may indicate a kinship tie. There were three marriages in 1775, one in 1776, and another in 1778. Of these marriages, Abbie Scot, who married Charles Howel in June 1775, may have been related to the above-mentioned Stephen. The Jacob Banks who married Susannah Jones in August was the younger brother of Judith Banks, who married Isaac Howell the same year, and of Mary Banks, who solemnized her relationship with James Johnson in 1776.[24]

Whether partners cohabited or legalized their marriages, a web of conjugal and blood ties developed within the early free Black population. David Granthum, for example, married Elizabeth Mealy in 1778. His wife came to the union with a son, James Mealy, who had been born out of wedlock. At his death in 1804, Granthum willed much of his property to his stepson, whom he referred to as his "wife's child," and to his "granddaughter" Jennie Mealy, who was James's daughter.[25] Siblings and their in-laws, cousins, aunts and uncles, stepfathers, and stepchildren lived near one another and formed enduring ties. At its very base, the free Black community grew out of these familial bonds, with roots and branches in the slave and white communities. Only as a consequence of these overlapping relationships could the free Black community survive and grow.

These official marriages document the establishment of dyadic ties between free men and women of color and the extensions from those relationships to children and neighbors. Baptismal records also permit some consideration of the meaning of family in the prerevolutionary period. Less than five months after their marriage, William and Elizabeth Lansford brought in their four-month-old daughter Milly to be baptized. Given Milly's birth in May 1762, Elizabeth was certainly pregnant at the time of her marriage to William. While we are unable to know the length of their premarital courtship, Milly's baptism attests to her parents' desire to legitimate her birth. Further, by having her baptized, they affirmed their commitment to one another and to the continued connection of the new family to the church.[26]

With these marriage and baptismal documents, some light is cast into the shadows. Admittedly, many questions cannot be answered. For example, little may be said of marriages and births not legitimated in the Episcopal church during Reverend Douglas's tenure. Indeed, individuals sometimes appear in later records as being legally married with adult children who would have been born before 1782, but no evidence of these unions appears in the early records.[27]

Some free Black persons may have joined Baptist congregations where they were married and baptized. By 1771, Baptists had gained a foothold in the county, establishing churches in Dover, Maniken, and Lickinghole. A contemporary observer noted that Goochland's gentry were among the most receptive to the Baptist message in Virginia. So too did enslaved and free African Americans claim membership in the county's Baptist congregations. During annual revivals, hundreds of African Americans were converted to the faith. Although the sources do not distinguish among celebrants, some of these individuals were probably free people of color. It is likely that some free Blacks joined other Protestant denominations active in the county during the prerevolutionary period. Marriages and baptisms noted in the records of the Dover Episcopal Church offer only a partial, though significant, account of the ways in which free Blacks solemnized the important events in their lives.[28]

The obverse side of the social nexus for free Blacks was of course their relationship with slaves. Evidence of the nature and extent of these relationships is fragmentary for the prerevolutionary period. But we can gain some insight both in the abstract and in particular cases by examining statutory law and the public records from the county. In absolute terms, the General Assembly opposed and attempted to stifle the growth of the free Black population. The presence of this anomalous group provided a constant reminder that the connection between color and status was a mutable one. Planters and their representatives feared that a mobile, free Black population would not serve as a buffer between whites and slaves but would instead promote dissension and insurrection.

Yet if there was a general consensus about the dangers of free people of color among the populace, the legislative response suggests that there were contradictory and ambiguous viewpoints about how best to monitor and administer their behavior. The essential problem for planters concerned the status of free persons of color and uncertainty about the roles these individuals would take in a society based on racial slavery. Strict regulation of associations between free Blacks and slaves seemed to reflect one strategy. In 1723, for example, the same year in which the assembly eliminated private manumissions, it also delimited the interactions between free Blacks and slaves. It prohibited free Blacks from attending "meetings of great numbers of negros and other slaves."[29]

Moving from the public to the private sphere, the law further attempted to drive a wedge between free Blacks and slaves. Not only were mass meetings declared illegal but domestic associations also came under scrutiny. The assembly imposed severe penalties, including fines and whippings, for free Blacks who "harbor[ed] or entertain[ed] any negro or other slave whatsoever, . . . without the consent of their owners." A related statute, enacted in 1798, further raised the specter of free Black and slave collusion. It reaffirmed the penalties for those who would associate with slaves without permission and invoked the death penalty without benefit of clergy for any free person found guilty of encouraging or participating in any slave unrest or for being an accessory to murder.[30]

Other measures and circumstances just as forcefully pushed the two groups together. For example, laws that required up to thirty-one years' service for juvenile apprentices no doubt resulted in the close interactions of free Blacks and slaves on a daily basis over extended periods of time. The blocked economic opportunities for free Blacks inevitably placed them in close association with slaves. They too were dependent on plantation agriculture, and in many instances other than their legal status could not be distinguished from slaves. Thus, ties of family, work, race, and economic dependency all were factors that subverted the carefully crafted legislation to ensure the maintenance of a social distance between these two groups. Some planters may indeed have recognized that efforts to keep these groups apart were impossible to enforce.

At least in the prerevolutionary years, their small numbers and relative incorporation into the daily life of rural Goochland County probably rendered free Blacks, in whites' views, a much less potent force. On the ground, therefore, the situation was a great deal more complex. Neither statutory law nor the explicit intentions of planters prevailed in predictably shaping the multiplex interactions of free Blacks, slaves, and whites.

Most free Blacks residing in the county before 1782 probably spent a significant portion of their lives as dependent laborers on plantations. The form and duration of this dependency varied according to law, customary practices on plantations, and the abilities or fortunes of individual free Black men and women. In the case of apprenticed free Black children, depending on their age of indenture, terms of servitude could be as long as thirty-one years or less than a year.[31] For individuals who were not under any formal terms of indenture to a specific master, plantation life and labor was still a dominant part of daily existence. In 1746, Daniel Cooper, for example, lived on the plantation of Anne Scott with her two adult sons and five slaves. Mary Banks resided and worked on Walter Leake's estate in the company of one slave, Tamer, an adult woman. By contrast, Daniel and William Banks lived on their own, perhaps as tenants but possibly owning their own plots.[32]

On some plantations, planters employed free Blacks as overseers. During the first half of the eighteenth century, in Goochland as in other Piedmont counties, many Tidewater planters shifted or established additional holdings in the uncultivated western lands above the fall line. Often such planters did not relocate but administered from afar, depending on overseers for the day-to-day management of the estate and slaves. But the absentee planter did not have to have resided in the Tidewater. Many lived in the Piedmont and sometimes in the county but maintained outlying quarters. We find that in Goochland, a few free Blacks found employment as overseers on such estates. In the tithes, they are either identified as overseers or in other instances appear as the only free Black tithe on a holding owned by a white planter.

The relationships between the free Black overseer and slaves, or between these individuals and the white planter, cannot be mapped with any attention to the subtleties of the loyalties and antagonisms that may have developed under these conditions. We can acknowledge, however, the presence of James Mealy, a free Black man, listed as overseer on the Beaverdam estate of a Colonel Phillip Lightfoot in 1746. Besides Mealy, ten male and three female adult slaves resided on the plantation located in the county's southern section in the area of the courthouse. On his Dover estate, also in the lower district but more to the southeast, Lightfoot employed Gervas Burdette, a white overseer responsible for twelve slaves (nine men, three women). John Christian, also an absentee owner (living in Charles City), relegated the management of an auxiliary quarter of his main estate to a free Black overseer, David Granthum. Granthum first appears in the 1746 tithe and maintained his position through 1755. Throughout this period, Granthum worked the plantation with three enslaved adults. In 1755, however, two other free Blacks, Will and Sam Granthum, joined the quarter's labor force.[33]

Structurally, no matter what the individual personalities, slaves and free Black overseers found themselves on opposing ends of the plantation social structure with differing perceptions of commitments to the white owner. At the same time, however, the opportunities for cooperation and the creation of personal and familial ties likely increased in situations where African Americans worked closely together. None of the plantations with free Black overseers exceeded twenty slaves. Thus, both slave and free inhabitants would have been familiar with one another, interacting closely on a daily basis. Planters' individual decisions to hire free Black overseers may have done more to broaden the social distance between free persons of color and their enslaved kindred than any calculated legislative directives from the colonial assembly.

The situation of John Cousins, a free Black overseer working on the modest holdings of William Pledge, suggests the range of variation in the configuration of the relationships among slaves, free Blacks, and whites in the prerevolutionary years. Cousins was listed as an overseer in the 1755 tithe lists along with two female slaves (Patt and Phillis). He worked closely with the slave women in the cultivation of corn, wheat, and tobacco and in raising livestock (horses, sheep, cattle, hogs) on Pledge's farm.[34]

What is somewhat puzzling was the need for an overseer, given the fact that Pledge resided on the estate and worked only two female slaves. The answer to the puzzle is perhaps to be found in the 1756 and subsequent levies. While he lived on his estate, Pledge's employment as the main caretaker for the jail and its inmates as well as for the courthouse buildings and public grounds meant that he would not have been able to attend to the hands or the operation of his plantation. In John Cousins, Pledge found both an overseer and a male adult worker to supplement the labors of his two female slaves. With Cousins responsible for the daily running of his estate, Pledge could devote his attention to his courthouse duties.[35]

The dimension of the mutual dependency between Pledge and Cousins was tested in 1755 when Charles Bates, himself a small planter and slaveholder, brought charges of assault against John Cousins. The county justices found the defendant guilty of a "breach of peace" and required him to pay thirty pounds' security to guarantee his good behavior, especially toward Bates, for "a year and a day." Perhaps to prevent Cousins's imprisonment and to avoid the loss of a valuable worker, Pledge stood the entire security. Thirty pounds was a considerable sum. His guarantee may have served to bind Cousins more firmly to the estate because, at least for a year, he was indebted to his employer and benefactor. Cousins's encounter with the law thus drew him into a tighter set of obligations to Pledge, but he had not fared too poorly with the local justices.[36] Indeed, had the justices followed the provisions laid out in a 1705 statute, punishment would have been far more severe. According to this statute, "any negro, mulatto, or indian, bond or free" found guilty of "lift[ing] his or her hand in opposition" against a white person was to be given thirty lashes "well laid on."[37] Given Pledge's familiarity with the workings of the court and the justices, Cousins may have convinced his employer to intercede on his behalf.

Tensions existed between free Blacks and middling and working-class whites. In 1754, Obadiah Smith and his wife, Mary, accused Frank Cousins, a "free mulatto," and two slaves, Myrtilla and Squire, belonging to the estate of William Randolph, deceased, of attempting to poison them. Apparently, these individuals had been involved in some longstanding conflict.

In such situations, the shared bonds of status or color did not always lead to the expected alignments. The accused pleaded not guilty but Murrocker, a slave, testified against Myrtilla, implicating her in the alleged poisonings. No other witnesses took the stand, and in the end the justices found the two slaves not guilty of the charges that had been brought against them. Similarly, at the same court, Frank Cousins was also found not guilty as charged. Thus, in spite of the corroborative testimony of a slave, the Smiths were unable to get satisfaction from the courts. Nonetheless, by virtue of being accused, Frank served twenty days in jail, while Myrtilla and Squire spent ten days awaiting their trials.[38]

The matter did not end with this final judgment of the courts. While the two slaves were returned to their owner's estate, Frank faced additional maneuvers on the part of Obadiah Smith. Smith testified to the justices that he "verily believe[d]" that he went "in Danger of his life by the said Frank Cousens, and that he does not, make this oath out of any Malice, Envy, but only thro apprehension of Danger."[39] The use of poisoning or threat of poisoning to frighten or take revenge against an enemy was a well-documented pattern among African Americans, both slave and free, in Goochland and throughout the Piedmont.[40] It is entirely likely, therefore, that the three accused employed or pretended to employ this technique against the Smiths.

In the end, the couple failed to convince the local justices. Although judged not guilty, Frank was required to post security in the sum of fifty pounds to guarantee his good behavior toward the Smiths for a year. Frank, in turn, had his supporters. Unable to post bond, he avoided further imprisonment when Paul Michaux and James Holman, two planters and slaveholders, guaranteed payment. The justices had in a sense reached some compromise, punishing Frank but not to the full extent available to them under statutory law.[41]

The cross-hatching of alliance and conflict may have occurred around a number of variables including race, status, and class as well as the individual reputations of the parties involved. In the prerevolutionary years, fears of collusion between free Blacks and slaves did not appear to have led to a wholesale repression of the free Black community. Its members, after all, were for the most part dependent on the patronage of planters. They were certainly not inclined to jeopardize their standing, however marginal, by instigating unrest.

In fact, where we are able to find sources of antagonism among free persons of color and whites, they appear to have been focused on personal animosities rather than any attack on the system as a whole. Perhaps these occasional flare-ups of conflict among free Blacks, slaves, and whites masked underlying collective tensions. Planters could afford to be lenient and the courts occasionally to give the benefit of the doubt to Black defendants because the mechanisms for more stringent suppression could always be brought into play. The county courts on occasion used the most brutal and repressive measures to ensure their hegemony over slaves and free Blacks. In one such instance, slaves declared guilty of murdering a white planter in 1733 were hanged, quartered, and burned. Their severed heads were displayed at the county courthouse.[42]

The year 1782 provides a useful point of division between the early and later periods of free Black population growth in the county. This division, however, is somewhat arbitrary. The "Act to Authorize the Manumission of Slaves," discussed in the next chapter, profoundly altered the society. But in spite of the dynamics of the American Revolution and subsequent ideological and structural changes, patterns set in an earlier period continued to have saliency for individuals and the society as a whole. Individual as well as familial lifespans bridged the two periods. Indeed, a free Black individual born in 1728, at the county's founding, would have been only fifty-four in 1782. Their daily routines need not have varied greatly over these years. A slave born in the prerevolutionary years and freed after 1782 experienced a significant transition in status, but if they remained in the county, their lives would have continued to center around the plantation and enslaved kin.

· 2 ·

Manumission and Planter Response

The passage of the private manumission act, the "Act to Authorize the Manumission of Slaves," in 1782 reflected both the changes that Virginia had undergone as well as the continuities between the pre- and postrevolutionary periods. State and county responses to the democratization of the manumission process provide a clear illustration of the dynamics at work. Although it constituted a dramatic shift in the terms under which the society had operated since 1723, private manumission had considerable support as expressed in the positive votes of county representatives in the assembly. These representatives, most of whom were from counties with large slave populations, could not have voted in this manner had they not had some assurance of the support of their local constituents.

A substantial number were vocal in their distaste for any changes that would allow for liberalized manumission and growth in the state's free Black population. They feared that passage of the 1782 act was the precursor to universal abolition and lobbied for a return to the controls extant in an earlier period. Underlying these tensions were similar assumptions about the negative impact of freed Blacks on society, assumptions that had their antecedents in the colonial period. To understand the situation in Goochland County and the consequences for the development of a free Black community, the contradictory push and pull of radical change, on the one hand, and reactionary conservatism, on the other, has to be acknowledged.[1]

Our initial entry point is the larger stage of the newly formed state. Opposition to private manumission took many forms. It began immediately after passage of the 1782 act and continued through the period under study.

Slaveholders railed against passage of the act, calling for its repeal in petitions to the assembly. Intense vitriol was directed against free Blacks, the most vulnerable of persons. By contrast, opponents showed surprising restraint toward planters who manumitted slaves and who were therefore partly responsible for the growth in the free Black population. Indeed, by the act of manumitting, they demonstrated disdain for the strident opinions of their anti-manumission counterparts.

Manumission opponents viewed free Blacks as disruptive social elements. They described them as lazy, subject to unprovoked viciousness, unmanageable, a potential drain on local fiscal resources, and, perhaps most damaging, predisposed to align themselves with slaves during insurrectionary activities.[2]

Although persistent, anti-manumission petitioners met with failure on each occasion that the issue of a repeal came up for consideration. Nonetheless, their strong arguments undoubtedly convinced some representatives to initiate debates about the feasibility of private manumission and to consider legislation that would require all freed slaves to leave the state. Such a vote took place in 1785, again in 1787, 1788, and 1791. Goochland was among counties whose representatives voted in the majority against any changes to the private manumission statute in 1785. Three years later, however, the county's vote was split among those who supported and opposed the same bill.[3] Shifts in sentiments were evident in the overall voting pattern over these years. By the late 1780s, not only did increasing numbers of representatives vote to overturn the 1782 act but the option to place harsh restrictions on the state's free Black population gained favor.[4]

The first salvo in the latter initiative occurred in 1793 when free Blacks were prohibited from entering the state. Furthermore, in a companion statute, the assembly ordered that every free person of color register with the court clerk of their place of residence. It was the responsibility of the clerk to handle the bureaucratic details of the registration process, maintaining a separate book "for that purpose." Once registered, the free Black person received a certificate of freedom that in the case of rural counties had to be renewed once every three years at a cost of twenty-five cents.[5]

In the context of domestic upheaval with Gabriel's aborted rebellion in 1800, the insurrectionary scare of 1802 following close on, and the events of the revolution in Saint-Domingue that stretched from 1791 to 1804, the darkest nightmares of Virginia's slaveholders were confirmed. Strict administration of the free Black presence extended to an amendment of the rules governing private manumission. Planters were still able to manumit at their discretion, but after 1806 freed slaves were legally bound to leave the state within twelve months of their manumission. Historians of the period speak of the 1806 law as a repeal of private manumission. Its terms confirmed planters' rights over property while it eroded the security and status of freed and free Black individuals, families, and communities.[6]

Passage of the 1782 act signaled a return, after more than half a century, of the individual planter's full authority over their chattel property. Planters once again moved center stage as the ultimate arbiters of any transformation in the status of their human chattel. While the legislature never completely absented itself from policing the freed Black population, and indeed increased the means of monitoring this segment of Virginia's population, it turned its attention away from any direct prohibition of planters' actions in matters concerning the disposition of their slave property. Part of the rhetoric of those opposed to liberalized manumission was that it would lead to mass emancipation.

Contrary to expectations, however, the total number of freed persons in Virginia always remained small in number when compared to the population of slaves. Perhaps from the perspective of those opposed to liberalized manumission, one additional free person of color was one too many. Nonetheless, the historical record indicates that the rate and course of manumission was relatively controlled. It was restricted, for the most part, to a limited number of planters with strong religious or secular beliefs against the ownership of slaves.[7]

In Goochland, an individual planter's release of chattel by legal instrument was the most common manumission procedure.[8] Slaveowners notified the public of the transition in the status of their slaves and gained final official sanction. Thomas Massie's deed of manumission of James (alias James Barrett) in April 1794 was typical. Massie used the first person, named the individual to be freed, and made reference to the law that gave him authority to take such action: "To all whom these presents shall or may concern. Know ye that I Thomas Massie of the County of Goochland have and do by these present Emancipate my man Slave named James alias James Barrett, and do hereby vest him with all and singular the previledges and immunities of a free born Citizen as far as the Laws Usages and Customs of the Commonwealth will admit."[9] The deed was signed by Massie and three witnesses, including the county clerk. Three months later, the document was officially recorded in the deed book "in solemn form" with the testimony of two of the witnesses that it was genuine.

The transition from slavery to freedom, at least at the procedural level, involved the mediation of the manumitter with the county bureaucracy on behalf of the enslaved persons. Of necessity, most of our subsequent discussions of private manumissions focuses on these "formal" cases. But in Goochland, as in other counties, the official court records do not tell the entire story.[10]

There is evidence of manumissions that fall into more nebulous categories. These are the most difficult to document. A slave's change in status from slavery to freedom was not always officially recorded in the form of a will or deed. In some instances, planters may have given slaves a written or verbal acknowledgment of their release from bondage but stopped short of filing any document with the court clerk. Subsequent action to formalize these emancipations was left to the individual freed person's discretion, the exercise of which may have varied from person to person, with the laws governing registration, and with the changing practical merits of being officially documented as a freed person of color. Furthermore, newly manumitted slaves who migrated into the county also registered with the courts. A "book" of free Black registrants is extant for a consecutive thirty-year period from 1804, comprising roughly 500 free persons, 148 of whom were manumitted. Many of these registrants migrated to Goochland from elsewhere. It is often difficult to sort out those individuals freed in the county and those coming from neighboring areas.[11]

For Virginia as a whole, historians have noted that only a small percentage of the free Blacks registered under the terms of the 1793 law.[12] Such was the case in Goochland County where registration rules were applied with great inconsistency and it was not unusual to have free Black residents who never registered or who effectively neglected to abide by the triennial registration requirement. Nevertheless, local county authorities and free Blacks did not completely ignore the mandated registration process. These registrations allow some means of identifying freed slaves whose manumissions were not recorded by will or deed. In September 1796, for example, Sam brought in a deed of manumission from his unidentified former master. The court acknowledged the deed and certified that he was a "free negro." Five years later, Robin, a free Black man, registered with the county court and presented a certificate of manumission from his deceased master Samuel Couch. After the document had been inspected, the court ruled that Robin was entitled to his freedom. In May 1824, Eliza, with her children (Martha Emmalina and Robert Washington Chancellor), presented a deed of manumission from one William Morris to the local county court. The deed was dated seven days earlier. By bringing in the deed of manumission, Eliza ensured that there would be official recognition and proof of her family's right to freedom.[13] Evidence of the presence of informal manumissions must be inferred from cases like this one and from the sizable number of free Blacks living in the county for whom no documents of manumission or freeborn status exist.

The acknowledgment of "informally" emancipated slaves alerts us to the variety of ways by which individuals experienced the transition from slavery to freedom. Indeed, once private manumission was legalized and as greater numbers of free persons of color entered the population, there were increased opportunities (some legal, some extralegal) for slaves to slip across the boundary that separated them from their free counterparts. Writing of the fallout from a Richmond Quaker's emancipation of his entire estate of slaves in 1795, historian Ira Berlin notes, for example, that "when news of a large emancipation in Richmond reached Petersburg, several slaves immediately left their owner and tried to pass as part of the negroes that obtained their freedom under the will of John Pleasants."[14]

At times, similar ventures on the part of slaves in Goochland County met with ill luck, and as a consequence they reached the attention of the authorities. The case of Peter, a Goochland County slave, and Frank Brown, "a free man of color," points to the capriciousness of fate at the same time that it suggests a degree of manipulation of status boundaries. Details emerged from the trial of the latter in 1827. Frank Brown was "charged with feloniously furnishing Archer Payne's negro man . . . with a copy of the said Brown's register of freedom for the purpose of Peter's posing as a free man."[15]

On the first day of October 1827, at the Louisa courthouse on Goochland's northern border, James Ferguson noticed Peter "passing on horseback." His suspicion raised, Ferguson, according to his deposition, "called back and further examined the [negro]." Peter insisted that "he was his own man." Unsatisfied with that answer, Ferguson continued to press the Black man, who finally admitted that he was a slave, the property of a Goochland planter named Archer Payne. It is unclear whether Peter presented a register of freedom as proof of his status or whether Ferguson conducted a search of the hapless slave, but in any case, such a document was found in his possession. The register was identified as belonging to Frank Brown, "a free man of color," resident of Goochland.[16]

Peter claimed at the time of his confrontation with Ferguson that he had found the "the said paper."[17] Willingly or by accident, Frank Brown became Peter's accomplice. Brown's case was referred to the Superior Court where the eventual verdict is lost to the records.[18] As to Peter's fate, beyond his being imprisoned during the period of the trial, the record is also silent. Slaves who attempted to pass as free were treated as runaways and returned to their masters. No judicial proceedings appeared to have been mounted against Peter, however, and no mention was made in the court proceedings of whether he owned the horse he was riding. It is assumed that since no charges of theft were brought against him in the court of oyer and terminer, the horse could have been his own property or belonged to his master, who probably meted out punishment to Peter once the slave was returned to the plantation.[19]

If it was indeed the case that Frank Brown loaned his free register to Peter, then such interaction is evidence of the continued relationship of free people of color and slaves. Perhaps these encounters fostered the movement of slaves into free status, if only, as in Peter's case, temporarily. But even if the assumption is made that he had indeed "found" the free paper, the implications are no less revealing. First, Peter was well aware of the power of the certificate of freedom. Second, Ferguson's ability to stop and interrogate the slave suggests that, when they ventured outside the familiar limits of their own neighborhoods, free people of color were extremely vulnerable.

Under these circumstances, Peter's assertion that he belonged to none but himself was a response that must have been heard and indeed used frequently in such interactions and may have sometimes been accepted without demands for further proof. In these situations, individuals took calculated risks. Again, Berlin describes the context within which slaves judged their chances for liberating themselves. "With so many newly (and illegally) freed blacks traveling through the countryside, it was no longer possible for whites to know every Negro in their neighborhood or realistically assume that every unknown black was a slave."[20]

Not everyone would have been as "committed" as James Ferguson, who, one suspects, would have left the slave unmolested had Peter not been traveling on horseback by the courthouse, the very center of Louisa's social and political life. Berlin notes that Virginia's system for policing the slave and free Black populations was not without flaws: "Although many whites automatically stopped every strange or unsupervised black man and woman and demanded proof of their status, the number of unknown free Negroes doubtless taxed the zeal of even the most vigilant white."[21]

Surreptitious exchange of registers from free people to slaves must have occurred. Support for this interpretation of the negative evidence is to be found in the seemingly perfunctory manner with which the county clerk issued duplicate certificates of freedom. At the least, it is certain that there were many such certificates available in the system.

Free persons of color often presented themselves to the county clerk to receive duplicate certificates of freedom that they claimed to have lost, accidentally destroyed, or worn out. Typical entries included that of one Diana Cooper, who reported in 1823 that her registration had been stolen. The clerk provided her with a copy. Two years later, she again appeared, this time because the copy had been "accidentally lost." Another copy was made and given to her.[22]

In the same year that Frank Brown was brought to court, Frank Moss, William Cooper, and Maria Cousins reported that they had lost their registrations and had them replaced. In a ten-year period from 1822 to 1832, the clerk "furnished" fourteen replacement certificates.[23] Although some investigation was made to ascertain the veracity of individual claims, it is likely that additional certificates made their way into the system and were put to use by slaves and free people. Some literate slaves may have forged registrations for themselves and perhaps for others.

What was a heavy burden—the necessity to prove one's free status to any enquiring white and to carry a certificate of freedom—could also have provided a means of subverting the mechanisms of social control. Given these possibilities, formally registered and acknowledged manumissions were special instances of a process whereby enslaved African Americans in Goochland County found divergent paths to free status.[24]

Given the existence of a formal and informal manumission process, therefore, the numbers of slaves manumitted provides an index of the methods, procedures, and motivations of activity that occurred above ground, so to speak, at the level of legally constructed and recognized social action. The informal means of gaining free status are less accessible to the historical eye.

The course of manumission was characterized by intense activity in the months following passage of the 1782 act. The earliest known response to the law came a few months after its passage in October of that year when James Hunnicutt emancipated Lettis James, a forty-three-year-old woman; twenty-three-year-old Edy James, most likely Lettis's daughter; and five other unnamed slaves. These individuals constituted all the slaves Hunnicutt owned. On the same day, in a cluster of manumissions by Quakers that autumn, Benjamin Watkins filed a deed of manumission for nine slaves. Two weeks later, Mary Pleasants, her daughter Mary Younghusband, and son-in-law Strangeman Hutchins together manumitted twenty-three slaves. In the largest single manumission of the year, and only two days following his family's divesture, Thomas Pleasants, another of Mary's children, emancipated his holding of fifty slaves. By the end of the first year of private manumissions, eighty-nine slaves, all formerly belonging to Quaker planters, gained free status.[25]

Altogether, forty-three Goochland slaveowners were identified as manumitting more than 191 slaves in the half century from 1782 to 1832. The characteristics of this pool of emancipated and emancipators offer some indication of the patterning of the manumission process in the county. No pattern of gender selectivity seems to have been operating in Goochland County emancipations. Fifty-four percent (103) of those freed were men, and 46 percent (88) female, a ratio of 1.1 to 1. The slight preponderance of men to women reflected that of the slave population as a whole, rather than any gender preference on the part of emancipators. For example, in the 1810 census, a year in which slave men and women were listed separately, the sex ratio was 1.1 (2,914 men and 2,607 women). Likewise, in 1830, the ratio remained about the same (2,964 men compared to 2,752 women). Thus, as far as the sex ratio is concerned, manumission seems to have been a fairly random process. A man was just as likely to be freed as a woman.[26]

By contrast, the population of emancipated slaves were predominantly children and juveniles, with the next largest category of persons being individuals between twenty-one and forty-five years of age. Only a few emancipated slaves were forty-five years or older. In a sample of 158 persons (83%) for whom age can be determined, 56 percent (89 persons) were under the age of twenty-one. Thirty-six percent (56 persons) fell between the ages of twenty-one and forty-five, and the remaining 8% (13 persons) had reached or passed their forty-fifth birthday. In his cross-regional study, Peter J. Albert found that in most instances emancipated slaves were under the age of twenty-one. The pattern in Goochland was similar.[27]

That older slaves were less likely to receive their freedom was due to a proviso in the 1782 law that required masters to provide financially for their former bondspersons over the age of forty-five.[28] Wanting to escape such obligations, emancipators likely retained property rights in older individuals or manumitted before the individual reached the mandated age. In 1797, for example, Thomas Fleming manumitted forty-five-year-old Ceasar, only one of his twenty slaves. Caesar had been manumitted just under the wire.[29] There were exceptions to the slaveowner's hesitation to manumit older individuals, for in the situation where manumission was a reward for long service, the slave tended to be a more mature individual. Under these circumstances, a planter could justify emancipation and ward off criticism by indicating their intention to provide the upkeep of the superannuated slave. But of the thirteen older slaves emancipated in the county, only in one instance did a planter offer any written acknowledgment of his legal obligation to provide for the welfare of the emancipated slave. William Webber made such a promise when he emancipated Hannah, a fifty-year-old woman, in 1797. An addendum to his deed of manumission noted that the "said Webber agrees to keep her [Hannah] free from any charge from the Parrish of Goochland County." Given the absence of anything in writing in the remaining cases, it is apparent the state had not stringently enforced the conditions outlined for the manumission of elderly slaves.[30]

At the other end of the age scale, the proportionate imbalance in favor of younger freed slaves was a consequence of planters' tendency to emancipate in family groups. Children were manumitted at the same time as their parent or parents. Individual records of emancipations suggest that this is a fair description of many of the earlier releases of slaves from bondage. Quaker planters who divested themselves of their entire estates liberated families with young children. All but one of the twelve slaves freed by Strangeman Hutchins, for example, shared the last name Scott. In this group there were six adults and six children. Included in Ursula Mosby's 1794 deed of manumission for all seventeen of her slaves were four adults and thirteen children among whom were nine- and four-months-old infants.[31]

The lineage of Thomas Pleasants's emancipated slaves and the series of manumissions undertaken by members of his family bears out this pattern. In the listing of slaves to be freed in his 1782 deed of manumission, Bridgett, an elderly slave about seventy years old, appeared first; then in descending age order from fifty years to six months old, the remaining slaves were named with an indication that they were "her increase."[32]

The records indicate that the Pleasants family had owned Bridgett since at least 1743. In that year, Thomas Pleasants Sr. willed Bridgett, then thirty-one, and six of her children (Maria, Aggy, Ben, Cupid, Judith, and Fanny), as well as "those thereafter should be born," to his wife, Mary Pleasants.[33] Subsequently, in 1782, Mary, by deed of gift, transferred ownership of Bridgett and her considerably expanded family to Thomas. Through some legal maneuver that is obscured in the records, these slaves under the age of majority, who had by this time legally passed from owner to owner a number of times, were once again deeded to Mary Pleasants, who was to derive benefit from their labor under the terms of the manumission act.[34]

The fate of the slaves owned by the Pleasants family suggests yet another consequence of the relative youth of freed Blacks. By the terms of the 1782 law, minors, though emancipated, continued under the authority of their former masters until the age of majority, twenty-one for boys and eighteen for girls. The conditions on the upper and lower age limits for private emancipation introduced contradictions that are evident in the manumission records of Goochland County. For one thing, the positive response of some slaveholders to the private manumission act did not necessarily lead to their permanent disassociation from the exploitative practices and cultural assumptions associated with the institution of slavery.[35]

At the same time that he officially manumitted all his human chattel, for example, Thomas Pleasants still legally retained primary control over twenty-nine provisionally emancipated slaves who were still in their minority. It is possible that Pleasants saw the legal restriction on fully liberating juveniles either as a burden or as a serious compromise of his religious convictions. As part of the legislative structuring of private manumissions, however, even planters who were philosophically or religiously opposed to owning property in persons found that the decision to manumit did not necessarily mean they surrendered all claims to the labor of their former chattel.[36]

More than half of the persons manumitted by Thomas Pleasants, to continue with this example, remained putative slaves until they became of age. That Pleasants calculated the benefits of such arrangements is reflected in a deed of gift recorded seven days after the initial deed of manumission in which he divested himself of all his human property. He transferred all the "slaves" who had not yet reached the age of majority to his mother's estate, giving to her "all his interest in the labor and profit arising from 29 negroes during their minority."[37] Thus he transacted his affairs as if these "negroes" were still property. In turn, for all practical purposes, Mary Pleasants, who had herself emancipated eight slaves, continued in her role as a slaveholder. This meant that Ovid, the youngest child in this group, who was only six months old, would not have been entitled to freedom until 1803.

In his deed of manumission for seven slaves, James Hunnicutt wrote that it was "right" that he "reserve the prerogative of acting as a guardian over them [two slaves still in their minority], until the males arrive to the age of twenty one, and the female to the age of eighteen."[38] Here, guardianship replaced ownership, but on a fundamental level the relationship of labor expropriation continued.

The argument is not that it was legislative intent to encourage planters to emancipate younger slaves but that the formal liberation of these individuals did not terminate access to their labor as a result of the stipulations laid down by the assembly. While officially free, these de facto slaves were either placed by executors in apprenticeship relationships with county planters or, if their masters were alive, continued in their service. Given the relative youth of the slaves emancipated in the county, it is probable that their contributions to the plantation workforce of their emancipators helped to offset the economic losses suffered by the emancipation of adult slaves.[39] Furthermore, planters must often have retained the parent or parents who chose to stay in close proximity to their children in some form of economic dependency. The 1782 law was intended to ensure that neither elderly nor juvenile freed slaves would become a burden on local resources. Slaveholders likely viewed the injunction that they support elderly freed slaves as a burden. Yet, from their perspective, the possibility of maintaining the services of "manumitted" juveniles entailed substantial benefits.[40]

I would caution, however, that the situation in which juveniles labored for their emancipators was not the result of any well-considered legislative design. But were there ways in which emancipators actively sought to lengthen the terms of service for the slaves they emancipated or intended to emancipate? Did planters try to have their cake and eat it too? When he examined the situation for Virginia as a whole, Peter Albert argued that the choice of manumitting instrument, whether by will or deed of manumission, provides one indicator of emancipators' attitudes toward the loss of slave labor. The will, according to this argument, was the method of choice for those emancipators who wanted to extend the services of their chattel for as long as possible. By contrast, the deed of manumission provided an expedient means of freeing slaves during their owners' lifetime.[41]

In his analysis of nearly one thousand documents from nineteen counties and towns, Albert has found that in those areas "which lacked a strong antislavery religious denomination" wills predominated: "Slaveholders who were moved to free their bondsmen postponed their emancipations so as to profit from their labor."[42] This was possible, in Albert's explanation, because slaves emancipated by wills did not receive their freedom immediately but were held in bondage through the lives of their masters or mistresses. In counties with strong antislavery elements, on the other hand, the preponderance of deeds of manumission meant that planters wanted the quickest and least encumbered route to manumitting their slaves.

The preponderance of deeds of emancipation among the sample of Goochland County's manumission documents supports Albert's findings insofar as the majority of planters who manumitted slaves were either Quakers or otherwise supportive of Quaker religious tenets opposing chattel slavery. Of the forty-three emancipators in the county, more than 80 percent used deeds of manumission, and in a few cases they used this method on more than one occasion.

Once the private manumission act was enacted, therefore, the deed of emancipation provided a means to register one's opposition to the institution of slavery or to free a particular slave selected from among many others. But as we have seen, counter to Albert's logic, the deed of manumission did not necessarily mean the slaveowner completely relinquished control over the body and labor of their former slave or slaves. The deed of manumission ofttimes offered only a provisional liberation to be delayed for up to twenty years. Thus, in Goochland County, although a deed of manumission may have reflected the intention of a slaveholder to terminate ownership of a slave or slaves, in practice, even with a deed, outright manumission could be postponed. The smaller number of wills from the county (eleven) do not accord neatly to Albert's rationale. Only one will directly indicates that a manumitter used the promise of freedom as a bargaining chip to ensure loyalty and continued good service. In his 1829 will, John Webber bequeathed to his wife, Martha, a slave by the name of John. Webber directed that if the slave "continued his faithful service to his mistress as he has to me," then at Martha's death he was to be given twenty-five acres of land and a horse. Although not specifically stated, one may assume that the enslaved John was also to be manumitted.[43] In most instances, however, where wills were used as a method of manumission, the emancipators drafted their wills shortly before their deaths. This had the effect of providing the slave with freedom almost immediately.

Although planters who emancipated by will were not necessarily antislavery sympathizers, they nonetheless used the will to give specific instructions to legatees and executors regarding the welfare of the slave or slaves to be freed. Two years before she died in 1825, Judith Shoemaker drafted a will in which she named her slave Guy and his sister Jenny and her children as legatees of her estate. They were to receive a house, "household furniture," "stock of every kind," and "all her [Shoemaker's] land and other property" for the rest of their lives.[44] By way of contrast, none of the deeds of manumission expressed any concern about the material welfare of the slaves to be manumitted. For these reasons, wills allow us to draw a rather more intimate portrait of the connections between slave and emancipator than most deeds of manumission. They do not suggest that the planter's motivation in using them was to delay the liberation of slaves so as to profit economically from their labor. In sum, the ways in which wills versus deeds of manumission were used in Goochland does not confirm Albert's argument.

If not yielding to easy formulations, the question of planter motivations in their responses to the private manumission act is nonetheless a vital one. Both methods of manumission provided the formal means by which slaves were released from bondage. Whatever the method chosen, planters often attempted to explain their decisions to emancipate. These explanations—some taking the form of intensely personal statements, others following standardized formulas—provide an important measure of planter attitudes toward slavery. They also suggest the nature of the role these planters expected to play in reshaping the contours of Virginian society, slave and free. Moving from the political to the personal, these statements of purpose also reveal much about the multifaceted relationships that existed between slaveowners and their former slaves. In the case of African Americans and some white planters, familial bonds more than political ideology or religious conviction motivated them to liberate their slaves.

Admittedly, the highly self-conscious statements expressed in deeds of manumission and wills never tell the complete story about the underlying reasons behind planters' decisions to manumit. On the one hand, religiously or politically motivated manumissions likely present an idealized version of planters' worldviews. Similarly, as public documents, they may obscure the exact nature of the relationships between planters and their former slaves that may have led to manumission.

The passage in 1806 of more restrictive legislation may have also influenced planters' discourse about their decisions to manumit slaves. Recently freed persons could be exempted from this new restrictive ruling if they made successful application to the Virginia Assembly and after 1815 to the local county court. An important criterion for the success of such petitions was the testimony of former masters or other whites, who vouched for the good character of the freed person. In the wording of emancipation documents, planters may have been responding to the likelihood that these documents could be useful in supporting their former slaves' petitions to remain in the state. Slaves used the statements of masters regarding their meritorious service to support their efforts to stay in Virginia. Behind the explicit statement of motivation for manumitting rests more complicated explanations of planter behavior and responses to changing sociopolitical and economic conditions.[45]

Quakers comprised the majority of emancipators in the county in the initial groundswell of manumission activity. Perhaps as important as the common bonds of religious conviction were the familial links among these early manumitters. By extension, the slaves they emancipated were also related by kinship, marriage, and geography, having labored on neighboring plantations owned by Quakers. Many, as I have indicated, continued to work on these holdings long after their official transition to free status. What was the patterning of Quaker involvement in manumission activity? Virtually all the slaves emancipated in the county before 1800 lived on plantations owned by Quakers. During the eighteen-year period from 1782 to the turn of the century, dates are available for 137 slaves freed by 22 planters. Of these slaves, a large majority (122 or 88%) had been formerly owned by Quakers.

Thomas Pleasants expressed a traditional Quaker viewpoint in the preamble to his deed of manumission. He challenged the institution of slavery as immoral and as a betrayal of the tenets of natural rights. Throughout Virginia, Quakers had actively campaigned against slavery in their ranks and supported the passage of the 1782 statute. Thus Pleasants, the eldest son of one of Goochland's most prominent Quaker families, immediately divested himself of his human chattel. "It is my duty," he wrote, "to do unto others as I would desire to be done by in the like situation." In this formulaic statement of Christian admonition to love your neighbor as yourself, Pleasants acknowledged his own humanity in that of his slaves. This was at once radical and conservative. His explanation was conservative because neither Quakers nor any other Virginian had ever taken up the banners of revolutionary abolitionists who had advocated immediate and general emancipation. Yet Pleasants's assumption that slaves had human qualities deserving of recognition was extraordinary. He lived in a society that relied on the belief that Blacks were only marginally human as one means of maintaining hegemonic control of those in bondage. Pleasants based his decision to free all his slaves on his philosophy of shared humanity. In addition, members of his family in Goochland, Henrico, and Powhatan Counties, as well a number of his close associates, together freed hundreds of slaves. Many of these were emancipated before passage of the 1782 act. Pleasants also drew on a related secular philosophy of natural rights in explaining his motivations, for he was "fully persuaded that freedom is the natural right of all Mankind."[46]

From 1782 to 1796, by which time all Quakers had either divested themselves of their slaves or left the Society of Friends, the mix of religious and natural-rights philosophies predominated as the most frequently cited reasons for voluntary manumission of slaves. In her 1782 deed of emancipation, Mary Pleasants Younghusband echoed her brother's preamble when she stated that "freedom is the natural right of all mankind and it is my duty to do unto others as I would desire to be done by in the like situation." She emancipated the slaves (Parrot, Sophia, Sall Cooper, Sarah, Ovid, Dinah, and Arthur) willed to her in 1781. Likewise, other Quakers justified their acts by reference to natural-rights philosophy.[47] Invariably, Quakers used the identical explanatory phrases, and all freed their slaves by deed rather than by will. In final testimony of their links through meetinghouse and familial and marital bonds, they witnessed by affirmation one another's deeds of manumission in the courts.

Beginning in the 1790s, planters only occasionally offered any systematic philosophical or religious reasons for freeing their slaves. With a few exceptions, they now freed individual slaves who had provided long or faithful service or were biologically related. No longer did they attempt to place their actions within a broader ideological context. In 1796, Archibald Cary Randolph, "for divers good causes . . . but more especially for the many and faithful services rendered to me," freed his "negroman" Juba and for the same reason Nanny, a "negro woman," probably Juba's wife.[48] In another instance, John Curd, "taking into consideration the extraordinary merit and general good character and conduct of [this] man slave," emancipated John Pierce. Pierce had apparently served long and well, for he was fifty-eight years old at the time of his manumission in 1816.[49] No doubt, he had been a lucrative source of income for his master. Even before his manumission, however, he had enjoyed a measure of freedom rarely experienced by most slaves. Hiring himself to the county, he was responsible among other duties for victualing white and Black prisoners and maintaining the jail and courthouse square.[50] As a free man, he continued to perform these duties. While Curd's rationale for manumitting Pierce was relatively straightforward, the motives of some planters are more difficult to discern in their emancipation documents.

Such was the case with Gideon Cawthon, who freed his "negro woman" Kate in a will dated July 1797. Cawthon spent almost a third of the document "bequeath[ing] his soul to God that gave it." In giving his soul to God, he hoped that this, his final "gift," would not be "despairing of [God's] kind reception of the same through the merits and mediation of my most compassionate redeemer."[51] Yet in this impassioned religious bargain, Cawthon failed to make any overt connections between his decision to free Kate and the salvation of his soul. Indeed, Kate's emancipation seemed to be as far as he was willing to go in compromising the institution of slavery. Although he owned seven slaves, one of them Kate's son, he freed only Kate while stipulating that the remaining six be given the opportunity to choose their own master. Because of their status as property, Cawthon's slaves had no legal voice in their own disposition. Yet it is likely, given their master's wishes, that they were able to choose informally among his friends. At the very least, James Holman, Kate's benefactor, took possession of her son Gideon, whom Cawthon had failed to emancipate. Tax records indicate that soon after the probate of Cawthon's will, Holman's slaveholdings increased by three, further suggesting that other slaves in Cawthon's estate may have chosen Holman as their master. These slaves' ability to choose their own master may have been facilitated by Cawthon's lack of any surviving white relations to contest this codicil.[52]

While he did not manumit all his slaves, Cawthon's provisions for Kate extended well beyond simply manumitting her. Not only did he "give unto my Negroe woman Kate her freedom," but he also left her "one sow and pigs and one cow and calf." Furthermore, in a highly unusual provision, he loaned "the said negroe Kate the land whereon I now live during her natural life." Only after Kate's death did he wish his friend James Holman to assume ownership of the estate. Kate appears to have been a relatively young woman, considerably younger than Holman. Cawthon must have realized that Holman would most likely not gain ownership of the land during his lifetime. Indeed, five years after her emancipation, Kate, not satisfied with Cawthon's arrangement, purchased twenty acres of the original parcel from James Holman at a cost of seventy-five pounds.[53]

Cawthon requested that "if my negroe woman Kate have any children born after my death that my friend James Holman or his heirs do inherit them."[54] Because Kate was manumitted this request appears, at first, to be a useless codicil. Her offspring would legally have been free because the status of children followed that of their mother. But this seemingly irrational request provides a clue to the nature of the relationship between Kate and her former master: for reasons that can never be fully understood, these directives reflected Cawthon's posthumous attempt to control certain aspects of Kate's life. His attempt to provide for Kate while indirectly restricting her mobility and condemning her future offspring to slavery suggests a strong but twisted emotional bond. In 1800, just three years after her own manumission, she purchased and immediately emancipated her "youngest" son, Woodson Granthum, who was born after his mother was emancipated. Contrary to law, James Holman had Kate's future "increase," even though she was a free woman. Later, in 1802, it appears that she purchased and manumitted an older child, Gideon, named after Kate's former owner but also the property of James Holman.

Also in 1802, Kate, now calling herself Catherine Granthum, purchased, again from Holman, for seventy-five pounds an adult slave, Phillip Granthum, whom she emancipated, intending "shortly [to] marry him," having "cohabited" with him "many years as his wife." The two sons appeared to have been the offspring of Phillip and Kate. At the time that she purchased Phil, the enterprising Kate also bought a sorrel mare from Holman.[55]

As with most intimate interactions between white planters and their slaves, it is difficult to ascertain the exact nature of the ties between Kate and Cawthon. Very soon after Cawthon's death, Kate gave birth to a child, Woodson, who appears to have been Phil Granthum's child. Perhaps she was not Cawthon's concubine. Even before her liberation, she had "cohabited" with Phil, who lived on a nearby plantation belonging to James Holman, Cawthon's close friend. Given Phil's proximity, it would have been difficult for Kate to hide their relationship had she also been intimately involved with her master. Furthermore, in her will and deed of manumission, Kate did not attempt to obscure her longstanding connection with Phil. Perhaps, therefore, rather than being sexually involved with Kate, Gideon Cawthon was her father.

Whatever the nature of the bond between these two individuals, however, the basic point is that Gideon Cawthon's decision to manumit Kate and to provide her with an estate and livestock was predicated on a close emotional relationship rather than on any philosophical belief that slavery was immoral. It was Kate's status that, for whatever reason, he wished to alter permanently and dramatically. Without explicitly acknowledging the nature of his relationship to her, Gideon provided the means by which Kate could support herself and also eventually purchase her children, her husband, and the land on which she lived. The terms of Cawthon's will illustrate the complex motivations, often in conflict with one another, that led planters to manumit selectively.

Yet in what at first seemed the most personal of motives, the political was also evident. In some cases, planters were well aware of the broader implications of their individual actions. Such was the case with Thomas Gray. Although not a Quaker and explicitly avoiding any political or religious rhetoric, he drew an immediate connection between his decision to manumit and the possibilities for dynamic change in the demography of the free Black population, and by implication in Virginia's social structure. In Gray's view, the growth of a free class of African Americans was a positive rather than negative consequence of liberalized manumission laws.

In a letter written to his brother William and recorded in the court order book in 1815 as his last will and testament, a dying Thomas Gray freed his two "servants," Nancy, thirty-four years old, and her daughter Tempy, nine. In taking such action, he expressed the hope that "none of my brothers or sisters will be dissatisfied with the manner in which I have directed my little estate to be disposed of." In anticipation of possible opposition to his decision, he addressed himself to those who might "dislike this part of my conduct." Gray's defense combined his religious conviction that slavery was immoral with an impassioned yet calculated vision. Individual manumissions, he hoped, would lead to the peopling of the society with free persons of color. He wrote,

> I can only inform them [those who would oppose his actions] that it has been my opinion for several years that our maker never intended any of his people to be slaves; by giving these two their freedom it may be the means of giving two thousand their freedom as their increase forever will be free and by keeping them in slavery there might be that quantity kept in slavery and as there will be no person injured by it[.] It is my last wish will and desire that the before named Negroes, Nancy and Tempy be free and they are hereby declared to be free after my death.[56]

In his modest letter, written in lieu of a legally witnessed will, Gray mounted a radical defense of manumission. While he sought empathy from his siblings, assumed a supplicatory posture in asking his brother William the "favour" of executing his last will and testament, and acknowledged the meager status of his estate, he openly challenged the very foundation on which Virginia's slave society had been built. It is important to remember, however, that Gray's manumission letter appeared seven years after the 1806 legislation which severely discouraged private emancipations. In effect, he advocated a form of civil disobedience by which the private acts of individuals would bring about growth in the free Black population—the very outcome the reimposition of restrictive clauses was meant to discourage.[57]

Beyond Gray's optimistic view of the long-term consequences of his decision to manumit Nancy and Tempy, his letter and other supporting documents strongly suggest that his motives extended beyond the religious and political to the personal. It appears that he fathered Tempy. Fourteen years after the writing of Thomas Gray's letter, Tempy registered with the court as a free person in 1827. She was twenty-three years old and about to leave the state, according to the document of registration. On the eve of her departure, the court records described her as "a mulatto woman about five feet high with long straight hair with many Black freckles in the face." Her mother, Nancy, registered in 1816, a year after being manumitted. She was described as "thirty-five years old, dark yellow, five feet one inch tall, and with dark curled hair." There was, of course, no similar policing measure that would have provided a description of Thomas Gray. And in any case, one cannot authoritatively impute paternity based on phenotypic descriptions. But when these descriptions are considered in the full context of Gray's manumission letter, his reference to the two women as "servants" rather than as "slaves," and the almost conjugal nature of his "little estate," they provide strong evidence of Gray's biological relationship to Tempy and his intimate relationship with Nancy.[58]

Thomas Gray not only freed Tempy but left detailed instructions about her future maintenance and welfare. "After my debts are paid which are very trifling," he wrote, two hundred dollars were to be set aside for the young woman's "support and education." Thomas further directed that his brother William "was to retain in his hand" this sum of money for that purpose.[59]

Obligations to other family members were not ignored. William Gray received a short gun and a horse, and William's son was supplied with a long gun. Perhaps as a conscious effort to mollify his siblings, Thomas Gray left a watch for his sister Lucy and further directed that the rest of his estate be divided equally among his siblings. Gray apparently left nothing to Nancy. Any benefit to her would have been derived from Tempy's relatively sizeable inheritance or William's generosity.[60]

William apparently did not share his brother Thomas's view of slavery's immorality nor his vision of a new society. In 1821, six years after Thomas's death, the tax records show that William owned an estate of eight slaves. His signature also appeared in an undated document from the late 1820s or early 1830s that petitioned the General Assembly for the removal of free Blacks from the state.[61] It is impossible to say whether he fully carried out the terms of his brother's bequest as it related to Tempy's maintenance and education. But it is likely that, notwithstanding his proslavery sentiments and opposition to the growth of the state's free Black population, William Gray felt a fraternal if not legal obligation to faithfully execute his brother's will.

In any case, Thomas's arrangements for Tempy's welfare placed her in a continuing dependent relationship with his brother William. That she left the county perhaps points as much to the difficulty of her relationship to her guardian and the impossibility of a free Black woman gaining an education in Virginia as it does to Tempy's obedience to the 1806 law that required free Blacks to leave the state. Indeed, if the strictures of the 1806 law had been her only motivation, Tempy would have been forced to leave the county a full five years earlier when she reached the age of her majority.

Thomas Gray decided to free his slaves for both personal and ideological reasons. Gray's case and the complex motives that led him to release Tempy and her mother suggest the range of attitudes toward slavery and the reasons behind the impulse to manumit. This case underscores the importance of examining planters' motivation as they evolved over the course of the history of manumission legislation. Just as importantly, it would be analytically shortsighted to discuss the motivations of white emancipators from any single religious, political, or personal perspective, or to see their actions as solely determined by economic variables. Liberalized legislation created the possibility for slaveowners with divergent values and intentions to free their slaves.

A return to the data on the patterning of manumission activity suggests the evolution of planter attitudes. Four periods of manumission activity can be identified. The first, characterized by an immediate wave of Quaker manumissions, reflects the brief primacy of religious concerns. Of short duration, such activity lasted only through the end of 1782. Once this pressure valve was released, there was a considerable slackening off in the numbers of slaves manumitted. The second period, lasting from 1782 to 1792, saw very little activity: only three deeds of manumission surfaced in the records. In summary, when the figures are taken as a whole, the Quaker response in 1782 may be described as anomalous. The overwhelming majority of the county's planters chose not to participate in private manumissions. After the initial peak, therefore, the spiral in the number of slaves manumitted was generally downward.

There was, however, a limited upswing in the fifteen years from 1793 to 1807. Planters once again began to manumit slaves. There was an increase in numbers that, though not coming close to the intensity of the first months following the legalization of private manumissions, constituted a marked shift. Twenty-four planters emancipated a total of seventy-six slaves, at a rate of about five slaves annually.

It has been a historical commonplace to argue that the Haitian Revolution and internal slave unrest directly affected the prevailing attitudes and actions of Virginia's slaveholders. Not only have historians posited a direct connection between slave rebellions and the increasing severity of legal restrictions on free Blacks and slaves, but they have also shown that planters felt individually threatened by the possibility that disenfranchised Blacks would destroy property and lives.

Historian Robert McColley, to take one example, notes a series of related actions taken by white Virginians in the wake of Gabriel's Revolt and the insurrection in Saint-Domingue. In addition to increased interest in colonization societies that called for the "removal of free persons of color," he cites the passage of a more stringent manumission law in 1806, "the removal of mandatory education for apprenticed Negro orphans," the closing of schools for free Blacks, and the "choking off [of] the small, but promising progress of gradual, voluntary emancipation as indicators of this repressive response." According to McColley, in an overall consolidation of power, there was also a "strengthening and stabilizing of the institution of slavery," a process that, he suggests, began during this period.[62]

One of the benefits of a county study is the opportunity to detect the subtler trends within broader patterns. In this regard, it is somewhat puzzling that there would have been an upturn in manumission activity in the county from 1793 to 1807. These are the years when one would have expected to find significant dampening of private manumission activity. Yet it is precisely during this period of slave unrest and legislative initiatives to impose more stringent controls on the state's free Black population that we begin to see an upturn in the numbers of emancipations and emancipating planters in Goochland. This trend is even more unexpected because emancipators at this time were probably among those least committed to challenging chattel slavery on philosophical or religious grounds. They were *not* in the vanguard of the private manumission movement.

Slaves from the county participated in at least two insurrectionary plots occurring in or near Richmond during this period. Gabriel's insurrection plans were betrayed in the late summer of 1800, and a similar scheme was exposed two years later in spring of 1802. In both situations, slaves from the county were directly implicated, and no doubt this information must have been disseminated to the county's planters in the subsequent revelations.[63]

The names of Goochland slaves poised to aid Gabriel in the burning and capture of the capital remain lost in the records. We do know, however, that boatmen, wagoners, blacksmiths, and other skilled slaves who moved about the countryside successfully recruited fellow conspirators throughout Piedmont counties, including Goochland, Louisa, and Buckingham.[64] Just two years later, slaves from the county were once again involved in rebellious activity. This time the depositions taken in the subsequent investigation do allow for identification of two key conspirators from Goochland, Arthur and Lewis. Arthur, a carpenter hired out in Richmond, belonged to Richard Farrish of the county; Lewis had recently escaped from his master John Brown after having served as a hired cook on at least two Goochland plantations. According to his own testimony, Lewis actively recruited slaves to the cause in Dinwiddie and Petersburg.[65]

Correspondence related to his capture and interrogation indicated that Lewis "passes under a free pass written by himself."[66] Lewis embodied all the worst fears of planters and the general white populace—a literate runaway slave who successfully assumed the identity of a free person and helped to instigate rebellion. Threat of revolt, therefore, was not merely a distant or abstract notion for Goochland's planters: the reality of insurrection intruded into everyday county life. This was particularly so for Lewis's owner, John Brown. Nonetheless, Brown seemingly ignored the obvious lessons offered by recent events when, in 1804, he emancipated Jack, one of his two remaining slaves.[67]

John Brown's actions reflected the paradox that is brought out in the patterning of manumissions from 1793 to 1807. During this period, Goochland planters manumitted slaves in numbers that worked in opposition to proslavery and anti–free Black sentiment, much of which was concerned with the heightened unrest of Blacks in the commonwealth and the impact on overall security. All this suggests that local responses to events occurring in the state and elsewhere did not always follow a predictable or easily decipherable course. Indeed, it is at the level of the local and personal that historians have had the greatest difficulty in explaining the persistence of emancipations when logic would have dictated otherwise.

Part of the answer to the pattern of manumission activity in Goochland during this period might rest in the nature of the relationship between manumitter and manumitted. After the last decade of the eighteenth century, a greater number of the county's emancipators began to emancipate preferentially—that is, with a few exceptions, they manumitted selected slaves. The tendency to manumit selectively was reflected in the ratio of emancipators to emancipated. Fewer than three slaves were manumitted per emancipator over this span of time, compared to a ratio of nine slaves to one emancipator in 1782. The diffusion of private manumissions over a greater number of planters suggests that emancipation became a primarily individual rather than collective option. Planters with narrower intentions, not related to religious ideology, came to represent the typical emancipator.

In Goochland, personal assessment of the slave or slaves to be emancipated came to play an increasingly important role in the decision of individual emancipators. The apparent lack of correspondence between slave rebellion and the numbers of emancipations indicates, therefore, that planters, while not oblivious to domestic turmoil, based their decisions to manumit on other considerations.

After 1807, manumission activity in Goochland went into permanent decline. Only twenty-two slaves, belonging to eleven masters, gained their freedom over the twenty-five-year period from 1807 to 1832: the rate of emancipation was less than one slave per year. Furthermore, in seventeen of these years planters did not manumit a single slave. The decline in numbers was a result of restrictions outlined in the 1806 law that required emancipated slaves to leave the state after a year or other sociopolitical factors.[68] The passage of the law reflected a strengthening conservative movement that sought not only to discourage manumissions but also to place new restrictions on free persons of color. Now more than a quarter century from the liberal rhetoric of the Revolution and vigorous antislavery evangelicalism, the very few planters who emancipated did so because of their particular relationships with individual slaves.

It is within this context that the 1806 removal law influenced the actions of some emancipators. Some free Blacks refrained from manumitting kinsmen for fear of separation should the new law be consistently enforced.

Their reasoning is best understood within our subsequent discussion of free Black manumitters in the next chapter. For white slaveowners, the issues were not as personally pressing. If the only issue had been their right to dispose of property, then the law did not constrain them. There is indication, however, that some emancipators took the issue of removal into account when they drafted their wills or deeds of emancipation. Masters who, to some extent, held themselves responsible for the material well-being of those they had enslaved constituted a group of about nine individuals. Of these, it is not surprising that seven manumitted after 1806. Slaves themselves may have informed their potential emancipators of their preferences concerning the problem of relocation outside Virginia.[69]

In 1807, when Sally Coley emancipated Lucy and her seven children, she acknowledged the possibility that they would have to leave the state. Lucy and her children were named primary heirs. They were to receive, "equally divided among them all," the use of Coley's plantation for one year after her death. Further, they received the estate's livestock (including two horses), "household and kitchen furniture," and the "growing crop and the crop that may be already made."[70]

At the end of the prescribed year, the land was to be sold to the highest bidder and part of the proceeds from the sale set aside to pay for the "transportation" of Lucy and her family out of Virginia. Further to this end, Coley wanted a portion of the money to go toward the purchase of a "lite horse carte" and "one horse worth about fifteen pounds." Coley moreover instructed that if the horse that was already part of the estate should "be dead or not able to help [the] within mentioned negroes move of out of the state as the law of the land calls for them so to do," the executors were to buy another horse, in addition to two saddles and bridles. Having provided transportation, Coley turned to the wishes of individual members of the family. Lucy had apparently given some indication that she was reluctant to leave the state. In the event that she did not change her mind, Coley specified that "if my negro woman Lucy will not goe oute of the state with her bigest children that Burton, James and Lewis shall have the two horses and saddles . . . and goe of oute of the state."[71]

The minor children—Frankey, Harrison, Martha, and Mary—supposedly would remain under the jurisdiction of their mother. Thus, for this slaveowner and for the slaves she emancipated, the 1806 law placed additional obstacles in the path to freedom. Sally Coley attempted to mitigate likely hardships by providing financially for her slaves after her death, while at the same time ensuring that they would not be unduly affected by the 1806 law. The well-laid plans of Coley may not have been necessary. Two years after their emancipation, Lucy and all of her children still lived in the county. Their names appeared in the free Black register. Apparently, they registered without having officially petitioned the assembly to allow them to remain in the state.[72]

When Martha Peers manumitted "all" of an unspecified number of slaves in 1829, she expressed apprehension about their "future comfort and safety." Her will directed that if the newly emancipated slaves wished to remain in the county, they had the option of petitioning the court. Failing that, they could choose to remain titular slaves under the supervision of her brother Thomas and his wife, Sally. Alternatively, she instructed that if they so desired, her slaves could use funds from the estate to move to a free state or be colonized to Africa. But Peers did not "wish" her slaves to "be colonized contrary to their wish." Thus, she offered her soon-to-be-emancipated laborers a number of legal and extralegal options from which to choose.[73]

Even without the safeguards attached to Martha Peers's instrument of emancipation, most of Goochland's emancipated slaves stayed in the county. The means of social control employed by authorities were not uniformly or consistently applied to coerce compliance with the removal law. As importantly, the different systems of administration of free Black residents did not necessarily entail the same social goals and agendas. Thus, for example, when the issue was tax collection, the county commissioners were probably unconcerned about whether the free Black taxpayer was a legal resident. The same may be said for the county clerk whose responsibility it was to maintain the free Black register. The clerk may well have seen his role as a passive one: to record the pertinent information for those individuals who presented themselves at the courthouse but not necessarily to seek out and prosecute those individuals who chose not to register.[74]

The resort to the extralegal compromises in which a slave could choose a master or work for wages points to ways in which white and Black Virginians circumvented the 1806 law. It is possible that in order to skirt the legal prohibitions, the number of informal manumissions increased. Ira Berlin suggests that "slaveowners, imitating the Quaker practice, frequently sold or willed bondsmen to a friend or a free Negro with the provision that the 'slave' be allowed to work on their own, keep their wages and enjoy all the rights allowed free people of color."⁷⁵

Apparently, Joseph Cross, a Goochland planter, adopted just such a strategy when he manumitted Moses and Tom in the summer of 1814. In his will, he cautioned that if the law prohibited manumission, then either his son Joel Cross or "someone that Moses may choose should act as master for him and pay him wages as his labors shall be worth." In this instance, the would-be emancipator required that some sympathetic individual act in cooperation with his "slave" to ensure that he would enjoy at least the benefits of free status, if not its legal recognition. The consideration shown to Moses came with a price: he purchased his freedom from Joel Cross for $450.⁷⁶

Tom's master laid out a different set of terms for him. He was not slated to gain his freedom at Cross's death. Instead, Tom was required to remain a slave for nine years, until December 1822. At that point, Cross indicated that "if the law will not allow his [Tom's] freedom," he bequeathed the "slave" to Phoebe, a free woman of color and Tom's wife. Under her ownership, it would not be necessary for Tom to leave the state. Should Phoebe die before the end of her husband's term of service, then he was also entitled to the options offered to Moses Cross. Tom's emancipation, therefore, like that of Moses, was based on a series of contingency plans that took into account possible changes in manumission law. Joseph Cross's consideration of the fate of his slaves was not without its own internal contradictions. He exacted a heavy price in labor and in cash before he consented to manumit these two men.⁷⁷

The patterning of and responses to manumission in Goochland County confirm that, despite the small number of cases proportional to Virginia's slave population, the social consequences were significant. Counties throughout the state, especially in the Piedmont, Tidewater, Northern Neck, and Southside, experienced growth in the numbers of free Black residents after 1782.⁷⁸ The exact nature of the responses to the presence of free Blacks varied at the local level. But in every instance, the introduction of private manumissions as a fact of life had an effect on relations among the three main social groups—whites, slaves, and free people of color—and brought into question the formerly sacrosanct meanings given to the categories "slave" and "free."

The wills of manumitters who freed slaves after 1806 and who made provisions for their slaves in case the law requiring transportation out of the state were strictly enforced revealed one form of response. In these documents, the fate of manumitted slaves emerges as still subject to the whims of their former masters. Another set of documents counters this view, however, enabling the historian to observe the actions and strategies of individuals as they made their own arrangements to gain exemption from the 1806 law. These documents suggest that free Blacks took an active role in defining their lives outside of slavery and in crafting means to make the transition from bondage to freedom. In the next chapter, I continue the examination of the relationship between institutional and legal structures, the free Black individual and the development of community, by refocusing on the question of manumission and the acquisition of free status from the point of view of Goochland's slave and free Black residents.

· 3 ·

Securing Freedom

Free persons of color purchased and emancipated their enslaved kinsmen. On occasion, through freedom suits, they challenged those who held them in illegal bondage, and they petitioned the Virginia Assembly and later the county court in order to remain in the state. When taken together, these actions indicate that slaves actively participated in securing freedom for themselves and others. Once freed, they had to be vigilant to protect their free status. Enslaved and free African Americans always had to negotiate and renegotiate their status and the degree of their freedom within the terms set out by Virginia's planter class.

Most Goochland slaves manumitted after 1806 did not formally request leave to stay in the county. They simply ignored the stipulations laid down by the assembly. Of the thirty-seven slaves manumitted after 1806, only seven persons filed formal petitions to remain in the county. In order to be successful, white residents with some standing in the community had to vouch for the free African Americans' good character and service. The need for white patronage and affidavits may have played a role in the small number of petitions from the county. For those freed Blacks who had not established ties to whites, the improbability of having a petition approved discouraged them from making any such applications.[1]

From 1806 to 1815, the assembly heard and decided on all petitions to gain exemption from the removal law. After this period, although it continued to hear petitions, the legislature gave local courts jurisdiction to decide cases on exemptions to the removal law.[2] Free Blacks immediately took advantage of both avenues of possible redress, one at the state level and the other locally.

The five extant petitions from Goochland County are dated after the shift in jurisdiction. Three of these were directed to the assembly rather than to local county justices. In one instance, a petitioner took his case to the assembly after the Goochland County Court denied him exemption from the removal law. Perhaps other free Black petitioners perceived that they would receive more sympathetic hearings from the state legislature than from the gentlemen justices who made up the Goochland courts. Comparing the details of these petitions provides a means of understanding them as a category of documents that expressed in agonizing clarity the dilemma of status and personhood which confronted free Blacks in the county.

Jacob Sampson, a free man of mixed race who had been manumitted in 1810 when he was fourteen years old, first applied to stay in the county in 1827, seventeen years after his manumission. Sampson had remained in the state in violation of the law for approximately ten years (his manumission took effect at his twenty-first birthday).[3] Subverting the law, however, was not without its risks. A manumitted slave who stayed in the state beyond one year could be resold as a slave. Although the evidence for Virginia indicates that this sanction was not applied with any consistency, it nonetheless could be brought to bear on individual free Blacks by the policing authorities.[4]

Such was the situation with Sampson. He was summoned to appear before the local justices in March 1827 to "show why he should not be sold as a slave." The considerable delay between Sampson's manumission and the court summons suggests there might well have been a hidden set of circumstances that made him suddenly vulnerable to the full letter of the law. Sampson appeared in court two months later in the company of his attorney. Apparently to the satisfaction of the justices, Sampson presented firm evidence of "his right to remain in the county as a free man." The charges against him were dismissed. By the time he successfully countered the threat to his status, Sampson was well on his way to establishing himself as among the most successful free Black residents in the county. He owned slaves, a lucrative public tavern, extensive acreage, and livestock.[5]

Although not initiated by his own petition, Sampson's defense resembled those of other petitioners. The success of an individual's petition depended on their ability to convince the presiding justices that the person was of good character, that they would not become an economic liability to the county, and that they were capable of making a substantial contribution to the local or state economy. In some instances, the supporting proof included testimony of whites to the indispensability of the free Black petitioner's skills as a worker. The weight given to this evidence by the local and state legislatures varied considerably.

John Pierce had proven himself a hardworking and loyal slave during his tenure as hired labor at the county courthouse before his manumission in 1816 and successful petition for residency the following year. He and his wife had worked for over two decades at the courthouse, purchased land and slaves, and had ties to powerful planters in the county. In this respect, both Pierce and Sampson could show that they were unlikely to threaten the social or racial order.[6]

Of the three petitioners to the county court, one was denied an exemption on the basis of his failure to provide any adequate evidence of "specified" "acts of extraordinary merit." Moses Cross had purchased his freedom in 1820 and first brought his case to the county court two years later. The local court's refusal to approve his petition reflected its interpretation of an earlier act of the assembly. In 1815, the assembly gave local courts jurisdiction over granting exemptions to the 1806 law provided the free Black individual had performed "acts of extraordinary merit" to remain in the state.[7]

That local justices adhered to strict interpretation of the law is revealed in the text of Cross's appeal of the county court ruling. He informed the assembly that those justices of the court who voted in favor of his petition counseled him to appeal the negative decision. As required, Cross had publicly announced his intention to petition the court two months before, but for some reason two local justices denied his petition because of "scruples relating to the construction of the law." Rather than expressing any objections to Cross as an individual, these opposing justices voiced their concern that correct procedures had not been exactly followed. According to Cross's petition, he had been told "by a Member of that [Goochland's] court [that] his general character was unimpeached, and but for those scruples the court would with sincere willingness have given its unanimous assent."[8] There was, therefore, some form of interaction between either Cross or his representative with the local justices. In response, Cross prepared a revised statement about his exemplary conduct as a slave and resubmitted his plea to the General Assembly in Richmond.

Free Blacks from Goochland who petitioned the assembly for exemption betrayed deep anxiety about their success in the passion of their pleas and successful mobilization of white supporters. Conscious of the high stakes involved, petitioners took every precaution to ensure that their case would be given sympathetic attention. When Cross presented his petition to the legislature, he included an extensive autobiography and a separate affidavit from the son of his former master attesting to his fine character and his expertise as a plantation and factory manager, miller, and boatman.[9]

The trajectory of Cross's life, as presented in the petition, revealed the white society's ideal portrait of a "desirable" slave and irreproachable free Black. The petitions to stay in the county reflected the view seemingly held by white planters that the loyalty of a slave before manumission was an accurate predictor of their behavior as a free person. Only those slaves who had demonstrated a high level of comfort with and accommodation to the institution of slavery would make desirable, permanent free Black residents. Besides providing insight into the kinds of strategies Cross used to convince the legislature of his own merits, his petition offers an intriguing portrait of the life of one freed slave living in the county in the first half of the nineteenth century. He was at least minimally literate for he signed his petition. It is likely, however, that he employed the services of an attorney to assist him in drafting and presenting his petition to the assembly.

Cross's transition to free status and then to the security of legal residence in the county began during the period of his enslavement. Inherited by Judith Peers after the death of her husband, he took on many of the responsibilities formerly undertaken by his deceased master. The breadth and substance of the duties he assumed on the estate provided the necessary evidence of his fidelity and great skill.[10] Thomas Peers, Judith's son, recalled that Cross "had in great degree the management of the plantation business," and to his knowledge was "always an uncommonly trusty slave." Peers further testified that the petitioner "was never known to drink a drop of ardent spirit part of the time that he belonged to [his] mother." In what must have been the greatest compliment that he could conceive of paying a Black man, and perhaps the most meaningful recommendation to the legislature, Thomas Peers affirmed that Moses Cross had carried out his responsibilities as a miller and plantation manager to the "general satisfaction to all concerned, or as much as could be expected in such a capacity from any man white or black."[11]

If being compared favorably to a white man in his capacity for work was not enough grist for the mill, Peer's affidavit confirmed Cross's narration on his own behalf that he had risked his own life in a successful effort to rescue the Peers family and their property from a fire. Told in the third person, the account of Cross's heroism combined humility with self-congratulatory drama: "[Your petitioner] begs leave with humility to mention that on one occasion his mistresses' house was on fire at a late hour of the night when all the family were asleep. He discovered it, gave an alarm and with great personal danger rushed to the fire, extinguished the flames, and rescued the family, who otherwise probably would have perished."[12]

In yet another account of his "acts of extraordinary merit," personal heroism spilled over into betrayal of his fellow slaves. Here we have a freed slave who in order to secure his own status and residence in the state described how he, while himself in bondage, unhesitatingly made every effort to reveal "suspicious" behavior on the part of Blacks living in the neighborhood. Cross's description emphasized his selfless vigilance in these matters: "Your petitioner begs leave to say that he has always been watchful to detect and desirous to suppress those mischiefs and vices in slaves and free persons of color." He further stressed his concern for the protection of the greater white community as well as that of his mistress: "In times when there were frequent alarms of insurrections of the Blacks in the neighborhood, where there number was great being near large estates and extensive coal mines your petitioner has more than once secretly made known to his mistress the whispers of such plots being agitations and concerning them. He was always distressed and anxious to make discoveries."[13]

Before her death, Judith Peers told her son of Cross's solicitude. During the rumors of insurrection that Cross himself had "communicated" to her, she "directed [him] to sleep in a room of the dwelling house and that she felt as secure from danger and her fears and apprehensions were as much relieved, as they would have been by being guarded in a similar manner by any individual white person." In yet another striking substitution, comparisons between Cross and a white person drove home the singularity of his character to the legislature. His physical proximity to his mistress during these moments of "anxiety" confirmed his essential loyalty and difference from the "dangerous black mass."[14]

Only after having provided overwhelming evidence of his worthiness to remain in the state did Cross make reference to the interests of his family and his personal needs. Although he set himself in an adversarial relationship to slaves and other free Blacks in his petition, his anguish no doubt mirrored that experienced by many others of his race who found themselves in like circumstances. He starkly laid out the choices he felt himself bound to make. If the assembly refused his request, then he would be forced to choose between "a return to slavery" or retention of his free status "by an involuntary exile, the remainder of his life, from his wife and children and the land of his nativity." For Cross, then, exile would be no less repugnant than relinquishing his freedom, "already purchased by his labour" and acquired at great personal cost. The Virginia Assembly responded positively to this long and impassioned petition. Moses appeared in the county records until his death sometime before 1831.[15]

Moses Cross was by all measures an immensely capable individual. He had established a family and a degree of economic independence. Besides purchasing himself, he had managed to save $150 during the time he was enslaved. The power of his petition, however, derived from painting himself as independent within a narrowly defined sphere, emphasizing his acceptance of the racial and social status quo and of his aloofness from the county's slave and free Black communities. Whether he had indeed practiced the measure of vigilance of his brethren that he claimed may be questioned. Claims to a high level of social and psychological distance from his peers and close identification with whites suited the requirements of his petition. In reality, such claims seem highly unlikely given his long years as a slave (almost forty-five) and daily interactions with other African Americans. Unless he lived a pariah existence, Cross must have balanced his life in a manner that allowed him to live in the slave, free Black, and white communities with some level of comfort.[16]

For the audience that he wished to convince, the meaning of Moses Cross's free status could never entail resentment of the oppressive nature of racial slavery. Yet as his petition made clear, he walked a very thin edge. In his petition, he emphasized the ways in which slavery had provided a civilizing and educative component, enabling slaves to demonstrate their loyalty and work ethic. But he had to be careful not to overvalue the condition of bondage, for then it would be difficult to make a compelling case for freedom. The ritual reference to his love for Virginia and his willingness to choose slavery over exile provided a key set of cultural references that would have resonated even with proslavery elements in the assembly.

Indeed, the language of Cross's petition was strongly reminiscent of those heard by the governor and council in the prerevolutionary period.

The petition of a slave couple who wished to stay in the county after their manumission in 1820 reveals a different species of entreaty to the assembly. It is the only one of the five petitions in which the voice of the free person was replaced by that of an advocate. We can assume that Harry and Mary, the freed slaves in question, supported the movement to gain them legal residency; however, in the petition they remain in the background. With this petition, the stress is less on any "extraordinary acts of merit" than on their advanced age and long years of service to their deceased manumitter, Martha Symes.[17]

John S. Fleming, executor of the will in which Martha Symes emancipated her slaves, acted as spokesperson for the couple. In addressing the assembly in the petition drafted in 1824, Fleming expressed his "sacred" obligation to carry out the testamentary wishes of his aged aunt. His tone was apologetic, informing the legislature that he "regret[ted] the necessity" of having to ask for an exemption of the 1806 removal law. And he acknowledged that he was aware of "the great reluctance with which applications of this sort [were] received." This comment may have been rhetorical, reflecting the formal language of entreaty. But when taken alongside the other petitions, it suggests that the entire issue of who should be exempted from the removal law was carefully deliberated within well-understood guidelines.[18]

At least in the bureaucratic attention to procedure, legislators wanted to make clear that discouraging the growth of the free Black population in the commonwealth was a pressing concern. Unlike Moses Cross, John Fleming bypassed the local courts because, as he wrote in his petition, "he was advised that under the working provisions of the law," the emancipating instrument in which Martha Symes expressed her wish to have her freed slaves remain in the county would not be recognized by the local courts. Although she had directed her nephew to pursue every avenue to gain the couple's legitimate residency in the county, she had not specifically stated that her slaves were of exemplary character. It is within this context that John Fleming made his excuses and brought Harry and Mary's case to the assembly for special consideration.[19]

Having spent most of their adult lives together as the only slaves of an elderly mistress, it is understandable that the couple would not want to leave the familiar surroundings of the county. They may well have expressed these sentiments at the time they were informed that they were to be manumitted in Symes's last will and testament. According to that document, Mary had been purchased "on [Harry's] account" by his mistress.[20] The couple had cohabited for upwards of fifteen years since that time. According to the testimony given by John Fleming, the couple had been manumitted because of their "faithful and exemplary deportment" toward a mistress "who had the misfortune to be entirely deprived of sight."

The familiar theme of slaves who worked without complaint and in a trustworthy manner emerged in this petition: Harry and Mary's "general honesty and propriety of demeanor" were lauded. Fleming further informed the assembly that the couple would cause no "injury" by remaining in the state because they were childless and were not expected, given their ages, to have children in the future. Fleming went to the heart of the matter that had provided the catalyst for passage of the 1806 law: Harry and Mary's presence in the county was unlikely to engender any "inconvenience from their posterity as they [had] lived together 10 or 15 years without any issue."[21] The fear of the free Black community in Virginia, as John Russell has pointed out, was not focused so much on particular individuals as on unchecked population growth resulting from natural increase. In their barrenness, Harry and Mary represented no such threat.

No wonder, therefore, that fifty of the county's planters saw fit to signify their support of the petition drafted by Fleming. The brief statement of support preceding their signatures is worth citing: "We the undersigned have been long acquainted with a negro man named Harry emancipated by the last will of Miss Martha H. Symes, and feel no hesitation in saying that his conduct has been as far as we know entirely unexceptionable, nor are we aware of any man of colour who enjoys a reputation superior to his, we have no doubt that if the legislature permits him to remain in the state, the example he will set to those in his situation will be beneficial."[22] Harry had managed to build up extensive linkages to planters in the county. He actively brought about his emancipation and eventually gained legal entitlement to reside in the county with his wife. He accomplished this considerable feat by convincing his white benefactors that his "character" was substantially different from those of other slaves and free Blacks. In his willingness to accept the terms set forth by county slaveowners, Harry secured a status denied to most other free Blacks. Just as Moses Cross was compared favorably to a "white man," so too Harry was depicted as "beneficial" to the society because of his potentially "civilizing" influence on other free Blacks. In these petitions, the figure lurking in the shadows was always the unruly and potentially destructive free Black individual. These petitioners exploited the contrast, presenting themselves as exceptional free Blacks who were fully adjusted to their fate and station.

It was not entirely contradictory for white planters to sign such petitions and at the same time endorse the 1806 removal law and other legislation that relegated free Blacks to the social and economic margins. These same individuals supported measures that limited the development of the free Black community and called for the enactment of mandatory colonization schemes. Such colonization schemes were expected to rid the commonwealth of its population of free persons. One such document, circulated in Goochland County and presented to the General Assembly sometime in the late 1820s or early 1830s, argued that free Blacks were neither free people nor slaves and as such were "incompatible with the tranquillity of society."[23]

Planters who supported Harry and Mary's continued residence in Goochland also attached their names to a petition that referred to the "degraded, profligate, vicious, turbulent and discontented" free Black populace.[24] While having vastly contradictory agendas, there was a parallel notion that in the same way that exceptional free Blacks could have a benign impact on local communities, the colonization of such exemplars would redeem "a barbarous and benighted" African continent. But the assumption in both cases was that dangerously large numbers of ordinary free Blacks were an unwanted and negative influence on the institutions and values of Virginia society.[25]

Freedom suits were another means by which "slaves" in Virginia actively attempted to achieve and maintain free status. These suits appeared sporadically in colonial Virginia and with increased frequency in the postrevolutionary period. They took two basic forms. Persons of color who believed themselves descended from free maternal parentage could sue for their freedom. In other cases, individuals who believed they had been manumitted by legal instrument, whether by will, deed, or decree of the courts, could bring suit against those who held them in illegal bondage. Such slaves were permitted to file claims *in forma pauperis* and would not be liable for the costs of filing or pursuing these cases in court. They were also eligible for appeal to district and superior courts.[26]

In his discussion of the relationship between law and society in the Chesapeake, Duncan J. MacLeod argues that freedom suits illustrate the contradictory application of ideas of equity in a system based on racial slavery. "Perhaps the most fundamental issue of Southern society," he writes, came to the fore in such cases. The "very existence of the suits, brought by 'slaves' not normally able to maintain an action in law," reflected the continuous need to redefine the interactions of the colony's and then the state's inhabitants with judicial institutions.[27]

Besides the question of the legitimacy of a slave's access to the court, the nature of evidence brought by plaintiffs in these cases tended to fall within the realm of "hearsay." Such evidence was by tradition not allowed in a court of law, except in the case of freedom suits. The courts faced an overriding question: "Was traditional procedure to be modified in the interests of freedom or was it to be maintained in the interests of property ownership?" McCleod further points to the tendency of the courts to rule in favor of freedom in the period immediately following the Revolution.[28]

But any such leniency proved short-lived. By 1795, the General Assembly had responded to the increase in the numbers of successful freedom suits and the consequent blurring of the racial line that had so clearly distinguished between free and enslaved. Sanctions were brought to bear against whites, particularly Quakers, who aided in the introduction and support of freedom suits brought to the courts. It became more difficult to have cases heard. Quakers or those in favor of abolition could no longer represent slaves, nor could they serve on juries in such cases. The height of favorable rulings in freedom suits occurred between 1782 and 1795. Thereafter, it became very difficult for a slave to receive a favorable ruling. Ira Berlin suggests that the greater involvement of the county courts in freedom suits meant that local slaveowners served on juries and were more likely to decide in favor of masters over their slaves.[29] Historians thus track the history of freedom suits from an early, liberal phase when all but the most trivial evidence was admitted and many slaves gained their freedom to a more restricted, punitive phase when suits were actively discouraged and the courts emphasized the preeminence of slaveowners' property rights.[30]

Only six persons in the county gained free status through this legal avenue. Two of the cases, coming as they did after the conservative backlash, diverged from the regional pattern. Nonetheless, these freedom suits offer insight into the procedures and kinds of evidence used when a "slave" or "slaves" contested their enslavement. The specifics of these circumstances confirm the view that the courts were especially concerned with the contextual particulars of individual claims. These cases also indicate the ways in which Blacks inserted themselves into the system to make their claims for freedom under situations that were rarely propitious.

In 1755, James Hoosling, a mixed-race slave, apparently petitioned for his freedom from his purported owner, whose name appears in the suit as "Mullins." References to the existence of Hoosling's claims did not appear in the court records but rather in the account book of his lawyer, John Fleming. Whether Hoosling was successful in his freedom suit is unclear. In his account book, however, Fleming noted charges for court appearances for the prosecution of the slave's petition between 1755 and 1756. Fleming also served as John Russell's attorney in 1759 when Russell claimed his freedom from William Drumwright's executors; the outcome of that suit is also unknown.[31] The importance of these cases is that they are relatively early, far removed from the subsequent rise in freedom suits after the 1770s. Given the timing, then, and the description of Hoosling as "mulatto," it is likely that his claim to freedom was the result of descent from a free white woman. The records do not allow speculation about the provenance of Russell's claim.

The remaining two cases came from the postrevolutionary period, with the plaintiffs both filing their suits *in forma pauperis*. Although the cases were filed at different times, one in April and the other in July 1800, the justices of the court appointed the same attorney to act in the slaves' defense at trials, which were scheduled only a day apart that November. Two separate juries were impaneled to hear the cases. In the first, the justices and jury heard the complaints of a single individual, while in the second, a woman and her four minor children brought charges of illegal enslavement against a Goochland planter.

Only fourteen years old, Samuel Miles first appeared in court on July 21, 1800, and claimed that William Smith, then of Goochland County, held him in illegal bondage. As the suit was *in forma pauperis*, the court appointed William Pope, gentleman, to be the boy's attorney. Given his youth, it is likely that Miles was encouraged by older, experienced persons to initiate his suit. The unusual circumstances of his bondage also support this conclusion as the young boy had not resided long in the county. Samuel had been born to Hagar and Solomon Miles, free Black residents of Philadelphia.

Apparently, the plaintiff's presence in Goochland was the result of his having been brought there by his peripatetic "owner," whose proprietary claims were now being challenged.[32]

Heard in two different sessions, four months apart, the case first revolved around the question of whether Goochland courts had legitimate jurisdiction to rule on the merits of the freedom suit. Fleming Payne, the defendant's attorney, argued that the county had no jurisdiction over the "action" because Samuel Miles "does not reside in the county aforesaid." His client, therefore, was under no obligation to answer the charges brought against him. In reply, the court ruled that jurisdiction had been determined when the freedom suit had been accepted *in forma pauperis*. Thus, in the first round, the proceedings to determine the validity of the plaintiff's claims resulted in an outcome favorable to the claims of freedom over property rights.

The justices of the county court, all of them slaveholders, used strong wording to bolster this decision: "The opinion of the court is in favor of the said plaintiff it appearing to the court that the said plaintiff has resided as great a length of time in the county of Goochland, as in any other county of the commonwealth, and the court is of the opinion that from the manner in which the plaintiff was carried by the defendant from place to place, he had a right of action in any court within the limits of whose jurisdiction he might be at the time of setting up his claim to freedom." Failing in his bid to have the case thrown out on jurisdictional grounds, Payne argued that no action should be taken since Samuel Miles was legally a slave. In support of this position, Payne informed justices that the defendant, William Smith, could "verify" ownership to their satisfaction. At some time during these proceedings, Miles testified "in his own words." He told the justices that he was "not a slave but [was] free" and placed himself "upon the countrey." Having heard the testimonies of both parties, the justices impaneled a jury of twelve men and proceeded with the freedom suit.[33]

If historians are correct about the general hostility to freedom suits in Virginia at this time, Samuel Miles's chances of regaining his freedom were rather dim. All four justices owned large estates with a large slave labor force, and at least eight of the jurors were themselves planters with substantial holdings in slaves.[34] Notwithstanding his initial success, therefore, the linked property and racial interests of William Smith and these individuals could have been expected to weigh the outcome against the young boy. Yet, in turning to the evidence at hand, slaveowners sometimes made decisions in opposition to their ideological and economic interests. Historians have observed that the general investment of the planter class in the sanctity of the legal system occasionally worked to the welfare of free Black individuals, and slaveholders were not always given the benefit of the doubt in freedom suits. At the same time, however, slaves had the burden of providing clearcut evidence of their claims if they were to prove successful in their bids for freedom.[35]

Samuel Miles was officially declared "free and not a slave." His travails, however, did not end with this verdict. The jury determined that he had been indentured under contract for twenty-one years to Emanuel Walker, a Philadelphia merchant. Although judged free from chattel slavery, the jury directed that the plaintiff be returned to his master in Philadelphia, where he was to continue his term of service.

The jury had reached what must have been a satisfying compromise. On the one hand, they had confirmed the absent merchant's limited rights to the person and labor of the young apprentice, while on the other they had given precedence to freedom over property by denying William Smith's fraudulent claims. No free Black person had been set loose "on the county," no one had been falsely enslaved, and at the same time the jury could comfort itself that it had not diverged from the letter of the law. Although Miles and his attorney could also claim success, victory was bittersweet. During the four months that the case worked its way through the courts, the young boy was imprisoned in the county jail. Furthermore, although he had escaped permanent bondage, he would not be fully free until 1816, when he would be thirty-one years old. On the positive side, his return to Philadelphia meant that he would be in some proximity to his parents and in familiar surroundings. Most importantly, he had escaped chattel bondage.[36]

Close attention to the evidence also characterized the court's approach to the freedom suit brought by Hannah and her four children, "slaves" residing in Goochland County who, according to their attorney, William Pope, had been illegally held by John McCrae. The central issue when the freedom suit was brought to the Goochland courts was whether McCrae possessed a deed of ownership for the four contested slaves.[37]

To understand the full ramifications of this suit and to place Hannah's actions in context, events occurring outside Goochland County twenty-four years earlier have to be taken into account, as they were by the presiding justices and jury. Hannah's claim to freedom derived from her being among a group of thirty-three slaves who had been manumitted in 1778 by Charles Moorman, a Quaker planter of Louisa County.[38] Since private manumission had not yet been passed into law, Moorman drafted a deed of manumission, as well as a will in which he gave specific instructions as to the disposition of his slaves if the assembly did not accept his petition or if the anticipated changes in the manumission law did not occur.[39]

As one of the minor children of Moorman's estate, Hannah found herself in the possession of her master's son Thomas Moorman, who was given temporary ownership until she reached the age of eighteen. According to the instruments of manumission, the elder Moorman intended that all the "increase" of his slaves were to be considered freeborn. Along with the other thirty-two slaves, Hannah remained in this liminal legal status until 1787, when by an act of assembly Charles Moorman's instruments of manumission were deemed legal and recorded as an "act to confirm the freedom of certain negroes late the property of Charles Moorman, deceased." Like other Quakers, Moorman had acted in anticipation of the passage of the 1782 act by manumitting his chattel despite the state's procrastination in enacting a law that would allow individuals to divest themselves of slaves in accordance with their religious or secular beliefs.[40]

Whatever the altruistic motivations of her former master, part of the problem for Hannah was that she had been freed in this transitional period as a child and one of four minors from the original estate who were "lent" to Thomas Moorman. In his will, the elder Moorman had distributed his slaves among six of his children and his widow. Hannah thus came to the estate of Thomas Moorman in a vulnerable position. That vulnerability contributed no doubt to the circumstances which threatened to deprive her of her freedom. Although it is not immediately clear how the chain of stewardship/ownership passed from Thomas Moorman to John McCrae, such a transfer did occur. Furthermore, during the intervening years between 1776 and 1800, Hannah bore four children whose status was in jeopardy along with their mother's. The task for the local Goochland justices was to untangle the evidence and to determine if McCrae could legally claim property rights in these five individuals.[41]

Before the jury was impaneled, the justices heard from Robert Freeman, a witness on McCrae's behalf. He testified that he "heard Charles Moorman say he had given the plaintiff Hannah to his son Thomas Moorman." The issue at hand revolved around whether Charles Moorman had "given"

Hannah to his son or lent her to be held in guardianship as a provisionally freed slave. Although the justices did not make direct reference to the assembly's confirmation of Charles Moorman's act of manumission, the immediacy with which they dispensed with Freeman's testimony suggests that they were aware of the assembly's decision. The jury was not allowed to hear Freeman's evidence.

The justices acted in similar fashion when McCrae's attorney argued that his client had purchased Hannah from Thomas Moorman in 1776. Hannah's children were born while she was in the possession of McCrae and therefore were also his possessions. William Pope's objection to this testimony was sustained by the justices of the court. They were unconvinced, it appears, because McCrae was unable to produce a deed of purchase for Hannah. When the jury was impaneled, none of this evidence was admitted into the official proceedings. The jury therefore found that "the plaintiffs were free and not slaves," and the court ruled that Hannah and her children were to "recover of the defendant their freedom."[42]

Having lost in the local courts, John McCrae took his case on appeal to the district court in Richmond. These records are not extant. But the presence of Hannah and her children in the free Black register and in other county records for the period after 1800 indicates she prevailed in the higher court as well. Hannah had taken the surname Moorman and named her children likewise.[43] Hannah's success was predicated in large part on documents that recorded her emancipator's intentions and the absence of competing evidence supporting the defendant. But only with her persistence and the cooperation of her legal counsel could she have successfully challenged the claims of a white planter. John McCrae may well have believed himself to have legally purchased Hannah from Thomas Moorman, who apparently did not share his father's opposition to chattel slavery.[44]

The outcome of Samuel Miles's and the Moormans' freedom suits encapsulated all the contradictions that faced free people of color in Virginia. Their free status came at great cost and was never fully guaranteed. In various guises and with always shifting currents, the law offered more constraint than opportunity. Only with extraordinary creativity and with the ability to seize the moment when the courts offered some semblance of equity could a few individuals hope to gain a measure of justice.

Another means of securing freedom involved self-emancipation or the emancipation of fellow slaves. For the period from 1782 to 1832, six instruments of emancipation involving free Black masters and their slaves were registered in the court records. Of these, all involved the liberation of family members. Catherine Granthum purchased and immediately manumitted both her husband and child while at the same time recalling the "love and affection" that she held for them. Free Black men, at least in the late eighteenth century, were more likely to have the wherewithal to purchase their slave spouses; the remaining five free Black manumitters were male. Roger Cooper, a free Black carpenter, emancipated his wife, Clarissa, and children, John, two, and Agnes, five years old, in 1793. In a not unusual pattern, particularly in the early years of the growth of the free Black community, he had "married" Clarissa while she was a slave. Two years later, Titus Freeman manumitted his wife, Molly, by deed. In 1801, Jack Baker freed his wife. Hoping to secure their future, he also emancipated his two children, eight-year-old Hannah and five-year-old John, three years later, "lest someone might make claim to them after me."[45] In his deed of manumission in 1816, Francis Cousins, citing the "love and affection" he bore for his daughter Ridley and her three children, Frank, William, and Lucy Ann, granted them their freedom.[46]

Jacob Sampson, affluent owner of a popular tavern on Three Chopt Road, one of the county's main trading routes, freed his wife, Franky Cross, and five children by deed of manumission in 1831 but stipulated that the emancipation was to take effect only after his death. By all the evidence, he lived for a good forty years after the drafting of this agreement, at least to the early 1870s. Apparently Sampson had considerable incentive to free his wife and children, if only on paper. He was married to Franky Cross, the only daughter of Moses, the freed slave who had worked so assiduously and at such great sacrifice to emancipate himself and maintain residence in the county. Moses must have been mortified to see his daughter and grandchildren remain in bondage.

The details of the relationship between Moses Cross and his son-in-law are not fully evident. But for some reason the final deposition of Cross's estate was decided by the assembly. By that 1831 ruling, Jacob Sampson could only take possession of the deceased's property if he agreed to emancipate Franky, "the natural child of the said Moses," and all her children. This stipulation helps to explain the simultaneous appearance with Moses Cross's will of Sampson's carefully hedged deed of emancipation in the Goochland County records for that year.[47]

It is not necessary to accuse Jacob Sampson of self-interested calculation in the matter of his family's manumission to see the contradictions in his relationship to the institution of chattel slavery. He too was caught in a bind. If he manumitted his family outright then they too would have had to get permission to remain in the state, a distasteful process that he had himself experienced and that had become increasingly difficult in the 1830s. By 1831, the legislature, for example, had restated its earlier position mandating public sale of free Blacks and people of mixed race who remained in the state "contrary to the law."[48] Jacob Sampson's dilemma regarding his family's status did not mean that he was opposed to owning slaves for profit. During his lifetime, he purchased a number of slaves who worked in his tavern and as agricultural laborers on his extensive landholdings.[49]

The case of Jacob Sampson's ownership of his family and of unrelated slaves illuminates the social contradictions that developed once the boundaries between bondage and color became more porous in the post-1782 period. Notwithstanding the other onerous legal constraints on their liberties, until 1832 free Blacks were not restricted in any manner from owning slaves. Ironically, therefore, at the same time most free Blacks lived on the economic and social margins of county life, a few owned slaves primarily to profit from their labor. John Pierce was among that number. In 1828, twelve years after his emancipation, he is listed in the tax records as owning fourteen slaves. His wife, a free woman, was also a slaveowner, owning up to four slaves. There is no evidence that the Pierces ever manumitted any of these slaves.

The difficulty in untangling the implications of this phenomenon is that the outward similarities with white ownership of slaves may hide fundamental differences in the ways these relationships functioned on an everyday basis. The interpretive focus shifts when master and slave were of the same race. For white planters, historians are likely to ask, "What motivated some individuals to manumit?" For Black slaveowners, on the other hand, the question is upended: "Under what circumstances did free Black slaveowners *not* manumit their chattel property?"

Scholars have long referred to the distinction between "benevolent" and "commercial" ownership of slaves by free persons of color. Early on, Carter G. Woodson proposed that of the relatively few free Black slaveowners enumerated in the federal census of 1830, most owned members of their family or friends in a protective rather than exploitative capacity. Woodson based his conclusion on the fact that the majority of free Black slaveholders owned only one or two slaves. Thus, for Woodson, free Black ownership of chattel property bore little resemblance to that of white ownership. According to this argument, only by virtue of legal, economic, and societal restrictions on manumission did free Blacks retain property in one another. In his study of free Black property-holders in Virginia, Luther Porter Jackson reached similar conclusions.[50]

For the Lower South, including South Carolina, historians have recently challenged the "Woodson thesis," arguing that a substantial number of free Black masters purchased and owned slaves primarily for labor exploitation. In a reexamination of free Black slaveowners in Virginia, Phillip J. Schwarz finds evidence of slavery as an economic investment among free Blacks but concludes that for the most part, these slaveowners "possessed [slaves] to protect them; they usually intended to emancipate their chattel when possible." Moreover, "they were doing all they could to safeguard their loved ones." Thus, according to Schwarz, from "1782 to 1806, most ownership of blacks by blacks was temporary, having as its object the manumission of that 'species of property.'"[51] Only with the passage of the 1806 removal statute did free Blacks refrain from manumission, fearing that their emancipated relatives would either be forced to leave the state or be reenslaved. When possible, Schwarz concludes, emancipation of their chattel property was the option of choice for most free Black slaveowners.

The small numbers of deeds of manumission for free Black slaveowners in Goochland County belie the frequency with which free Blacks married and purchased their wives and children. Between 1806 and 1830, about 10 percent of Goochland's free Blacks owned slaves. The 1806 state law, however, constrained those who would have otherwise preferred to emancipate family members. The decision to manumit could jeopardize family stability. The removal law, though only sporadically enforced, always loomed in the background. Increasingly, as restrictions were placed on all free Blacks, the right to property and thus to jurisdiction over one's slave family provided a limited guarantee. Yet on the other hand, maintaining family members as slaves was not without its own risks. As Jack Baker so perceptively realized, there was always the danger that spouses or children who were slaves could be sold if the free head of household died intestate or indebted: the family could be sold or their ownership revert to the state.

Given the many considerations that a free Black family owner had to take into account in making the decision to manumit, the patterning of manumissions and its underlying meanings were necessarily different from those of white manumitters. The data in Goochland does not allow for any systematic organization of free Black slave ownership into neat categories. At the level of analysis possible, it is difficult to distinguish the underlying motivations for manumission, on the one hand, and slave ownership on the other.

The data from the county does support, however, Schwarz's finding that the majority of free Black slaveowners in the state owned slaves for a relatively short period of time. In Goochland, fifty-six free Black slaveowners can be identified. Of these, only nineteen (34%) kept slave property for more than a year, and even in these instances ownership rarely extended beyond three years. Other indications that free Black slaveowners predominantly held family members or non-kin as a means of protecting them from expulsion from the state is reflected in the temporal patterns of ownership. Of the total number of free Black slaveowners, only thirteen (23%) held slaves before 1806.

The involvement of African Americans in Goochland County in struggling to achieve and maintain free status is evident throughout the period under study. But especially after 1806, they must have had to exercise constant vigilance in order to negotiate the labyrinth of legislative and social arguments and policies that hemmed them in on all sides. Part of the uncertainty stemmed from the ambivalence with which they were regarded: courted and at the same time denounced, recognized as free people but denied the rights and privileges of their white counterparts, the constant objects of policing measures that were selectively and unpredictably enforced. Yet they were also able to establish roots in the county and perhaps even develop a sense of their "native" ties to the county and the state.

· 4 ·

Youth and Bound Labor

Despite focusing on the North, a quite different socioeconomic and demographic setting, W. J. Rorabaugh's characterization of craft apprenticeship captures the situation in Virginia. Apprenticeship was "complex, diverse, and amorphous," he writes. Its stated and unstated objectives were often in conflict, yet not so much so that they explicitly challenged existing institutions and ideologies. For the historian it is the institution's mutability that intrigues and confounds at the same moment.[1]

Statute law relating to juvenile apprenticeship encapsulated the multiple dimensions of the institution in Virginia. But it is at the local level that the connections among coercive, reformative, training, charitable, protective, and racist functions are more clearly illuminated as juvenile apprenticeship adapted to particular social and economic contexts.

In a manner similar to ownership of slaves, the institution of juvenile apprenticeship illuminates the many ways free African Americans were able to use a system they were unable to overturn. But what does it mean to speak of opportunity in such a context? And does free Black engagement with the laws that so constricted their actions and the lives of their children indicate strategies of resistance or merely confirm the inherent power of the system to incorporate and exploit disenfranchised members of society?

Once set into a legal framework, juvenile apprenticeship brought into play actors with different investments in and experiences of the system. These would have included free Black and white mothers and their African American children, slaves, apprentices and masters, county officials and the assembly, the free Black community, and the wider community of white

Virginians. These levels of interaction illuminate the interlocked domains of race and status that free Blacks inhabited.

Free Black apprentices appeared early in the history of Goochland, with indentures registered in the court records only two years after the county's founding in 1728.[2] By the time of these indentures, juvenile apprenticeship had been well institutionalized in Virginia. I briefly examine the origins and development of legislation before turning to a discussion of free Black apprentices in Goochland County.

The antecedents for an indentured labor system rested with the English, but in Virginia, as David Galenson points out, the institution underwent significant transformations built on a substrate of traditional forms.[3] The same may be said of juvenile apprenticeship in Virginia with its foundations in English pauper and craft apprenticeship. As a part of this tradition, boys and girls were indentured to the households or shops of artisans and craftspeople to learn skilled trades. For Galenson, the distinction between indentured servants and juvenile apprentices is an important one. But in Virginia, the boundaries between these two categories of labor were not clearly articulated.[4]

Mention of the presence of juvenile apprentices first occurred in a 1619 letter written to city officials from the Virginia Company of London. It thanked them for their help in recruiting a hundred of London's homeless children to serve Virginia planters and outlined plans for transporting an additional hundred apprentices the following spring. The company promised that indentured children would be "educated and brought up in some good Trade and profession whereby they may be enabled to gett their liveinge and maynteyne themselvs when they shall attain their severall ages."[5]

When imported into the colony these children stood on the threshold between apprentice and indentured servants-in-husbandry. After serving a minimum term of seven years or until they reached age twenty-one, they then served an additional seven years as tenants before receiving their freedom dues and a parcel of land. In its earliest manifestation, then, juvenile apprenticeship had already been adapted by the Virginia Company to serve specific labor functions and to help populate the new settlement.

By 1646, when the Virginia Assembly drafted the first indigenous laws, the focus was no longer on immigrant children but on those born in Virginia during the intervening years. The text of the law linked the colony's prosperity to God having "vouchsafed increase of children ... who [were] now multiplied to a considerable number." Natural increase was itself a sign of demographic health, but it also meant that the colony had a divine duty to control and manage the growing juvenile population. The act gave local jurisdictions the authority to take impoverished children from their parents and to bind them to "tradesmen or husbandmen."[6]

The colony and later the commonwealth distributed care for the indigent out to localities and then to individual households and citizens. In her discussion of seventeenth-century attitudes toward the poor, Virginia Bernhard argues that such responsibilities were shouldered without complaint by an emerging gentry willing to assume its obligations for those less fortunate.[7] And to some extent the language of apprenticeship legislation hints at a certain *noblesse oblige*.

While no specific instructions were given as to the length or terms of service of these children, the 1646 statute justified the codification of apprenticeship practices. Its language contained the elements of a moral architecture that acknowledged the polity's responsibility to mold its young into proper and useful citizenship. It referred to the "sloath and idlenesse" of young children for whom no provisions for education or training had been made. Apprenticeship would alleviate the burden of indigent parents unable to care for their children and reduce demands on parish coffers.

But even in setting out the earliest mandate, the assembly seemed aware that the poor might not be well disposed to accept either the externally imposed definition of their plight or the remedies offered. The 1646 act referred to the inherent problems in separating children from reluctant parents, who through "fond indulgence or perverse obstinacy" resisted the incursions of county officials into domestic life. In light of these tensions, the act justified the coercive elements in a binding-out process that would serve the greater end of bringing "honor and reputation" to the country.[8]

At its inception, apprenticeship legislation primarily functioned as a remedy for the problem of idle and indigent white youth and an instrument of social rather than racial control. There was nothing, however, that barred the application of the law to free Black children when either their numbers or "sloath" became problematic. Although modified over the years, the 1646 law provided the groundwork for the institutionalization of juvenile apprenticeship in Virginia. Evidently, free Black children were apprenticed under the terms of the early laws, even though the law made no specific provisions for these children.[9]

Race did not become the determining factor in binding out children until 1691. And when the distinction was made, it took on the characteristics of indentured servitude rather than juvenile apprenticeship. As part of a far-reaching codification of slave laws ("An Act for Suppressing Outlying Slaves"), the legislature gave church wardens the authority to bind all the mixed-race children of white women to terms of thirty-one years. Moreover, any children born to female indentured mulattoes were also bound for the same period. Nothing more closely resembled slavery than the inherited servitude visited on these children.

This encroachment on the lives of white mothers of mixed-race children occurred regardless of their ability to support them. In this respect, the legal classification of mixed-race children of white mothers differed from that of others. While the distinction blurred over time, and may not always have been made at the local level, the law seems to clearly indicate that these offspring were to be indentured as servants, not as apprentices. Masters were not required either to train or instruct them.[10]

Clues to the assembly's anxiety about slave-white interactions include a five-year term of servitude and a substantial fine levied on white women who bore the children of Black men, and perhaps even more telling, its unequivocal prohibition of interracial marriage. Women who joined in such unions risked permanent banishment from the colony. As with juvenile apprenticeship proper, the binding out of mixed-race children became a ready instrument for social, sexual, and racial control. The assembly intended to maintain the distinction between mixed-race offspring of white mothers and other free Black children.

Only in 1765 did mixed-race servants indentured under the 1691 statute obtain relief from the terms that had set them apart as a separate category. Recognizing the "severity" of the thirty-one-year term, the assembly reduced the years of servitude established for all other bound children. This modification points yet again to the ambiguity characterizing the entire body of law regulating Virginia's free Black population. The pendulum seemed to swing in the opposite direction when in 1805, the assembly made it illegal for Overseers of the Poor to "require the master or mistress to teach . . . reading, writing or arithmetic" to Black or mixed-race children who were bound out. It did not, however, explicitly forbid such instruction.[11]

At the same time that it severely restricted children of color, Virginia's apprenticeship legislation provided a framework of rights that confirmed the apprentice-master relationship as contractual. Apprentices, or their representatives, had the right to complain to the Overseers of the Poor if they were mistreated or if they believed that other terms of the apprenticeship indenture had been violated.[12] Masters in turn had wide powers over the apprentices' conduct, mobility, and labor.[13] As Winthrop D. Jordan has observed for apprenticeship as a labor system, it "permitted compulsion" but did not "permit so total a loss of freedom as lifetime hereditary slavery."[14]

The major sources for reconstructing the quantitative aspects of free Black apprenticeship are the listings of binding orders registered in county court records. These binding orders identified masters and gave the names, gender, and, less frequently, the ages of the children. They provided the names of the child's or children's mothers. Sometimes they designated the specific training a child was to receive. In addition to these court records, a range of primary sources including manumission records, free Black registers, inventories, marriage records, and court cases involving masters, apprentices, and their parents allow us to secure full characterizations of participants in the apprenticeship relationship as well as to examine the overall role of apprenticeship in the county through 1832.

In all, 262 free Black children were apprenticed from 1730 to 1832. Immediately conspicuous is the relatively small proportion of children apprenticed in the half-century before the private manumission act of 1782 dramatically increased the numbers of free Black residents of the county. Churchwardens apprenticed between one and four children annually, with a total of forty-three children bound. Except for a thirteen-year period in which there were no registrations of apprentices, this pattern was consistent, suggesting a small mixed-race presence in the county. Free Black apprenticeship in Goochland, therefore, was primarily a postrevolutionary phenomenon with more than 80 percent of apprenticeship contracts occurring after 1782.

While a precipitating factor in the rise in the free Black population, the manumission law did not lead to an immediate increase in the activities of the Overseers of the Poor. For the first decade, the level of apprenticeship did not depart from the earlier pattern. This trend is somewhat unexpected since within months of the 1782 law more than half of the slaves manumitted in the county had received their freedom. A good many of these came from families with children. In October 1782, for example, thirty-five of the fifty-five slaves emancipated by Quaker families were children. A major reason for the decade's lag before a significant rise in juvenile indentures is that the manumission act required masters to forestall the release of emancipated children until the age of twenty-one for boys and eighteen for girls. These children, therefore, did not come under the direct supervision of the Overseers of the Poor but were assigned to a quasi-apprenticeship or, perhaps more aptly, to a condition of delayed emancipation.

What had been a trickle of free Black children brought into the apprenticeship system turned into a steady flow in the final decade of the eighteenth century. The Overseers of the Poor indentured ten free Black children in 1791, thirty-six children in the following four years, and seventy-six over the entire decade. Many of these children were the offspring of those freed individuals who reached adulthood in the 1790s and established independent taxable households. The transition from slavery to freedom, however, had not allowed them to consolidate the resources to maintain their children financially. Thus, in a great irony, this first generation born outside of slavery found themselves, as had their parents, inextricably bound to the plantation.

Apprenticeship levels declined overall as the free Black community established itself in the county. Through 1830, proportionately fewer children of a growing free Black population were apprenticed out. One possible explanation is that more free Blacks had achieved sufficient economic stability to shield their children from the stringent terms of apprenticeship indentures. Data from the federal census and the county tax records show a marked decrease in dependent free Blacks residing in white households. Despite legislation specifically intended to restrict free Black rights, reduce their numbers in Virginia, and tax them at a punitive rate, significant numbers maintained some economic independence.

The situation for free Black apprentices may also have mirrored a general pattern noted by Rorabaugh. He argues that during the antebellum period, fewer and fewer localities, especially in the South, drew on apprenticeship as a system for handling indigent youth. Many young people who might otherwise have been apprenticed were attracted to urban industries.[15] Falling numbers of apprentices in Goochland also reflected these new socioeconomic realities. No clear conclusion may be drawn, however, until scholars undertake further research on free Black labor patterns in rural Virginia counties.

In the sample of apprenticed children, county clerks recorded the apprenticeship of 148 boys and 114 girls (a ratio of 1.3:1) from 1731 to 1832. The slight overall disparity in the ratio of males to females masks the increasing likelihood of boys being apprenticed in later decades. From 1803 to 1812, for example, the male-female ratio reached as high as 3:1 and remained at 2:1 through 1830. These ratios persisted despite a greater number of girls under eighteen years old in the nineteenth-century free Black population.

What were the factors that led to the greater proportion of boys in the population of apprenticed children? In explaining a similar pattern for North Carolina, John Hope Franklin argues that masters preferred male apprentices. Boys were favored, he suggests, because they could perform a wider range of tasks than girls and could also be trained in skilled crafts necessary to the economy of their masters' households.[16] Another incentive from the perspective of masters, perhaps, was the longer term served by boys.

Another possibility is that free Black mothers may have chosen to place their sons rather than daughters in other households. Because girls were usually trained in skills such as sewing and spinning that the mother herself could teach, it made sense for boys to be apprenticed out to learn skilled trades such as smithing, coopering, and carpentry.

A letter to the Overseers of the Poor in the 1790s suggests the hesitation some planters may have felt when taking on responsibility for indigent free Black children, especially girls. Philip Pleasants, a Quaker, wrote of the dire circumstances of three children—the son and daughters of Aggy Cooper, a free Black resident of the county. "There was," he wrote "a general order made some years ago to bind them all to Thomas Pleasants. I have a few weeks ago conversed with his representative on the subject. They decline altogether taking any but the boy so that there will be two girls remaining." Phillip agreed with some reluctance to take the oldest girl, Sally, to "make her a weaver" but asked the Overseers to place her younger sister, Betsy, elsewhere. He urged quick action: "I think it would be right not to delay the business, as the necessaries of life are scarce and . . . they must suffer."[17] The Quaker planter was adamant about not accepting the younger sister, despite his awareness of her dire circumstances.

Church wardens and later Overseers of the Poor apprenticed children as young as two and as old as nineteen for boys and seventeen for girls. Age at apprenticeship could be ascertained for sixty-three children. In this sample, age of apprenticeship for most boys was between three and five; for girls, between seven and ten years old. In other words, the length of indenture for boys was fifteen to eighteen years and for girls eight to eleven. Although representing only a fourth of the total number of children apprenticed, this sample strongly suggests a general pattern in which boys were apprenticed out earlier and thus for longer periods, while girls remained with their families for slightly longer periods and served relatively shorter terms in their masters' households.

Who were the masters to whom free Black children were apprenticed and under whose authority they spent a significant portion of their lives? Masters figured as central participants in the apprenticeship process, with Goochland County Quakers playing a key role. The Overseers of the Poor often indentured free Black children to Quakers who formerly had been slaveholders. The Pleasants family is a case in point. Throughout the eighteenth century, family members had owned a large number of slaves; after 1782, one branch of the family emancipated nearly one hundred slaves. In subsequent years, the Overseers indentured out many of the children of these freed slaves to the family. By taking on apprentices, the Pleasantses reimposed a form of servitude even as they acted in accord with the dictates of their faith to eschew ownership of human property and serve the poor. Quaker involvement may be interpreted from these opposing perspectives.[18] There were strong correspondences between manumitters and those who eventually became masters in the juvenile apprenticeship system.

Of the 105 masters identified, fifty-one appeared in the tithe and tax lists. More than 50 percent of individuals owned between zero and five slaves. Seven masters owned between six and ten slaves, and four owned between eleven and fifteen slaves. These masters took on an average of one or two apprentices, and when two children went to the same master, they often were siblings.[19] Typically, therefore, most planters who used apprentices were of a middling socioeconomic status.

The juvenile apprenticeship arrangement fit the needs of these middling planters and artisans. It provided them with access to laborers who received no wages and for whom no initial capital outlay in the form of a purchase price for slave labor was necessary. For those who owned a small number of slaves, apprentices supplemented the labor force. Yet unlike their poorer counterparts, middling planters and artisans could afford to support the minimal costs of food and board due to the apprentice. Among this group were a few free Black artisans who appeared to have been unrelated to their free Black apprentices.

When middling planters decided to take juvenile free Black apprentices, they must have considered a number of factors. Since most children were indentured out before they were eight years old, they initially could contribute little to the overall production of any agricultural or artisanal unit. Further, if a master intended to train a young person, the terms of the apprenticeship contract required that the apprentice be released at precisely the moment they entered adulthood. Small wonder that free Black mothers and apprentices often appeared in court to pressure reluctant masters to terminate overdue indentures. These circumstances help to explain what at first seems a paradoxical situation in which the Overseers of the Poor sometimes failed to find masters willing to take indigent children who had been identified as candidates for apprenticeship.

It appears that the courts did not assign apprentices to large slaveholders. Or, from another view, affluent slaveowners did not normally take free Black children as apprentices. Of our sample of masters, only two owned more than twenty slaves. William Bolling owned ninety-three slaves in 1820 when he took on three brothers. But these indentures occurred at the request of the boys' dying father.[20] Less is known of the possible motivations of David Ross, a planter with sixty slaves, substantial livestock, and large landholdings, who took three brothers, the sons of Franky Barnett, in 1795 and another male apprentice a year later. Ross's involvement in the apprenticeship process is partially explained since he lived in the county's upper district and rented land to a community of free Blacks who worked as watermen, grooms, planters, and spinners for planters in the vicinity. Ross, therefore, may have apprenticed these children as an extension of his direct involvement in the hiring and tenancy of free Black adults.[21]

Ira Berlin notes that in the South some farmers insisted that indigent free Black children be apprenticed without the consent of their parents. "In some places," he writes, "the advantages of holding free Black apprentices became so great that authorities had trouble binding out white children." In Goochland, the "market" for free Black apprentices did not appear to have been so intense. The binding of orphaned or illegitimate white children was not diminished by the existence of free Black apprenticeships.[22]

By giving free Blacks access to the courts and codifying the reciprocal relationship between master and servant, the juvenile apprenticeship system sometimes produced unintended consequences. After the American Revolution, the system subverted the strict dichotomy between enslaved Blacks and free white citizens. The institution as it evolved in Goochland County combined a strong element of compulsion with a degree of flexibility that free Black individuals could sometimes exploit. For the county's white elite, success in using apprenticeship as a means of social and racial control often came at the expense of making free Black individuals conscious of the rights afforded them by law: they inserted themselves into the apprenticeship process as soon as they were able to do so.

How did parents (primarily mothers) retain some level of authority over their bound children when apprenticeship laws required them to relinquish their authority? They used their knowledge of the judicial process. If a master was unscrupulous and parents were not vigilant, young Black apprentices could lose their free status while under indentures. The case of Billy and Jesse Cooper illustrates the dangers of unregulated apprenticeship. Overseers of the Poor first apprenticed the two brothers to a county planter, Samuel Couch, in 1791. By some sequence of events, the boys were taken to Richmond, without notification of the courts or consent of their mother, Rachel Cooper. After Couch's death in 1801, the court "directed the Overseers of the Poor . . . to send to the City of Richmond for Billy and Jesse Cooper." The boys were then reapprenticed separately, Jesse to Charles Hopkins and Billy to Robert Saunders. Rachel Cooper's complaint apparently only reached the courts some six years later. On hearing testimony, the court ruled that the apprenticeship order was to be rescinded because "Jesse and Billy had been removed out of the said County more than twelve months before the time of making the order binding them to the said Saunders and Hopkins."[23] Thus, only by pressing her suit based on a legal technicality was Rachel successful in shortening the duration of her children's forced apprenticeship.

For the family of Lucy Lynch, dissatisfaction with her indenture stemmed not from the fine points of law but rather from the "moral character" of the household to which she had been bound. On her mother's death, Lucy had been ordered apprenticed to Samuel Jackson, a "free man of color." In 1819, sometime after the original binding order, John Lynch, whose relation to Lucy is not known, came to the court on her behalf. He acknowledged that Lucy had been "duly bound by the Overseers of the Poor" but requested to have that indenture rescinded. On hearing testimony, the court ruled that "the sd. Jackson is an improper person on account of the character of the sd. Jackson's wife." As requested by John Lynch, Lucy was discharged from Samuel Jackson's authority and bound out to John Lynch.[24] These cases point to the importance of family support in mitigating abuses in the apprenticeship system.

Proximity to apprentices even when they were not resident in the household allowed the wider kin network to remain connected. In the above situations, it is likely that the children first complained to their families, who then brought their concerns to the county court. Although there was no guarantee of success, the orders passed down by the Overseers of the Poor could be and sometimes were challenged.

Except in the four instances where fathers were listed, single mothers appeared as the primary guardians of children to be apprenticed out.[25] While this focus on unmarried women may be an artifact of Overseers' refusal to recognize slave and common-law marriages or marriages performed by nontraditional ministers, it does indicate that mothers bore the responsibility for dealing with civil authorities in matters related to the placement of their children.

Rachel Cooper exercised this responsibility in 1783 on behalf of her two sons, Daniel and David Cooper, who had already served five years of their indenture to Japheth Towler. The boys' master had "ill-treated" them, she testified, and further charged that he had threatened to move them out of the county without her consent. Like many of his eighteenth-century contemporaries, Towler planned to relocate in search of greater prosperity. Rachel Cooper asked the court's intervention to prevent Towler from "removing (the children) to a distant county." On hearing testimony from both sides, the court rescinded the original indenture, asked Towler to surrender the children, and ordered them apprenticed to "some tradesman." Cooper knew of and acted on her right to complain about Towler's physical abuse of her children, but more vitally she knew enough of the law to intercede to prevent permanent separation from her children.[26]

Some mothers tried and succeeded in convincing the courts that they could provide adequate care for their children and therefore objected to the placement of their children outside the household. Evidence from the tax lists, occupational registers, and the U.S. Census suggests that most of the mothers listed, particularly those with more than two children, were economically constrained to accept the mandates of the courts.[27] These women responded to the court summons in order to modify rather than rescind initial binding orders. Mothers offered names of preferred masters and mistresses for their children, registered children's ages, and sometimes indicated the craft in which they wished their children to be trained.

In 1816, for example, Charlotte Freeman convinced the courts to apprentice two daughters, Nancy and Henna, to a member of her family. When she appeared, Charlotte requested that her daughters be bound to Judith Scott, a free woman of color. It is probable that Judith was either her mother or sister-in-law, both named Judith, and that she formally agreed to take financial responsibility for the children. When they were bound out three years later, Freeman's youngest children, sons John and Josiah, aged six and three, had the surname Scott, while her older children with Nathan Freeman shared their father's last name. It appears that the indentures and change of surname were occasioned by the separation of Charlotte and Nathan in 1814 or 1815. The records do not say to whom Charlotte's five children were bound in 1819 but, as in 1816, she probably managed to keep part of her family together. Extended kinship networks enabled mothers not only to cushion the impact of court-ordered apprenticeships but also to maintain some parental authority according to the letter of the law.[28]

Anxieties about the binding out of children intensified for sick or dying parents. Such considerations might lead them to make arrangements to apprentice their children to neighboring planters who were willing to assume the role of a guardian. Daniel Cooper, working as a carpenter, moved to William Bolling's land with his wife, Nancy, and young family in 1811 when their oldest child, Burwell, was just seven years old. Although not landowners, they appear to have enjoyed a measure of financial stability and had avoided having Burwell bound out. Court actions suggest that Daniel made such an arrangement with William Bolling, a wealthy planter who served as a justice on the Goochland Court prior to his death in the winter of 1816–17. That Burwell was bound out to Bolling the same day Bolling was appointed administrator of Daniel's estate is significant. After a father's death, or abandonment of family as with Charlotte Freeman, a court order was normally issued to the Overseers of the Poor to find a suitable master for the orphan(s). An agreement between Cooper and Bolling is likely because Bolling undertook the duty of Burwell's apprenticeship the same day he agreed to administer Daniel Cooper's estate.

When Bolling accepted these responsibilities he acknowledged and continued into the next generation the patron-client relationship with this free Black family who had been tenants on his land for six years. Equally significant, Nancy was allowed to keep the younger children at home until they arrived at ages where they could begin training in a suitable trade. Nancy was not called into court to prove she had the means to support her orphaned children. Apparently, and perhaps with Bolling's influence, the court felt that even though they were technically orphans, Nancy could support them. Although documents defining the exact nature of Bolling's role in this sequence of events have not been encountered, there can be no doubt that the intercession of an influential person like Bolling provided some protection from the indenture of Daniel and Nancy's children as infants. They were not bound out to William Bolling until 1827 and 1830. It seems the court felt that Nancy, with Bolling as her patron, had the means to care for her children and raise them properly.[29]

Indentures signed by Overseers of the Poor, who thereby assumed the role of master, concretely expressed the links among branches of the local government, the white freeholding class, and the state while making explicit the relationship among these groups and the free Black apprentice. The October 1804 apprenticeship contract between William Clarke and Peyton and Austin Isaacs included the signatures of Clarke, Thomas Bates, Humphrey Parish, two Overseers of the Poor, and John Hunnicutt, a gentleman justice. And in what appeared to have been a normal occurrence, the document was "sealed and delivered in the presence" of the two brothers. Given their ages (nine and eleven), it is likely that their mother, Molly Isaacs, mentioned in the indenture, also attended the proceedings.[30]

Without neglecting the element of coercion in the practice of binding out, it is fair to say that apprenticeship contracts offered free Blacks tangible evidence that they had rights under the law; that the relationship of apprentice-master provided some measure of obligation on the master's part; and that, however constricted, they too were part of a class of free Black Virginians.

The recognition of contractual arrangements was not an abstraction for free Blacks but a deadly serious issue. Given the strong practical resemblance between juvenile apprentices and slaves, these indentures offered critical evidence of a legal difference that mattered. Mothers of apprenticed children and apprentices themselves appeared in court to complain about poor treatment, illegal indentures, and other abuses. These were no strangers to the failures of the system to uphold their rights. Nonetheless, people with precious little access to judiciary processes succeeded on occasion.

Free African American mothers in Goochland responded to court summons "to shew cause if and why [their] children should not be bound," and presented their points of view to a court that had "been informed that [they were] not able or does not provide for them according to law." When acted on, these summonses gave free Black mothers an official voice in the disposition of their children.[31]

By definition, slavery entailed the purchase of rights in persons. Apprenticeship, on the other hand, allowed only for the temporary transfer of the right to the labor of free Black minors. That this distinction created a basic difference of approach to the expropriation of apprentice and slave labor is most clearly illustrated in the extant apprenticeship contracts drawn up by the churchwardens and after 1785 by the Overseers of the Poor. Whether for white or free Black apprentices, indentures from the eighteenth and nineteenth centuries did not differ in content before 1805. Such agreements specified the nature of the apprentices' responsibilities and obligations to their masters or mistresses. Binding orders were recorded in the county order book, while the formally written indenture constituted the written contract.[32] The indenture included covenants specifying "some art, trade, or business" as well as "reading and writing, and if a boy, common arithmetic, including the rule of three, and to pay to him or her £3, and ten shillings at the expiration of time."

An indenture written out on the occasion of the binding out of Frank James to James Hunnicutt in 1812 contained the conventional language. The statute eliminating covenants regarding instructions in letters and numbers had already been passed. But in other respects, this indenture remained essentially similar to earlier ones. Hunnicutt should teach Frank or "cause him to be instructed in" the "trade and mystery of a farmer," as well as provide adequate food, clothing, and shelter. The indenture required that Frank reciprocate by "fully serving," "keeping [his master's] secrets," and "obeying his commands." Another covenant, typical of extant indentures of both white and free Black apprentices, obligated the apprentice to "do no damage to his said master, nor suffer it to be done by others without giving notice thereof to his said master, and in all things behave himself as a faithful apprentice during said term."³³

In its everyday meaning, "obedience" for the free Black apprentice might well have been oceans apart from that for his white counterpart; so too for the other elements in the indenture contract. The distinction between a set of limited rights and the concept of full equality is an important one. Neither Overseers of the Poor nor masters, nor for that matter free Blacks themselves, assumed that identical contractual arrangements conferred equality on the ground.³⁴ The essential point is that for the free Black apprentice and his family, the existence of the indenture contract affirmed and marked free status in a legal and public way—that the apprentice was free, that he had access to the courts, that his master's authority had specific boundaries, and that the appropriation of his person and labor should not exceed the limits set by law. Free Blacks drew on these basic contractual rights when they presented themselves to the Overseers of the Poor and the courts.

· 5 ·

Work and Freedom

In an economy based on the labor of enslaved Black persons, free African American workers should not have existed. As one approach to reconciling the seeming contradiction, many historians have argued that for the most part these individuals were slaves in all but name. Indeed, free Blacks were as embedded in the plantation system as were slaves: the majority lived on the socioeconomic and political margins of Virginian society. Yet they found many ways to develop a sense of autonomy within these margins.

Goochland's rural plantation economy used workers wherever it found them—whether they were free or slave, Black or white. Planters acknowledged the presence of free Black labor and took their "difference" into account. On the one hand, fearful of the natural affinity they believed existed between free and enslaved Blacks, whites found administrative and political means of creating distance between them. On the other hand, for purposes of expropriating labor, and because they were fearful of the assumption of equality on the part of free Blacks, whites wanted to reduce the status distinctions between these two groups. The history of restrictive legislation against free Blacks in Virginia after 1782 reflected the General Assembly's ad-hoc and ultimately unsuccessful efforts to define and categorize precisely the "species" of the free Black person and of free Black labor. On occupational lists women were simply listed in most instances as "houseworkers" or "spinners" with no further distinctions.[1] Married women's names always followed that of their husbands, an indication of their subordinate relationship to the assumed head of household. In the occupational register of 1811, for example, Ned Guinn is listed as a shoemaker, "his wife Jenny" as a spinner/weaver. Only on investigation of a set of plantation accounts does Jenny's additional skills as a midwife emerge: in 1827, she was paid a two-dollar "midwife's fee" for attending Granville Smith's slave.

Jenny combined a number of skills that took her beyond the confines of her own home and involved her in the lives of slave women. Work was not merely what she did as a weaver, nor did it always entail the production of goods for market. In turn, it is probable that her contribution to the family equaled that of her husband and that in fact their roles were complementary rather than unequal. Whatever the arrangement between them, however, the commissioner responsible for registering this couple inevitably assumed that Ned Guinn was the "head of household." Using the occupational list as a self-supporting document would have obscured the occupational diversity of free Black women and hidden the manner in which individuals created multiple economic ties to the plantation while maintaining their residential independence.[2]

By focusing on a single dimension of the free Black experience—that is, on the patterns of work and the conditions under which free Blacks exchanged their labor for goods and services—it is possible to trace individuals and families as they pursued their livelihoods and attempted to negotiate the economic realities of the county. More than any other aspect of their lives, the work activity of free Blacks resulted in diverse interactions with all levels of the county hierarchy, from white planters to slaves. Furthermore, the criteria for judging the character of free Blacks usually reflected the nature of their contributions to the economic well-being of the wider community.[3] For these reasons, local county records most often refer to free Black individuals because of their participation in the local economy. This diversity and frequency of appearances allow historians to bridge the distance between the public and private worlds of free Blacks and so begin to delineate the patterns of social action that motivated and influenced their economic activity.[4]

The occupational and residency lists are extant for five years between 1804 and 1817 for the county's lower district, while tax lists that identify the occupations and residences of free Black taxpayers in the upper district are available for the years between 1804 through 1815. Together these sources provide an overview of the range of occupational options available to free Blacks. When considered along with estate accounts, they provide a window into the occupational strategies used by these individuals. And while the paths taken varied, one is immediately struck by the value placed on the creative flexibility of free Blacks in the county economy. This ability to adapt was borne out of the restrictions within which free Black workers had to maneuver.[5]

Most free African American men were listed as planters or farmers. In a sample of ninety-eight men who lived in the lower district, twenty-four (24%) were listed as planters or farmers. These terms appeared interchangeably and seemed not to indicate any distinguishing characteristics. In the county's upper district, an identical sample yielded an even higher proportion of individuals who worked in agriculture. Forty (41%) of ninety-eight free Black men worked their own land or tenant-farmed.[6]

The differential number of planters in the two districts is explained by the county's geography. In the upper district, creeks such as the Lickinghole and the Tuckahoe flowed southerly into the James River and provided water to the district's plantations and residents, but they were not commercially navigable. By contrast, the James River on the lower district's southern border and later the James River Canal were major commercial routes that provided free Black men with an alternative and often lucrative occupational option.[7]

Some men owned and operated their own licensed boats or worked on the river commercially. Thirteen free Blacks (13%) from the lower district were listed as boatmen licensed to navigate the river from the falls at Richmond to those in the western town of Lynchburg, while one person was listed simply as a waterman. The records do not indicate if there was a significant difference between watermen and boatmen, although it is possible that a waterman might have worked on the river without owning or operating his own licensed boat. Given the absence of navigable waterways in the upper district, it is not surprising that only two free Black men were listed as being boatmen and that only one worked as such full-time.

For Richard Adams, who resided in the upper district, boating was one of four crafts that he pursued from 1804 to 1828. In addition, he farmed his own land and that of others and worked as a carpenter and a cooper. In 1820, he manufactured six hogsheads for Thomas Miller, a local planter, at the rate of $1.00 per barrel and in 1821 received $5.50 for similar work on another estate. Perhaps the profits from such transactions enabled Adams to enter the James River trade. In 1828, he was listed as owning his own boat.[8]

The accounts bear testimony to the singular importance of these workers (out of all proportion to their numbers) and to the subsequent independence boating offered to those who could afford the initial costs or were able to find employment with boatowners. As intermediaries between the city and its markets and planters along the river as well as inland, boatmen wielded considerable power, both in Black and white communities. Without them and their counterparts—the wagoners who used the overland routes along the county's major turnpike—planters would have found it immeasurably more difficult, if not impossible, to move their tobacco and grains to market. Middling planters would have been particularly vulnerable because they could ill-afford their own boats or slave boatmen.

As a category, wagoners do not appear in the occupational registers but accounts identify a number of individuals who transported goods within the county and along the roads to Richmond and Charlottesville. Some free Blacks may have worked in one primary occupation with wagoning as a secondary livelihood. John Lynch, for example, was a fairly successful blacksmith who also owned his own wagon and ferried goods throughout the area. Wagoners were important along the river as well. They were hired to transport goods to and from plantations situated at some distance from river landings.[9]

In order to avoid insolvency and secure some measure of economic independence, free Blacks often found it necessary or advantageous to pursue one or more skilled and unskilled craft. In both the upper and lower districts, farmers in particular pursued alternative means of livelihood. Thirty-two men in the sample changed or combined occupations. Of these, nineteen farmed at some point in their work history. No discernible pattern seems to have guided the individual's choice of a second or third trade. For example, five farmed as well as participated in the active river and canal transportation and trading network, as either watermen or boatmen. John Johns, a riverman and farmer from the upper district, also worked as a wheelwright. Two individuals worked as ditchers, a profitable skill closely related, though not identical, to farm labor. One man was a hostler and a groom, while another was a well-digger and mason.[10]

Free Black ditchers were important in their own right. An essential component in plantation agriculture was the construction of well-situated ditches to provide drainage for tobacco and grain fields. The low-lying areas of the county's lower district in particular were subject to flooding. Some free Black men were specialists in the digging and maintenance of these open culverts. Their presence in the records offers yet another glimpse, from the perspective of the free Black worker, of the social relations of labor and of the ways in which work was organized in the county. Fourteen ditchers worked lower district plantations, while nine ditchers resided and worked in the upper district. Ditching entailed a combination of specialized skill and hard manual labor.

In late December 1824, Francis Harris contracted with Frank Coley, providing specific instructions concerning the length, width, and depth of the ditches. Coley was paid $127.80 for "cutting 2,130 yards of ditch at six feet wide and two feet deep @ 6 c[ents] p[er] yd" on Harris's Powhatan plantation.[11] Free Black ditchers seem to have been responsible for mobilizing and paying their own workforce to supplement that of the plantation. The seven jobbers listed in the upper district would have been hired for the ditching crews.

While occupational lists offer a view of the "official" occupations of free Blacks in the formal economy, glimpses of an active subterranean economy occasionally emerge in other sources. For example, Nathaniel and Jacob Banks manufactured and sold illegal liquor. In 1818, "from the information of John Banks, Jnr.," the county's grand jury indicted them for "retailing spirits at their residence to be drank at the place where [they] sold without license." The normal fine for such an infraction, whether committed by Blacks or whites, was thirty dollars. Ultimately, the prosecution against the Bankses was "dismissed by the attorney for the Commonwealth," and while their encounter with the court possibly discouraged further activity of this kind, the risks of being apprehended may well have been worth the extra income such an enterprise might generate.[12] Tavern licenses were relatively expensive, ranging between eighteen and twenty-four dollars a year, and applicants were required to provide evidence of good character. Over the half century from 1782 to 1832, few free Blacks were able to afford licenses, and only one, Jacob Sampson, was allowed to operate an establishment of "private entertainment." For the county poor of either race, extralegal activity was always an available economic option. Whites also were tried and fined for violating retail liquor regulations or for buying and selling stolen goods.[13]

Many of the county's free Blacks sought to supplement their income by pursuing a variety of overlapping and interrelated activities, taking advantage of economic opportunities as they arose. This is not to suggest that free Black individuals in Goochland County were ceaselessly market-oriented or that they were oblivious to issues of morality. Perhaps it is more appropriate to think of their actions as constituting part of a moral economy in which a primary aim may have been to maintain their status as free persons by providing themselves with a flexible margin of economic security.

Take a criminal case brought to the county courts in October 1817 involving the interactions of free Blacks and slaves in the far western part of the county, on the banks of the James River. Peyton, the property of Jesse Norris, stood trial for "feloniously stealing, taking and carrying away 16 bushells of wheat the property of Warner Lewis of the value of $24." Lewis, who filed charges, was a substantial planter owning twenty-one slaves and a large plantation. But after hearing the evidence, the justices found Peyton not guilty.[14]

At the same court but in separate trials, two free Black men, boatmen by trade, were charged with having received the wheat on the night it was stolen. The county court further charged that they agreed to take the wheat, knowing that it had been stolen. David Cousins, the first boatman tried, was accused of having taken aboard twelve bushels of the wheat on Thursday night, October 9; Tarlton Barnett, whose boat was also moored in the vicinity, allegedly received four bushels of the same lot of grain that night. The justices determined that neither Cousins nor Barnett had conspired with Peyton either to steal or fence the wheat. In fact, the court's failure to convict Peyton suggests that, lacking sufficient evidence, the justices were unable to prove that the slave had acquired the wheat by dishonest means. Warner Lewis's claims against Peyton and the boatmen could not be substantiated in court.

Imagine the meeting in the dark of night on or near the river and the negotiations about who would get what portion of the wheat and at what cost. Both Barnett and Cousins were experienced boatmen. It is likely this was not the first time they had encountered such a situation. If they were not personally acquainted with Peyton, they may still have been aware of his status as well as the restrictions that accompanied it: by statute, slaves could not own, much less sell, property, particularly not such a large quantity of wheat.[15] The clandestine nature of the transaction suggests that the parties recognized the need to avoid detection and were well aware that they might be discovered and apprehended. Yet both men were willing to jeopardize their licenses as well as their freedom to supplement the income from their regular river trade.

The larger point here is not to establish the boatmen's guilt or innocence but rather to suggest that they made a reasonable decision to participate in a transaction that promised a fair return on their investment. Further, by 1817, free Blacks, especially men as mobile as these were, had wide experience with the law and its applications. They understood the significance of testimony, the reliability of witnesses, and the nature of evidence. And, not coincidentally, at the time of their trial, relatives could afford to post a one-hundred-dollar bond for David Cousins. Thus, their decision to take on the wheat was not haphazard but based on a wide knowledge of many aspects of the society in which they lived. As much as their officially recognized trades and crafts, the ability to apply their social skills and common sense enabled free Blacks to maneuver in a social terrain full of risks and obstacles.[16]

Goochland, like other Piedmont counties, was thoroughly agricultural. Throughout the colonial period, tobacco was the main crop planted in both the upper and lower districts. After the American Revolution, there was a demonstrable shift toward the cultivation of mixed grains (corn, wheat, and oats), with tobacco becoming only a complementary crop.[17]

By the first census in 1790, slaves constituted 55 percent of the total population. That percentage increased steadily, reaching almost 59 percent by 1810, and by 1830 the slave population that had earlier showed signs of leveling was 63 percent of the total number of people residing in the county. It is against this demographic and economic backdrop that free Black labor must be considered. In spite of the growing numbers of free Blacks after 1782, they still represented a relatively small proportion of the whole population. Most white planters used and depended on slave labor. Free Blacks augmented this labor force, providing whites who did not own their own slaves with skilled and unskilled labor.[18]

Free Black labor served the needs of yeoman and middling farmers who required a reservoir of laborers who could perform a range of skilled and unskilled tasks but for whom the planters did not have to bear either the cost of the initial capital investment or the ongoing expenses of a permanent chattel labor force. The percentages are telling. On average, between 1782 and 1831, 45 percent of the total number of tithables (of which free Blacks made up only a small proportion) did not own slaves. And of the remaining 55 percent who were slaveholders, only 10 percent owned more than ten slaves.[19] In a sample of thirty-five planters who hired free Blacks and kept accounts, 52 percent owned fewer than ten slaves and 32 percent of these employers had between eleven and twenty slaves on their estates. Two people who hired free Blacks owned no slaves, and two planters held more than ninety slaves.[20]

Consistent with their increasing presence in the county, free Blacks began to appear with some frequency in estate accounts after 1800. Two such accounts suggest the ways in which planters used the labor available to them and how free Blacks integrated themselves into the economy of these estates.

When Frederick Argyle died, his account for a period of six years between 1804 and 1810 was filed with the court clerk. Argyle's holdings included twenty slaves of which nine were small children and eleven tithable adults (six men and five women). At the end of August 1811, when Argyle needed to transport his tobacco harvest to Richmond, he hired an unnamed boatman, the slave of a fellow planter, Benjamin Anderson. In the following month, Argyle again required the services of a boatman and on this occasion used John Pierce to take 180 bushels of wheat to market in the city. He would again use Pierce in January 1814 to ferry an unspecified amount of tobacco.[21]

Pierce was still a slave during this period, but as we have previously noted, he was an independent contractor who in an agreement with his owner, John Curd, hired his own time and lived with Milly, his free wife. A few years after this transaction, Pierce gained his freedom but continued to ferry goods to and from Richmond and within the county. He may have owned his boat in 1811. But it was not until 1828 that he licensed "Boat #2," possibly a second boat, under his own name.[22]

Frederick Argyle, in this short period, had drawn on the services of two individuals, both of whom were slaves but who by the nature of their craft were relatively independent. Pierce, in particular, was in the process of securing his freedom. In December 1811, Argyle once again employed another of John Curd's slaves, a blacksmith whose work was valued at $33. Two years later, he paid Anthony Jenkins, a free Black shoemaker, a sum of $14 on two different occasions. For medical care, Argyle engaged Doctors Vaughn and Galt, white physicians, at a cost of $42 in 1811, and a free

Black midwife hired in midsummer of 1812 received fees of $3.75 for attending a slave woman during childbirth. In addition to these expenditures for services rendered, Argyle hired out labor to his compatriots. In 1812, he charged $10 for the short-term hire of an adult slave. In the following two years, he hired out four "negro boys" for much longer periods of time, for a total fee of $165. The mix of services contracted and the flexible use of free and unfree labor in Argyle's account was typical.[23]

In the final decade of the period under study, Francis Harris's account reveals even more elaborate use of free labor (both Black and white). According to the tax list, he owned fifteen tithable slaves in Goochland. This figure would not have accounted for children under twelve and elderly slaves nor for those slaves on his Powhatan County estate. In a series of transactions between 1823 and 1830, Harris engaged skilled workers to provide clothing and shoes to the plantation. In 1824, he contracted with James Cowig, a free Black shoemaker. Ten years earlier Cowig had been apprenticed out by the Overseers of the Poor to "be learnt the art and mistery of a shoemaker." Still living in the county, he was hired to make "two strong pair [of] shoes" for Harris's sons Alexander and Edgar, at a total cost of $2.75. The father was apparently satisfied with Cowig's workmanship for in January of the following year the shoemaker delivered thirty-nine pairs of shoes to the plantation for a cost of $13. Less durable and cheaper footwear, these were slated for the use of the plantation's slaves. At $0.33 a pair, Cowig was competitively remunerated. For exactly the same fee, four years later a white shoemaker, Daniel Utley, made forty-one pairs of shoes at a total cost of $13.66, while John Harvey, a white shoemaker, was paid $4 for making two pairs of shoes for Edgar and Alexander.[24]

Two white carpenters made coffins for the estate, one for Mrs. Harris, who died in 1823, and the other for Sarah, likely a child, who passed away the next year. A white boatman, Henry Pralst was engaged in 1824 to take wheat to Richmond and paid $13.66. In the same year, Peter Sublett and Mingo, two free Black boatmen who owned their own boats, ferried wheat and bran "at sundry times" in either direction between Goochland and Richmond for a total of $48. Charles Howell, another free Black boatman, transported goods for Harris some years later. Planters took advantage of the frequent trips these boatmen made up and down the river and to Richmond. In 1828, for example, Mingo sold a rawhide in Richmond for Harris's estate. On another occasion, he purchased cloth in the city for William Shelton, another planter. Here, these boatmen acted as mediators between urban merchants and consumers and rural planters.[25]

Although Harris depended on his slaves for much of the agricultural labor, he also hired free workers on a seasonal basis and for specialized tasks. This hiring took place even in instances where the estate had an apparent surfeit of labor. At the same time Harris's estate sold James, "a negro man," for $300, it also expended considerable sums taking on wage laborers. From this perspective, slaves may have proved a good source of ready cash, while workers could be paid their wages over an extended period of time with no maintenance costs. In 1824, Thomas Conway, a white laborer, and James Tyler, a free Black, cut wheat over a period of ten days. Conway received $10 and Tyler $13.25 for ten days' work. Tyler's higher wages suggest that he was responsible for providing the animal power for the thresher. He was taxed for two horses shortly after he appeared in this account. Holman Shoemaker, a white mechanic, repaired the threshing machine during the harvest, while Frank Coley, a free Black laborer, was hired to stack wheat. Besides this work, Coley was again hired by Harris later that winter to cut ditches on the Powhatan estate. In their work for Harris, whites and Blacks were bound to interact, if only to coordinate activities connected to their duties. They also certainly would have worked alongside the estate's slaves.[26]

The plantation hired Nancy Jennings, a free Black weaver, in 1823, but the bulk of the estate's cloth was contracted to slaves belonging to Lucy Crouch, an independently wealthy plantation owner. White women who did not have the wherewithal of Crouch were engaged to sew clothing for Harris's children. Except for Nancy, no other free Black woman appears in the estate's accounts.[27]

What patterns, if any, may be discerned from the records of such accounts? First, middling planters combined a number of strategies in handling the labor needs of their estates. They hired the slaves of neighboring planters; they contracted out work to larger plantations; and they hired skilled, semi-skilled, and unskilled free workers for specialized tasks and during the peak harvest months. Free Blacks, in turn, took advantage of the labor needs of these planters, who represented a significant portion of the county's landholders. Second, the accounts point to the likelihood that for many rural free Blacks, particular work assignments were intermittent rather than sustained. In response, they necessarily developed ties to more than one client. Thus, within a few months a carpenter, for example, can be seen plying his trade on more than one plantation, often at some distance apart. It is not coincidental that horses were most frequently listed as property owned by free Black men: in a randomly chosen year (1813), of 111 free Black male taxpayers, approximately half owned a total of 74 horses. While also useful as farm animals, these horses offered essential mobility.[28]

Besides mobility, the presence of these horses, coupled with the marked absence of free Blacks working in agriculture except during the labor-intensive months of harvest, evokes yet another pattern. Rather than working as plantation hands, after 1782 most free Blacks were independent taxpayers who either farmed their own land or rented land from whites in some form of tenancy. Before this period, the small free Black population often lived with slaves on plantations.[29]

Planters' accounts offer a view of work in the county that diverges from the model constructed by historians, who have looked primarily at urban free Black communities in the Upper South. In their use of free workers, plantation owners hired both white and free Black skilled and unskilled workers and remunerated them at roughly similar rates for comparable tasks. Thus, in the above case, Daniel Utley received the same payment as James Cowig for making shoes for slaves and children on Francis Harris's estate. There were apparently no skilled crafts in which free Blacks did not have to compete with white craftspeople.

Some Virginia planters preferred to hire free Black workers for particularly arduous work that they considered too dangerous for their valuable slave property. It is plausible that planters' use of free Black ditchers reflected this thinking. While not necessarily dangerous, ditching was back-breaking work, especially when the ground was wet or frozen. But a reverse argument provides as convincing an explanation: By its nature, ditching required gang labor, a pattern and rhythm of work that must have provided uncomfortable associations with slave labor for free Black workers. In return for their services as ditchers, therefore, free Blacks bargained for competitive wages. They also expected their employers to meet the customary obligation of providing additional remuneration for the purchase of whiskey. For example, when John Martin contracted to cut ditches on Alexander Fowler's plantation, he received $112.18 to pay his crew and an additional $15.17 to provide "whiskey for the ditchers." In this manner, they mitigated what might have been considered a degradation of their status as free Blacks.[30]

There was one occupation that free Black workers appeared to avoid deliberately, despite its availability. The Dover coal pits in the western part of the county required large numbers of unskilled workers for its underground mines. Ronald Lewis describes the strict work regimen under extremely hazardous conditions. Hired slaves rather than free Blacks provided the greatest proportion of the workforce. The view that free Blacks were placed in the most dangerous work situations in order to save valuable slave labor seems particularly inappropriate in this case. Had there been a systematic effort to place free Black workers in the most dangerous occupations, one would expect a preponderance of free labor at the mines. In Goochland, despite the Dover mines' proximity, only three free Black coal diggers appear in the records. By contrast, the 1850 census, the first census to specify the occupations of whites in the county, documented the presence of fifteen white miners. The assumption that free Blacks provided a pliant, readily available pool of workers may only be relevant in counties where free Blacks had fewer employment opportunities.[31]

Skilled artisans and craftsmen among the free Black male population provided essential services to county plantations. The skilled crafts, much more than unskilled work, represented a departure from the norms of slave labor. Unlike slaves, skilled workers negotiated their own contracts and could discriminate among prospective clients. Skilled artisans constituted 28 percent of those free Black men listed as having occupations. The largest proportion worked in four trades, as carpenters, coopers, shoemakers, and blacksmiths. Wheelwrights, harness-makers, well-diggers, and masons made up a smaller percentage.[32]

Free Black representation in these crafts has been the subject of some discussion in the literature. According to historians, the growth of a white artisan class was significantly retarded in the South by the close association of slaves and free Blacks with the building and service trades. Whites, in this view, refused to pursue these skilled and semi-skilled occupations because they believed that performing "nigger work" would degrade their social and economic status as free white men. In his version of this argument, Ira Berlin argues that in order to maintain the distinctions between "nigger" and white work, and to preserve interclass solidarity among whites, slaveholders only reluctantly employed white laborers "for jobs normally done by blacks."[33]

There was considerable regional variation in the occupations considered demeaning by their association with Blacks.[34] Some attitudes were more typical of urban settings in which competition for employment, housing, and other amenities may have intensified racial and class antagonism. In Goochland, however, many whites and Blacks shared identical skilled occupations, and white planters hired and remunerated these individuals at the same rates.

Plantation accounts offer a partial view of the range of occupations practiced by white artisans. Rather than a strict compartmentalization of skilled crafts by race and status, there was considerable overlap, especially in the first three decades of the nineteenth century. For example, free Blacks competed for jobs and contracts with free white shoemakers, blacksmiths, carpenters, weavers, boaters, and wagoners. Plantation accounts provide the most direct evidence of the permeability of boundaries among many forms of white, free Black, and slave labor.

In 1808, for example, the executor of Robert Lewis Jr.'s estate recorded that "Dr. Bob," a free Black "physician," had been paid a sum of fourteen shillings in May 1802 and in August of that same year three pounds, the balance of his fee "in full," for administering a "physick" and attending to Lewis's slave Mitch. In the same account, lesser sums were recorded as due to Drs. Vaughn and Carter, two white physicians who had also attended slaves on the estate. Perhaps in spite of the availability of Vaughn and Carter, Lewis's slaves requested the services of Dr. Bob. It may also have been true that when it came to the health of his six valuable slaves, Lewis could ill afford to discriminate between the skills of white and Black physicians if the latter's remedies proved more effective.[35]

After all, Dr. Bob was hired to administer a "physick," hardly a task that would have been outside the domain of white physicians of the period. The establishment of a working relationship between the free Black physician and the white estate formed part of a wide network of similar exchanges of skills, labor, and goods that occurred in the county from its settlement but especially after the liberalized manumission act of 1782. Lewis's tardy final payment, some three months after Dr. Bob's work, may be interpreted as characteristic of the mutual interdependence of long-term patron-client ties. Indeed, I argue in the next chapter that the work of free Black apprentices on plantations in return for training, room, and board represented the institutionalization of such interactions.

Estate accounts suggest that planters frequently employed independent free Black workers to perform a variety of agricultural and ancillary duties. For example, when Nancy, a slave on Charles Houchin's plantation, died in the winter of 1830, blacksmith and carpenter Bartlett Isaacs—who, with his brother Austin, had been a juvenile apprentice—constructed her coffin for a fee of three dollars. Isaacs's duties did not extend beyond making the coffin. Another "blackman," perhaps also free, was paid fifty cents for "digging the grave." For a much larger sum, Peter Gabbin, a free Black ditcher, charged William Shelton fifteen dollars for cutting ditches in January 1826. Gabbin's ditching was much needed, for in August 1826 he received twenty dollars for similar work.[36]

While Isaacs and Gabbin provided occasional services as coffin-maker and ditcher, other free Blacks arranged lengthier contracts with their employers. For example, over a two-year period between 1826 and 1827, William Howell received a total payment of $17.53 for providing cotton cards and weaving cloth for the Shelton estate. Over approximately the same period, Henrietta Gray was paid $21.24 for services as a weaver on the same plantation. The document is unclear about the intended use of this cloth, though it was probably for clothing the plantation's slaves. An inventory of Shelton's estate taken in 1826 indicates that he owned twenty-five slaves. Of this number, ten lived on his plantation in Goochland and the rest on a Nelson County property. Did Shelton provide the cotton and equipment or did the sum paid include costs for materials and labor? The details of the transaction between the free Black weavers and Shelton are lost. Yet the absence of raw cotton from either estate inventory and of any equipment for the manufacture of cloth on the Goochland estate suggests that the free Black weavers may have provided much of their own material and tools.[37]

In the winter of 1826, Samuel Cocke, a white carpenter, received $4 for making a coffin for the estate of Granville Smith. The following November, Woodson Cocke was paid $4.50 for making two coffins for Frank and Little Stepney, two slaves belonging to Smith. Two years later, for a considerably larger fee, Kenneth McRae, another white carpenter, was paid $21, "the balance for repairs on [the] dwelling house" of William George. William McRae was hired by the same estate to make a coffin at a cost of $5. Whether making coffins or engaging in work requiring greater use of their skills, white carpenters' employment opportunities seemed to parallel that of free Blacks. James Fuzmore, for example, a free Black carpenter, completed repairs on the house of William Mullins in 1814.[38]

Only one craft related to fishing appears in the records. After twelve years in which he was listed solely as a planter, Thomas Christian in 1817 changed his official occupation to that of fishtrap maker.[39] Perhaps most county residents made their own fishing equipment. Yet in the very singularity of some trades lies an indication that free Blacks managed to gain some limited entry in crafts generally restricted to whites. For example, one free Black miller appears in the record, along with a hatter and tailor-barber. Given the importance of grain production and the number of licensed mills in the county, however, one would have expected to find more millers in the free Black skilled workforce. The 1850 census counted fifteen white millers resident in the county. Here, perhaps, was a craft to which free Blacks had limited access. Yet again the situation is rather more complex than it first appears, because a number of slaves in the county were in fact employed as millers. In the case of barbering, the situation in this rural county sharply diverged from the pattern in the cities of Richmond and Petersburg, where free Blacks almost monopolized this industry. Only one barber appeared in the free Black occupation list for Goochland County, and he combined this skill with tailoring. The variations in patterns of work for free Blacks and whites in different counties and regions of Virginia well illustrates the need to examine the specific roles of free Black workers in local economies.[40]

Blacksmithing offers yet another counter to the argument concerning "stigmatized" crafts. White blacksmiths regularly appeared in estate accounts (sixteen were enumerated in the 1850 census). Yet free Blacks like John Lynch, a blacksmith described as mixed-race, also appears in the records. Part of a family whose members followed the trade, Lynch worked regularly for at least two plantations over a period of five years. From 1824 to 1829, the records indicate that William George, a white planter, paid a total of nearly one hundred dollars to Lynch's shop account and that Thomas Matthews similarly used Lynch's services for four years.[41]

Planters' decisions to hire either a white or Black skilled worker reflected individual values and preferences, race being one possible consideration, level of skill and experience another, and proximity to the plantation site a third. Whites and Blacks competed for long- and short-term work on the county's plantations. What is immediately obvious in this community study is that all whites, whether slaveholders, middling farmers, or unpropertied and unemployed, did not share the same normative perceptions about stigmatized and unstigmatized work.

While free Blacks exchanged goods and services among themselves and with slaves, their success in establishing these reciprocal economic and service relationships with planters formed the greater part of their livelihoods. Historians examining these bonds often discuss such reciprocal links as those in which free Blacks were inevitably the lesser partners. Although structurally disadvantaged, free Black individuals often negotiated terms of employment that worked to their benefit. Unable to use legislative means to challenge the racial dichotomization of the larger society, free Blacks may have to some extent mitigated the imbalance in their face-to-face economic and social interactions with whites. The existence of reciprocity for individual free Blacks, however, in no way presumes that the county's free Blacks generally were ever able to overcome their economic marginality. In acknowledging the presence of a system of customary obligations, dependencies, and duties between free Black workers and their white employers, therefore, we have only scratched the surface of the place of free Black wage labor and the ability of free Black workers to maintain a livelihood in the county's plantation economy.

Resentment and racial exclusion were facts of life for rural free Black residents. In addition, the demand for the work of skilled craftspeople must have been relatively intermittent. To gain economic independence, free Blacks, including skilled craftspeople, sought to gain title to land of their own. Land meant permanent shelter, food for subsistence, and goods for the market. Compared to their unskilled counterparts, free Black craftspeople had skills they could use as a form of surety in transactions with whites.

Austin Isaacs, a free Black carpenter who had learned his trade as a juvenile apprentice, purchased twenty acres of land from Humber, a white planter, for $250 in 1813. According to the terms of that agreement, he was to pay the sum in full with interest in a year's time or ownership of the land would revert to Humber. Unable to make good on that agreement, Isaacs renegotiated the terms of purchase in January 1814.[42]

As part of that renegotiation, Isaacs acknowledged his indebtedness to Humber. This time around, the two men crafted a new agreement in which two hundred dollars plus interest on the purchase price was to be paid within a year. William Williams, another white planter, stood security in the sum of two hundred dollars for Isaacs. The final part of the deed of trust was a detailed description of the terms of barter, with Isaacs's carpentering in exchange for the remaining balance on the land.

The language of the 1814 deed, written from Humber's perspective, makes it difficult to ascertain the nature of Isaacs's input in hammering out either the exact specifications of the structure or the timetable for its completion. Furthermore, he had the least leverage in this agreement. Yet he was the expert, and even in this document the expectations that came with the craftsperson-employer relationship emerged. All materials, including nails, were to be provided by Humber. Isaacs was to "provide himself with provisions" and was to be "allowed forty dollars for the barn." On completion, this sum was to be credited toward payment on the purchase price for the twenty acres of land.[43]

Isaacs "engaged to build a barn . . . sixteen feet by eighteen . . . and have it ready by next harvest [probably by September 1814]." Besides specifying the size of the barn, Humber made clear his expectations on materials and workmanship: "The said Isaacs is to make use of the framing & plank of the old barn as far as it is sound having it as nearly the pitch of the old barn as the timbers will allow, it is to be well sheeted & shingled & all done in a good workman like manner including every thing usually appertaining to such houses, with a good floor." Should the barn not be built or the balance on the land not paid, Humber could sell the land in part or full at public sale.[44] If the terms were met, however, Isaacs was to gain clear title. The records do not disclose the eventual outcome of this agreement. Contractual arrangements of this sort, however, document the involvement of free Blacks in the local economy. They indicate that free Blacks engaged in multistranded exchanges of goods and services with whites and with one another.[45]

Another set of issues is immediately obvious. Although sharing the anomalous position of being free and Black in a society for which race and enslavement were normally coterminous, free Blacks had different experiences of work and divergent levels of material well-being among themselves. Consider, for example, that in 1826, when thirty-five free Black residents appeared on the insolvency lists as unable to pay personal property taxes of $1.11 per person, Daniel Moss, a licensed boatman, remitted $1.65 on three slaves and two horses, while Henry Lynch, described as a mulatto and most likely a blacksmith, paid property taxes of $2.12 on four slaves and two horses and owned nineteen acres of land valued at $54.[46]

By way of crude juxtaposition, we might note the acknowledgment in the June 1814 county records of new state legislation requiring "all free negroes and mulattoes that have been returned insolvent to be summoned to next court, to shew cause why they should not be hired out as the law direct in such cases for payment of their taxes." Free Blacks employed as wage laborers or skilled craftspeople received competitive remuneration, but individuals hired out by the court could expect at most a legal minimum daily wage of sixteen cents. In March 1823, the court ordered sheriff John Underwood to hire out "all the free negroes" who "had been retained . . . as insolvent on the county levies and poor rates."[47] Some measures seemed to have been taken to limit abuses of the system. In 1820, the court required that when "hiring out insolvent free negroes and mulattoes," the sheriff was to "make report of such hires to the court" so that "he does not hire them out for a longer time than will be sufficient to pay his or her taxes and levies at the rate of 16 c wages by the day."[48] Within the letter of the law, therefore, a free Black insolvent could typically expect in the 1820s to work approximately seven days to pay off average yearly taxes. By itself such a term of forced labor was relatively short, but it reveals the powerlessness of economically marginal free Blacks. They had few means to protest their temporary bondage. White insolvents' labor, by contrast, was not forcibly expropriated.[49]

Although insolvent free Blacks appeared annually in the tax lists, it is difficult to judge the degree and consistency with which the law itself was used to punish them. Legislation rarely is a perfect reflection of social realities and attitudes. Nonetheless, the appearance of this and other laws reducing free Black autonomy allows us to delineate roughly the extreme ends of a continuum. On the one end, there were impoverished individuals at great risk of being "retained" and their labor conscripted; on the other, free Black workers actively and freely exchanged their labor for wages in the manner of their white counterparts.

The conditions that allowed some free Black workers to take advantage of the wage labor system also meant that the labor of many others was appropriated and that still others found themselves permanently disfranchised, landless, and dependent.

· 6 ·

Kin, Neighbors, and Community Consolidation

Buying land and securing their relatives' freedom took on great significance for Goochland's free African Americans. In the antebellum period, increasing numbers purchased land. Sixteen percent of free Black adults in 1860 owned acreage—a figure that had tripled in three decades. Expansion of the community at this historical point can be measured not in terms of increases in the numbers of people but in terms of the ability to accumulate and hold onto land and personal property.

By contrast, distinctions based on relative wealth in the period between 1800 and 1830 revolved less around land ownership and more around the reconstitution of families through the purchase of family members. For example, in 1815, 125 tax-paying free Blacks in the county owned a total of 21 slaves, most of them kin-related. Surplus funds also purchased horses and cattle, essential to agricultural production and transportation. Ownership of horses was a high priority as is evident in taxes paid on 97 during this same year. Livestock not only provided food for the household and tilled rented land for cultivation, but along with horses was a form of savings—an immediately available source of potential income. Levies were paid on 135 head of cattle in 1815. Surplus capital consolidated family ties, sustained household production, and was reinvested in the domestic economy.

When they did not own land, free Blacks negotiated tenancy arrangements with white farmers as an economic bridge from slavery to freedom. For the majority of the free Black community, different tenancy arrangements provided the best attainable compromise between outright land ownership and residence within white households. In 1810, slightly over a quarter of free Blacks lived in white households. Single individuals rather than families lived in these arrangements and half of them were children under the age of twenty. A substantial percentage were people over forty years old. These were highly mobile individuals, rarely appearing in the same household in consecutive census years.

Distinctions among dependents, tenants, renters, and skilled artisans evident before 1830 took on greater salience in the antebellum period. Free Blacks came into their own as independent heads of households, and those who could afford it bought land. Parcels ranged in size from one or two to upwards of five hundred acres, owned by a free Black planter and tavern-owner. Collectively, free Black ownership of land increased from approximately six hundred acres in 1830 to approximately two thousand in 1860. Landowners, particularly those with parcels above fifty acres, constituted the county's free Black elite, not unlike the status accorded their white counterparts. Free Black landowners often rented or entered into tenancy arrangements with poorer members of their community. Data from the 1830s through the 1860s reinforces the portrait of a maturing free Black community of increasing complexity.

If property ownership gives a sense of the emergence of an elite, examination of family structure gives a fuller sense of those at the broad base of the pyramid. The relative ease or difficulty with which free Black persons established their own households was directly related to their degree of independence from white planters or the occasional Black landowner. For many individuals the situation was not necessarily clear cut. While many families managed to maintain separate households, they nonetheless lived precariously on the margins of the local economy. Throughout the postrevolutionary years there was considerable variation in the ability of free Black households to prosper. As we have seen, some families were relatively successful, accumulating property, benefiting from association with important white planters, and using knowledge of the county legal and political structure to solidify their gains. At the other end, families struggled to obtain the basic necessities. Surviving racial exclusion and economic deprivation was a hopeless struggle for many. Single women lost their children to the apprenticeship system, and men and women regularly found themselves on insolvency lists, forced to work for little more than room and board. In response to the pressures in the external world, free Blacks turned to their families and networks of kin, near-kin, friends, and neighbors. Reliance on family and social networks was reflected in the patterns of residential clustering in five of the county's eleven districts—in Dover Mills and Johnson Springs in the southeast, in Gumsprings and Fife in its center, and Caledonia district in the west. These are still the centers of present day African American life in Goochland County.

The majority of free Black households in each census year were male-headed. There was considerable variation, however, in the relative proportion of female- to male-headed families. The range for female-headed households grew from 18 percent in 1820 to about 45 percent by 1860. This radical shift in women's roles within the family has no discernible single explanation. The pattern of gender and family formation would suggest the impoverishment of a greater number of free Black households, given the absence of two income-producing adults. But what seems to be occurring simultaneously was the growth in family size and in the numbers of adults living in a single household. The pattern seems to have shifted with increasing numbers of women heading extended families including their adult children and minor grandchildren; there was also a rise in apparently unrelated adults living in these multigenerational families. In 1830, for example, only 1 percent of independent households contained one or two people. Household size of between six and ten persons was the norm, a pattern that persisted to 1860. Whether male or female headed, the experience of free Black families in Goochland County was of the greater economic insecurity of persons living alone or in small family units. Rather than gender, the important factor may well have been the relative success of households to capture the productive and reproductive resources of its members. Consolidation rather than isolation in smaller units appears to have been the most successful organizational strategy. Additional adults contributed to household resources. This pattern was as true of elite free Black households with personal and real property of above five hundred dollars as it was for those with incomes below twenty-five dollars, or with extended families where the majority of members were nonproductive children.

The domestic and household histories of three free African American families in the county illuminates the ways in which families established themselves. Households were interdependent, drawing on collective material and human resources. Mary Banks's family was typical. A free Black woman born in the early phases of the county's settlement, Banks, like many of her male and female counterparts, lived on the estate of a white planter who increased his holdings of property and slaves over the course of her residence.[1] Banks's labor and later that of her seven children no doubt contributed to her master's ability to make the transition from small to middling planter. But in the meantime, his upward mobility was accompanied by her downward trajectory as she struggled to maintain some independence and regain primary jurisdiction over at least some of her children. Born at midcentury, they were obligated to repeat their mother's story of forced dependency. But coming of age during the revolutionary years, they could envision a life of expanded opportunities. Remaining in the county, they pushed the societal, racial, and economic boundaries constructed to confine them to their place as far as they could. The Banks's family history provides one indication that free Blacks living in rural areas explored a variety of options, none of which necessarily included migration to urban areas.

Described as a free mixed-race woman, Banks first appeared as the mother of Jane Banks in a 1744 apprenticeship order and two years later as a tithe of Leake along with one slave (Tamer). Over the course of two decades, all seven of Banks's children would be apprenticed to a Leake, sometimes exchanging masters but staying within the same family. As a free woman on this small holding, she would have had close contact with Tamer as well as with the white members of the plantation household, which included Walter Leake's adult sons.[2]

Banks continued to work on the Leake plantation, and in a familiar pattern, the church wardens bound her second child, Jane, to the same master in 1744, the year of her birth. Five years later, Louisa was apprenticed to Leake. By 1755, Banks had apparently left Leake's employment, no longer appearing as a tithe. She continued to reside in the county and during this period gave birth to three additional children (one girl and two boys). Mary's fate was once again linked to the Leake household in 1757, when the church wardens apprenticed four of her children (John, Judith, Jacob, and Agnes) to Walter Leake, and again in 1759, when they were apprenticed to his widow.[3]

A mere two years later, on Walter Leake's death, the church wardens placed Jane and Louisa, Banks's older children, in the household of Judith Leake. Both Walter Leake's wife and daughter were named Judith. If their new mistress was the daughter, then, it is likely the two children moved to a new household. If they remained with the widow, then the transfer in indenture would have been in name only. In either case, the Banks children continued to serve in a household connected to their deceased master, and probably in close proximity to their mother and siblings. We do not know if Mary Banks had any say in her children's placement. Once the court declared them indigent or "unfit," free Black mothers rarely could prevent the apprenticeship of their minor children as paupers. Such women were occasionally successful, however, in determining where their children served their indentures. Banks may well have exercised that option because all her children were bound to the same individual. Another explanation is also possible: because the Leakes were small planters and unable to purchase slaves, they may have actively sought to have the Banks children placed in their household.[4]

The children's ages at the time of their apprenticeship indicates that for more than a decade Banks had been successful in keeping the oldest out of the juvenile apprenticeship system. But with the burden of each additional child, or perhaps as a consequence of some drastic change in the family economy, she was eventually forced to relinquish her parental authority. Jane was fifteen years old at the time of her placement with Judith Leake but Jacob, the youngest, was only four years old.

Juvenile apprenticeship, regardless of the personal relations or resulting benefits to the apprentice, was always a coercive institution. When Jane's term came to a close in 1763, Judith Leake refused to give up control over the young woman. In response, Jane Banks, apparently well aware of the limits of her mistress's power, petitioned the courts. Having heard testimony by the involved parties, the local justices ruled against Leake. They "discharged" Jane "from any further service" and required that the recalcitrant mistress pay three pounds' freedom dues as required by law. This sum was small reward indeed for the years of Jane's labor but nonetheless must have provided her with some satisfaction, as must the court's decision to acknowledge the termination of her indenture. Mary Alsup, another young woman apprenticed to the Leakes, testified on Jane's behalf. Jane's success in the courts may have been a direct result of her personal vigilance as well as her family's long experience with the apprenticeship system and the rules by which it was regulated.[5]

The youngest of the Banks children also used the courts to resolve conflicts with a member of the Leake family. In 1772, Jacob, whose indenture appears to have been informally transferred to one Elisha Leake, complained that his master had neglected to teach him a trade as specified in the original terms of his contract. By this time, Jacob was eighteen years old and may have become concerned about his inability to support himself once he became independent. On Jacob's behalf, his attorney asked the justices to terminate the arrangement with Elisha Leake. For the remaining years of his indenture, Jacob wished to be reapprenticed to a master who would teach him a trade. Again, the justices considered the evidence presented on both sides and subsequently ordered the church wardens of St. James Northam Parish to "bind the said Jacob to Peter Pollock to learn the trade of carpenter."[6]

Jacob Banks apparently accomplished his goal in the three or four years remaining in his indenture. With the independence that a skilled craft afforded, he saw his way clear to begin a family. Unlike his mother, who was unable to maintain a household and never formalized her union with the children's father, Jacob married Susannah Jones as soon as his contract with Pollock came to an end in 1775. Jacob may well have terminated ties to Leake precisely because he wanted to acquire a craft that would allow him to start and support a family. He was the first among his siblings to marry, though his two sisters followed soon after.[7]

Events on a broader scale engaged Jacob and his brother John, who both joined and fought in the Continental Army.[8] The brothers returned to the county after the war. At a time of social upheaval and uncertainty for both free Blacks and slaves in Virginia, Goochland was a known entity. At least for these two brothers—with wives, children, extended kin; well-established links to the free Black community as well as some white planters; and a firm sense of the rights accorded them under the law—the return to rural Goochland seemed the appropriate step to take after the war's end.

If the return to the county marked an affirmation of the Banks brothers' ties to the familiar, it also signified confidence that they could better support their families by staying put than by uprooting themselves and moving to nearby Richmond, some other rural place, or one of the growing number of non-slaveholding states. The latter possibility may well have presented itself, given the brothers' access to wider knowledge of what lay outside the county and the commonwealth resulting from their war experience. Jacob's initial success at gaining some familial and economic stability is indicated in the presence of six adults in his household in 1782. John and Jacob established themselves in the county's upper district, the former as a planter and the latter as a carpenter. An 1806 occupational list described both men as mixed-race: John lived on and worked his own land, while Jacob plied his trade as a carpenter while renting land from Dabney Wade, a white planter.[9]

The gender-specific occupations of both men were paralleled by those of their wives: Susannah was a weaver while Sally, John's spouse, was a "houseworker." The two couples maintained their relationships into the third decade of the nineteenth century when they disappeared from the records. Given their advanced ages, it is likely that their absence from tax lists after this date suggests either that they were infirm and therefore exempt or that they had died within that decade.[10]

Both brothers moved frequently within the upper district but their lives always intermeshed, as they raised children, witnessed marriages among kin, quarreled among themselves and their neighbors, and occasionally ran afoul of the law. The two brothers accumulated livestock and personal property and paid taxes—a small measure of their accomplishment. Perhaps most importantly, given their childhood experiences, they managed to shield their sons and daughters from the juvenile apprenticeship system.[11] This is not to say that the lives of the third generation of Bankses were substantially easier than that of the first and second. They continued to face economic hardships and discriminatory legislative policies.

The benefits of the extended family are clearly seen in the case of the Banks brothers and their wives. The two couples began to have children at the end of the war. Because both families depended on farming for subsistence and, in John's case, for a livelihood, a large family was an advantage rather than a drawback. Jacob and Susannah had seven children while John and Sally had at least five. The developmental cycle of these two families followed a pattern that became increasingly familiar in the postrevolutionary years.[12]

The children remained in their respective households until young adulthood, when most married and established their own families near to their parents and other kin but in separate dwellings. For example, in 1811, Jacob's sons Martin and Elisha rented land for farming from Rice Innes, a white planter. Twenty-four and twenty-one years old, respectively, when they moved from under their parents' roof, both men lived in separate households but near to one another. At this time, they may have been cohabiting with their future wives or planning to start families, for just two years after they left their father's household, they solemnized marriages to local women.¹³

On the same day in March 1813, Elisha wedded Nancy Lynch and Martin married Betsy Ann Howell. Both women were described as mixed-race. In another extension of family ties, Betsy Ann may well have been related to Isaac Howell, the uncle-in-law of the two men and the husband of their Aunt Judith. Jacob's third son, John, named after his uncle, left his father's household sometime after 1815, marrying Biddy Ann Tyler eight years later in 1823. As with the older generation, family ties were reaffirmed at critical rites of passage.¹⁴

John's son, John Jr., followed a similar though delayed cycle. He did not leave his parents' household until he was in his mid-twenties, marrying a few years later at the age of twenty-eight in 1819. His cousin Elisha stood security at his wedding. John Jr.'s slightly advanced age at the time of his marriage could have been connected to the fact that he was an only son. More so than his cousins, his labor may have been essential to the maintenance of his parents' household.¹⁵

Jacob's three daughters, together with John's three, all married free Black men, at which time they left their parents' households. Their brothers, by contrast, normally worked a few years on their own before taking a spouse. The pattern exhibited by the Banks daughters followed a common trend. Without the skills and earning capacity of their male counterparts, young single women may have found it economically and socially beneficial to remain in the parental household when feasible, contributing to the domestic economy and receiving board, shelter, familial support, and protection in return.

The youngest daughter in John Banks's family, Jane, started her own household at fifteen, and it appears that Judith remained at home for the longest period, marrying when she was twenty-five years old. The earliest marriage among the Banks daughters occurred in 1797 when Jacob's eighteen-year-old daughter Polly married John Tyler, six years her senior. Eighteen years after Polly's marriage, Judith Banks, the last of the daughters to remain single and at home, left her parents' household to marry Elijah Day.¹⁶

Consciousness of color and caste seems to have operated in the choice of partners for the third generation of Banks women. With one notable exception, they married men who were freeborn and mixed-race, a preference that influenced their brother's selections of mates as well. In this respect, these women followed a pattern with origins in the prerevolutionary period and ongoing significance for the development of the free Black community. If the Bankses can be defined as forming a familial clan, much of their decision-making resembles collective rather than random behavior as they consolidated long-held ties to other freeborn families. We cannot dismiss the possibility that parents may have attempted to direct their children's choices of spouses. Eliza Banks, for example, married Drury Farrar in 1801, whereas Polly and her brother John married siblings in the Tyler family. They thus became related through blood and marriage to the Farrars and Tylers, two other free Black families with early roots in the county. Other daughters similarly formed unions with men whose families were freeborn in the eighteenth century.[17]

Records of marriages in the Banks family reveal the interconnections among families and neighbors, slaves, whites, and free persons of color in their sphere of social relations. Typically, marriage bonds listed the wife's parents, at least one witness to the ceremony, and persons designated to stand security. Occasionally, persons giving affidavit of the age, provenance, or parentage of one or both partners were also named. We can presume that the individuals named in these bonds were present at the marriage ceremony and probably already familiar with one or more of the main participants. For the most part, those involved in the ceremonies of the Banks children were free persons of color. Jacob and John Banks were present and vouched for their daughters at the time of their weddings. (The one exception to this custom occurred when Jacob's daughter Jane married a formerly enslaved man.)

On the occasion of the marriages of their daughters to the Banks sons, Francis Tyler, Charles Howell, and Robert and Polly Lynch attended the marriage proceedings. Francis Tyler had also been present more than two decades earlier when his son John married Polly Banks. He was thus connected to the Bankses through both his son and daughter. Only in two instances did whites stand security for these marriages, and only in one case was there a white witness. Ira Berlin argues that planters' participation in these ceremonies was an extension of free Black dependency and had the effect of diminishing free Black independence. Reliance on whites to "vouch" for the good character of a free Black individual, he suggests, was yet another form of coercive paternalism. Such dynamics may certainly have played a role in other aspects of the Bankses' lives. But the predominance of free persons of color as witnesses and security would argue against the power of whites in legitimating the ceremonies that joined families to one another. For the most part, the Bankses relied on friends and kin to acknowledge and legitimate their children's transition to adulthood.[18]

We are left to wonder about the nature of the relationship between the Banks and Leake families. In spite of their involvement on opposite sides of court disputes, they appeared to have maintained close contact. Altogether four children (Judith, Eliza, John, and Elisha) in the households of Jacob and John Banks shared names with members of the Leake household. Further, in 1787, Josiah, Walter Leake's son, stood security at the marriage of Mary Banks to Henry Isaacs.[19]

The dynamics of the relationship were further revealed when in August 1803, Jane Banks married Richard Adams, a former slave, described as a "mulatto cooper." Not coincidentally, Adams had gained his freedom from Josiah Leake just two months before his marriage to Jane. His former master stood as security, but John Banks, the bride's father, was absent. Perhaps he disapproved of the union, for he had been present when his daughter Sally was married and would also participate in the later marriages of his other two daughters. In the absence of the father, Josiah Leake vouched for the bride and groom. Here, perhaps, parental authority may have been overridden by the willingness of a white planter to act as security.[20]

What could have been the source of John's disapproval? Jane was only fifteen at the time of her marriage while her sisters had all reached the age of majority before starting their own households. Further, the previous status of Richard as a slave, especially on the Leake plantation, may have conjured up unpleasant memories of previous dependency. Richard Adams, known as "Dick" while a slave, lived on the Leake plantation near the Bankses and rented land from James Holman, a white planter whose name appears frequently in the records in connection with the free Black community. Perhaps it was during this period of tenancy that the young Jane made acquaintance with her future husband. In a rather tangled web of overlapping intrigues, Holman mediated between Richard Adams and his owner, for it was he who provided the catalyst for Adams's emancipation by purchasing the slave for four hundred dollars and then freeing him. Adams, we can presume, was indebted to Holman and expected to reimburse him. Among the fifteen adult slaves on the Leake plantation, Richard Adams was the only one who legally gained free status. And even then, he did so by virtue of his own ability to purchase himself. Although Adams showed considerable initiative in negotiating his freedom, was a skilled cooper, and, in a bid to mark his new status, dropped the diminutive "Dick" for "Richard," this was not enough. John Banks appears to have been reluctant to accept him as a son-in-law.[21]

Tensions in the family persisted well after the couple took their vows. In December 1803, the parties appeared in court when John Banks complained that his son-in-law Richard had "breached the peace" toward him. No details of their quarrel are on record. Richard Adams, however, was taken into the sheriff's custody where he remained until he could post bond for his "good behavior" for the "space of six months." Adams's relationship with the Leakes may well have initiated or reflected a fracture in the connections between the white family and members of the older generation of Bankses. Only with the help of Walter Leake and James Holman, who together posted the sum of thirty dollars to supplement thirty dollars placed by Adams himself, did the sheriff release the prisoner.[22] While the evidence does not allow for deeper interpretations of the sources and motivations of the conflicts between parents and children, former master and apprentices, by marrying Richard Adams, Jane Banks had clearly shifted her loyalties, throwing in her lot with the opposite side. In the end, as we discuss in a later chapter, Richard Adams would rise to some prominence in the free Black community as a wagon and boat owner responsible for much of the county's ferriage back and forth to Richmond, and as a skilled craftsman, slaveowner, and landholder with a wide range of economic links to Goochland's planters.[23]

No matter what efforts they made to create strong and cohesive family bonds, internal circumstances, together with the outside pressures placed on free Blacks, contributed to fission and dissension in the by now complex cluster of households connected to the Banks family. One instance of a major breakdown in family relations occurred when the courts received information that Jacob and Nathaniel Banks had been illegally retailing liquor without a license "at their residence." At the grand jury presentments in December 1818, one of the primary witnesses was John Banks Jr. He testified against his uncle Jacob and against Nathaniel, who was likely his aunt's child. John Jr. may have been the "informer" who alerted the justices to the illicit behavior.[24] Perhaps, he had been compelled to betray his close relatives, but it is also likely that this action could have been a means of expressing dissatisfaction, jealousy, or revenge.

John Jr.'s complicity with the county justices did not help his own situation when three years later he ran afoul of the law. Again, he had betrayed the trust of someone who was related to the family by marriage and who had served in the Continental Army with John and Jacob Banks. According to the indictment against him, John Banks Jr. "forg[ed] and counterfeit[ed]" George Tyler's name in order to purchase "groceries" valued at five dollars from a local retailer. John Jr. was obviously literate. George Tyler, who must also have been literate, maintained an active account with the white proprietor of a store in the upper district. In his deposition, Tyler testified that the signed request for groceries was not in his hand but belonged to that of Banks. On the basis of this deposition and testimony by white residents, Banks, who initially pleaded not guilty, was remanded to the jail for trial at the superior court in Richmond. In light of the evidence against him and on the advice of his counsel, John Fleming, Banks acknowledged his guilt, perhaps to lessen his punishment. Nonetheless, the justices denied him bail.[25] Many free Blacks in the county, including the Banks patriarchs, resorted to illicit activities to supplement livelihoods gained on the margins of the plantation economy. That this involvement would lead to confrontations with the courts as well as to intrafamilial disputes comes as no surprise.

The life course of the Banks family provides ample evidence of the opportunities and constraints available to free people of color in the county. It is apparent that the basis of the family's long-term prosperity depended on the solidarity of its members, proximity of their households, and close ties to whites and other free Blacks. Dissension threatened but did not undermine their sense of group solidarity. This consciousness helped them survive and increase their numbers through the nineteenth century. One must resist, however, any inclination to wax sentimental about this family's endeavors. In the end, while they achieved a certain stability, few family members ever accumulated substantial property or significantly challenged the status quo. Indeed, their success was based on seemingly conscious efforts to establish an identity separate from the larger African American community that included slaves and freed Blacks. Although the third generation of the Banks family coming of age after 1800 made overtures to the growing numbers of manumitted slaves that swelled the ranks of free people of color, they did so with some reluctance.

Color, generational differences, relative residential stability, geography, and economic status were all factors that influenced consolidation as well as division within the free Black community. The smaller numbers of free persons of color in the prerevolutionary period and the ambiguity of their free status meant that they interacted closely and on intimate terms with slaves. On the other hand, the fact that there were smaller numbers may have stimulated free Blacks to seek one another out in order to maintain and pass on their status to the next generation as well as to mark their difference from slaves. Undoubtedly, both processes operated in the early formation of free Black families and the free Black community.

The evidence from the postrevolutionary years indicates that as greater numbers of emancipated slaves made the transition from slavery to freedom, there was an intensified connection between slaves and free people. In fact, those individuals freed after 1782 retained closer and more long-lasting ties to the slave community that they had only recently left. Exhilaration must often have been coupled with intense despair at having to abandon close relatives and friends. Individuals who gained their freedom did so at considerable personal loss and pain.

This most certainly was the case for Thomas Ford. Born in the late colonial period, he gained his freedom with passage of the 1782 manumission act. Ford was emancipated, but his family, apparently owned by different masters, remained in slavery. Almost as if he wished to deny the impact of slavery on his personal conduct and on his bid for autonomy, he crafted at his death a final symbolic gesture to reaffirm his essential humanity and that of his children. This gesture encapsulated the dilemma faced by manumitted slaves. Whereas free status represented opportunity and stability for the Bankses, for Ford it offered only an empty victory.

In 1810, when he registered as a free person of color, Thomas Ford was sixty years old, "dark" with "black curled hair," and five feet five and a half inches in height. He had been freed by Peter Sublett, a planter. So far, the instruments of social control used by the state to monitor the free Black population suggested nothing out of the ordinary about this man, except perhaps his relatively advanced age when compared to other slaves freed during this period.[26]

An entirely different view of Ford emerges in his last will and testament, drafted during the final years of his life. The presence of a will is itself unusual. Few residents in the county, whether free Black or white, formally bequeathed their estates through the courts. The will provided Ford with a means of expressing his concerns as a father. William Miller, the court clerk, witnessed the will and probably wrote it because Ford was illiterate. With all the barriers preventing Ford from gaining control of his children, the will served as a means of extending some of the fruits of his liberty to them. Written in November 1813, the will was officially recorded three years later at the May court in 1816. Ford died sometime during this period, only a few years after his manumission.[27]

Devoid of any of the usual religious preambles, the will confirmed that Ford was well along in years—being sixty-three years old in 1813—and then moved immediately to the matter at hand. His modest holdings totaled $26.66, $14 of which "was in money" and the "balance in property" held in safekeeping by Francis Cousins, a free Black man who Ford appointed as his executor. Ford's son Moses, a slave "belonging to Jordan Harris of Powhatan," and his three other children, Judy, Gabriel, and Squire, all the property of the Goochland estate of Charles F. Bates, were to benefit from the division of the estate. The father singled out Judy, his only daughter, for special treatment. She was to "take in her share, a red cloak at $6.66 and a new fur hat at $5." The total value of Judy's inheritance at $11.66 was more than double that of her brothers. No doubt the "property" referred to by Ford as being "now in the hands of Frank Cousins" were these two items, which he must have purchased in advance for Judy, perhaps even at her request.[28]

As if to assert his parental authority and to diffuse any possible tensions between the siblings, Ford confirmed that his daughter should have the fur hat and red cloak "even if my estate is not sufficient to make my sons' equal with her in value." Indeed, if Frank Cousins abided by this directive, Moses, Gabriel, and Squire only received five dollars apiece. It is somewhat poignant that Ford, at the beginning of his bequest, expressed the desire that his estate and "everything due at my death" were to be "equally divided."[29]

This last will and testament raises a number of questions and provides an intriguing glimpse of the relationship between a free father and his slave children. It is important to point out that this is the only will of its kind in which slave children not owned by their parents were officially recognized and bequeathed property. No one challenged the legality of Ford's will, even though slaves by definition could not own or inherit property. Customarily, however, slaves did possess material wealth, but their ownership claims were not protected by law. The point here is that the sanctity of Ford's rights to disburse his estate according to his wishes seemed to have superseded other legal considerations.

When his will was recorded in the court records and witnessed and signed by the clerk, the county played an equally important role in legitimizing the transfer of cash and goods to four slaves. As required by law, Francis Cousins posted thirty dollars' security, more than the amount of the estate, to ensure that he would carry out his responsibilities as executor. The singularity of Ford's will, the modesty of his estate, and perhaps the consent of his children's owners must have contributed to the court's willingness to go along with his bequest. One free Black man's transfer of property to his slave children would not have been perceived as threatening the status quo. But perhaps it was.

One wonders about Thomas Ford's motivations. It was more common for most fathers of his class, whether white or Black, to give gifts directly in order to avoid the bureaucratic complications and expense of drafting a will. Perhaps Thomas Ford believed that by participating in the formal process of transferring property by will, he would somehow protect his offspring's rights to his estate. For his sons, the small amount of cash was less problematic than the more ostentatious gifts of a fur hat and red cloak to his daughter. Her possession of this finery would surely have made her stand out from other slaves and certainly from many white women in the district, who would have found the purchase of such clothing far beyond their means. Official recognition of Judy's ownership of these personal items, though not having any legal weight, nonetheless must have given Ford some comfort. In their almost blatant frivolity, Ford's gifts to his daughter signified a reversal of the assumed social order. Certainly, he could have chosen any number of more functional goods or simply given Judy cash.

But we should look beyond the actual gifts to the underlying meaning of the exchange. During his lifetime, Ford enjoyed no parental authority.

He could neither give his children his name, determine where they lived, nor freely participate in their upbringing. Most importantly, he did not have the financial means to liberate them. By passing on his estate through the legal system, he extended to them a small share in his freedom. At the same time, the registration of his last will and testament inscribed his relationship to his children in the county records. If only symbolically, he affirmed his links to them and their relationship to one another as offspring of the same father. Given the structural restraints on the slave children and their father's poverty, they were unable to constitute themselves as a domestic unit. Ford's will suggests, however, that his impossible situation did not negate either his sense of obligation or affection for his children. The father's ultimate failure to reconstitute a family in freedom reveals the extraordinary difficulties that confronted free men and women, especially when their families straddled the boundary between slavery and freedom. They had constantly to strategize to mitigate the punitive effects of economic, racial, and political restrictions.

The records provide no other mention either of the origins or fate of this family. We do not know if Thomas Ford fathered his children while a slave or afterward. Were the children of the same mother and did they at any time live in the same household? The only clues available are the names of Judy, a girl valued at $75, and of Gabriel and Squire, young men worth $120 each, who were listed along with nineteen other slaves in the 1808 inventory of Charles Bates, deceased.[30]

The other clue to the history of this family lies in the 1809 tax list. Ford is listed as owning a slave on whom he paid forty-four cents tax. Manumitted slaves often purchased family members when they accumulated sufficient funds. It is likely that the slave mentioned in the 1809 tax list was Ford's wife and the mother of his children. Ford, a ditcher who was far advanced in age, did not own any other property. A search of subsequent tax lists yields no further mention of Ford's ownership of a slave. As to the children, their valuation in Bates's 1808 inventory suggests that the sons were adults or near adulthood, while Judy was about fifteen years old. By the time of her father's death in 1813, she would have been a young adult and her brothers in their mid-twenties or early thirties. Had Ford's intent been to purchase first his wife and then his children? Did the continued enslavement of his offspring reflect his inability to follow through on such plans? The evidence does not allow us to answer these questions.[31]

If we juxtapose Charles F. Bates's inventory with Thomas Ford's will, we begin to gain some insight into the complexity of the world in which free Blacks and their slave kin attempted to create stable relationships. On the one hand, the inventory listed the cost of human property; on the other, the will evoked the essential humanity of these slaves, the sons and daughters of other human beings. The dilemma faced by Thomas Ford no doubt repeated itself in other families in which either children, parents, or other close kin were enslaved by nonfamily members. His experience was typical of the segment of the free Black community that had been manumitted after 1782. But in his regard for the welfare of his children, Ford shared common ground with many free persons of color, whether freeborn or manumitted, male or female. Scholars have all too frequently neglected the active involvement of African American men in the nurture of offspring and in the building of cohesive family bonds. That insurmountable odds frequently thwarted them should not diminish the seriousness of their efforts.

By nominating Frank Cousins, a free Black man and landholder, as his executor, Ford expressed confidence in a trusted friend. In 1801, Frank and Chloe Cousins served as witnesses to a will in which a white planter was nominated executor of the estate of a free person of color. Given his previous participation as a witness to a will and his involvement in an intricate suit in the court of chancery that legalized his manumission and that of other slaves held by legatees of John Pleasants of Powhatan County, who resisted manumitting them according to the terms of his will, Frank Cousins was no stranger to the legal bureaucracy.[32]

As executor, Frank Cousins was an apt choice. Thomas Ford and Frank Cousins had a longstanding relationship and shared experiences as slaves and freed people. They were close in age and had both been manumitted from plantations in Powhatan. It is highly likely, therefore, that their friendship predated their emancipation and residence in Goochland. Both Frank and Chloe Cousins were familiar with the circumstances surrounding Ford's separation from his children. Like Ford, they also had close relatives who were bondspersons. Unlike Ford, however, the Cousinses succeeded in their efforts to purchase and manumit family members. The three friends may well have supported and influenced each other's attempts to maintain strong ties to their enslaved brethren.

At the same court session in which Frank Cousins filed his friend's will, he also recorded a deed of purchase and manumission for Ridley Cousins and her two children, Frank William and Lucy Ann. Having played a central role in the creation and administration of his friend's final bequests, Frank Cousins attended to his own affairs. Although the deed does not mention the degree of relationship except to say that the manumitted slaves were the "relations" of Cousins, a marriage bond from 1824 offers firm evidence that these were Frank and Chloe's daughter and grandchildren.[33]

Thomas Ford chose an individual whose experiences most closely paralleled his own and who would likely carry out his wishes. The camaraderie that these friends developed during their enslavement no doubt cushioned their introduction to the vicissitudes of life as free people of color.

In choosing a free Black executor, Thomas Ford acted on a preference shared with other free Blacks who chose persons of similar race, status, and experience to carry out their last wishes. During important rites of passage, free persons of color often turned to one another to witness, vouch for character, stand security, or, in the case of wills, administer their affairs. Certainly, whites also performed these functions but not predominantly so. In the small group of seven wills made by free Blacks, three included participants of the same race and status as the legatees: two individuals served as executors and two as witnesses for these documents. In one instance, both whites and free Blacks participated in the filing of a will.[34]

What do these choices reveal? For one thing, they indicate that free Blacks did not necessarily turn to white patrons to mediate their dealings with the legal system. In the apparent ease with which free Blacks chose their compatriots as executors, the emergent values of a free Black consciousness may be discerned. Certainly, these individuals did not perceive themselves as either powerless or without the capacity to take actions on their own behalf.[35]

The circumstances surrounding Thomas Ford's last will and testament suggest the intricacies of the links forged among individuals who had in their lifetime experienced both slavery and freedom. The idiosyncrasies of individual behavior cannot be ruled out. But evidence in the case of Ford and Cousins suggests that within the commonalties of race and class, individuals may have enjoyed closer associations with those with similar life histories. At the end of his life, Thomas Ford, for example, turned to Frank and Chloe Cousins. Until 1813, he lived on and rented land in another part of the upper district, and, as we have suggested, for some part of that period a slave shared his household. But in 1813, in the same year that his will was drafted, he is listed as being a member of John Cousins's household.[36]

In addition to Ford, this household included Frank, Chloe, and at least nine other adults and children. It is likely that Thomas Ford, now alone, moved to this large household because of old age and illness. He must have been fairly certain that he would receive care. While the sources do not reveal the exact nature of the events leading up to Ford's decision to change his residence, the pooling of economic and familial resources, as we have earlier noted, was one of the recurring strategies used throughout the period. Ford's dismantling of his own household and move into the Cousinses' home may have been based on his deteriorating health. In other situations, economic need as much as the cultural emphasis on kin-based cooperation encouraged the elaboration of mutual helping mechanisms within the free Black community.

Viewed in microcosm, the Banks, Cousins, and Ford families represent distinct points on a continuum. Slavery precluded formal recognition of Ford and his children as a family. Indeed, his children were dispersed between two masters and two counties. Geography as well as the slave code prevented him from claiming his parental authority. By contrast, Frank and Chloe Cousins managed to purchase and manumit members of their family. Jacob and John Banks were also constrained by virtue of their race, but within the narrow field of maneuver they were actively involved in the lives of their family, especially their children. Put another way, the Banks and Cousins families could plan for a future, if only within the domestic sphere: children would be married, skills passed on, family names maintained, and, most importantly, rights in one's person and property were confirmed. The majority of free persons of color living in the county through the early national period fitted somewhere along this continuum.

Marriages between free Black women and slaves rarely emerge in the records. The men remained invisible for the most part, and marriages between such individuals were always informal. Perhaps for this reason, the two instances of such unions in the county records provide fascinating glimpses into the intricacies of family formation and the links between whites and Blacks and across status boundaries. Paradoxically, these exceptional cases tell us much about the overall patterns of the free Black experience of family in the county. These include relationships between parents and children, the political economy of the domestic unit, and relations between the sexes.

Catherine Granthum, like Chloe and Frank Cousins, successfully united her family in freedom. Manumitted in 1797, she purchased and manumitted her oldest son, Woodson (six years old), in 1800, and her husband, Phil, in 1802. In the deed of manumission for Phil, she revealed that she intended to solemnize her longstanding common-law marriage. As a slave Phil had been referred to only by his first name but now legally took his wife's surname. Thereafter, until his death in 1838, he appeared in the county records as Phil Granthum. At the time of Catherine's manumission and purchase of her spouse, she also wrote a last will and testament as well as a deed of loan contingent on her marriage to Phil. It is apparent that Catherine was unusually cognizant of the legal system and perhaps a bit cynical about Phil's intentions once he was freed. She was a woman of considerable property, having purchased more than two hundred acres of land from the executor of her former master's estate. Phil, on the other hand, was propertyless and, but for his wife's affection, would have remained enslaved. The two legal documents reflected the economic imbalance between the two partners.[37]

In a deed of loan rivaling any modern prenuptial agreement, she laid out a stringent set of conditions under which her new husband was to have access to her property during his lifetime. He gained full use of her "estate, real and personal" in order to "raise, clothe and school" their two sons and any subsequent offspring "born of [her body]" as well as provide himself with "decent support." This arrangement became null and void if, after Catherine's death, Phil remarried or "cohabited with another woman as his wife or harlot." Her property would then revert to her executors and chosen trustees, Richard Bates and John Herndon, two white planters and slaveholders, who were to manage the estate until the children reached the age of majority.[38]

Catherine died five years after the writing of her will. In the event of her death and Phil's remarriage or death, all property and personal estate was to be divided equally between the two boys after all debts had been paid. Ever conscious of her children's future, Catherine directed that "should it be necessary to bind them out," she wished the boys to be "kept together," under the tutelage of "some mecanic of respectability." The records do not indicate that Gideon and Woodson Granthum were ever apprenticed. But had circumstances demanded it, their mother hoped they would pursue crafts outside those traditionally occupied by the county's free Blacks.[39]

For Catherine Granthum the decision to marry a man of lesser means must have entailed a good deal of soul-searching. She wished to protect her considerable wealth and her children's welfare. Virginia law followed English common law in which "marriage brought an automatic transfer" of a woman's real and personal property to her husband.[40] Thus, the deed of loan represented for Catherine Granthum a finely orchestrated hedge, as she gave her husband use rights to her property without relinquishing full control.

The Granthum family lifecycle progressed from slavery to freedom. Essential to its relative success was Catherine's connections to influential whites in the county: her manumitter and benefactor, Gideon Cawthon; James Holman, a white neighbor who sold her land and, ironically, her children and husband; and the executors of her will and trustees of her children and estate, Thomas Bates and John Herndon.

For whatever complex reasons, these middling and wealthy slaveholders were willing to facilitate Catherine's efforts to gain a firm economic footing and reunite and stabilize her family. Perhaps their motivations were not entirely altruistic. As trustees, Thomas Bates and John Herndon stood to control a substantial estate and possibly the labor of two young apprentices. Yet Phil managed to retain parental authority and the records do not suggest that his wife's white executors ever challenged his rights as widower. At the same time, we cannot define these planters' motivations as entirely humanitarian. They owned slaves at a period in the county's history when other options were available. How do we account for their behavior? We return to the distinction white planters seemed to make between free Blacks as individuals with whom they had established reciprocal relations and as faceless members of an alternately threatening and disposable mass. Ambiguity was at the heart of the formation of free Black families in a slave society and of the relationships that developed between free Blacks, whites, and slaves.[41]

Between 1803 and 1832, the Pierce family also established deep roots in the county. Much of their strategizing involved the creation of economic and social ties to influential whites. John Pierce, we know, was owned by a white planter but had somehow convinced his master to allow him to contract his own work and to retain a portion of his wages. He was forty-five years old in 1803. The county employed him continuously for twenty-five years from 1803 to 1828 as the person responsible for the overall functioning of the courthouse buildings and grounds, the provisioning of prisoners, and the fueling and furnishing of the jail and public halls. Further, Milly, his wife, provided the meals for prisoners, for which service her husband was reimbursed. After more than fourteen years as a slave, Pierce was manumitted for "extraordinary merit and general good character and conduct." He received special dispensation to remain in the county, where he continued his duties.[42]

It would be hard to overstate the importance of Pierce's position during his tenure at the courthouse. A typical levy taken in 1807 showed payments to him for purchasing and installing in the courthouse windows "nine panes of glass," for the replacement of a stovepipe, as well as for the usual maintenance of the courthouse and jail and supply of wood for heating. Pierce's relative power extended well beyond the specifics of his responsibilities. One can certainly imagine that as he moved between the jail, the courthouse, and the square where litigants as well as onlookers gathered, he shared confidences, carried information between parties, and developed a wide and influential network of connections with gentry and common folk, Blacks and whites.[43]

Milly Pierce, John's wife, was a free Black spinner. Her origins are obscured in the records but she may have been freeborn. The couple, though not legally married, had a longstanding, stable relationship and shared a household with their six children, five daughters and a son. Given her husband's legal status for the greater part of their union, Milly conducted the couple's economic transactions. Until 1817, it is her name that appears in official records. As early as 1804, the Pierces lived near the courthouse but owned twenty-three acres in the county's upper district, which they rented to other free African Americans. In the residential hierarchy of the county, Blacks rarely lived near the courthouse. But, given the convenience of having John Pierce near the courthouse, an exception must have been made.[44]

The Pierces used their connections to county government and to individual whites in a number of instances. A set of agreements between the family and John Fleming, a large landholder and county justice, reflected their ability to bargain successfully to ensure their family's long-term stability. In May 1825, Milly, called "Mildred Pierce" in the documents, paid sixty dollars to Fleming for the two acres of land where the family had resided near the courthouse. Fleming owned a tavern near the property that was rented to other tenants. The deed, therefore, did not transfer the land outright to the Pierces. Instead, Milly purchased the right to reside on the property during her lifetime and that of her husband.

In order to protect against competition, Fleming's conveyance was made on the condition that neither Milly nor John would "keep a house of entertainment." His assumption that this free Black family had the potential to establish a competitive tavern is revealing. Furthermore, the compromise worked out by the parties, though placing restrictions on the Pierces' use of their house, nonetheless meant that they secured an agreement that would allow them to continue living at the courthouse, even when John Pierce ceased being the county's "employee."[45]

Obviously dissatisfied with the arrangement limiting the tenure of their residence to their lifetime, the Pierces, two months later, renegotiated the agreement. In an addendum to the deed, Fleming wrote, "I have this day had a conversation with John Pierce and have promised him that when he and his wife Mildred shall die if his children living with him shall wish to reside on the land [to] which his wife now holds a life estate in they may do so as long as it may be agreeable to them." He cautioned, however, that they were to be held to the same conditions of the original deed, "behav[ing] in such a manner so as not to incommode [him] or the tenants that [he] had on the Goochland Courthouse farm." The Pierces thus ensured, as far as they could, that their adult children would have a measure of security and residential stability.[46]

Free African Americans in Virginia performed a kind of balancing act: one act of indiscretion on their part, a twist of fate, any explicit acts of resistance by their enslaved brethren, or the weighing of political arguments in favor of a more strictly administered slave regime would send them toppling over. Free African American families worked to attain family stability and continuity. Their efforts were expressed, for example, in the use of the same first names over four generations, in an increase in tenancy and land ownership through the antebellum period, in the creation of customary areas of free Black residential clusters, and in the community's relative success in holding on to its marginal economic and social position in the county. At the level of the household, evidence suggests that family units expanded and contracted as a result of the natural domestic cycle, as individuals gained better or at least different employment and tenancy arrangements and sought greater autonomy.

Courthouse Custom as an Archival Filter

Comparing Goochland Sources with Other Central Virginia Counties

ROBERT VERNON

The Forest

Reginald Butler's book on Goochland County opens with dramatic testimony detailing two infanticide cases from the late eighteenth century. This is a good place to begin, he writes, because the "murder of two newborn infants opens a window into the interior worlds of free African Americans and their white neighbors."[1] It is also a good place to begin a discussion of how his narrative was both informed and limited by the sources to which he had access. Naturally, this is a question that must be addressed with respect to what was readily available in the 1980s, the years in which he made frequent trips to Goochland Courthouse and the Library of Virginia. The limitations of discovery and access to primary sources certainly had an impact on the historical narratives he developed and on which he based his analysis and conclusions about the lives of free people of color in Virginia. However, despite these limitations, his study of free Black life in rural Virginia during the eighteenth and early nineteenth centuries remains an essential source for understanding the history of race and racism in Virginia.

An examination of how Butler interpreted one of those events reveals the limitations of the sources that were available prior to 1989, when he completed his dissertation, and how such limitations can affect historical interpretation. Butler states that Bridgett Cooper resided "in a house in the 'forest'" near her family. He emphasizes the term "forest" to represent the symbolic landscape of Bridgett's world.[2] Specifically, the "location of household, garden, and the world beyond—the forest or woods—provided important cognitive categories.... The garden represented domestic space where behavior could be easily scrutinized. Outside of that domain—out of sight—in the forest or the woods, behavioral norms could not be monitored as closely."[3] This is a powerful metaphor of liminality, a fence separating the domestic space of the garden from the shadowy realm of the forest symbolically coalescing with the transitional states of birth and death in this account of infanticide. But a source not available to Butler demonstrates that "forest" had an entirely different meaning within the context of the criminal charge that Bridgett faced.

Butler's analysis of the case against Bridgett is based on a transcription of an inquisition, a commonwealth, or criminal, cause recorded in Goochland's county order books. The "Forest" is mentioned twice in that source with ambiguous spatial contexts. Bridgett's sister Becca testified "that she came to the Forest to live at the House where the prisoner [Bridgett] then lived." And, according to Elizabeth Lawson, Bridgett's "child was born between the Forest and her mothers that morning as she was returning Home."[4] Bridgett's case was scheduled to be tried in the district court, which at that time was in Richmond. We know nothing of her fate because papers from the district court were destroyed in the April 1865 evacuation fire. There is, however, another source for this case that would not have been readily available to Butler at the time he was researching Goochland County records.

As part of the procedure of court business, papers associated with any issues that were heard in open court were filed and entries on the matter were made in court record books. The papers stored in file boxes at the courthouse were kept for future reference. Actions or decisions taken on criminal cases like Bridgett's were occasionally summarized in county order books. The collections of documents in these cases are commonly referred to as "loose papers" and might consist of summons, depositions, receipts, court judgments, or any written evidence relevant to the cases recorded in the order books. The documents created in the process of gathering evidence for civil and criminal cases in Goochland, Albemarle, Louisa, and some other counties are now flat-filed chronologically at the Library of Virginia and constitute a series of records called "Judgments."[5]

When Butler researched his dissertation in the 1980s, most Goochland manuscripts were stored as bundles of folded papers in large cardboard boxes at the Library of Virginia. That finding relevant information was difficult is indicated by the fact that he cited Goochland County Miscellaneous "Old Papers" only five times, primarily for records of the Overseers of the Poor involving apprenticeships for poor children of color. In order to find these documents, Butler might have used an inventory of Goochland records that were transferred to the library.[6] Prior to flat-filing manuscripts, these county inventories were the primary finding aid researchers used to determine which cardboard box might contain relevant documentation. For Butler to have discovered other papers related to his research would have taken great perseverance and no small amount of luck.

In the years following Butler's research, the manuscripts from Bridgett's case were processed at the Library of Virginia and are now filed in a collection called Goochland Judgments. They include much information not available to Butler. Of particular interest is the coroner's inquisition. On January 2, 1794, about a week after the death of Bridgett's child, twelve "good and lawful men" met at the house of Phillip Lawson to examine the infant's body. They concluded that the child "came to his Death by Violent means but when or by whom they know not."[7]

But perhaps the most important document in the case papers is another version of the "Examination of Bridget Cooper," similar to the transcription recorded in the Goochland order book but with one very significant difference. It clearly states that the child's death occurred "at The Forrest, the House of William H. Pleasants."[8] This changes the context Butler created describing the locality for the death of Bridgett's child from a location in nature to adjacent to a white family's home, thereby tying the event more intimately to the relationships that existed between William H. Pleasants and the Black people his father had emancipated twelve years earlier.

"The Forest" was constructed a few years after Thomas Pleasants purchased the 653-acre tract in 1776.[9] The house may have been built for his son William, and Bridgett Cooper's case verifies that William was living in the house as early as 1793.[10] The tract, known as "Charlie Forest," was divided following the death of Thomas Pleasants, and a 1808 survey shows a sketch of the house and two nearby structures.[11] It is likely that one of the outbuildings was the residence of Bridgett's mother, Chloe Cooper, whereas Bridgett lived in the Forest itself, where she was probably employed by William as a house servant.

Additional places of residence must have been a necessity for the free people of color living on the Pleasants estates. Lists for "Mulattoes and

Free Negroes" from the years immediately before and after the 1804 death of Thomas Pleasants give the names and occupations of those that lived at the Forest, where William resided, and "Beaverdam," where Thomas and James lived.[12] They show considerable movement of free people of color between the two residences (table 1). Changes of residence between plantations owned by the Pleasants would not have been unusual. The lists also confirm that most of those living on the Pleasants estates were, like Chloe Cooper and her daughter Bridgett, former enslaved workers who had been emancipated by Thomas Pleasants in 1782.[13]

Collectively, these sources describe a physical and social setting very different from Butler's. Rather than a house "in the forest," they reveal that the dwellings of Chloe and others were near the residence of William H. Pleasants, a substantial house called the Forest. Further, we learn that Bridgett, who was then about twenty-two years old, resided in this house with Pleasants, who was unmarried and twenty-seven at the time Bridgett became pregnant.[14] Her pregnancy must have been a topic of some discussion in the neighborhood among people of both races, and there must have been speculation about who had fathered the child.

Beyond the facts of their ages, knowing each other since childhood, and living in the same house, there are other circumstances that suggest William was the father of Bridgett's child. The papers filed in Goochland Judgments provide suggestive omissions. First, William was not called upon to serve on the coroner's inquisition "to Enquire how & in what manner the sd Negroe child came to his Death" on his property, perhaps owing to some concern regarding a potential conflict of interest. Also, William was summoned along with seven other individuals to appear at the courthouse on January 9, 1794, to give evidence in Bridgett's case, but there is no evidence that he did so.[15]

TABLE 1. Numbers of adult free people of color residing at "The Forest" and "Beaverdam," 1802–1807

RESIDENCE	1802	1803	1804	1805	1806	1807
William H. Pleasants, "The Forest"	11	12	14	6	11	8
Thomas Pleasants, "Beaverdam"	2	3	4			
James B. Pleasants, "Beaverdam"				16	9	9

Source: GC, "Free Negro and Slave Records," oversize box 2, barcode 1149995, LVA.

And although these considerations raise questions about William, it is far more important to consider what motives Bridgett might have had if William was the father. Was there shame in bearing the child of her former owner's son? Did she and William have a disagreement over her status and that of the child she was expecting? The issues are complex; if there was a sexual relationship between William and Bridgett it might have ranged from rape to a consensual relationship based on a lifetime of shared experiences. Butler discusses at length the supportive interactions between Bridgett, her mother and sisters, and Polly Younghusband Maddox and Debra Pleasants. These women treated Bridgett's situation with compassion based on long familiarity with Bridgett and William. Even without the advantage of having the manuscripts from Goochland Judgments for his analysis, Butler must have suspected unusual motives for Bridgett's desperate solution when he wrote that the "white women's depositions suggested that the Coopers and Pleasants had maintained patron-client links that may well have extended to more intimate interactions."[16]

Sources

As Bridgett's case demonstrates, conclusions drawn by researchers from historical accounts are shaped by the documents they encounter. But what factors determine the access and availability of those documents? To answer this question, we must look to the past and understand the historical circumstances of their original creation and subsequent curation and preservation. Are they readily available to researchers? These are critically important questions for assessing and appreciating Butler's history of communities of color in Goochland County.

Goochland County holds a special place among central Virginia counties because almost all county records have survived.[17] The county was established from Henrico County in 1728 and has a complete set of deeds, wills, and order books from its founding. In addition, a parish register, kept by Reverend William Douglas, provides a unique record of births, deaths, and marriages for the period between 1750 and 1797, including the marriages of many free people of color and the births of their children. Butler made extensive use of the so-called *Douglas Register,* which enabled him to identify many families of color, a difficult task because eighteenth-century records seldom identify people as such.[18] Although there is a much smaller register containing only births for Louisa County spanning the years 1764 to 1778, no other surviving parish register from central Virginia documents births, deaths, and marriages.[19]

Hanover County, to the northeast of Goochland, was established in 1721 and, like Goochland, extended to the Blue Ridge Mountains when it was formed. There was much movement of families, Black and white, between Hanover and Goochland. Unfortunately, Hanover record books and most loose papers were removed from the courthouse and taken to Richmond for protection during the Civil War, where they were burned in April 1865. Only two eighteenth-century deed and will books survive.[20]

Because of population growth and the inconvenience of traveling long distances to attend county court sessions, two new counties were created from Goochland and Hanover in the 1740s. Louisa County was formed from Hanover in 1742 and Albemarle County from Goochland in 1744. The dates of changes in county boundaries are key to knowing where to find records on families and individuals. For example, information on residents for Fredericksville Parish can be found in the Louisa court records prior to 1761 and in the Albemarle records after 1761.

Butler's research during the 1980s predated the online collections of indexed document images. In fact, the manuscripts, or "loose papers," from Goochland County had come to the Library of Virginia in Richmond only a few years before he began working through order, deed, and will books at the Goochland Courthouse. During those years, most of the Goochland materials at the library were folded sheets of paper, tied together with string or ribbon and grouped in the "bundles" that clerks used to store records at the courthouse. A few collections, such as lists of taxpayers or "tithe" lists from colonial Goochland, had been pulled from boxes and were flat-filed in folders. Butler made good use of these in locating the residences of many of the mid-eighteenth-century free people of color he studied. However, the bulk of the manuscript sources that could have supplemented the record books that Butler consulted were scattered among hundreds of cardboard boxes storing the work of Goochland clerks over some two hundred years.

What we encounter here thus exemplifies the two factors determining the availability of archival resources: the idiosyncratic ways clerks in different jurisdictions organized, recorded, and transcribed court documents relating to civil and legal matters as well as their later disposition, preservation, and curation. In effect, two archival filters exist, one in the past which selectively preserved paperwork considered relevant to the business of law and local administration, and the other, in the present, grouping these records into useful categories for the researcher. The advent of digital technologies not available to Butler is making an expanding range of surviving materials more easily accessible to future scholars. We might consider this emerging digital regime a third "filter," one that reveals the severe constraints Butler encountered and overcame in the 1980s. What we can now see and know gives us a fresh perspective on the pioneering research that produced his remarkable dissertation. It is important to note here that this crucial digital work also fulfills Butler's vision and is an outgrowth of and testament to his work at the Woodson Institute.

As for the first filter, various Virginia laws specified that counties were to maintain a series of record books, to be kept "in good order," although the exact procedures clerks adopted for recording county business and administering justice varied from county to county, depending on local customs and the quirks of successive incumbents. Researchers must be aware of these local procedures, for they are rarely clearly articulated. In most cases they must be inferred through immersion in the broader corpus of manuscripts and record books in each locality.

The historian must also know where to look. Albemarle County's "loose papers" were transferred from Charlottesville to Richmond in February 1984 in hundreds of cardboard boxes. A similar process occurred in Goochland and other Virginia counties. This vast quantity of unprocessed material sent to the Library of Virginia and no longer available in county courthouses made it virtually impossible for researchers to systematically review many important record groups at the courthouse. However, Butler did benefit from the peculiar practices of Goochland's county clerks. Many significant criminal cases in Goochland were recorded as inquisitions in the county order books and included good copies—sometimes verbatim—of the actual documents that county officials collected as evidence for those cases. Such transcriptions are seldom, if ever, seen in the order books for Louisa or Albemarle Counties.

As staff at the Library of Virginia began to organize the material found in the many cardboard boxes from Goochland and other counties, they created flat-filed collections researchers could access without requesting the large cardboard boxes of miscellaneous bundles. The processing of undifferentiated bundles of manuscripts into chronologically arranged flat-filed collections organized by document type constitutes a second filter. Many documents are still unprocessed, but important collections, such as Goochland Judgments, can be found by using county order books as a case index. Examination of these manuscripts reveals that not everything was transcribed and that some transcriptions were inaccurate. As Bridgett's case demonstrates, this can alter the interpretation of historical events.

Recently, large collections of manuscripts related to African American history have been placed online, both as images and as transcribed and indexed PDFs. This constitutes a third filter for manuscripts. Posting documents related to African American history on the Internet was initiated at the Virginia Museum of History and Culture in 2011 with their "Unknown No Longer" project. This was followed in 2016 at the Library of Virginia when "Virginia Untold: The African American Narrative," was launched online. The Central Virginia History Repository, which went online in April 2019 and is supported by the University of Virginia's Institute for Advanced Technology in the Humanities, hosts a collection of images that include records of the Overseers of the Poor from Albemarle, Fluvanna, Goochland, and Louisa Counties. It was renamed the Reginald D. Butler Local History Archive following his death in July 2019. Finally, in the last few years FamilySearch.org has placed images from Virginia county record books online. Extraordinary resources like these make it possible to find and examine documents, especially those at the Library of Virginia, which are indexed by name, county, and record type.

Many documents will never be recovered, of course, including those destroyed in war and by fire. Records from Albemarle and Henrico Counties were destroyed by British raids during the Revolutionary War. And court documents from adjacent Hanover County, the entire collection of district and superior court cases sent from Goochland and other counties to Richmond, as well as records of the Virginia General Court were all destroyed during the Richmond evacuation fire on April 3, 1865. The Library of Virginia has a "Burned Jurisdiction Database" that hosts the few records that have been found in other collections from localities that suffered document loss.[21] Goochland is unique among central Virginia counties in possessing the civil and ecclesiastical records essential to the documentation of free Black families and their interactions with white neighbors.

Reginald Butler's innovative account of free Black life in Goochland County is constructed through the integration of careful genealogical reconstructions of families of color with historical narratives that illuminate the fabric of everyday life in Goochland County. Genealogy alone builds from individuals to families but seldom blossoms into a community study. Butler's work is notably successful in revealing the intimate interactions that intertwined Black and white families as communities. These interactions extended beyond the local level. Free Black migration to nearby counties was common, and families of color maintained kinship connections even though they became separated by days of travel. I offer a review of the status of county records in central Virginia below—now that archival consolidation and digitization are in full bloom and allow research across counties—to promote future regional studies of free Black life in Virginia in Butler's spirit.

The study of free people of color in Virginia primarily stands on five principal sources of information that specify race: tax lists, registers of free people of color, registration papers, indentures of apprenticeship, and freedom suits. A significant part of our understanding of the lives of free people of color comes from these sources. To be sure, a few very rare autobiographies, diaries, or journals can illuminate the lives of particular individuals. Store ledgers and the papers of physicians also provide fascinating glimpses into the experiences of people of color. Free people of color and enslaved laborers appear in these documents, both as purchasers of services and goods, and as laborers who bartered their time and skills when cash was not at hand. But these sources of information are atypical.

More typical are the five source groups enumerated above. To provide a quick overview, county tax lists give an annual count of all heads of families, usually a male, residing in a district and an inventory of taxable property that can be indicative of economic status. Depending on the time and locality, race was sometimes recorded. Personal property taxes were collected starting in 1782, although tithe lists are available for some counties and provide earlier information. Between 1793 and about 1805, most counties and cities had begun to register their free people of color. County registers of free people of color provide physical descriptions of individuals, including their sex, age, height, hair, and skin color to identify particular individuals. When venturing beyond their neighborhood, free people might be required to produce their registration papers to prove they were not enslaved and had the right to travel between jurisdictions.

Indentures of apprenticeship have roots going back to the seventeenth century and beyond to England. Orphans and poor children were enrolled with craftspeople to learn a trade so that they would not become a financial burden on the community. When apprenticed, a child went to live in the household of the craftsperson; this established bonds between white families and families of color that reinforced customary expectations of the proper roles and behavior for people of color. Relevant information can also be gleaned from a miscellaneous array of official documents. In his work, Butler presents a lengthy discussion of manumissions by deed or will and addresses the complexities of freedom suits, which contain numerous depositions that are goldmines for historians for reflecting individual and community values and perceptions.

To properly understand and make use of these records it is necessary to look at how and why these records were collected and maintained from jurisdiction to jurisdiction. Although laws required that the same records be produced in all jurisdictions, there was great variability in the way local officials gathered and recorded information. Understanding the traditions and practices of county and parish officials and reconstructing their practices during different periods of time are the contextual keys to properly interpreting surviving records.

County Tax Lists

Virginia began collecting annual personal property taxes in 1782. Tithe lists are available for some years in Goochland, Louisa, and Fluvanna Counties prior to 1782. Free people of color are occasionally found in them, but race is never specified and must be inferred from other sources. Butler made excellent use of the Goochland tithe lists, identifying many individuals and families from mid-eighteenth-century Goochland who appear in later county records and in personal property tax lists. Unlike tithes, entries in personal property tax lists may identify the race of individuals by tagging them after their name with an "N" or "FN" for "negro" or "free negro," or an "M" for "mulatto." In very rare instances people are identified as "Indian." Depending on the commissioner taking the list, FN might mean that a person was emancipated or it could simply mean that a person had very dark skin. Similarly, M generally meant that a person was born free, but emancipated people with a light complexion might also be identified with an M.

The race implied by identifying a person as a "mulatto" can be bewilderingly complex. In the eighteenth and early nineteenth centuries, most Indigenous people were identified as mulattoes. Prior to the considerable effort over the last twenty-five years to discover and document individuals in county records identified as Indian, it was generally assumed that the term "mulatto" simply referred to mixed-race children of white women.[22] It has become apparent, however, that the racial tags employed by commissioners varied widely according to contemporaneous usage and personal idiosyncrasies. A commissioner might only serve for a few years before a successor deployed a different template for racial identification. For example, because of multiple freedom suits in Richmond and in Albemarle and Louisa Counties, most members of the extended Kinney family were tagged as "mulattoes" because of reputed Native American ancestry, and not as "free negroes," even though they had been enslaved.[23] The challenge was expressed concisely by Peter Crawford in the undated list he returned in Louisa County: "All those [listed] above are free Negroes, & those that follow below are Mulattoes Agreeable to the best distinction I have been able to make."[24] In addition, most larger counties had two districts, each with its own commissioner, and one commissioner might tag a person with FN one year and M the next.

An even more challenging situation occurs when no tags are used. This was the case in Albemarle County between 1782 and 1788. In 1789, some but not all people of color were identified in St. Ann's Parish. In Fredericksville Parish this tagging does not appear until 1805. Lacking any racial identification, the only way to identify a person of color is through a broad knowledge of the families of color in a region over many decades. In Albemarle, Hanover, Louisa, Goochland, and Fluvanna Counties, Bowles and Farrar were common surnames among white families and families of color. At least three individuals named Zachariah Bowles lived in Hanover, Goochland, and Albemarle Counties in the eighteenth century. One was a white man who served in the Revolutionary War, whereas another Zachariah was the son of Amy (Bowles) Farrow and, born in 1769, too young to serve.[25] To make such distinctions requires much tedious work with lists and records from adjacent counties, a compelling argument for using regional studies—now made possible by digital tools.

Some people of color rarely or never appear in tax lists. Catherine Foster, who owned property adjacent to the University of Virginia, was not listed as a woman of color in any personal property tax list and never registered in Albemarle County.[26] There were people like Foster in Goochland County who were inconsistently listed and never registered, and there is no obvious explanation for these omissions. Were they so well known that they did not have to be listed, despite the legal requirement? Did some officials view them as white? Joshua Rothman presents a list of sixty-one skin tones from Richmond police records, demonstrating a continuum of color that could shift into different racial categories over time based on changes in law.[27] Any attempt to identify all people of color in a jurisdiction is probably futile, but it would nonetheless be useful to analyze and explain lacunae in the documentary record that studies of free communities of color such as Butler's reveal.

Occasionally separate lists of free people of color were made for some districts and placed at the rear of the annual personal property tax list, rather than mixing them alphabetically with all district residents. This would have made it easier for the district commissioners to maintain a list of free people of color. Louisa County has such compilations at the ends of personal property tax lists for both districts between 1813 and 1818. And free people of color are listed in the books for both districts in Albemarle County in 1813 and 1814. The reason for these special lists is that higher taxes were levied on free people of color in those years in order to help pay expenses for the War of 1812—although it was collected unevenly, sometimes from both men and women, and sometimes from men only.[28] The 1813 personal property tax is one of the few sources that list single free women of color and the wives of free men of color. The variation in the collection of this capitation tax is an excellent example of inconsistent local enforcement of acts passed in Richmond that would bear heavily on free communities of color in Goochland County and throughout the commonwealth.[29]

Lists of Free People of Color

In addition to personal property taxes, separate surviving tax lists of free Blacks in Goochland County offered Butler an invaluable resource for reconstructing the history of its free population of color. Lists from the upper and lower districts identify the wives of free men of color in the early nineteenth century. Both districts have lists for 1804 through 1812, excepting 1808. But the lower district has additional lists for 1802, 1803, 1815, and 1817, while the upper district has a list for 1813.[30] Entries for free people of color in the personal property tax lists for Goochland County were usually recorded with the same information that was recorded in the district lists of free people of color. This means that missing years can be supplemented with entries from the personal property taxes, and that they can be compared to verify the information recorded.

A review of an act passed in January 1801 reveals why two lists were made, one for personal property taxes and one enumerating free people of color. Unlike Goochland County, in Fluvanna County the personal property taxes for at least the first decade of the nineteenth century do not record race. Free people of color were listed as though they were white. In Fluvanna, at least, a second list conforming to the 1801 act was necessary. This act required that "every commissioner of the revenue, annually, to return to the court of his county or corporation, at the time he returns a list of taxable property, a complete list of all free negroes or mulattoes within his district, together with their names, sex, places of abode, and particular trades, occupation or calling, a copy of which list shall be fixed by the clerk of the said county or corporation, at the courthouse door, and the original be deposited for safe keeping in his office."[31] The form and frequency of lists of free people of color mandated by the 1801 act vary considerably. Goochland County has an impressive collection of these lists that run from 1802 to 1817. Powhatan County has lists for 1801, 1805, 1811–13, 1815, 1817–23, and 1833.[32] Fluvanna County has what is probably the most impressive collection of lists in Virginia, covering every year from 1801 to 1850 except 1803, 1808, and 1843 to 1846.[33] No lists created in accordance to the 1801 act are known to exist for Albemarle County, although an entry in the order books states that "Thomas Garth Commissioner of the County made a return of the list of the people of Colour & free negroes" in October 1802.[34] A special census of free people of color regarding emigration to Liberia taken in 1833 is the only list of free people of color conforming to the 1801 requirements available for Albemarle County.

Almost all the lists for Goochland County contain information on residence, occupation, and the names of wives. The Goochland lists generally give residence in relation to a landowner. They also make a distinction that Butler considered significant, distinguishing residence between "at" and "on." In this, he was following the observation of Luther Porter Jackson that "on" was derived from "on his own land" and distinguished owners from tenants.[35] The early Powhatan County lists also make this distinction. By way of contrast, the Fluvanna lists generally state residence in terms of a geographical feature rather than by landowner. These lists are also remarkable for naming children with their mothers in every year from 1801 to 1836 or 1837, after which they simply note the number of a woman's children. It is therefore possible to determine the birthdates and parents for most free people born in Fluvanna County during that period.

One of the great advantages of annual lists, whether derived from personal property taxes or created as a separate list for documenting the population of free people of color, is that they show mobility or migration. Aaron Barbour is listed in Albemarle's Fredericksville Parish in 1807 and 1809 and was probably there in 1808 when no taxes were collected.[36] According to the Goochland personal property tax lists, Barbour was living in the upper district of Goochland County in 1810 and 1811, where he was described as being an "Indian" and working as a wheelwright and cooper.[37] From 1813 to 1816, Barbour appeared in the Fluvanna lists of "free negroes" and "mulattoes" living near Union Mills, which was a stage stop and where he would have found employment as a wheelwright for wagons and as a cooper for the kegs that transported tobacco and other goods along the Rivanna River. Barbour never registered in any of the three counties in which he resided, despite being required by law to have a registration, or "free papers." Although he never registered, Barbour seems to have been able to move about freely in these counties without being apprehended and jailed.

Although Albemarle and Louisa Counties do not have a series of annual lists of free people of color, like those of Goochland and Fluvanna, Albemarle does boast an exceptional list taken in 1833. In response to the 1831 Southampton County insurrection led by Nat Turner, a bill was proposed in the Virginia House of Delegates in December 1832 to fund a report "to the general assembly, shewing the ages and sex of such free persons of colour as may be transported from this commonwealth."[38] In March 1833, "An ACT Making Appropriations for the Removal of Free Persons of Colour" was passed that funded surveys of free people of color in Virginia's counties and cities to determine who might be willing to emigrate to Liberia. It also funded their removal.[39] Responding to this act the Albemarle Court ordered two commissioners to compile "a complete list of all the free Negroes or

Mulattoes in their respective districts together with their names, sex, places of abode, and particular trades, occupations or callings—distinguishing in their lists the free mulattoes from the free blacks," and to "ascertain what numbers, if any, of the free Mulattoes & free blacks . . . are willing to emigrate to the Western Coast of Africa, together with their names, ages and sex, how long they have remained within the limits of this County, and whether they were free before the 4th of March 1833."[40]

I met Reginald Butler in early 1995 when I contacted him to enquire about this court order to take a "census" of free people of color. He said he knew of no such census but wanted to accompany me to the Library of Virginia to see if the returns existed and, especially, if they contained a list for Goochland County. The requested auditor's manuscripts contained the lists of free people of color taken in Fredericksville and St. Ann's Parishes in Albemarle and many other localities in Virginia. But much to Butler's disappointment, there were no lists for Goochland County.

The letters from the county clerks to the auditor in response to the act are significant because they illuminate prevailing attitudes of free people of color regarding their possible removal to Liberia. Although Goochland did not return a list, in September 1833 its clerk of court replied that "no report has been made, and it is confidently believed, that not one free person can be found in the County willing to accept the benefits and provisions of the aforesaid Act." From Fluvanna County a Mr. Crewdson wrote that "I could not find one that seem to have the most distant idea of leaving their native land to go to Libera or elsewhere unless compeld."

Responses from counties beyond central Virginia were more pointed. Greenbriar County's clerk wrote that "it appears to me that the free people of Colour in this County are hostile in the extreme to the Project." The response from Amelia County was similar: "Several of the free negroes of the County have told me they would prefer being sold as slaves and remain here than to be sent to Liberia." An equally emphatic reply was sent from Prince William County: "The unvarying and unhesitating answer has been 'NO' I cannot trust myself among Negroes I wou'd sooner be a slave here, than a free man in Africa or Liberia.'" The letters from these clerks of county courts and the results of the survey are an example of disenfranchised people "voting with their feet." Lists were returned from 28 cities and counties across Virginia, which enumerated some 7,896 free people of color. Of these, only 43 expressed a willingness to emigrate.

The 1833 lists varied greatly in form and content. Some were mere lists of names, while others, including from the two Albemarle districts, took the form of detailed censuses giving age, sex, occupation, and place of residence.[41] The format and content of lists could even vary within a county, as the returns from Fredericksville and St. Ann's Parishes in Albemarle County demonstrate. The lists for Albemarle and other counties are organized to display family structure, listing the male or female head of household first, then followed by spouse and children. Ages and occupations are given in most of the lists, whereas the personal property tax and district lists of free people of color seldom provide ages. The Fredericksville Parish list included information about "how long they have remained within the limits of this County."

Apprenticeships are also represented in the Fredericksville list. For example, John Goen is listed as the twelve-year-old son of Mary Goen, a washerwoman living in Charlottesville, and as "bound to A. Whitehurst." John was indentured to Arthur Whitehurst in July 1830 when he was nine years old to be trained as a cooper.[42] There are numerous entries in the Fredericksville list for young people of color not living with their families while serving an apprenticeship. That the commissioner knew of, or was able to find, these young people of color living and working with white families was a reflection of his intimate familiarity with families of color in his half of Albemarle County.

Registration Papers

In his discussion on registrations or "free papers," Butler notes that "registration rules were applied with great inconsistency and it was not unusual to have free Black residents who never registered or who effectively neglected to abide by the triennial registration requirement."[43] This inconsistency in registering free people of color is common to all central Virginia counties, and probably to all Virginia counties. It is one of the poorly understood phenomena of the registration process. How did free people of color evade these laws on registration? Or, to flip the question to the administrative side, why did county officials register some and apparently ignore others?

I earlier noted that Aaron Barbour was listed in personal property taxes in Albemarle, Goochland, and Fluvanna Counties, but there is no record that he ever turned in his free papers in any of those counties or was issued new ones. We cannot know why individuals like him failed to register: perhaps they enjoyed a peculiar—and to us, unknowable—social status that exempted them from the requirement; they viewed themselves and were viewed as something other than persons of color. After all, Barbour was described as an "Indian" in some tax records.

Occupation may be a useful area of research on why some people registered and others did not. Free people of color working as boatmen or wagoners usually had free papers because their work took them to counties where they might not be known. Occupation also suggests individuals' social networks. Apprenticeship indentures provide both occupational information and connections between their families and those of their masters. Significantly, the free papers all adult persons of color were required to carry did *not* document occupation.

Davy Cooper's interaction with the Goochland County clerk regarding his registration is a rare case where a reason for nonregistration was given. In October 1831, Finch Scruggs provided Cooper with an affidavit that he could use as a pass to certify that he was a free person until he had an opportunity to go to court and register. Scruggs wrote that he had known Cooper "for a number of years" and "never heard his right to freedom questioned." The Goochland clerk had told Cooper that because "he was a cripple he supposed it was not necessary for him to have any." Cooper was a "shoemaker by trade" who risked "disappointing his employers" by not finishing his work for them. Scruggs had "no doubt" Cooper "will go to Goochland and procure his papers" in due course.[44] In December, Cooper proceeded to register in Goochland County. According to his register, he was a fifty-eight-year-old "black" man whose swollen right leg was shorter than the left.[45] While no reason was given for the change in Cooper's requirement to register, the date of the affidavit is significant. It was written two months after Nat Turner's Rebellion in August 1831.

Document counts in "Virginia Untold" for central Virginia counties indicate the wide range of county court practices regarding registration.[46] For example, when Darkas Brown presented her Powhatan County free papers in Goochland County court in 1823, she was issued a new register for Goochland and her Powhatan register was copied into the Goochland Free Negro Register. Below the entry of the transcription is a note stating, "A copy from the original register was received and destroyed. 20 Jany 1823." Similar entries in 1823 show that the destruction of registers presented in court by free Black migrants to Goochland County was routine and continued to at least 1833.[47]

The types of documents related to specific actions or steps in the registration process preserved in county collections of loose papers indicate additional variations in local administrative practices. Of the fifty-six images for Goochland registration documents in "Virginia Untold," sixteen are affidavits that free papers were lost. To support his contention of the "seemingly perfunctory manner with which the county clerk issued duplicate certificates of freedom," Butler recounts how Peter, an enslaved man, used another man's free papers to run away. Reviewing entries in the Goochland order books, Butler concludes that the clerk issued eleven replacement certificates between 1823 and 1829.[48] The surviving Goochland manuscripts in "Virginia Untold" confirm this practice.

However, the county order books and the surviving papers for Albemarle County that our digital age has made accessible and searchable now present a very different picture of the practice of issuing replacement certificates. There are no entries in Albemarle order books for replacement registrations during the six-year period that Butler reviewed for Goochland; only around ten documents refer to lost freedom papers in the much larger Albemarle collection (468 images) in "Virginia Untold."[49] Of these, most are from counties where free Black residents lived before moving to Albemarle.

The manuscripts in "Virginia Untold" relating to West Gardner show how Albemarle officials responded to requests for replacement registrations. In July 1855, one West Gardner published an advertisement in the *Milton Chronicle* in Caswell County, North Carolina, for his lost free papers. Not long after this he moved to Richmond where, in July 1856, he was confined in the Richmond jail and applied to the Albemarle court through an attorney for a copy of his free papers. According to the order book entry, "inspection of the register of free negroes produced in open Court that no person is registered by the name of *West* Gardner," though "a certain Meriwether Gardner was registered." Two people testified in court "that they knew the said West Gardner," a "free negro" and former resident, and believed that "Meriwether Gardner and West Gardner are one and the same person."[50] A receipt, dated July 14, 1856, showed that West Gardner paid "for getting a certificate from the County Court of Albemarle" certifying his freedom. Gardner's new registration was issued on August 5; a copy was kept in Charlottesville and is now posted in "Virginia Untold."[51]

By being able to search through new digital databases such as "Virginia Untold," researchers can today ascertain that the registration process in Albemarle was not as "perfunctory" as it was in other counties. In Goochland, new registrations were simply copied from the county Register of Free Negroes; in Albemarle, all the steps for issuing a new register were repeated. The first step was to have neighbors certify an individual's free status. The next step was to measure an individual's height, a task frequently assigned to Charlottesville cabinet maker Washington Chiles in the 1820s and 1830s.[52] Slips of paper with height measurements signed by Chiles can be found for at least fourteen individuals from Albemarle in "Virginia Untold." No such documents appear among the Goochland images. Another important step in Albemarle's registration process was to look for scars, moles, or other identifying features, usually including skin color; age and status at birth were also recorded. Gardner's 1843 register thus indicated that he was "born free," and the 1856 register added he was "born free of parents emancipated prior to the 1st of May 1806." There are other notable differences between Gardner's two registers. According to the earlier document, he was 5 feet 9½ inches high with a dark complexion; in 1856, he was only 5 feet 8 inches and his complexion was described as light.[53] These discrepancies show that re-registering in Albemarle involved much more than simply copying an old registration.

The images in "Virginia Untold" are from manuscripts in the Library of Virginia's county collections of "Free Negro and Slave Records."[54] The most frequent entries in the "type of certificate" field are attributes for affidavit, certificate, description, and register, but the attributes related to specific functions performed by county administrators are limited. For example, none relates to lost free papers. A researcher would have to review all the affidavits, certificates, and registers in a county and reclassify them with appropriate attributes. Locating documents concerning specific actions taken by the county clerks would require new metadata tags such as testimony regarding freedom, measurement, description of appearance, recording registers, re-registering, lost free papers, or proof of age. A flowchart like the one I constructed on the management of apprenticeship (see fig. 1, below) would be a useful heuristic for understanding how the registration process was managed in different counties. In the 1980s, Butler made excellent use of what was available in the Goochland County Register of Free Negroes and the entries he encountered in order books; at the time, the

Goochland manuscript sources on registration were unprocessed and effectively unavailable.

Now, the Virginia Open Data Portal enables research on free Black migration. Table 2 lists central Virginia counties and cities whose registrations were turned in at other locations. The second column indicates the number of registrations of free Black residents for each county in the Library of Virginia's "Free Negro and Slave Records." Because free Black men and women coming into a county were required to turn in prior registrations, it is possible to determine the number of migrants and their home counties. Combined with data in the county registers, this source would reveal local patterns of migration.

Registrations from prior counties of residence were preserved in Albemarle, Henrico, and Lynchburg but destroyed in Goochland. A researcher would have to identify transcriptions from free papers generated elsewhere that were recorded in the Goochland County Register of Free Negroes to construct a list of migrants to Goochland. Certificates given to migrants in the Albemarle County order books generally did not indicate former counties of residence. Assembling old registers in "Virginia Untold" or among

TABLE 2. Migration of free people of color derived from registrations in the Virginia Open Data Portal

COUNTY	RESIDENTS	IMMIGRANTS	EMIGRANTS
Albemarle	654	102	8
Amherst	0	?	9
Buckingham	0	?	23
Cumberland	686	11	16
Fluvanna	31	10	20
Goochland	109	7	31
Hanover	0	?	10
Henrico	390	184	40
Louisa	40	10	19
Lynchburg	173	127	7
Nelson	0	?	3
Powhatan	1,248	23	27

Source: Virginia Open Data Portal.

free papers in the Library of Virginia's "Free Negro and Slave Records" for Albemarle is therefore essential. The filtering effects of local practices for recording registrations of immigrants and preserving old registrations, such as those of Albemarle and Goochland, likely vary for other counties as well.

Finding migrants who left a county is more complicated. The table must be sorted on the "locality of origination" field. Former residents of Buckingham and other counties where records were destroyed by fire can thus be identified. A total of twenty-three migrants from Buckingham have been found, with eleven relocating to Lynchburg, five to Albemarle, three to Prince Edward, three to Powhatan, and one to Charles City County.[55] Migration is a critical component of free Black history that is covered anecdotally in family histories but has not been studied in a sustained fashion on the local or regional levels. Registration data organized in the Virginia Open Data Portal now raises the possibility of detailed geospatial studies on free Black migration, especially if combined with transcriptions from the indexing of free registers now underway at the Library of Virginia.[56]

Apprenticeship Indentures

County court and parish records in Virginia relating to apprenticeship also constitute a major source of documentation for the history of free people of color that span a period from the seventeenth century into the twentieth. Juvenile apprenticeships established important bonds between white families and the families of people of color whose children learned a trade while residing with or near their assigned masters. Beyond instruction for a trade, apprenticeships provided a social education for children of color so that they might better know the societal norms and behaviors that were expected of them in a society controlled by whites. Butler's chapter on "Youth and Bound Labor" is a thorough description of the history of this institution and how it was modified over the years as a means of controlling the free population of color and providing a labor source for white planters and tradesmen. Indentures of apprenticeship were drafted as contracts defining certain duties and responsibilities between apprentices and masters. But juvenile apprenticeship "was always a coercive institution," Butler concludes, "regardless of the personal relations or resulting benefits to the apprentice."[57]

The role of adjudicating the complaints and petitions that might arise during an apprenticeship fell to the county courts. These disputes produced a substantial collection of cases recorded in court order books and were occasionally more thoroughly documented in county judgment papers, a potentially rich source that can illuminate interactions between families of color and the white craftspeople to whom their children were bound. Because there is no other continuous and intimate source of documentation for the study of relationships between white and Black Virginians for so long a period, understanding how this institution functioned at the local level is critical.

Butler presents a detailed discussion of the relationship of the free Black Banks family and the family of Walter and Judith Leake.[58] The court orders for the indentures and petitions for Gideon, Jane, Louisa, Agnes, Jacob, John, and Judy Banks span a period of thirty years.[59] Butler suggests that Jacob Banks's successful petition for a release from his indenture to Elisha Leake so that he could be apprenticed to carpenter Peter Pollock demonstrates the Goochland court's responsiveness to complaints of indentured people of color.

Because Goochland Judgments were still unprocessed, Butler did not have access to nineteen-year-old Jane Banks's 1762 complaint "that she ought not by Law to be compelled" to continue serving Judith Leake. She had been advised that she should have been "discharged from her service" at age eighteen and paid her "Freedom Dues," but that Leake had refused to do so. The court decreed in July 1763 that "the petitioner recover her freedom & that she is discharged from any further service by the said Judith and that the said Judith pay her Three pounds ten shillings currt Money for her Freedom dues."[60] This newly available source further underscores Butler's point.

The indenture of Benjamin Via recorded in the vestry book of Fredericksville Parish also illuminates relationships between white and Black families, where neighbors availed themselves of apprenticeships and Black apprentices were able to negotiate terms, to a degree, with their white masters. In 1755, Via, a one-year-old "poor mulatto boy" was bound "by and with the Consent of his mother Mary Via" to Andrew Ray "until he shall attain to the age of thirty-one years."[61] Mary Via and Andrew Ray were neighbors and lived on the Rivanna River, near where the Rivanna Reservoir is now located, in a part of Louisa County that was incorporated into Albemarle in 1761. A second apprenticeship indenture between

Andrew Ray and Benjamin Via was recorded in Pittsylvania County in 1775, just before Via reached his twenty-first birthday.[62] It stated that Andrew possessed the services of Benjamin "bye Indenture descending to" Andrew—who was not the Andrew referred to in the 1755 indenture but probably a younger son.[63]

This second Andrew was styled a "planter" in the Pittsylvania deed; Benjamin Via probably engaged in the same agricultural routines as his master and was incorporated into the plantation "family." Because Via's labor would have been vitally important on a farm, it was in Andrew Ray's interest to secure as much of the remaining ten years of his apprentice's indenture as possible while avoiding the risk of provoking him to run away or sue for his freedom under the terms of a 1765 statute that limited apprenticeship indentures for males to the age of twenty-one.[64] For his part, it was unlikely Via would win a freedom suit, and running away would forfeit his freedom dues and probably result in additional years of service.

Some sort of compromise was in order and the two agreed to split the difference. Ray's deposition in the Pittsylvania County Deed Book suggests that more was involved than the value of Via's labor. Citing "divers Causes and Considerations but more Especially" his "Good will" toward "the sd Benjamin Via," Ray thus discharged his apprentice "from all former Indentures" in exchange for a new indenture, agreed to by "Via of his own free will" that he would "faithfully and truly . . . Serve" Ray from the present date (May 19, 1775) until Christmas day 1779, when Via would "pass a free man."[65]

Like Via's original thirty-one years, Butler writes about indentures to the age of thirty-one for illegitimate mixed-race children of white women as encoded in Virginia law between 1691 and 1765.[66] The term or length of indenture was occasionally recorded in court orders or in apprenticeship indentures. In June 1749, Bathsheba Holloway, a four-year-old "mulatto bastard girl," was indentured in Louisa County until she reached the age of thirty-one years. In Albemarle County, twins Janey Brown and Lucy Hagar, "mulatto bastards" of Ann Brown, were bound out as infants, Janey at three months and Lucy at six months. Both were indentured to serve thirty-one-year terms.[67] As noted above, service to the age of thirty-one was eliminated in 1765 because it was viewed as "an unreasonable severity towards such children."[68]

The Virginia General Assembly passed an act in 1786 requiring the Overseers of the Poor in each district to compile monthly lists of orphans.[69] However, there are the only two lists in the papers of the Overseers of the Poor for Albemarle, Fluvanna, Goochland, and Louisa Counties that comply with the assembly's 1786 directive. At some point in the late 1790s, the Goochland Overseers submitted a list to the county court naming fourteen children, their parents, and their dates of birth. This and other eighteenth-century lists do not identify people by race but other records indicate that the children of two of the mothers listed were people of color and the children of the third mother listed were white. Similarly, in 1787, the Overseers of the Poor in the northeast district of Albemarle County presented a list of six orphans to the court, including at least one young man of color.[70]

The provenance of these documents exemplifies the evolving nature of historical research. The Albemarle list comes from an "unprocessed" box of documents that contains a miscellaneous collection of court papers, including lists of insolvents (people who did not pay an annual tax), and an odd assortment of records for the Overseers of the Poor. The Goochland list is from a collection now titled "Apprenticeship Indentures," with a note indicating that these are miscellaneous papers of the Overseers of the Poor. The Goochland papers include an important letter Butler cites from Philip Pleasants concerning the son and daughters of Aggy Cooper that he found among "Goochland County Miscellaneous Court Papers, 1728–1740," an extensive collection of unprocessed manuscripts stored in large cardboard boxes during the years of Butler's research.[71] It is a testimony to the thoroughness of Butler's research that he ever encountered this document. Since then, the Library of Virginia has catalogued hundreds of such boxes, sorting manuscripts into categories like "Free Negro and Slave Records," "Judgments," "Overseers of the Poor," and many other groupings that facilitate research. As noted above, the Library of Virginia has also placed online large collections of indexed images related to the history of free and enslaved people of color. Needless to say, researching African American history now is nothing at all like it was when Butler reviewed primary sources at the Goochland Courthouse and worked his way through countless boxes of dusty, unprocessed papers at the Library of Virginia.

The examples of Banks, Via, and the listing of orphans are indicative of steps in a logical organization to the processes followed by local courts in deciding who would serve an apprenticeship, resolving problems occurring during a child's apprenticeship, and assuring that the apprentice was freed from the indenture and received freedom dues at the end of the term of service. These procedures can be displayed as a flowchart showing the sequential steps in the process for managing juvenile apprenticeships. Because the processes derive from the implementation of laws regulating the care and training of poor children, we see the same functions employed in the court records of Goochland, Albemarle, and Louisa Counties.

The steps shown here followed the traditional legal process of hearing and issuing decrees on controversies that came before the county justices on court days and were recorded in county minute and court order books. The court would issue an order that a child be bound out, and it fell to the vestry before 1786, and to the Overseers of the Poor thereafter, to carry out the order. They had to find a suitable person to whom the child could be bound and then draft an apprenticeship indenture formalizing the

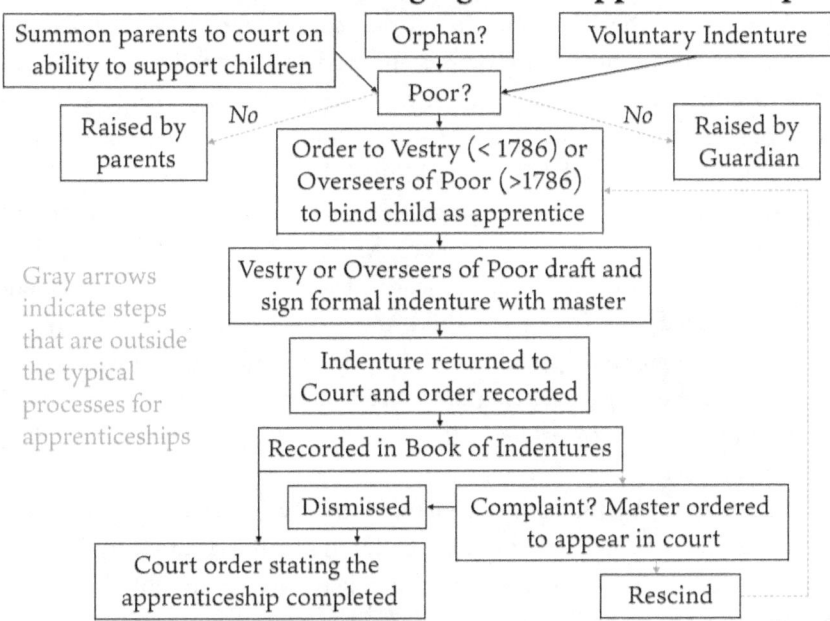

Court processes for managing child apprenticeships

apprenticeship. This document was supposed to be returned to the court. Most counties preserved string-bound bundles of apprenticeship indentures, similar to bundles of manuscript wills and deeds. Originally stored in file cabinets at the courthouse for future review, they now can be found for many counties among the county loose papers at the Library of Virginia.[72] The indenture might also be copied into parish registers or, after 1786, into books maintained by the Overseers of the Poor that might be called the "Orphan's Book," "Book of Indentures," or some similar title. As a result, there was significant variation in how different counties maintained their records of apprenticeship indentures. It is worth noting that the apprenticeship indentures transcribed into the vestry book of Fredericksville Parish (1742–87), which was part of Louisa County before 1761 and fell into Albemarle after that year, are unique among local surviving parish vestry books.[73]

The following paragraphs describe each step in the flowchart. While county courts exercised considerable power over the care and education of children, the welfare of the poor was in many ways a community endeavor, the common responsibility of neighbors, the parish, and the vestry or Overseers of the Poor. The stated purpose of juvenile apprenticeship was to provide instruction in some useful trade so that children would become productive members of the community, rather than paupers. Three ways of recruiting juvenile apprentices are shown at the top of the chart.

When the male head of household died, his children were considered orphans, even if the widow survived. If the estate of the deceased parent was insufficient to support an orphan, the court would order the orphan child bound out to a craftsperson to learn a trade. If the estate was sufficient to educate, feed, and clothe the child, the orphan could be raised by the mother with a guardian appointed by the court to manage the estate until the child reached legal age. Guardians were supposed to return an annual account of the orphan's estate to the county court during a session called Orphan's Court.

Actions taken by the county court and the Overseers of the Poor were framed as being for the benefit of the children and the community. Parents occasionally objected when a child was taken from them, however, complaining that the court had intervened against their will and contrary to the child's best interests.[74] The court could also summon parents to appear in court and demonstrate that they had the means to support and properly raise their children.[75]

With the replacement of the parish vestry by the Overseers of the Poor in 1786, efforts to evaluate the situation of certain poor or problem families were apparently renewed. Although no Louisa County order book for 1786 survives, tickets for court orders from 1786 summoning Joseph Hawkins, Charles Sprouse, and Joseph Ore, "being disorderly persons," and two tickets summoning Mary Thacker were issued.[76] There is no evidence that their children were indentured as apprentices. In 1798, the Albemarle court bound out George and William Booth because "the estate was not sufficient for support."[77]

Occasionally a parent would request that their child be bound out. In 1758, Catharine Martin wrote to the Goochland court requesting "an Order of Court Directing the Church Wardens of Saint James Northam Parish to bind my Son Francis Martin unto William French to Learn the trade of a Taylor." The county court responded favorably to her petition.[78] Voluntary indentures appear more common among white parents than free women of color. None were encountered in the eighteenth-century orders of known families of color in Albemarle, Goochland, or Louisa Counties. They might have existed, but as Butler observes, free women of color who were in a common-law marriage or married to enslaved men were liable to have their children indentured, regardless of their financial status.[79]

Juvenile indentures were not the only court function in which race played a significant role. There were racial differences in the ways county courts, parish church wardens, and later the Overseers of the Poor confronted the problem of illegitimate children. A grand jury presentment was the first legal action taken against a woman delivering a "bastard child." Since illegitimate children did not have legal fathers, they were considered orphans and required by law to be bound out. The mother might be fined five hundred pounds of tobacco or fifty shillings to cover costs to the parish for caring for a bastard child if the "reputed father" did not give security.[80] A bastardy bond could be issued if the father was identified, and he would be required to pay the parish for maintenance of the child until the child was bound out. Grand jury presentments, fines, and bastardy bonds in the records of Albemarle, Goochland, and Louisa Counties appear only for single white women. Why there are none for single free women of color is a perplexing question because the laws on illegitimacy applied to all women. This is a topic ripe for further investigation, made possible by the digitized sources now available.[81]

Between 1746 and 1782, Louisa County order books and the Fredericksville Parish Vestry Book identify twenty-eight children described as a "bastard child" or a "base born child."[82] Because there are gaps in the Louisa orders, it is likely more illegitimate children were indentured there. In Albemarle, George Welch, a "bastard child," was bound out in 1745; the same order book entry bound Joseph Welch and Hannah Welch, the "mulatto" children of Eleanor Welch, to Edwin Hickman. Although this court order does not explicitly state that George was Eleanor's "mulatto" son or that Joseph and Hannah were "bastards," it is likely that all three children were people of color and illegitimate.[83] Fredericksville Parish became part of Albemarle after 1761 and the apprenticeship indentures for four "bastard" children were transcribed into the vestry book between 1761 and 1763. In addition, nine illegitimate children, one described as a "natural son," were recorded in Albemarle order books between 1791 and 1799. In all, at least sixteen children were recorded as being illegitimate in Albemarle records between 1744 and 1799 and another thirteen were so identified between 1817 and 1844. In Albemarle and Louisa no grand jury presentments, fines, or bastardy bonds are known for determining the reputed fathers of illegitimate children of color. The children's status is identified only through apprenticeship records.

Freedom Suits

Butler discusses the freedom suits of four individuals: James Hoosling, John Russell, Samuel Miles, and Hannah McCrae, also known as Hannah Moorman. Butler cites a 1759 court order for Russell, "a Negro & poor person who supposes he is entitled to freedom & is detained as a Slave by David Mimes & Thomas Drumwright."[84] Aside from the entries in an account book, he offers no further information on the suits by Hoosling and Russell, concluding that "the records do not allow speculation about the provenance of Russell's claim," and that the outcome of his suit was unknown. However, these two suits were important, he suggests, because they were "relatively early, far removed from the subsequent rise in freedom suits after the 1770s."[85]

The organization of Goochland records at the Library of Virginia when Butler worked there made it highly unlikely that he would encounter papers from the Russell suit among the many boxes containing bundles of loose court papers. The papers have since been flat-filed and are now located in the boxes of Goochland Judgment papers. John Russell's petition claiming that he was illegally detained as a slave was supported by five depositions, revealing that Russell claimed descent from a Native woman through the female line. Willmouth Starke testified that fifty-five years earlier, in about 1710, her father, Thomas Turner, purchased a woman, "Indian Mary," and that her mother "seem'd to be displeased with her Father . . . for buying an Indian." Willmouth was not aware that Mary had filed any claim to freedom, but her daughter Nann, John Russell's mother, unsuccessfully petitioned the King and Queen County court for freedom around 1746. Citing "her long black hair & Tawny Complexion," deponent James Farguson confirmed "Indian Mary's" identity. Although Russell's suit abated with his death in June 1762, it documents a prior freedom suit and an ambiguity about the legal status of enslaved Natives between 1710 and 1720.[86]

An earlier suit in Goochland County reveals additional details about mid-eighteenth-century petitions for freedom. In September 1750, Jack Hatcher, known as "Indian Jack," filed such a petition against John Parish.[87] Hatcher's petition claimed that he was "the son of Sarah the Daughter of an Indian free Woman," who "by Circumvention & indirect practice was kidnap'd into servitude in this Colony" and "detained in Bondage . . . contrary (as he humbly apprehends) to all Natural Right, Equity & Justice."[88] Asserting matrilineal descent from a free Indigenous woman, an essential element in successful freedom suits based on Native ancestry, Hatcher also invoked a conception of natural rights later deployed by Thomson Mason in the 1772 landmark case *Robin v. Hardaway*.[89] Mason then argued that enslavements of Native peoples were "infractions of the federal as well as natural rights of those people." As historian Honor Sachs observes, "The possibility of abolition unleashed by natural rights thinking remained in the realm of intellectual exercise" until Mason "applied such arguments to a case involving the actual liberation of slaves."[90]

Another aspect of this case deserves greater attention. Deponents Robert Napier and John McQuarry were asked specifically about the status of Native Americans brought into Virginia: were they to serve as slaves or as indentured servants? According to Napier, Jack Hatcher's grandmother Betty was "was brought in to this Collony By the said Edward Hatcher an Indian trader & sold by him to serve according to Law." Napier had purchased a teenaged Indigenous boy from "the same company," understanding "that he expected he was to serve only to the age of thirtyone or thirtythree." McQuarry told the court about "three Indian men" brought "into New Kent County" and sold there some forty years ago who successfully sued for their freedom. He also knew of a Native woman with two daughters who was said to have "served her time," but he could not say whether she "died a servant or free."[91] In evaluating "Indian Jack's" petition, the Goochland court sought relevant precedent on the status of Natives brought into the commonwealth.

At the time of Jack Hatcher's suit, the exact dates on which Betty and other Natives arrived in Virginia had no special legal significance. In the 1750s, the act of 1705 codifying the law of slavery in the commonwealth was not thought to repeal the 1682 act legalizing Indian slavery.[92] As might be expected, the evidence regarding status could be ambiguous. Robert Napier said that Betty, Jack's grandmother, was sold "to serve according to Law." Whether Betty was sold as a slave or as an indentured servant is unclear. Napier himself illustrated this fluidity of status when he purchased a Native boy as an indentured servant, bound to "serve only" into his early thirties.

McQuarry's deposition is noteworthy because it demonstrates that even in early eighteenth-century Virginia, enslaving Native people might be challenged in court. In 1754, he described a freedom suit "about forty years past" against John Aldridge in New Kent County where three "Indians Imployed Alexander McKinney to get them free, which he did."[93] In July 1754, a jury found Judith Parish guilty of falsely imprisoning Jack Hatcher. But Parish made a plea to stay judgment and the case was in court again in February 1756 when she was ordered to pay forty shillings' damages.[94] The court learned that Hatcher had not yet been freed in June 1756, and noted that "it still remains undetermined whether the said Jack shall obtain his Freedom."[95]

Perhaps the most challenging aspect of freedom suits is not documenting the fascinating genealogies that connect an enslaved person to a free mother but rather the mechanisms employed by traders, planters, and merchants to transform free people into slaves. Moving indentured children from one county to another was a common tactic, discussed by Butler in his account of Japheth Towler's attempt to move Rachel Cooper's sons out of Goochland County without her consent. In another county the free status of children might not be known and they could be sold as slaves. Certificates attesting to freedom or indentures of apprenticeship could be lost or destroyed, making it necessary to consult a lawyer and petition the court for freedom. It could take years to gather depositions and present a case to the court: Jack Hatcher petitioned for his freedom in 1750 and a jury ruled in his favor in 1754, but he was still held in bondage in 1756 pending an appeal. As Butler found in Goochland County, "only six persons in the county gained free status" through freedom suits.[96]

Butler's thorough review of Goochland court orders indicates that he was aware of Jack Hatcher's case but decided not to include it in an otherwise comprehensive review of Goochland freedom suits. Why? The eighteenth-century statutes regulating the free population of color almost always enumerated them as applying to "negroes, mulattoes, and Indians."[97] To understand why this case was excluded and why Butler did not include a discussion of Native enslavement we must consider the context of Native American slavery within the larger study of slavery at the time Butler wrote.[98] As the title of his study suggests, his focus was on "the *free Black* community." In conversations we had on the topic in 2001 after I encountered *Hatcher v. Parish's Adm'x* in Goochland Chancery Records at the Library of Virginia, Butler insisted on the distinction between African American and Native American identity. He certainly knew that many African Americans claimed Native American ancestry and that it had sometimes opened a window for "passing" into white society. But as a person who came of age during the civil rights movement of the 1960s, Butler felt that a fragmentation of identity was a threat to African American solidarity and to the political, social, and economic progress of African Americans. I think it fair to say that Butler's strong focus on Black identity and the relative novelty of publications on Native American ancestry within the Black population at the time he was working on his dissertation influenced his decision not to pursue questions concerning Native American slavery and freedom that emerge from research in the records of Goochland and other central Virginia counties.

Genealogies

The section that follows gives a detailed account of the family of William Scott, a Goochland apprentice described as a "mulatto" who was the plaintiff in an unusual suit initiated against his blacksmith master on his behalf by a Quaker member of the Overseers of the Poor. Interestingly, the research recently made possible by digitized sources reveals that the Scotts were Butler's ancestors. Butler always wrote with discerning sensitivity about the intimate lives of ordinary people, their personal relationships, and the communities in which their families were embedded. I offer this section in this very spirit, to demonstrate what kinds of stories we are able to reconstruct now, using all the sources that have become available in this century.

William Scott

The suit styled *William Scott, assee. v. James Quigg* is one of only two court cases with depositions involving apprenticeship encountered thus far in central Virginia.[99] Scott's case was filed in March 1801 in Goochland County and abated in May 1805 with Quigg's death.[100] Scott was a young man of color, although he was not so identified in his indenture. When I first encountered this suit in 2013, it was filed in a box of Goochland County "Miscellaneous Papers" that included apprenticeship indentures, court orders to bind out children, bastardy bonds, and other documents related to the care of poor children by the vestry and Overseers of the Poor. This collection contained many documents from the 1760s and 1770s, with the earliest dating to 1738. Papers in this collection were recatalogued recently, and the Library of Virginia now has digital images for *William Scott v. James Quigg* posted on "Virginia Untold."[101] Given the importance of apprenticeship in revealing intimate interactions between free Black families and the families of the white craftspeople to which they were bound, one of the goals of this discussion is to spur the search for similar cases.

The suit was initiated by Thomas F. Bates, a Quaker and one of the Overseers of the Poor for Goochland County. Bates had drafted and signed the apprenticeship indenture that constituted a contractual agreement between William Scott and James Quigg. On the reverse side of the indenture Bates wrote that he wished "a writ to issue directly" against Quigg for breaking the "Covenant." Bates sought to assess Quigg five hundred dollars for damages because "Quigg has totally neglected his education, Teaching the Trade," and failed to pay Scott his "freedom dues." This copy of the original indenture noted that Scott "was born 18th July 1779" and therefore had reached the age of twenty-one and the termination of his apprenticeship.[102] "William did in all parts comply with the said covenant," Bates charged, and had kept "the same towards the said James Quigg." On March 26, 1801, a summons was issued to Quigg to appear in court and respond.[103]

Our understanding of why Bates charged Quigg with breaking the indenture covenant depends on two depositions and a receipt for medications. The deposition of teacher Samuel Cosby as a witness for Scott, taken in November 1803, addressed the failure to educate Scott and suggests that many masters hired teachers to instruct free children of color but that instruction time was very limited. Cosby recalled that Quigg "entered a mulatto boy by the name of William Scott as a schollar under him" in 1796, but "the said boy never attended his school but twenty days the whole year, & that he never heard of the boy's going to any other school whatever." Cosby's deposition included an extraordinary exchange between the teacher and Scott (the plaintiff), followed by questions from Quigg (the defendant):

> Question by the Plaintiff—How did I behave while [in] your school,
> Answer—there was no remissness
> Question by the Plaintiff—How did I learn while at your school
> Answer—pretty well
> Question by the Plaintiff—what time did I generally get to school
> Answer—some times late
> Question by the Plaintiff—what time did I return from school
> Answer—some times you were calld on rather early
> Question by the Defnt—Was not your school ended early in the Faul
> Answer—Yes
> Question by the Deft—Did I not send the Plaintiff till the end of the School
> Ansr—Yes
> Question by the Deft—Did I not enter the Plaint on the 5th of July of the above date
> Ansr—You did[104]

Virginia law stipulated that no "negro, mulatto, or Indian be admitted to give evidence but against or between negroes, mulattoes or Indians," but did not prohibit the examination, or questions from, people of color during a deposition.[105]

William Scott's schooling and training as a blacksmith apparently were limited due to health issues. Robert Smith testified for Quigg on the charge of failing to teach Scott a trade and Quigg's care of him. He said Scott began his apprenticeship as an unhealthy child and "was in such an ill state of health" when he "first went to live with the said Quigg that he was not able to work at the black smiths trade." Smith did not know how long the sickly apprentice had studied with Cosby but noted that he was "an idle boy & difficult to manage." Quigg had been "at considerable trouble in getting the said Scott cured of the complaint," and concluded, "instead of a profit to the sd Quigg," the "well fed & clothed" apprentice was in Smith's "opinion altogether a disadvantage."[106]

A receipt for medical treatment was the only other surviving evidence in the case.[107] Among the medications purchased were calomel (a mercury-based purgative sometimes used to treat worms), jalap (another purgative), camphor (a topical treatment for fungal infections), sulfur (used as a laxative and for topical treatment), and Rochelle salts (another laxative). Given the nature of these medications it is not surprising that Smith considered Scott "idle."[108] No verdict was returned due to James Quigg's death, so it is uncertain how the jury assessed the depositions.

The complaint of breach of covenant filed by Bates and the depositions in William Scott's case reveal the interactions and views of members of the Goochland community that are indicative of Butler's observation that "juvenile apprenticeship brought into play actors with different investments in and experiences of the system." It is unfortunate that the depositions of two other witnesses for Scott, Connerly Mullins and Wright Moreland, were not preserved with the papers of this case. Their statements might have further revealed what Butler describes as "levels of interaction [that] illuminate the interlocked domains of race and status that free Blacks inhabited."[109]

Although no information about William Scott's family was included among the papers in this case, Butler's goal of revealing the "interlocked domains of race and status" can be furthered by a reconstruction of the Scott family. The court order to bind out William recorded that he was Robert Scott's son, and his indenture described him as "a poor boy."[110] With the exception of 1794, Robert Scott was listed in Goochland personal property taxes for the upper district from 1791 to 1798; in 1798, he was also included

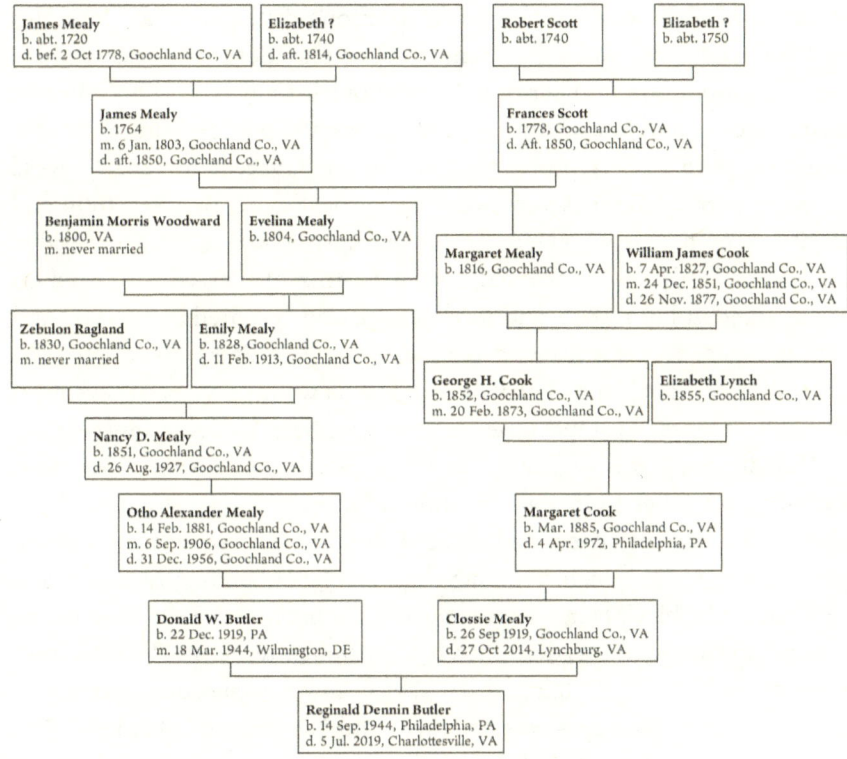

Reginald D. Butler's family tree

in a list of insolvents who did not pay the county levy.[111] Nothing is known of where Scott lived prior to 1791, although he may have been from Henrico County where a number of Scotts were identified as "Indian." His subsequent absence from the Goochland records suggests he may have died in 1798 or 1799, and a court order was issued in July 1805 to "bind out James Scott and Robert Scott children of Robert Scott deceased."[112]

By combining residences in the lists of free Blacks with the locations of property in the 1815 land tax, we can determine with some precision where William Scott lived after his apprenticeship with Quigg, whose property was located nine miles northwest of the courthouse near the northern branches of Lickinghole Creek, and suggest likely family connections. The first list of free people of color living in Goochland's upper district (1804) includes an entry for William Scott, a farmer, residing "at Samuel

Robinson's." Following Luther Porter Jackson's distinction, "at" indicates that Robinson was probably a renter.[113] The only deed in Goochland indexed for Robinson is an April 1805 deed of trust mortgaging his animals, farming tools, and household property to pay a debt.[114] In 1805, Scott was living on John Hicks's property, described as adjacent to Rice Graves's property and seven miles northwest of the courthouse. Between 1804 and 1809, several people who were almost certainly related to William resided on Hicks's land. These included Joshua Scott, a planter who is listed on Hicks's land in 1804, 1805, and 1809. Joshua also appeared in the 1800 and 1801 personal property taxes as living at Johnson Hodges's, about ten miles northwest of Goochland Courthouse.[115] Joshua would have been seventeen or eighteen years old at that time and may have been Hodges's apprentice.[116]

William Scott was registered as a free person of color in Goochland County in October 1805, a few months after the suit against James Quigg abated, and was then described as "aged about Twenty six or twenty seven years about [5' 5¾"] high, a bright yellow com[plex]ion (approaching near to white) strat black hair, was free born."[117] In his March 1806 Goochland register, Joshua Scott was described in very similar terms, as about twenty-three years old and 5'7 tall with a "light yellow complexion approaching nearly to white, blue eyes was born free and has straight black hair." The county clerk may have included the hair descriptions as a perceived feature of Native identity.[118]

Noel Smith, a carpenter, was also living on John Hicks's land in 1804. When he married Peggy Scott in January 1803, William Scott was the surety for the marriage. He was also the surety on Frankey Scott's marriage bond to James Mealy in January 1803. The two couples were married on consecutive days, January 5 and 6, and the fact that William Scott served as a surety or witness with their prospective husbands on the marriage bonds indicates that he was the brides' closest living relative who could fulfill this requirement.

William probably died in 1808 or 1809 because the last entry for him in the Goochland tax lists was in 1807. In the following years Joshua assumed the responsibility of serving as surety on marriage bonds. He was the surety when James Scott married Amey Bennett in January 1814. Joshua again served as surety when Christopher Scott and Patsy Sims were married in December 1817.[119]

Described in 1809 as "aged & infirm & can do but little housework," Eliza Scott, listed between 1806 and 1813, was probably Robert Scott's widow and mother of his children. Her care appears to have been shared among her children. In 1806, she was living with Noel and her presumed daughter Peggy Smith. In 1807, she lived with William Scott. In 1809, she appeared on John Hicks's land with Joshua Scott. There is no listing for her in 1810 but she reappeared in 1811, "Betty Scott mulatto at Joshua Scott housework," and in 1812 living with Joshua and Christopher on John Lewis's land. Nothing is known about her aside from these entries.[120]

Butler determined that Scott was one of the eight most common surnames among Goochland free Black residents.[121] Indeed, sorting the many Scotts into their appropriate families is an arduous task. The Scotts, like many free people of color, did not own land, but the family must have been well known during the twenty-some years they lived in this part of the county. Their rentals and the locations where they served their indentures were within walking distance of Betty Granthum's land, where James and Frankey (Scott) Mealy, Reginald Butler's ancestors, lived and which served as an anchor of stability and refuge for related families of color.

Butler's accounts of the lives of Goochland's free Black population are enriched and grounded in his meticulous reconstructions of families of color. This narrative of what is presented as the family of Robert and Eliza Scott is an example of what might be done to reconstruct free families of color in the spirit of Butler's work by using clues from the sources described in this essay. The combined details on the Scott family from Goochland records establishes a larger context for the suit Bates filed on behalf of William Scott. Likewise, Reginald Butler's painstaking research in the sources available to him established the foundation for further work on the history of free people of color in central Virginia and throughout the plantation South. His book provides a broad interpretative framework for newly accessible documents, enabling scholars to build on his compelling arguments. Butler would have been particularly interested in the elaboration of family networks that were central to his project—and which would have helped clarify his own family's genealogy. Utilizing the same sources Butler used, genealogy documents facts from the lives of individuals and groups them into interconnected families. Butler's Goochland study goes beyond the begats to reconstruct communities of interacting Black and white families, creating an intricate social context for illuminating and interpreting family histories.

Butler's Future for the Past

In 2001, Reginald Butler gave me a fat folder of his photocopies and research notes on Goochland County. He also shared files he created in Nutshell, an early database application. At the time I had been gathering information on free people of color in Albemarle County for about six years and sharing my finds with Butler and his students, who came to my house to work on genealogies of Albemarle families of color from the records I had transcribed. Butler thought his notes would help me identify individuals from Goochland and recognized that his study was incomplete without some account of people who migrated from Goochland to Albemarle and other counties. While attempting to define and address Butler's broad research interests for this essay and what future research in the spirit of his work would entail, I reviewed the old Nutshell files and discovered several text files from Butler's graduate school days at Johns Hopkins. These supplement the accounts of Gertrude Fraser in her preface above and Scot French in his essay below and describe Butler's developing ideas about history and historical explanation.

While at Hopkins Fraser describes Butler's exposure to a multidisciplinary approach to history that involved concepts from anthropology, medicine, linguistics, economics, and other fields that he integrated into his vision of social history. The development of these ideas is present in his notes from an American Anthropological Association meeting he attended in the late 1980s. They trace Butler's search for explanatory concepts for his research in Goochland County. The breadth of his interests is reflected in the notes. From the sessions on language he asked, "How is gender constructed in ordinary discourse?" and "Why do cultural models have power?" He continued, "Because they are embedded in larger models. They are parts of other cultural contexts." Considering context, he asked, "Were there differing views of midwives within the Afro-American community itself?" Finally, he listed some chapters, perhaps to be included in his dissertation:

- Social Representation of Death
- Midwives as a case study

- On memory and the use of history
- Illness and Health Modeling, the idea of control
- The Process of Devaluation vs Resistance
- Renewal, rebirth, religious experience at adolescence at revival time

The chapter list demonstrates a breadth of questioning about the social life of African Americans during this evolving phase of seeking models to integrate and explain what he was discovering about free Black life in the Goochland Courthouse.

The documentation of Butler's research is reflected in the scope of his Nutshell files. He created separate databases for census, land tax, manumissions, registrations, tithes, occupations, parents, masters, and free Black marriages. He did not use Microsoft Access but certainly would have integrated these separate data files into a relational database to better explore the records he recorded. And Butler would applaud the work at the Library of Virginia in scanning and indexing free Black and slave records, placing them online, and creating a search interface that enables users to find records based on a variety of filtering criteria.

Scot French's discussion of "Race and Place" provides a thorough account of Butler's focus on the importance of local history.[122] In 2004, Butler supported an innovative integration of database technology and local history when I discovered that property lines were inked onto 1937 aerial photos between 1940 and 1942 for the "Albemarle Mapping Project." On the reverse side of the photos the numbered parcels listed the landowners, with African American landowners indicated by placing "(col)" after their names. Steve Thompson and I photographed the entire set of aerial photos at the Albemarle County Real Estate Office. I used ArcGIS to georegister the photos and digitize the property lines, creating a geodatabase. Butler provided the funds to purchase an extension to ArcGIS that produced an interactive map of land ownership by race for Albemarle's Rivanna district. This map supported Boolean queries that allowed users to filter properties based on several criteria, such as race and acreage. The map was online from 2004 until about 2018, when Erik Irtenkauf updated it by digitizing the remaining Albemarle County property parcels and moving the data to a more robust map server, ArcGIS Online. African American communities and landowners can be explored through the Faded Contours project website (https://www.fadedcontours.com/albemarle1940/). Butler's support for such projects is indicative of a broad vision of methods of historical research that take advantage of new technologies to document and recreate historical African American communities.

The use of software tools to aggregate and publish data is more apparent in the projects Butler supported as director of the Carter G. Woodson Institute for African-American and African Studies than in his book. In his book we see an emphasis on organizing the information he collected on individuals and families into the broader themes that defined the legal, political, and societal institutions that structured and constrained free Black life in Goochland and, more broadly, in Virginia. The loosely related proposed chapters Butler considered as a graduate student were replaced by chapters that explicitly defined the boundaries between free and enslaved life and the resulting relationships between Black and white people as they navigated a complex legal landscape. What he retained from his graduate training was an appreciation of how explanatory models from other disciplines, in particular anthropology, could provide an interpretive context for social relationships.

Butler's prologue on infanticide is developed through the contexts of liminality and rites of passage, "larger models ... of other cultural contexts" that he uses as an interpretative framework.[123] The discussion of infanticide is narrated as a form of a "social drama," another concept developed by Victor Turner that provides an additional explanatory context for conflict and crisis resolution.[124] Although Butler does not cite Turner, the influence is clear and can be directly traced to Butler's multidisciplinary graduate education, especially in the first chapter he envisioned, the "Social Representation of Death."

"Thick description" is another technique for understanding social life Butler borrowed from anthropology and deployed throughout his Goochland study.[125] It involves understanding not just the actions but also the motivations of actors in a situation. It accounts for the richness of the narratives in Butler's book. For example, Butler's extended discussion of the financial arrangements of John and Milly Pierce with white patrons records the facts of these arrangements and describes how they were beneficial to both parties.[126] His account of the contractual nature of juvenile apprenticeship recognizes the reciprocal relationships between white planters and craftspeople and the parents of the children apprenticed to them. Parents could protest mistreatment to the court, and as we learn from the case of

William Scott, a member of the Overseers of the Poor could even act *in loco parentis* for the child's benefit. Such details might be found in the archival weeds, but one person's weed is another's flower when it blossoms into an understanding of personal motivations underlying documentary records.

In my essay I have attempted to emulate some of Butler's techniques and focused on detailed narratives of individuals that create a social context for the manuscripts used to document free Black life. Butler called his approach "social history" and played a leading role in the Central Virginia Social History Research Group; Joshua Rothman's essay describes Butler's years in graduate school as a period of florescence of "new social history" as a technique for understanding the past. As a student Butler wondered why "cultural models have power," and his words suggest a vision of nested models with each layer providing a unique explanatory framework. This approach suggests that Butler's path for future historical research would involve a cross-pollination of ideas and theory from an array of disciplines. For example,

- Demographic and economic determinants of migration
- Regional studies: what defines a region? See, for example, James River versus Southside
- Social network analysis to depict relations among individuals and groups
- Geospatial databases using a time slider to focus on place and date
- Expanding family genealogies into kinship networks
- Ecological models for settlement: soil types, available land, water
- Structural models for legal processes, for example, an apprenticeship flowchart
- Memory and the use of history (in Butler's 1980s chapter list)
- More indexed databases of primary sources (AI generated prosopography?)
- Religion and community organization
- Poverty

Other themes could be added to this list but none of the bullets captures the true strength of Butler's approach to history. Butler tells us that his family has deep roots in Goochland County and candidly discusses his own stake in his research.[127] But many individuals have roots in the areas they choose to study and have not produced histories as comprehensive or as insightful.

In *The Idea of History,* R. G. Collingwood may reveal the best answer for future histories done in the spirit of Butler's work as a historian of Goochland County and as the director of a major institution for academic research.[128] Collingwood asks, "What is history for?" and answers that it is for human self-knowledge. For me this succinctly sums up Butler's vocation as a historical researcher and his intense search for explanatory frameworks to make sense of the records he encountered. And so, I would suggest that lists of topics to study are less important than programs that inspire motivated students to look beyond the confines of canonical texts in their discipline, broaden the scope of their inquiries, and seek explanations that enhance their own understanding of the past.

A "Forceful and Effective" Leader

Reginald D. Butler's Intellectual Legacy as Director of the Carter G. Woodson Institute, 1996–2005

SCOT A. FRENCH

With all the different kinds of history we practice, there is still no intellectual history of academic administration—no awareness that administrators might intend their actions as argument by other means, might see their work as creating not just discrete possibilities for others' inquiries, but whole fields of inquiry.

> —PETER N. MILLER, "Argument by Other Means: Toward an Intellectual History of Academic Administration," *Perspectives on History* (2016)

In the sixteen years between the completion of his Johns Hopkins history PhD in 1989 and his retirement as director of the University of Virginia (UVa)'s Carter G. Woodson Institute for African-American and African Studies in 2005, Reginald D. Butler engaged in a fundamental "rethinking" of African American and African Studies (AAAS) in the digital age. Inspired by his fruitful collaborations with local researchers and archivists on his dissertation and book manuscript, Butler sought to institutionalize a new model of community-centered, digitally enabled research that would engage emerging scholars from underrepresented groups, incentivize cooperation between academic and lay scholars, and create publicly accessible digital platforms for shared research data and finding aids.

Butler articulated his argument for new directions in AAAS through a series of multiyear, grant-funded research and teaching initiatives spanning his nine-year tenure (1996–2005) as director of the Woodson Institute. Butler's administrative leadership merits attention as more than simply a biographical footnote to this posthumously published manuscript. The programs he designed, instituted, and directed were, in fact, an extension of his argument for broadly collaborative local-global studies grounded in sustained archival research and community-based networks of "local knowledge."

This essay connects Butler's self-narrated experience as a Philadelphia-born "native son" of Goochland County, interrogating the laws, customs, and cultures of segregation that prevailed in his family's ancestral homeplace from the early 1700s to the mid-1990s, to the democratizing mission he articulated as director of UVa's Woodson Institute and principal investigator on a series of grant-funded initiatives aimed at "Rethinking African-American and African Studies in the Digital Age." Part institutional history and part academic memoir, this study draws heavily on Butler's administrative correspondence—primarily grant narratives and foundation reports—and my own personal recollections of Butler as a close friend and mentor during our nearly decade-long collaboration at the Woodson Institute.

Butler hired me—then a recent Woodson Predoctoral Fellow and history ABD writing my dissertation on Nat Turner in American memory—as his assistant director in 1997, promoted me to associate director once I completed my PhD in 2000, and recommended me for appointment as interim director in 2005–6 after medical issues forced him to curtail his activity and reluctantly step down from his post. From this institutional vantage point, I observed firsthand Butler's determination to wield administrative power assertively and creatively as a means of transforming the academy from within. I shadowed him at meetings with deans and provosts, joined him on an early pilgrimage to Ford Foundation headquarters in New York City, and helped him to assemble faculty-led project teams that would carry out his vision. He welcomed me into his home, richly adorned with African and African American folk art; shared his love of music, particularly jazz and blues; talked history, culture, and politics; and occasionally invited me to join him on errands to the rural property he owned (and could not bring himself to sell) in Goochland. In later years, we traveled together to Salvador da Bahia, Brazil, and Cape Coast, Ghana, where we conferred with community leaders on the design of UVa study-abroad programs that would add a global, diasporic dimension to Butler's administrative legacy.

Reflections of a Black Scholar in the Goochland County Courthouse

Those who worked closely with Butler knew him to be an intensely private person, loathe to share personal details in public settings. Yet, in the introduction to this book, written in the mid-1990s, Butler revealed the self-consciousness he experienced as a Johns Hopkins–trained scholar returning to his family's ancestral home to conduct research in the historically white domain of the Goochland County Clerk's Office. He wrote,

> When I first entered the archival room at the Goochland County Courthouse, I was the object of much curious, perhaps anxious attention. Lawyers, real estate agents, the county clerk and his assistants, the sheriff, and an occasional genealogist—all white—worked confidently with the historical and contemporary records housed there. On the other hand, the few African American residents who came on official business invariably stood politely in the outer office and requested a clerk's employee to find whatever pertinent legal document they needed—whether for land transactions, criminal cases, marriage licenses, or traffic violations. Whites mediated access to these public resources.
>
> Though the county had been the home for generations of my maternal relatives extending back to the early eighteenth century, though I had lived there with my grandparents through adolescence, more than two decades later when I walked into that public space, I felt as if I had broken a taboo. . . . Eventually, by virtue of academic credentials, I gained access and a certain privilege in the clerk's office that remained unavailable to most African American residents.

Butler drew a direct line between the eighteenth- and nineteenth-century Black residents of Goochland and his own disruptive presence in that late-twentieth-century courthouse:

> The issue of a Black presence at the courthouse environs is of course not a new one. It proved sufficiently bothersome to nineteenth-century county administrators who, in an 1836 order, empowered the sheriff to "keep all slaves and free negroes out of the courthouse while the court is sitting unless they have business before the court." Black

county residents in the nineteenth century were strongly invested in the activities taking place at the Goochland courthouse....

By the late 1980s, however, an African American in the main archival room of the clerk's office was an oddity. What did I intend to do with the records? How had I become so familiar with the material housed within and what gave me the authority to break traditional racial and social boundaries? How would I interpret the records?

For Butler, accessing Goochland County's records to write a history of its free Black community represented a quiet victory in the everyday realm of the Black freedom struggle. It allowed him to assemble and collate the documentary records that would inform his study and reinforced his passion for archival research as the bedrock of good scholarship. In his acknowledgments, Butler thanked the county clerks by name, as well as the archivists at the Virginia State Library and Virginia Historical Society, "all of whom helped to smooth the often-rough terrain of the research process."[1]

Upon completing his PhD at Johns Hopkins in 1989, Butler was awarded a one-year Ford Foundation Postdoctoral Fellowship to work on his manuscript revisions. Later renamed Diversity Fellowships, the Fellowships for Minorities program was "designed to increase the diversity of the nation's college and university faculties by increasing their ethnic and racial diversity, maximize the educational benefits of diversity, and increase the number of professors who can and will use diversity as a resource for enriching the education of all students."[2] As an early beneficiary of the program Butler recognized the immense value of foundation support for minority recruitment and retention, and—in subsequent years, as an academic administrator at UVa—he looked to Ford and other foundations for critical funding and scholarly validation of Black community studies. As a UVa faculty member and later director of the Woodson Institute, Butler devised innovative programs to address stubbornly persistent cultural and socioeconomic barriers to graduate study and historical research among minority students. He showcased research methods in his undergraduate classes and recruited a cadre of emerging scholars to join in a systematic exploration of race and place in central Virginia and beyond.

Early Black Studies at the University of Virginia, 1969–1981

When Butler arrived at UVa in 1991, he joined a small cadre of faculty affiliated with the Woodson Institute, an interdisciplinary teaching and research fellowship program directed by Civil War historian and Black Studies pioneer Armstead L. Robinson. Robinson had been recruited by Paul Gaston in 1980 to join the History Department as an associate professor and to help create an institutional home for UVa's fledgling African American Studies program. "Armstead had a vision of what kind of program we should have," Gaston later recalled, "so although there were four people who designed the program, there was only one who dreamed it up."[3] Robinson brought impressive scholarly and activist credentials to his role as the institute's founding director. As an undergraduate at Yale University, he had helped design Yale's Black Studies program and coedited a critically acclaimed volume *Black Studies in the University: A Symposium*, published by Yale University Press in 1969. He went on to earn his doctorate in history with honors at the University of Rochester, where he studied under two leading historians of slavery, Stanley L. Engerman and Eugene D. Genovese.[4]

As a veteran of 1960s student activism at Western Washington University, Butler understood the struggle involved in creating Black Studies programs at predominantly white, recently desegregated institutions like UVa. In a brief institutional history prepared for the Ford Foundation, Butler placed the Woodson Institute's origins within that broader civil rights struggle. "The Afro-American Studies Program at the University of Virginia preceded the founding of the Woodson Institute by nearly a dozen years," he told Ford. In 1969, the university responded to student demands for minority faculty recruitment and new courses in Afro-American Studies by appointing a faculty-student Committee on Black Studies. The committee recommended establishing an introductory course and appointing an African American scholar to head an undergraduate program in Afro-American Studies, leading the College of Arts and Sciences Faculty to unanimously approve a new interdepartmental major in Afro-American Studies in March 1970. The Board of Visitors approved the new bachelor of arts degree program later that year. Here, Butler identified some of the structural weaknesses that he would later inherit as director of the Woodson Institute. "By 1980," he wrote, "a consensus had emerged among faculty, students, and administrators that the Afro-American Studies Program needed improvement," particularly in serving the needs of undergraduates: "Students and a vocal minority of Black faculty favored the establishment of a teaching-oriented Afro-American and African Studies Department."[5]

The university instead decided to create a research-oriented institute that would draw faculty from established departments to teach a few core courses while recruiting Black faculty and graduate students through various fellowship programs. In this way, planners hoped, faculty involved in the new Afro-American and African Studies program would not be isolated from their traditional disciplines or the rest of the university.

The new institute was modeled after six existing interdepartmental programs at the university: Political and Social Thought, General and Comparative Literature, Women's Studies, Linguistics, Asian Studies, and Latin American Studies. A steering committee—consisting of faculty members who taught AAAS courses or who represented departments that offered such courses—would set the curriculum, advise majors, read senior essays, and in general function like any departmental undergraduate committee. The chair of the institute would be a scholar, with a faculty appointment in a traditional department.

In April 1981, UVa announced the creation of an Institute for Afro-American and African Studies, promising that it would enhance both "teaching and research" in the field. The institute was named after Carter G. Woodson, the Virginia-born "father of Afro-American Studies." Robinson, an associate professor in the History Department, was named acting director; two assistant directors, one for curriculum and programming, and one for research and fellowships, would be named later.

The Woodson's founders offered a compelling vision of a university-wide institute, closely tied to traditional departments and actively engaged in teaching, research, and minority recruitment. Dedicated to creating and sustaining a community of AAAS scholars and teachers, it hoped to integrate its curricular and research programs into the center of UVa life. While augmenting the number of African Americanists and Africanists at Virginia, the institute would also serve as a vehicle for promoting community outreach.

From Butler's vantage point, however, "this 'utopian' vision never materialized." Without full faculty lines or teaching fellows, the institute could offer few courses of its own beyond the two large introductory surveys and a smattering of electives. Likewise, its residential research fellowship program, which averaged between six and eight fellows per year in the late 1980s, had dwindled to just three or four by the mid-1990s.[6] For the institute to thrive, Butler opined, it needed to rethink the relationship between its research and teaching functions and develop stronger ties with UVa students, faculty, and communities beyond the academy. He wrote,

> During its first fifteen years, the Institute became defined primarily as a graduate and post-graduate research center. The Institute never seized upon the opportunity to create formal alliances with traditional departments that would lead to collaboration in teaching and research. . . . At the same time, the Institute did little to foster a sense of community among University faculty teaching courses that counted toward AAS [Afro-American Studies] major. Several faculty members with joint appointments in the Afro-American and African Studies Program were allowed to drift away from the Institute, their formal commitments limited to the occasional Woodson Steering Committee or fellowship review committee meeting. Those who did teach AAS-designated courses on a regular basis rarely met to discuss the courses and their relationship to the curricular objectives of the major.[7]

Butler envisioned an institute that would foster community both within and beyond the prestigious—but programmatically insular—predoctoral and postdoctoral residential research fellowships. In the years immediately prior to his appointment as director, he found models for this kind of academic community engagement in the institute-led Venable Lane Task Force (1993–95) and an independent spinoff project, the Central Virginia Social History Research Group. Both projects engaged academic and lay scholars in the gathering and sharing of information vital to a more nuanced understanding of race and its shifting boundaries in central Virginia.

The Venable Lane Task Forces/Central Virginia Social History Project: Collaborative Research through Community Partnership

The Venable Lane Task Force emerged from an accidental discovery. In the summer of 1993, a University of Virginia construction crew grading land for the expansion of the B1/F8 parking lots on Venable Lane (then home to the Woodson Institute) unearthed what appeared to be a human grave shaft. Work was halted, and a team of UVa researchers—historians, genealogists, archaeologists—was assembled to investigate. Over the next several weeks they determined that the property had once belonged to Catherine "Kitty" Foster, a free woman of color, and that the site held as many as twelve graves. Records showed that Foster purchased the two-and-one-eighth-acre plot in 1833, and that she and her descendants owned the property until 1906. Based on the number and size of the known gravesites and their close proximity to the Foster homesite, the researchers tentatively concluded that they had stumbled on a family burial ground containing the remains of four adults and eight children.

Armstead Robinson, as director of the Woodson Institute and a leading historian of slavery and emancipation, was asked by the local newspaper to explain the significance of the site's association with an early nineteenth-century free Black family. "It's one of the least known areas for historians," he told the Charlottesville *Daily Progress*. "There isn't much known about the simple folk, black or white, because they don't leave large footprints like presidents, such as Jefferson or Monroe. There is so much that can be learned."[8] Subsequent archaeological investigations in the summers of 1994 and 1995 revealed the foundation and cellar of a house and the remains of an "elaborately paved" pedestrian walkway leading from the homesite to Jefferson Park Avenue. It was not until many years later, during archaeological excavations for the South Lawn project, that researchers discovered the full extent of the burial ground—thirty-two gravesites in all—and its connection to the surrounding free Black neighborhood known as "Canada."[9]

In June 1993, UVa established a fourteen-member Venable Lane Task Force to conduct site research, gather public input, and consider educational and commemorative possibilities for the Foster site and beyond. Robinson chaired the panel and moderated discussions at several public meetings; Butler served as one of four academic faculty members on the panel. This very public process of consultation and deliberation established an important precedent for university-community relations, long strained by the memory of slavery and segregation and the stark social inequalities between an elite university and its local labor force.[10]

Robinson's taskforce initiated a discussion of what the site *meant*—legally, politically, historically—and what value the site might hold as a commemorative space and educational resource. In doing so, the taskforce established a multidisciplinary, broadly collaborative research agenda that Butler nurtured and expanded during his tenure as Woodson director. With strong community backing, the taskforce insisted that UVa document and preserve the site without disturbing the graves or destroying the physical evidence of individuals, families, and communities of color.

Butler's scholarship on eighteenth-century Goochland County helped situate the Foster site within a long history of free Black community life and racial "mixing" in Virginia. Genealogical research further illuminated the fluid social identities of Foster family descendants, some of whom had left the region and passed as "white." Taskforce researchers—faculty, graduate students, and independent scholars—established racial "in-betweenness" and "liminality" as defining features of the Foster site, critical to its interpretation and commemoration. The Fosters inhabited a world somewhere between slavery and freedom, Black and white, citizenship and self-exile. The homesite itself occupied middle ground, beneath the sightline of the university's Jeffersonian-era Academical Village but well above the bottomlands inhabited by much of free Black and enslaved Charlottesville.

The discovery of a free Black family homesite and burial ground in close proximity to the university became a "teachable moment," activating the scholarship of Robinson, Butler, and others. It marked the beginning of a concerted effort to document, interpret, and commemorate the hidden history of nineteenth-century African American neighborhoods and communities in Charlottesville that had been "lost" in the twentieth century to UVa expansion, urban renewal, and post-segregation-era neighborhood gentrification.

Robinson did not live to see the Venable Lane project—or, more tragically, his magnum opus book project on the demise of slavery and the collapse of the Confederacy—through to completion.[11] His death from a brain aneurysm in August 1995 came as a great shock to the UVa scholarly community and left the future of the Woodson Institute in limbo. Robinson had been the institute's "first and only" director, a point emphasized in his *Washington Post* obituary.[12] The appointment of William Jackson as interim director did little to calm concerns among UVa faculty and fellows about the institute's status and survival.[13]

Deprived of institutional direction and critical resources, the Venable Lane Task Force disbanded shortly after Robinson's death.[14] Plans for memorialization of the Foster site and burial ground were put on indefinite hold while UVa administrators weighed options for future development around the site. Butler and Lucia (Cinder) Stanton, senior research historian at Monticello's Thomas Jefferson Foundation, sought to keep the work of the taskforce going through the formation of an ad-hoc group of local researchers dubbed the Free Black Forum (later known as the Central Virginia Social History Project). The group convened at the Monticello Gatehouse on September 19, 1995—three weeks after Robinson's death—with Butler, Stanton, UVa anthropology professor Jeffrey Hantman, UVa graduate student and Foster Site archaeologist Drake Patten, Thomas Jefferson Foundation research director Ann Lucas, and independent scholar Robert Vernon in attendance. According to meeting notes, Butler was an active participant. At one point he raised the ethical issue of digging into free Black family histories much like his own: "Are we thieves? Are we intruders?"[15]

Pressing forward with a second meeting on October 10, 1995, the group discussed several potential publications: a collection of articles based on Foster family research, genealogies for the entire free Black population of Albemarle County, databases for studying free Black social stratification and migration. The gathering also discussed the possibility of seeking funding for their work through the National Endowment for the Humanities (NEH) or the Ford Foundation. It is clear from their meeting notes that Butler and his colleagues envisioned an ongoing, grant-funded collaboration among UVa faculty, graduate students, and local researchers—some (like Stanton and Lucas) affiliated with Monticello and others (like Vernon) independent scholars with deep knowledge of local archives. Yet, absent institutional support from the Woodson Institute—then under interim leadership while a search for Robinson's successor took place—the pursuit of publications through a university press or grant funding from the NEH or Ford likely would have foundered.

As UVa faculty voiced their "concern about the status and survival of the Institute," Butler emerged as a leading candidate to replace Robinson. A search committee chaired by Paula McClain, a full professor in the Department of Government and Foreign Affairs, nominated Butler—then newly tenured as an associate professor in the History Department—as director.[16] In July 1996, UVa Dean of Arts and Sciences Ray Nelson appointed Butler to succeed Robinson as the institute's director.

Butler pledged to build a more active, outward-facing, locally and globally engaged institute that would fulfill the ideals of its founders while responding to the social, political, and intellectual challenges of the twenty-first century. He restructured the administrative staff and hired me—a UVa history PhD candidate who had recently completed a two-year Woodson Predoctoral Fellowship—as his assistant. Butler later explained that this critical staffing decision was driven by the unique demands of the position:

> This was a moment of transition for the Institute; the Dean had just appointed me to replace Armstead Robinson, the founding director, who led the Institute for fifteen years until his untimely death in 1995. As part of the reorganization of the Institute, the associate director, the director of undergraduate studies, and the computer systems coordinator—all of whom had served under the founding director—departed. These three administrative positions were collapsed into one newly created position of assistant director, with teaching responsibilities in AAS and the History Department. Scot's ties to the Institute as a former AAS 101/102 teaching assistant and Woodson predoctoral fellow, together with his scholarly focus on African American history and his unique strengths in humanities computing, made him the ideal candidate for the new position, and he was hired in 1997.[17]

Working closely together, Butler and I collaborated with faculty and community partners on a series of grant-funded initiatives that would lay the groundwork for a reconceptualized program of teaching, research, community outreach, and minority recruitment. Early initiatives (1997–2000) supported local and regional faculty seminars, while later projects (2000–2006) funded digital archives, community studies, visiting fellows, curriculum redesign, and study-abroad/field-learning experiences in Africa and its diaspora.

Changing Cultures of Race in the Modern World: Interdepartmental Seminar, 1997–1998

Butler moved quickly to address concerns raised in an external program review concluded shortly before Robinson's death. The reviewers—Stanley L. Engerman, University of Rochester; Robert J. Norrell, University of Alabama; and Allen Isaacman, University of Minnesota—hailed the Woodson fellowship program as "an outstanding success" in attracting attention and generating important scholarly publications in AAAS. Yet they also observed that the fellowship program, while facilitating the work of individual scholars, rarely generated a vigorous, sustained exchange of ideas between visiting scholars and the larger UVa community. Woodson seminars were "episodic and poorly attended," and residential fellows only occasionally interacted with UVa graduate students and faculty.

With seed funding from the dean's office, Butler established the "Changing Cultures of Race in the Modern World" interdepartmental seminar, a twice-monthly, interdisciplinary workshop/lecture series designed to bring students and faculty from various departments and programs together with visiting scholars and Woodson research fellows to discuss new scholarly approaches to the subject of race. Each session was moderated by one or more faculty members, who made brief comments on a selected topic and set the stage for discussion. The seminar addressed the following questions:

- How are scholars working in a variety of fields—cultural studies, social history, literature, anthropology, archaeology, architecture, to name just a few—grappling with issues of race? Can they find common ground for scholarly discourse?
- How can we make use of new information technologies to facilitate the teaching and research of these issues? What resources are available through the World Wide Web? How can we use electronic mail and moderated discussion lists to enhance scholarly discourse?
- How can scholars studying issues of race make connections between the local and the global? How have changing patterns of migration and immigration produced new perceptions of identity that challenge traditional definitions of race, ethnicity, community, and nationality? How have international geopolitical developments, such as the collapse of the Soviet Union, the disintegration of Yugoslavia, and ethnic conflict in Africa, reshaped the conceptualization of race?

Nearly one hundred faculty from thirty different programs, institutes, and departments at UVa subscribed to the Race Seminar (as it became known) mailing list; many became regular participants. Butler and his staff made extensive use of the new information technologies provided by the university to coordinate meetings and circulate readings among this large, geographically dispersed group of scholars. They worked closely with the technical staff of the various electronic centers at UVa—the Electronic Text Center, the Digital Image Center, the Digital Media and Music Center, the Special Collections Digital Center, the New Media Center, the Social Science Data Center, and the Geographic Information Center—to develop new resources for teaching and research.

The Race Seminar fulfilled several of Butler's immediate goals. It institutionalized a forum for the cross-disciplinary exchange of ideas among UVa faculty, graduate students, visiting scholars, and Woodson research fellows. It contributed to the development of an interdepartmental, team-taught, graduate-level seminar, which debuted in the spring 1999 semester. Finally, it gave the institute greater visibility in the larger scholarly community, thus making the university more attractive to prospective graduate students and faculty. Recognizing the value of the Race Seminar, the dean of arts and sciences awarded the Woodson Institute a two-year grant to support its continuation.

The Holsinger Studio Exhibit/Emerging Scholars Program, 1998–2000

At the same time, Butler moved quickly to secure funding for institute programming that would engage the local African American community—long excluded from UVa outreach prior to the Foster project—while immersing undergraduates in archival research. In 1998, the Virginia Foundation for the Humanities (VFH) awarded the institute a grant to research and mount an exhibit of African American photographs from the Rufus W. Holsinger Studio Collection and Digital Image Database in UVa's Special Collections. Roughly five hundred of the nine thousand images in the Holsinger Collection portrayed African Americans through studio portraits and other outdoor scenes—a remarkable window into African life in the region, circa 1900–1925. The grant supported publication of an exhibit catalogue and a traveling exhibit built around the theme "History, Race, and the Value of Place in Central Virginia."[18]

Butler cast the project as a community-engaging extension of his own scholarly research on African American community life. The theme "reflected our interest in 'placing' the African American subjects of Holsinger's photographs within a social and cultural history of the region," Butler explained. But "Holsinger's records tell us little, if anything, about their place in the community—their family and kinship ties, where they lived and worked, what churches they attend, what civic and social groups they joined," nor did these images reveal how "segregation—and, in the case of older African Americans, slavery—shaped their individual and collective identities." The challenge, Butler told the VFH, "was to separate the people in these photographs from the facile props and neoclassical backdrops of Holsinger's Studio and place them within more historically accurate social, cultural, and geographical settings." Researchers "would combine the limited information recorded by the photographer with a rigorous analysis of census data, local and regional newspapers, court files, tax records, deeds, wills, and other public documents." Seeking additional information from family and community members, the project promised to shed new light on the lived experience of Holsinger's subjects. Participants would be enabled to "interrogate our own notions of 'race' and 'place'" and share their insights with a broader public.[19]

Butler recruited students from the History Department's newly established Emerging Scholars Program (ESP) to conduct the research. Cofounded in 1996 by Butler and his colleague Brian Balogh, the program encouraged African American and other ethnic/racial minority students with outstanding academic records to consider graduate careers in the humanities and social sciences by immersing them in local research projects and connecting them with mentoring programs such as Phillips Academy's Institute for the Recruitment of Teachers.

To identify individuals and groups in the Holsinger Collection, students printed out the digitized portraits, put them in binders (by name, where available), and took them to the African American cultural festival in Charlottesville's once-segregated Washington Park. Area residents suggested about fifty possible identifications, and some offered to do follow-up interviews. The Washington Park "History Harvest" introduced students to the community and the community to the collection, while introducing Butler's more outreach-oriented institute to the community.

Beginning in 1998, all incoming third-year ESP students were required to take an upper-level digital history course with a special focus on issues of "Race and Place." Students were expected to learn basic HTML-authoring skills and contribute to the development of digital history databases and exhibits. The Woodson Institute offered two ESP/digital history courses— "Digital History and the Jim Crow South, 1900–1941," and "Race and Place:

Life after Emancipation in Central Virginia, 1865–1918." Noteworthy ESP alumni from that era include political scientists Andra Gillespie (PhD, Yale University, 2005) and Deva Woodly (PhD, University of Chicago, 2008), and historian Brandi Hughes (PhD, Yale University, 2009).

The Chesapeake Regional Scholars Summer Seminar: New Approaches to Teaching and Research in the Twenty-First Century, 1997–2000

As part of his expansive vision for the institute, Butler invited scholars at small liberal arts colleges and minority-serving institutions throughout the Chesapeake Region (North Carolina, Virginia, the District of Columbia, Maryland, and Delaware) to "rethink" African American Studies in dialogue with participating Woodson-affiliated faculty and leading specialists in the field.

In 1997, Butler secured a three-year, $250,000 grant from the Ford Foundation to host the Chesapeake Regional Scholars Summer Seminar, "Rethinking African-American and African Studies: New Approaches to Teaching and Research in the 21st Century." Thirty-five fellows, supported with stipends and UVa housing, participated over four summers. The program included presentations by Woodson-affiliated faculty, such as literary scholar Deborah McDowell, anthropologist Gertrude Fraser, and musicologist Kyra Gaunt, and outside speakers such as historians Herman Bennett, Ira Berlin, and Barry David Gaspar, whose work illuminated the complexities of race and ethnicity across time and space.

Butler saw digital humanities—with its emphasis on open-access collections and interdisciplinary collaboration—as a natural theme for exploration through the Chesapeake Seminar. In its fourth and final year (funded by Ford as a no-cost extension), the seminar paired past fellows with community partners to develop grant-funded digital projects for their home institutions. The week-long seminar "Building an African-American Digital History Archive: A Workshop for Principal Investigators and Project Teams" featured a keynote by Abdul Alkalimat, director of Africana Studies at the University of Toledo ("Cyberspace and the Black Experience: A Vision for Research in eBlack Studies") and a hands-on digital workshop led by William G. Thomas III, director of UVa's Virginia Center for Digital History. David Bearinger, associate director of the VFH, presented on "Finding Funding Sources/Writing Winning Grant Proposals." Butler himself led a "Research Roundtable: Finding Individuals, Finding Communities."

Project teams chosen to participate in the Chesapeake Digital History Archive Seminar reflected Butler's interest in supporting local/regional studies and data collection for community-based digital archives: "Princeville: The Town That Defied White Supremacy"; "Virtual Christiansburg Institute Digital Collection and Archive"; "Race, Time, and Place: African Americans in Tidewater Virginia"; "Public Education in Delaware, 1867–Present"; "The Richmond Police Guard Day Book Digital Archive"; "ABC's of the African-American Educational Quest"; and the "Chesapeake Region African American Census Database."

In their formal evaluations, participating fellows from historically Black colleges and universities (HBCUs) responded enthusiastically to the themes, structure, and content of the seminar. Flora Bryant Brown, a historian at Elizabeth City State University, said the seminar "caused me to 'rethink' my own conceptual framework for presenting African American Studies in my classes." Likewise, Clara Small, a historian at Salisbury State University, called it "an excellent program, in that it gave me the opportunity to read, discuss and rethink African-American Studies. Most of all, it afforded me the long-awaited opportunity to learn some computer techniques that I have wanted to learn for a long time."[20]

The Chesapeake Seminar placed Butler's Woodson Institute at the hub of a region-wide network of scholars, archivists, and educators representing a remarkably diverse range of institutions: Delaware State University, Morgan State University, East Carolina University, Lynchburg College, College of William and Mary, Virginia Union University, Norfolk State University, Loyola College in Maryland, Saint Augustine's University, and North Carolina State University, as well as James Madison's Montpelier, Old Salem Inc., Monticello, and the National Archives at College Park. By the turn of the twenty-first century, Butler's democratizing vision for the Woodson Institute—the building of digital communities—had begun to take form.

Building Digital Communities: A Collaboration with the Virginia Center for Digital History (1999–2002)

Butler's interest in developing digital archives and online resources for teaching and research in AAAS led to a major grant-funded collaboration with the Virginia Center for Digital History (VCDH), a leading incubator of digital projects at UVa. In September 1999, the NEH awarded the two centers a $100,000 grant to fund two concurrent and complementary projects:

- Building a digital archive, "Race and Place: An African American Community in the Jim Crow South," which combined searchable databases of primary sources with historical exhibits on African American life in Charlottesville and Albemarle County, Virginia, circa 1870–1940.
- Building networks of scholars at HBCUs to develop related digital history projects. The institute promised to share its technological experience and resources with faculty and archivists at HBCUs throughout the mid-Atlantic region, building on institutional ties established in the Chesapeake Regional Scholars Summer Seminar.[21]

In a UVa news release announcing the grant, Butler stressed the benefits to students enrolled in the Emerging Scholars Program and related African American Studies courses. "Both at UVa. and other institutions," he explained, "the projects offer African-American and other students opportunities to work on significant research and to prepare themselves for careers in technology and the humanities."[22]

Butler also saw the digital partnership with the Center for Digital History as essential to his vision of the institute as a hub between the university and underserved institutions and communities. In a 1999 Ford grant proposal, he explained the broader intellectual/philosophical aims of the "Building Digital Communities"/"Race and Place" archive project. This collaborative initiative, he told the foundation, promised "to 'democratize' history by giving the public greater access to archival resources and more input into the interpretation of the past." The opportunity to participate in developing a more inclusive history would be particularly meaningful to African American undergraduates as they prepared for careers in technology and the humanities and contributed "to the development of African American resources for use by teachers and students at HBCUs and other underfunded institutions of higher learning." Their work would also "address the 'racial gap' in the use of the World Wide Web by creating more sites of interest to African Americans, both locally and regionally."[23]

Modeled after Edward L. Ayers's *The Valley of the Shadow: Two Communities in the American Civil War*, an award-winning educational resource and digital archive, *Race and Place: An African American Community in the Jim Crow South* included transcribed newspaper articles, city directory and census data, letters and diaries, oral history projects, maps, and political materials with a focus on Charlottesville. While the VCDH ceased operations in 2009, a victim of state budget cuts, the *Race and Place* website remains active and accessible thanks to continued web support from UVa's Institute for Advanced Technology in the Humanities.[24]

"Rethinking African-American and African Studies": New Approaches to Teaching and Research in the Twenty-First Century, 2000–2002

Faced with stagnant university funding and a lack of support for an expanded African American Studies program, Butler saw external funding as the key to the institute's fortunes. In a March 1998 letter to the Ford Foundation's Alison R. Bernstein, vice president of the foundation's Education, Media, Arts, and Culture Program, Butler assessed the institute's progress under his leadership and set the stage for new, more sweeping grant proposals. "The Institute was founded upon an understanding of race as a immutable category of American life," Butler wrote Bernstein. "Today, a new understanding of race as an ever-shifting category has forced the Institute to reevaluate its mission and redefine its programs and curriculum accordingly. How will changing cultures of race reshape African American Studies programming in the twenty-first century?"[25]

Butler's framing question and its call to action resonated with Ford. In April 1999, Butler traveled to New York City to meet with a new program officer, Margaret Wilkerson, who encouraged him to submit a grant proposal. That September, the foundation awarded the Woodson Institute a three-year, $250,000 grant to develop model programs and initiatives related to teaching and research on race, ethnicity, and society in Africa and the Atlantic World. Titled "Rethinking African-American and African Studies: New Approaches to Teaching and Research in the 21st Century," the grant funded postdoctoral teaching and research fellowships, overload and summer wages for UVa faculty participating in the review of courses and curriculum, honoraria for outside consultants and guest lecturers, and miscellaneous costs associated with the development of teaching resources and orientation materials.

In an interview with *Diverse Issues in Higher Education,* Butler noted that the institute had embarked on a fundamental rethinking of its core curriculum, beginning with its introductory courses, AAS 101 and 102. "We've tended to follow a very traditional paradigm," he explained, telling "the story of African Americans in the New World in a very linear trajectory" from the trans-Atlantic slave trade to the American civil rights movement. It was time to think more hemispherically and comparatively, moving beyond the tightly bound national narrative, Butler argued. The grant would help refocus the program on three broad areas of study: (1) Africa and the Black Atlantic, (2) North America, and (3) South and Central America and the Caribbean. Butler hoped "to use the university's particular strengths—the legacy of Carter G. Woodson, the state of Virginia's extremely rich documentary resources and the university's high-tech multimedia capabilities—to attract more students to the program and to build bridges with faculty across the Arts and Sciences disciplines."[26]

Administratively, the grant enabled the institute to reinvigorate its dwindling postdoctoral fellowship program without additional state funds; it also provided pilot funding for the redesign of the African American Studies (AAS) major, with team-taught introductory courses that more thoroughly incorporated Atlantic World/African diasporic approaches and more thoroughly integrated online teaching resources. Most importantly, perhaps, the grant addressed some of the weaknesses inherent in the institute's original design as a program, with loosely affiliated faculty, rather than a department with full-time faculty lines. As Butler observed in a 2005 report, "Faculty from Anthropology, English, History, Religious Studies, and Sociology now routinely participate in the teaching of these [introductory] courses; their collaboration has fostered a new sense of collegiality among AAS contributing faculty and stronger ties to the Institute and its programs. Students now know that AAS has a core faculty that extends across the university."[27]

"Mapping Monticello's Diaspora": The Center for the Study of Local Knowledge in the Construction of Race, Gender, and Nation, 2002–2005

Butler's vision of the Woodson Institute as a research hub that nurtured local/regional community studies within an Atlantic World/African diasporic framework crystallized in 2002 with the establishment of the Center for the Study of Local Knowledge (CSLK). Funded by a three-year, $250,000 Ford Foundation grant and administered by the Woodson Institute, the CSLK promoted new ways of understanding and representing the construction of race, gender, and nation at the local, "everyday" level of experience.

Butler explained the conceptual framework for the center, and its geographical emphasis on central Virginia, in the grant abstract. "By local knowledge," he wrote, "we mean a community's understanding of its social relations, past and present, and the implications for the everyday ordering and reordering of society." The Monticello plantation and surrounding communities in central Virginia provided "a unique interpretive space on which to map discourses of race and gender in the construction of citizenship and national belonging."[28]

The project was animated by several key questions about how different academic disciplines understood and represented local knowledge as well as the role community members played in its production and reproduction. Butler was particularly interested in learning how "local knowledge informs discourses of race, gender, and nation over time," and in exploring ways in which new technologies could "map these discourses and make them meaningful and accessible to various publics."

Butler appointed Corey D. B. Walker, a Woodson-affiliated scholar and recent PhD from the College of William and Mary, to serve as inaugural director of the center. In the fall of 2002, Walker launched the CSLK graduate/faculty seminar and distinguished lecture series with a two-day campus visit by Duke University professor Walter Mignolo. The seminar focused on "Regimes of Knowledge and the Academy in the Age of Globalization" while the public lecture, held in the Rotunda Dome Room, addressed "Tomorrow's Universities: Global Coloniality and the Geopolitics of Knowledge." Walker's second speaker, François Weil, Director d'Études, École des Hautes Edudes en Sciences Social, Paris, delivered public lectures

("A Genealogy of Genealogy: The Quest for Ancestors in American History," at the Albemarle Charlottesville Historical Society and Miller Center Pavilion). The spring calendar featured the renowned anthropologist Clifford Geertz speaking on "Local Knowledge and Human Interests."[29]

When Walker stepped down to become an assistant professor of religious studies, Butler and I assumed co-directorship of the center. Moving away from the graduate seminar–visiting lecturer model, we initiated numerous public history partnerships that involved close collaboration among academic and lay scholars and institutional/community partners.[30] In one noteworthy case, CSLK's involvement transformed a UVa professor's project into a multiyear collaborative research venture centered on the theme of "local knowledge." Working in the Albemarle Charlottesville Historical Society archives, UVa architectural historian Daniel Bluestone discovered a cache of public records—including hundreds of photographs and property appraisals—documenting a 1960s urban renewal project that demolished the core of Charlottesville's African American business and residential district known as Vinegar Hill. Bluestone encouraged Butler and me to develop a CSLK project that would digitize the Vinegar Hill records and help place the site within a larger history of African American place-making and displacement in the city. With support from Albemarle Charlottesville Historical Society historian-genealogist Ann W. Carter, we embarked on a multiyear effort to digitize and transcribe all the records and make them publicly accessible, along with newly conducted oral histories with former Vinegar Hill residents.[31]

Over the next several years, CSLK grant-funded graduate project managers Schuyler Esprit (2004–6) and Luann Williams (2006–7) worked with undergraduate researchers and local residents, the Albemarle Charlottesville Historical Society, the Public Housing Association of Residents, the Charlottesville Redevelopment and Housing Authority, and the city of Charlottesville to digitize hundreds of photographs, property appraisals, and public records related to Vinegar Hill, with the aim of building an online archive and virtual tour of this urban "memoryscape." As project directors, Butler and I framed the Vinegar Hill Project around a "local knowledge" research question: "Can the thoughtful application of new technologies, informed by archival research and sustained civic engagement, reveal new understandings of urban renewal and its long-term impact on the health and welfare of a community?"

Custom-built by VCDH director of technology Bill Ferster using an elegant Flash-based web authoring tool called VisualEyes, the "Vinegar Hill Memoryscape" invited users—often with simple visual cues—to explore these questions in an intuitive fashion. An interactive map featured photographs and appraisal data for every home and business demolished within the twenty-acre redevelopment zone. Users could choose to highlight properties within a certain assessed value or condition. High-resolution aerial photos allowed for "flyover" views from every direction. A video player featured retrospective interviews with African American business owners and homeowners displaced by the project, while animated visualizations showed the razing of the neighborhood and the dispersal of its residents across the city. Student and faculty research projects explored specific themes, such as Black versus white ownership of property ("A Tale of Two Landlords") and the correlation of topography with housing quality.[32]

CSLK facilitated many other community-based research projects by simply providing institutional sponsorship and administrative support. For example, the center provided an institutional home for two studies of African American community life in central Virginia—Melissa Shore's Ivy Depot film project and Emma Edmunds's Oral History of the Civil Rights Movement in Danville, Virginia—enabling these independent researchers to raise funds from public and private sources. The Ivy Depot film project received $10,000 from the VFH and $10,000 from the Charlottesville Area Community Foundation; the Danville project received $72,000 over three years from the Elizabeth Stuart James Grant Trust. The center's directors (Butler, Corey D. B. Walker, and me) served as scholarly advisors to these projects, participating in planning meetings, suggesting research questions, and proposing alternative interpretations. Moreover, they facilitated the archiving of materials produced by these projects—including oral histories, photographs, and bank records—through the University Library's Digital Media Lab and Special Collections Department.

"Rethinking African-American and African Studies": Study Abroad/Field Learning in Cuba, Brazil, and Ghana, 2004–2007

Having successfully revamped the institute's introductory AAS courses in phase one of the Ford Foundation "Rethinking African-American and African Studies" grant, Butler looked to expand upper-level course offerings to include study-abroad/field-learning opportunities in Africa and diasporic regions of the Atlantic World. In 2004, he secured a three-year, $300,000 supplement to the institute's Ford-funded "Rethinking African-American and African Studies" grant with these local-global hemispheric cross-currents in mind. "It has been our goal," Butler told the foundation, to create a curriculum that would "attract outstanding minority students and faculty to U.Va. and better prepare all students for citizenship in a world of shifting racial and ethnic demographies." That meant addressing the conspicuous underrepresentation of Black undergraduates in language study, study abroad, and departmental honors programs, traditional "gateways to graduate study in the humanities and social sciences."[33]

Butler pledged to develop upper-level courses that combined traditional classroom experience "with community-based learning experiences in Africa and African diasporic areas, such as Cuba, Brazil, the French West Indies, and the American South." These interdisciplinary courses would "introduce students to historically situated constructions of race and national identities within the local-global matrix of 'everyday' experience." Over the course of five years (thanks to a two-year, no-cost extension from Ford) the grant funded a ten-day, January term study-abroad program in Cuba (2004); a six-week, language-intensive field-learning summer program in Bahia, Brazil (2005); and two ten-day January term study programs in Cape Coast, Ghana (2008–9).

Butler played a pivotal role in organizing these programs, recruiting faculty members in History, Latin American Studies, and AAAS to develop site-specific syllabi/itineraries and coordinate intensive field-learning experiences rooted in African/Diasporic/Atlantic World history. Although struggling with health and mobility issues related to the onset of Parkinson's disease, Butler traveled to Brazil and Ghana with participating faculty to meet with university and community partners vital to the success of the programs. In Salvador da Bahia—a primary destination of the Portuguese slave trade and a center of Black life in the Americas—Butler and the Ford grant team visited the Federal University of Bahia's Center for the Study of Afro-Orientals, the Steve Biko Cultural Institute (which created the first secondary school course for Blacks in Brazil), and the Ile Aiye Dance and Drumming Class. In the village of Cachoeira, they met with community elders, viewed student living quarters, and observed the Festa da Boa Morta, or Feast of the Good Dead.

To plan the UVa in Ghana January term program, Butler made his first and only trip to West Africa. He found it an intensely moving experience, made more so by the knowledge that Parkinson's would make a return trip impossible. Butler and January term co-instructors Maurice Cox and I met with Cape Coast's Oguaa traditional council and paramount chief, who greeted us with libation ceremonies. We toured Cape Coast Castle, headquarters of the British slave-trading operation in Africa, where tens of thousands of Africans languished in crowded pens before passing through the infamous "Door of No Return" to board ships bound for slave markets throughout the Americas. We conferred with Rabbi Kohain Halevi, an American expatriate and executive director of the foundation supporting the Pan African Festival of Arts and Culture, and visited the economically marginalized Muslim neighborhood known as the "Zongo," where we met with the Chief Imam and his family. During a brief stop at an Asafo military company shrine—a large, round, concrete structure with a tree growing out of it, decorated with a whale and the words "No. 7 Company"—Butler sat down to rest. A group of children quickly gathered around him, smiling and posing for a picture. The scene so inspired Togolese artist Samuel Tete-Katchan—a friend to Butler and the program—that he captured the moment in a painting.

Retirement and Institutional Legacy

In August 2005, Butler stepped down as director of the Woodson Institute, citing medical issues related to Parkinson's. His quiet retreat from academic life, coupled with an unexpectedly rocky search for his successor (which took two and a half years and concluded with the appointment of English professor Deborah McDowell), denied his many friends, colleagues, and mentees an opportunity to publicly acknowledge and celebrate his many accomplishments at the Woodson Institute.

At the twenty-fifth anniversary of the Woodson Institute in April 2007, Butler's nine years of academic leadership and innovative program-building—validated by more than $1 million in external grants—were briefly acknowledged but overshadowed by tributes to his predecessor, the late Armstead Robinson, whose founding vision for Black Studies gave birth to the institute.[34] Yet in that same year, unbeknownst to Butler or his colleagues, the Ford Foundation issued a 278-page report—*Inclusive Scholarship: Developing*

Black Studies in the United States, a 25th Anniversary Retrospective of Ford Foundation Grant-Making, 1982–2007—which placed Butler at the vanguard of the field.[35]

In a chapter devoted to Ford Foundation–funded AAS programs, reviewer Dianne M. Pinderhughes, a political scientist at the University of Illinois at Urbana-Champaign, praised Butler for his "forceful and effective" leadership at the Woodson Institute. Drawing on interviews conducted during a day-and-a-half site visit to UVa in 2000, Pinderhughes credited Butler with rejuvenating and enriching "the complex institutional environment of the Woodson Institute" after the untimely death of its founding director had put the institute's status and survival in doubt. "In the short time since Reginald Butler was named director in 1996," she wrote, the institute "has been reinvigorated and reconceptualized. . . . Butler has strengthened existing projects and added a number of important new ones."[36]

Butler accomplished these goals, Pinderhughes noted, despite a critical lack of staffing for institute activities, which included the administration of the undergraduate AAS program and supervision of the predoctoral and postdoctoral residential research fellowship program. "It can be said," she wrote, "that the university has been supportive of the *intellectual developments* within the Woodson. But it has been unwilling to provide ongoing support for the administrative infrastructure to manage those activities." Pinderhughes warned that "the complexity and the volume of the research-based projects associated with the Institute might lead, after a number of years, to burnout. The untimely deaths of Robinson and, within a short period, the director of University of Iowa's program (who was also about fifty) should send clear signals to University administrators and leaders in the field. Maintaining these programs is not only intellectually demanding, it is physically and psychologically stressful."[37] Indeed, both Robinson and Butler struggled to complete work on their manuscripts while directing the Woodson Institute; both suffered debilitating medical emergencies and died before seeing their manuscripts published.

Much has changed since 2007, when the Ford Foundation issued its program report on the Woodson Institute and the state of the field. In 2017, after years of student, faculty, and directorial pressure, the institute became a "full-fledged" academic department within the College of Arts and Sciences. "The Carter G. Woodson Institute has long distinguished itself for its signature contributions to the research and teaching of African and African-American studies in this country," Dean Ian Baucom said. "Its promotion as this University's newest academic department, built on the ambitions of [then-director] Deborah McDowell, her faculty colleagues, and the institute directors who preceded her [Butler and Robinson], marks a significant milestone for the College and Graduate School of Arts & Sciences."[38]

Today, Butler's tenure as director is widely and publicly acknowledged by his peers at UVa and beyond. When Butler died in July 2019, *UVA Today* memorialized his tenure as "the second director of the Woodson Institute" and a pioneer in "the study of local African American history using early digital technology." Kirt von Daacke, a UVa history professor and academic dean who was one of Butler's students as an undergraduate, cited Butler's work as an influence on two UVa presidential commissions studying slavery and segregation at the university. "His work at Woodson, with its insistent focus on promoting local history as a way to answer big scholarly questions, using emergent digital technology along the way, was frankly path-breaking," von Daacke said.[39]

Given Butler's early and sustained commitment to "Rethinking African-American and African Studies in the Digital Age," it is fitting that this posthumous publication of Butler's book on colonial and early national Virginia include a digital companion growing out of his original archival research, augmented with new data compiled and analyzed by Robert Vernon. As director of the Woodson Institute, Butler brought independent scholars like Vernon into the fold, supported their work, and acknowledged their enormous contributions. He institutionalized this broadly collaborative, community-based research model through the Central Virginia Social History Project, the Chesapeake Scholars Summer Seminar, the *Race and Place* digital archive, and—perhaps most ambitiously—the Center for the Study of Local Knowledge. Although the grants that funded these projects have long since expired, the work lives on.

"Home to a Very Old Place"

On September 14, 2019, family and friends from across the country gathered under a tent at the Butler family homeplace in Goochland County to share their loving memories of Reginald and to celebrate his life and legacy. I used my time to thank Reginald for his friendship and mentorship; for hiring me as his assistant director; and for shielding me from many of the job's most difficult, stressful elements. I also read a brief excerpt from Butler's book manuscript, focused on the role his mother and aunts played in shaping his character and feeding his passion for history. At the conclusion of the memorial service, participants walked to the gravesite where Butler's mother, aunt, and other family members lay interred beneath headstones. A swarm of bees soon chased us all away, to howls and laughter, a sharp reminder of life's sweetness and sting.

Butler affirmed his connection to this place—his family's ancestral "home place" in Goochland—in the introduction to his 1989 dissertation. "My mother and aunts," he wrote, "kept alive a sense of the 'home place' that has informed the telling of this story. That tradition, together with their patience and spiritual support, have buoyed me through the years."[40]

Yet, as noted by friends and family, Butler's consciousness was shaped as much by his travels—to and from Goochland County from his childhood home in West Philadelphia; across the country to Washington State for work and college; south to Mississippi as a voting rights activist; across the Black Atlantic to Cape Coast, Ghana, and Bahia, Brazil—as by his Central Virginia roots. Viewed diasporically, the full scope of his life and work can be more fully appreciated.

In March 2020, the Virginia General Assembly adopted a joint resolution "Celebrating the Life of Dr. Reginald Dennin Butler," which situated his administrative work at the Woodson Institute within the intellectual and political framework of his social justice activism and local-global scholarship. It reads,

> WHEREAS, Dr. Reginald Dennin Butler, a professor of history at the University of Virginia and former director of the university's Carter G. Woodson Institute for African-American and African Studies, died on July 5, 2019; and
> WHEREAS as a young man, Reginald Butler was active in the struggle for social justice both in Washington state and nationally, joining the Student Non-Violent Coordinating Committee and canvassing for voters in Mississippi; and
> WHEREAS, Reginald Butler graduated from Western Washington University in 1969, earned a master's degree and a doctorate in African American colonial history from Johns Hopkins University in

1989, and joined the University of Virginia Corcoran Department of History in 1991 as a scholar of early African American history; and

WHEREAS, Reginald Butler served as director of the Carter G. Woodson Institute for African-American and African Studies from 1996 to 2005, during which time he explored many emergent technologies for the study and dissemination of historical resources while also developing programs, research opportunities, and initiatives for students; and

WHEREAS, Reginald Butler conducted the Chesapeake Regional Seminar in Black Studies, organizing workshops and seminars focused on new directions in research and the teaching of African American studies; he also convened and coordinated the Central Virginia Social History Project, a group of area scholars examining race and ethnicity in Central Virginia from the 17th to the early 20th century; and

WHEREAS, Reginald Butler served on the Advisory Committee on African American Interpretation at Monticello, the Albemarle County home of Thomas Jefferson; and

WHEREAS, Reginald Butler will be fondly remembered and dearly missed by his children, Maya, Ishmael, Omar, and Alfred, and their families; his brother, Howard; his sister-in-law, Geri; and numerous other family members and friends; now, therefore, be it

RESOLVED by the House of Delegates, the Senate concurring, That the General Assembly hereby note with great sadness the loss of Dr. Reginald Dennin Butler, a civil rights activist and treasured professor of history at the University of Virginia; and, be it

RESOLVED FURTHER, That the Clerk of the House of Delegates prepare a copy of this resolution for presentation to the family of Dr. Reginald Dennin Butler as an expression of the General Assembly's respect for his memory.[41]

Recollections

Shomer Zwelling

I first met Reginald Butler in the late 1970s, when he was a research fellow at the Smithsonian Institution's Museum of American History, and I was a working historian in the Research Department of the Colonial Williamsburg Foundation. A colleague whom we both knew and respected mentioned to me that Reginald was completing his fellowship at the Smithsonian, was an up-and-coming historian with a first-rate intellect, and was looking for employment while completing his dissertation. Meanwhile, I was intent on and committed to bringing well-researched, eighteenth-century African American historical interpretation to the streets of Williamsburg's outdoor living history museum. I contacted Reginald and shortly after we met, a position in the Research Department was developed. He was interviewed, and several months later Reginald too was a member of the Research Department, renting a house on the Duke of Gloucester Street, the museum's main pedestrian throughway. It seemed simultaneously natural, incongruous, and ironic for him to be there, but then again Reginald had a fine sense for life's ironies, even those that sometimes grated.

From the start Reginald and I enjoyed, trusted, and respected each other both professionally and personally. Over the years we both grew and deepened from our connection and in our connection. Although Reginald had family roots in rural Virginia where he spent his boyhood summers, he grew up in Philadelphia. Meanwhile I was raised in a relatively small, ethnically diverse industrial town in central Connecticut but went to college in New York City and later to graduate school outside Boston. We were both strongly influenced by the politics of the 1960s and were leftist in our orientation but with a commitment to and love of rigorous inquiry. One special moment in the early phase of our relationship was when we discovered that we both very much liked the movie "Nothing but a Man." That realization seemed to open a door. Another was when we found out at approximately that same time that we also loved and respected *The Souls of Black Folk* by W. E. B. Du Bois.

Reginald lived in Williamsburg for two years and then moved to Richmond, later to North Carolina, and then Charlottesville. A shared interest and commitment to history as well as to honest, authentic communication was at the heart of our long relationship. A conversation with Reginald was a treasure and an exploration, perhaps an artform also—thoughtful, real, free-ranging, personal, interpersonal, fun, funny, and intellectually rewarding, rooted in the realities of life and the historical imagination.

As a scholar and a person Reginald was disciplined and fierce in his high standards, in the depth of his commitment to the historical reality of how "Black folk" actually lived their daily lives, their networks, and their strategies, both the subtle and the overt ways, the above ground and the underground. He was an artist and a seasoned craftsman in his work, able to combine the details of everyday life at the local level with the larger patterns of cultures within cultures interacting, changing, making demands, and finding channels.

Reginald had a questioning mind that respected the hard work of others while also pursuing and following the evidence and its traces in the historical record however challenging to unearth, discover, perceive, and understand. Although he became more seasoned, deft, and discerning with years of experience, his capacity for astonishment and incredulity remained intact throughout, testimony to his openness to ideas, new discoveries, emerging but well-wrought perspectives, and the unexpected fruits of ever-evolving human ingenuity.

Throughout, his appreciation for irony was exquisite, and while he well understood the power dynamics and rules of professional conduct in various situations, he did not suffer artifice in silence. He spoke his mind with grace, integrity, well-rooted courage, and conviction, a rare combination. In turn, he won the admiration and respect of colleagues, friends, and students without pandering to anyone but with a keen, understated sense of humor that was invariably a part of his mix. Along with many others, I remember and miss him with much affection, with deep gratitude and ongoing appreciation for his presence, as well as his enriching and innovative contributions to the life of both the mind and the heart in this field.

Kathleen Halley

Reginald Dennin Butler was a cherished friend for over a half-century. Although very different in so many ways, we appreciated, supported, and understood each other. When I first met him in 1966 at Western Washington State College (now University) in Bellingham, Washington, which is about twenty miles from the Canadian border and some fifty miles from Vancouver, Canada, I had just recently turned eighteen and he would soon be twenty-two. This mainly white, small college town was an unlikely and foreign feeling place for both of us. To our small band of quite directionless Black freshman, mostly from Seattle and known then as Negroes, Butler was the smart, studious, intense, serious, sophisticated, wise, very cool older guy from the East Coast.

I believe Butler was recruited to Western on both a basketball and an academic scholarship. While he was 6'4 and a decent player with a lean athletic build and a passion for basketball, sometime before I arrived he quit the school's basketball team, saying he felt they were just using his body and not seeing him as a full human being. He was also feeling the pull of a possible career in higher education. There were hints of racist treatment too. His love for basketball remained strong throughout his life, waning slightly in his last years. Watching a competitive game live or on TV was a joy for him. Still, he maintained a vigilance of the game and sports in general for their political and racial realities and implications.

It was the nascent years of the Black Power student movement across the country during that 1966–67 academic year. There had been the courageous freedom riders during the dawn of the decade. There was also Freedom Summer in Mississippi in 1964, where three young male civil rights activists working to get long-disenfranchised Black people registered to vote were murdered—two Black and one white. Their killings were a catalyst for the consideration and passage of the 1965 Voting Rights Act. But this was more campus-based and nationwide—less patient or willing to wait, often with tentacles into both rural and urban Black communities with tutoring and mentoring programs for young students. Black students, with the support of allies, were demanding the transformation of colleges and universities by greatly expanding Black student enrollment, increasing the numbers of Black faculty, and providing separate dorms and other housing options for Black students. A major demand was the establishment of Black Studies courses, programs, and ultimately departments to address the central role of Black history and culture in American life.

Foundational to these efforts was the study and retelling of the history and cultural practices of African Americans in the United States. Butler, who had been an avid reader of history and many other subjects since he was young, was well-positioned for this fight. Early on, he knew that American history was Black history, and of course this historical investigation and illumination became his life's work. He loved the idea and reality of Black people. He did not idealize our people. (An aside: I remember Butler telling me decades ago how he would tear out pages of books from his school library and stuff them down his pants so that they wouldn't be visible when he walked home to read them. Carrying books, reading, and studying were not viewed positively by many of his peers and was seen as acting white.)

I left Western at the end of my freshman year to attend a small private historically Black college in Ohio. I thought I might meet a larger number of Black folks that I didn't already know. In the following year Butler and his future wife, Barbara Madison, were very active in the Black student movement at Western—helping to bring about some crucial changes to that small, liberal-leaning college. Being older and having many experiences beyond his years, he mentored, encouraged, celebrated, and sometimes chastised other younger students who did or did not take study and scholarship seriously. This was a theme for him throughout his life.

Butler was a complex and complicated man who loved nature and the vibrancy and beauty of the natural world. He valued hard work and activity of the mind and the body. He tested himself constantly, both physically and intellectually. I believe it was a rare day that he did not engage in some type of physical exercise, usually a variety of vigorous exercises. He had a great curiosity about life and a zest for discovering new things. He would investigate how to do a task that he knew nothing about—from installing very large new windows in his house to tiling a bathroom to removing dams built by beavers from a stream on his beloved property in the country in Virginia. After reading about a task, he would complete it, sometimes getting both skilled and unskilled folks to assist. He also valued just being in the moment—often while listening to jazz (Sonny Rollins was a favorite), blues (especially early southern blues), and other music of whatever kind he found and appreciated.

In his thoughtful, considerate, interested-in-you way, Butler attracted all kinds of people into his circle. He cared for, respected, and loved people from every station of life—including strangers, students, neighbors, colleagues, support staff, top administrators, family, and friends. He also required solitude, content in its silence and indicating sometimes with humor (and not so subtly) that it was time for company to depart. He did not suffer fools gladly and could have stinging rebukes and flashes of you-don't-want-to mess-with-me anger when someone was unethical, disrespectful, unfair, mean to those they knew had less power, or were being racist or employing any of the negative -isms. He had a broad sense of the world, and while he traveled to more places than many, he wanted to travel more and for longer periods of time.

Butler loved to laugh, and his witty, deeply intelligent humor and storytelling might take you a few beats to realize how funny it was. He saw the absurdity in life that was often on full display and also was fond of the reliable, everyday certainties of life. Laughter and a skeptical view of the world helped sustain him.

Butler could also be stubborn and inflexible—set in his ways. Of course, his ways were the correct ones. But he was also generous and always doing something for somebody, handing out big and small unexpected kindnesses and wanting no acknowledgment for them. He was not a complainer and did not want to talk about problems as if talking about them gave them too much oxygen. He shared physical and emotional hurts and pains infrequently and not to seek interventions or solutions. He would work things out in his way and in his time. He wanted you to listen.

· NOTES ·

ABBREVIATIONS

AC	Albemarle County Clerk's Office, Charlottesville, VA
A.M.B.	Albemarle County Minute Book, original at AC, microfilm copy at LVA
A.O.B.	Albemarle County Order Book, original at AC, microfilm copy at LVA
FPVB	Fredericksville Parish Vestry Book, 1742–87, barcode 5620882, LVA
GC	Goochland County Clerk's Office, Goochland, VA
G.D.B.	Goochland County Deed Book, original at GC, microfilm copy at LVA
G.M.B.	Goochland County Minute Book, original at GC, microfilm copy at LVA
G.O.B.	Goochland County Order Book, original at GC, microfilm copy at LVA
Hening, Statutes	William Waller Hening, ed., Statutes at Large; Being a Collection of All the Laws of Virginia, from the First Session of the Legislature, in the Year 1619, 13 vols. (Richmond, VA: R. & W. & G. Bartow, 1819–23)
LVA	Library of Virginia, Richmond (formerly Virginia State Library Archives)
PC	Pittsylvania County Clerk's Office, Chatham, VA
P.D.B.	Pittsylvania County Deed Book, original at PC, microfilm copy at LVA
RV	notes added to the original manuscript by Robert Vernon

INTRODUCTION: RACE, STATUS, THE LOCAL, AND THE PERSONAL

1. See the discussion in Reginald D. Butler, *The Evolution of a Rural Free Black Community: Goochland County, Virginia, 1728–1832* (Charlottesville: University of Virginia Press, 2025), chap. 3.
2. Ibid, 74, 76.
3. Rhys Isaac, *The Transformation of Virginia, 1740–1790* (Chapel Hill: University of North Carolina Press, 1982).
4. Mechal Sobel, *The World They Made Together: Black and White Values in Eighteenth-Century Virginia* (Princeton, NJ: Princeton University Press, 1987); Edmund S. Morgan, *American Slavery, American Freedom: The Ordeal of Colonial Virginia* (New York: Norton, 1975); T. H. Breen and Stephen Innes, *"Myne Owne Ground": Race and Freedom on Virginia's Eastern Shore, 1640–1676* (New York: Oxford University Press, 1980).
5. John H. Russell, *The Free Negro in Virginia, 1619–1865* (Baltimore: Johns Hopkins University Press, 1913).
6. Carter G. Woodson, *Free Negro Heads of Families in the United States in 1830, Together with a Brief Treatment of the Free Negro* (Washington, DC: Association for the Study of Negro Life and History, 1925); Luther Porter Jackson, *Free Negro Labor and Property Holding in Virginia, 1830–1860* (New York: D. Appleton-Century, 1942); John Hope Franklin, *The Free Negro in North Carolina, 1790–1860* (Chapel Hill: University of North Carolina Press, 1943); E. Horace Fitchett, "The Traditions of the Free Negro in Charleston, South Carolina," *Journal of Negro History* 25 (1940): 139–51; E. Horace Fitchett, "The Origin and Growth of the Free Negro Population of Charleston, South Carolina," *Journal of Negro History* 26 (1941): 421–37; E. Horace Fitchett, "The Status of the Free Negro in Charleston, South Carolina, and His Descendants in Modern Society: Statement of the Problem," *Journal of Negro History* 32 (1947): 430–51.
7. Ira Berlin, *Slaves without Masters: The Free Negro in the Antebellum South* (New York: Pantheon, 1974).
8. Berlin, *Slaves without Masters*, xviii–xx. Other works on free Black southerners published around this time include Edwin Adams Davis and William Ransom Hogan, *The Barber of Natchez* (Baton Rouge: Louisiana State University Press, 1973); Herbert E. Sterkx, *The Free Negro in Ante-Bellum Louisiana* (Rutherford, NJ: Fairleigh Dickinson University Press, 1972); and Marina Wikramanayake, *A World in Shadow: The Free Black in Antebellum South Carolina* (Columbia: University of South Carolina Press, 1973).
9. Early New England town studies include John Demos, *A Little Commonwealth: Family Life in Plymouth Colony* (New York: Oxford University

Press, 1970); Kenneth A. Lockridge, *A New England Town: The First Hundred Years* (New York: Norton, 1970); and Philip J. Greven Jr., *Four Generations: Population, Land, and Family in Colonial Andover, Massachusetts* (Ithaca, NY: Cornell University Press, 1970).

10. Darrett B. Rutman and Anita H. Rutman, *A Place in Time: Middlesex County, Virginia, 1650–1750* (New York: Norton, 1984); Orville Vernon Burton, *In My Father's House Are Many Mansions: Family and Community in Edgefield, South Carolina* (Chapel Hill: University of North Carolina Press, 1985); Richard R. Beeman, *The Evolution of the Southern Backcountry: A Case Study of Lunenberg County, Virginia, 1746–1832* (Philadelphia: University of Pennsylvania Press, 1984); Robert C. Kenzer, *Kinship and Neighborhood in a Southern Community: Orange County, North Carolina, 1849–1881* (Knoxville: University of Tennessee Press, 1987).

11. Suzanne Lebsock, *The Free Women of Petersburg: Status and Culture in a Southern Town, 1784–1860* (New York: Norton, 1984); Barbara Jeanne Fields, *Slavery and Freedom on the Middle Ground: Maryland during the Nineteenth Century* (New Haven, CT: Yale University Press, 1985); Michael P. Johnson and James L. Roark, *Black Masters: A Free Family of Color in the Old South* (New York: Norton, 1984); Michael L. Nicholls, "Passing through This Troublesome World: Free Blacks in the Early Southside," *Virginia Magazine of History and Biography* 92 (1984): 50–70; Gary B. Mills, *The Forgotten People: Cane River's Creoles of Color* (Baton Rouge: Louisiana State University Press, 1977); Adele Logan Alexander, *Ambiguous Lives: Free Women of Color in Rural Georgia, 1789–1879* (Fayetteville: University of Arkansas Press, 1991).

12. *Return of the Whole Number of Persons within the Several Districts of the United States* (Washington, DC: U.S. House of Representatives, 1801), 51.

13. Butler, *Evolution*, 20.

14. On gender and free Black women, for example, see Wilma King, *The Essence of Liberty: Free Black Women during the Slave Era* (Columbia: University of Missouri Press, 2006); Amrita Chakrabarti Myers, *Forging Freedom: Black Women and the Pursuit of Liberty in Antebellum Charleston* (Chapel Hill: University of North Carolina Press, 2011); Emily Clark, *The Strange History of the American Quadroon: Free Women of Color in the Revolutionary Atlantic World* (Chapel Hill: University of North Carolina Press, 2013); and Jessica Millward, *Finding Charity's Folks: Enslaved and Free Black Women in Maryland* (Athens: University of Georgia Press, 2015). On free Black people and the law, see Ted Maris-Wolf, *Family Bonds: Free Blacks and Re-Enslavement Law in Antebellum Virginia* (Chapel Hill: University

of North Carolina Press, 2015); Emily West, *Family or Freedom: People of Color in the Antebellum South* (Lexington: University Press of Kentucky, 2012); and Kimberly M. Welch, *Black Litigants in the Antebellum American South* (Chapel Hill: University of North Carolina Press, 2018). On free Blacks, race, and labor, see L. Diane Barnes, *Artisan Workers in the Upper South: Petersburg, Virginia, 1820–1865* (Baton Rouge: Louisiana State University Press, 2008), and Warren Eugene Milteer Jr., *North Carolina's Free People of Color, 1715–1885* (Baton Rouge: Louisiana State University Press, 2020). An excellent recent comparative study is Alejandro de la Fuente and Ariela Gross, *Becoming Free, Becoming Black: Race, Freedom, and the Law in Cuba, Virginia, and Louisiana* (New York: Cambridge University Press, 2020).

15. Berlin, *Slaves without Masters*, 136.
16. Melvin Patrick Ely, *Israel on the Appomattox: A Southern Experiment in Black Freedom from the 1790s through the Civil War* (New York: Vintage, 2004), x, 456–57.
17. Kirt von Daacke, *Freedom Has a Face: Race, Identity, and Community in Jefferson's Virginia* (Charlottesville: University of Virginia Press, 2012), 8. Other recent work centered on stories of one family or community include Eva Sheppard Wolf, *Almost Free: A Story about Family and Race in Antebellum Virginia* (Athens: University of Georgia Press, 2012); Julie Winch, *The Clamorgans: One Family's History of Race in America* (New York: Hill and Wang, 2012); and Richard C. Rohrs, "The Free Black Experience in Antebellum Wilmington, North Carolina: Redefining Generalizations about Race Relations," *Journal of Southern History* 78 (2012): 613–38.
18. Warren Eugene Milteer Jr., *Beyond Slavery's Shadow: Free People of Color in the South* (Chapel Hill: University of North Carolina Press, 2021), 2.
19. Butler, *Evolution*, 133.
20. Ibid, 142–43.

PROLOGUE

1. "Examination of James Cooper charged with feloniously murdering and privately burrying a male bastard child issue of the body of Lily Ann Craddock," G.O.B. 16:429–36, May 7, 1787; "Examination of Bridgett for feloniously murdering her male bastard child," G.O.B. 19:432–34, January 15, 1794. For other infanticide cases in the county, see "Inquisition taken on the body of a child of Anna Jenkins, alias Anna Martin," G.D.B. 25:586–87, May 14, 1824; Frances Green "brought to the bar for murder of her bastard child," G.O.B. 1:50, November 20, 1728; Elizabeth

Hambleton "on suspicion of infanticide," G.O.B. 7:418–20, June 6, 1754; Jane McBride "charged with felonious murder of her bastard child," G.O.B. 20:349, September 5, 1796.
2. Depositions of Polly Cooper, Sophia Parrish, and George Tyler, G.O.B. 16:429–31, May 7, 1787.
3. Deposition of James Cooper, G.O.B. 16:429–36, May 7, 1787.
4. Depositions of Elizabeth Lawson and Becca Cooper, G.O.B. 19:432–33, January 15, 1794. My appreciation to Clossie Butler for information on the persistence of and rationale for such practices. She remembered that through the 1930s, rural African American women in Goochland County used this method for expressing breast milk and weaning infants.
5. For a discussion of eighteenth-century domestic space and dwelling size among the white poor and middling classes and among Afro-Virginians, slave and free, see Isaac, *Transformation of Virginia*, 33–34, 72–74; Sobel, *World They Made Together*, 72, 76, 100; and Phillip J. Schwarz, "Emancipators, Protectors, and Anomalies: Free Black Slaveholders in Virginia," *Virginia Magazine of History and Biography* 95 (1987): 317–38.
6. Sobel, *World They Made Together*, 100–126.
7. Deposition of Debra Maddox Pleasants, G.O.B. 19:433, January 15, 1794.
8. Ibid.
9. Isaac, *Transformation of Virginia*, 116–19.
10. Deposition of Polly Cooper, G.O.B. 16:429–36, May 7, 1787.
11. Gary B. Mills, "Miscegenation and the Free Negro in Antebellum 'Anglo' Alabama: A Reexamination of Southern Race Relations," *Journal of American History* 68 (1981): 16–34; Kathleen Brown, "Engendering Racial Difference, 1640–1670," paper presented at New Directions in North American Slavery Studies: An Informal Workshop at the Johns Hopkins University, October 1993; Martha E. Hodes, "Sex across the Color Line: White Women and Black Men in the 19th-Century American South" (PhD diss., Princeton University, 1991); Bertram Wyatt-Brown, *Southern Honor: Ethics and Behavior in the Old South* (New York: Oxford University Press, 1982).
12. Deposition of Sophia Parrish, G.O.B. 16:430, April 27, 1787.
13. For the Pleasants family manumissions, see G.D.B. 13:255–61, October 19, 1782; 13:246–48, October 21, 1782. For the genealogical history of the Pleasants family in Goochland and surrounding counties, see Norma Carter Miller and George Lane Miller, *Pleasants and Allied Families: An Historical Genealogy of the Descendants of John Pleasants (1644/5–1698) of Henrico County, Virginia, and of George Pleasant of York County, Virginia*

(DeKalb, IL: N. C. Miller, 1980), and William Wade Hinshaw, *Encyclopedia of American Quaker Genealogy* (Ann Arbor, MI: Edwards Brothers, 1950), vol. 6.
14. Miller and Miller, *Pleasants and Allied Families*, 10.
15. Laurel Thatcher Ulrich, *Good Wives: Images and Reality in the Lives of Women in Northern New England, 1650–1750* (New York: Knopf, 1980), writes of older women's roles as mediators in social conflict and stewards of the behavior of younger women.
16. List of Personal Property Taxes, 1791, GC.
17. Isaac, *Transformation of Virginia*, 347–50.

INTRODUCTION

1. Caleb Perry Patterson, *The Negro in Tennessee, 1790–1865* (Austin: University of Texas Press, 1922); Leonard P. Curry, *The Free Black in Urban America, 1800–1850: The Shadow of a Dream* (Chicago: University of Chicago Press, 1981); Johnson and Roark, *Black Masters*; Philip D. Morgan, "Slave Life in Piedmont Virginia, 1720–1800," in *Colonial Chesapeake Society*, ed. Lois Green Carr et al. (Chapel Hill: University of North Carolina Press, 1988), 433–84; Berlin, *Slaves without Masters*; Joel Williamson, *New People: Miscegenation and Mulattoes in the United States* (New York: Free Press, 1980).
2. Kathleen Brown, "Gender and the Genesis of a Race and Class System in Virginia, 1630–1750" (PhD diss., University of Wisconsin–Madison, 1990).
3. Allan Kulikoff, *Tobacco and Slaves: The Development of Southern Cultures in the Chesapeake, 1680–1800* (Chapel Hill: University of North Carolina Press, 1986), 432. On the incendiary potential of free Blacks in southern society, Ulrich B. Phillips observed that "many men of the south thought of themselves and their neighbors as living above a loaded mine, in which the negro slaves were the powder, the abolitionists the spark, and the free negroes the fuse." Phillips, *Slave Economy of the Old South: Selected Essays in Economic and Social History* (Baton Rouge: Louisiana State University Press, 1968), 60–61.
4. Herbert Bolton, "The Free Negro in the South before the Civil War" (PhD diss., University of Pennsylvania, 1899); Ralph B. Flanders, "The Free Negro in Ante-Bellum Georgia," *North Carolina Historical Review* 9 (1932): 250–72; Russell, *Free Negro in Virginia*; James Wright, *The Free Negro in Maryland, 1634–1860* (New York: Columbia University Press, 1921); Charles Sydnor, "The Free Negro in Mississippi before the Civil War," *American Historical Review* 33 (1927): 769–88; Howard Rosser Taylor, *The*

Free Negro in North Carolina (Chapel Hill: University of North Carolina Press, 1920); Harold Schoen, "The Free Negro in the Republic of Texas," *Southwestern Historical Quarterly* 39 (1936): 292–308

5. Flanders, "The Free Negro in Ante-Bellum Georgia," 250.
6. Russell, *Free Negro in Virginia*, 160.
7. Ulrich B. Phillips, *American Negro Slavery: A Survey of the Supply, Employment and Control of Negro Labor as Determined by the Plantation Regime* (Baton Rouge: Louisiana State University Press, 1918).
8. Morris Boucher, "The Free Negro in Alabama prior to 1860" (PhD diss., State University of Iowa, 1950); Donald E. Everett, "The Free Persons of Color in New Orleans, 1830–1865" (PhD diss., Tulane University, 1952); Fitchett, "The Traditions of the Free Negro in Charleston"; Jackson, *Free Negro Labor and Property Holding in Virginia*, 33; Franklin, *The Free Negro in North Carolina*.
9. Jackson, *Free Negro Labor and Property Holding in Virginia*, 229.
10. Johnson and Roark, *Black Masters*; Loren Schweninger, *Black Property Owners in the South, 1790–1915* (Urbana: University of Illinois Press, 1990); Lebsock, *The Free Women of Petersburg*; Alexander, *Ambiguous Lives*.
11. Berlin, *Slaves without Masters*.
12. For a recent summary of these debates, see Peter Kolchin, *American Slavery, 1619–1877* (New York: Hill and Wang, 1993), and Charles B. Dew, "The Slavery Experience," in *Interpreting Southern History*, ed. John Boles and Evelyn Thomas Nolen (Baton Rouge: Louisiana State University Press, 1987), 120–62.
13. Schweninger, *Black Property Owners in the South*, 69, chaps. 3–4, 235–37.
14. Johnson and Roark, *Black Masters*.
15. Michael P. Johnson and James L. Roark, "Strategies of Survival: Free Negro Families and the Problem of Slavery," in *In Joy and in Sorrow: Women. Family, and Marriage in the Victorian South, 1830–1900*, ed. Carol Bleser (New York: Oxford University Press, 1991), 90.
16. Fields, *Slavery and Freedom on the Middle Ground*.
17. Berlin, *Slaves without Masters*; Curry, *The Free Black in Urban America*.
18. Brown, "Gender and the Genesis of a Race and Class System"; Joseph Douglas Deal III, "Race and Class in Colonial Virginia: Indians, Englishmen, and Africans on the Eastern Shore during the Seventeenth Century" (PhD diss., University of Rochester, 1981); Breen and Innes, "*Myne Owne Ground*."
19. Goochland County Free Black Register, 1804–60, registration nos. 1–2 (1804), Goochland County Register of Free Negroes, 1804–64, barcode 1120353, LVA.

20. G.O.B. 1836–44:50, August 21, 1837.
21. Morgan, "Slave Life in Piedmont Virginia"; Philip Morgan and Michael L. Nicholls, "Slaves in Piedmont Virginia, 1720–1790," *William and Mary Quarterly*, 3rd series, 46 (1989): 211–51.
22. Morgan, "Slave Life in Piedmont Virginia."
23. Ibid.; Richard S. Dunn, "Black Society in the Chesapeake, 1776–1810," in *Slavery and Freedom in the Age of the American Revolution*, ed. Ira Berlin and Ronald Hoffman (Urbana: University of Illinois Press, 1986), 49–82.
24. Brown, "Gender and the Genesis of a Race and Class System"; Breen and Innes, *"Myne Owne Ground"*; Deal, "Race and Class in Colonial Virginia."

1. BORN INTO FREEDOM

1. Apprenticeship contracts appeared in the G.O.B. from 1730 to 1832. Unless otherwise indicated all county records dated are in GC. Marriages and birth records for the county through 1832 have been compiled from a number of genealogical collections. They include Kathleen B. Williams, *Marriages of Goochland County, Virginia, 1733–1815* (Alexandria, VA: City of Alexandria, 1960); Thomas P. Hughes Jr. and Jewel B. Standefer, *Goochland County Virginia Marriage Bonds and Ministers' Returns, 1816–1854* (Memphis, TN: N.p., 1972); *The Douglas Register: Being a Detailed Record of Births, Marriages and Deaths Together with Other Interesting Notes as Kept by the Reverend William Douglas, from 1750 to 1797* (Richmond, VA: J. W. Fergusson and Sons, 1928) (hereafter *Douglas Register*); and William Lindsey Hopkins, *Northam Parish Vestry Book, 1744–1850* (Richmond, VA: N.p., 1987). Other sources on the county's free Black residents include Goochland County Register of Free Negroes, 1804–64; Lists of Tithables in Goochland County, 173586, 1746–48, 1768, 1775, 1777; and Goochland County List of Personal Property Taxes, 1782–1832, all LVA. On revolutionary free Black veterans, see Luther Porter Jackson, *Virginia Negro Soldiers and Seamen in the Revolutionary War* (Norfolk, VA: Guide Quality Press, 1944).
2. Peter J. Albert, "The Protean Institution: The Geography, Economy, and Ideology of Slavery in Post-Revolutionary Virginia" (PhD diss., University of Maryland, 1976), 269.
3. These patterns are apparent in apprenticeship records and criminal and civil court proceedings. All records are in order books from 1730–1832; in the Lists of Tithables; and in the marriage and birth records of *Douglas Register*.

4. On eighteenth-century migration to the Piedmont from the Tidewater, Philip D. Morgan and Michael Nicholls, "Africans in the Virginia Piedmont, 1720–1790," unpublished ms., provides an excellent discussion. See also Kulikoff, *Tobacco and Slaves*.
5. See Berlin, *Slaves without Masters*, 51–52, 58; Gary B. Nash, *Forging Freedom: The Formation of Philadelphia's Black Community, 1720–1840* (Cambridge, MA: Harvard University Press, 1988), 20–21; Joan Gunderson, "The Double Bonds of Race and Sex: Black and White Women in a Colonial Virginia Parish," *Journal of Southern History* 52 (1986): 351–72, at 358; Herbert Gutman, *The Black Family in Slavery and Freedom, 1750–1925* (New York: Pantheon, 1976); and Sobel, *World They Made Together*, 154–64.
6. Many slave names for the early period reflected planters' whimsies and attractions to Roman and Greek mythology—Venus, Cesar, Atlas, Scipio, Hercules, Pompey, Cato, Jupiter, Parthena—as well as the perhaps African heritage or provenance of some slaves—Cudja, Shantee, Jallapa, Affee, Congo, Cowhey, Jolloff. By contrast, free Blacks appear to have had a collective aversion to either category of names. These and other African-derived names appeared in the 1746 tithes of Ann Mayo, Phillip Mayo, James Murray, Abraham Perkins, and Colonel John Fleming, and in the 1747 tithes of Alex Speir and Joseph Cotts. Greek and Roman slave names were prolific. See, for example, tithes of Ann Mayo, 1746; Phillip Mayo, 1747; Thomas Turpin, Richard Randolph, and Thomas Randolph, 1755; and John Hopkins, 1775.
7. RV: *Douglas Register*, 348.
8. Sobel, *World They Made Together*, 154–55; Gunderson, "Double Bonds of Race and Sex," 358–59; Eugene D. Genovese, *Roll Jordan Roll: The World the Slaves Made* (New York: Pantheon, 1974), 448–50.
9. Hening, *Statutes*, 3:86–88.
10. Ibid., 3:453–54.
11. Ibid., 3:87, 473–75; 6:548; 8:134–35. According to a 1662 statute, the status of children followed that of their mothers. Ibid., 3:170. A 1705 statute and a subsequent measure in 1748 made servitude intergenerational, that is, if the female children of white servant women themselves bore children during their thirty-one-year indenture, those children would have to serve for thirty-one years as well. Ibid., 6:548.
12. Apprenticeship orders appeared in the Goochland County Order Books for the year in which the child was apprenticed. Hannah, G.O.B. 2:13, July 1730; Tom, G.O.B. 2:179, August 3, 1731; Elinor Griffin (not identified by

race) and Moll, a "mulatto girl," G.O.B. 3:16, November 16, 1731; "mulatto girl," child of Elizabeth Griffin, G.O.B. 6:392, November 17, 1747.
13. *Douglas Register*, 348.
14. Ibid., 347–48.
15. Sobel, *World They Made Together*, 9. See also her introduction.
16. RV: Tithes of Reverend William Douglas, 1775, in Goochland County Tax and Fiscal Records, 1746–77, barcode 1184642, LVA.
17. Reciprocity, patriarchy, paternalism, and the power relations engendered in these forms of institutionalized and noninstitutionalized interactions among slaves, free Blacks, and whites have been the subject of much debate in the last two decades. These works include Genovese, *Roll Jordan Roll*; Eugene D. Genovese, *The World the Slaveholders Made: Two Essays in Interpretation* (New York: Pantheon, 1969); Gerald W. Mullin, *Flight and Rebellion: Slave Resistance in Eighteenth-Century Virginia* (New York: Oxford University Press, 1972); Sobel, *World They Made Together*; Anthony Parent, "'Either a Fool or a Fury': The Emergence of Paternalism in Colonial Virginia" (PhD diss., University of California at Los Angeles, 1982); and Berlin, *Slaves without Masters*, 194–95. Isaac, *Transformation of Virginia*, 308–10, discusses the shift from patriarchy to paternalism in the eighteenth century as the individual and his "quest for fulfillment" arrived on center stage. Isaac writes that "in the age of 'sensibility' patriarchy was being sentimentalized into paternalism in a social system that was less rigidly organized according to status categories and more attuned to the play of personal emotions, slavery became problematic. . . . In the realm of moral philosophy this change registered itself as 'humanitarianism.'" Thus, according to Isaac, some planters turned to selective manumission as one means of convincing themselves of their humanitarian bent. For a well-argued critique of the concept of paternalism, especially in its Genovese variant, see Fred Siegel, "The Paternalist Thesis: Virginia as a Test Case," *Civil War History* 25 (1979): 246–61.
18. James Hugo Johnston, *Race Relations in Virginia and Miscegenation in the South, 1776–1860* (Amherst: University of Massachusetts Press, 1970), 165–317; Breen and Innes, *"Myne Owne Ground"*; Deal, "Race and Class in Colonial Virginia"; Nicholls, "Passing through This Troublesome World," 52–56; Winthrop D. Jordan, *White over Black: American Attitudes towards the Negro, 1550–1812* (Chapel Hill: University of North Carolina Press, 1968), 137–44.
19. Berlin, *Slaves without Masters*, 6; Deal, "Race and Class in Colonial Virginia," 215; Nicholls, "Passing through This Troublesome World," 52.

20. For discussion of the disproportionate number of white men to white women in the seventeenth-century Chesapeake, see Morgan, *American Slavery, American Freedom*, 407; Lois G. Carr and Lorena S. Walsh, "The Planter's Wife: The Experience of White Women in Seventeenth-Century Maryland," *William and Mary Quarterly*, 3rd series, 34 (1977): 542-71; Russell R. Menard, "Immigrants and Their Increase: The Process of Population Growth in Early Colonial Maryland," in *Law, Society, and Politics in Early Maryland*, ed. Aubrey C. Land et al. (Baltimore: Johns Hopkins University Press, 1977), 88-97; and Kulikoff, *Tobacco and Slaves*, 32-37.
21. Morgan, *American Slavery, American Freedom*, 336.
22. Williamson, *New People*, 12-14; Deal, "Race and Class in Colonial Virginia," 213-16; Berlin, *Slaves without Masters*, 6-7. See also Parent, "'Either a Fool or a Fury,'" which offers a well-argued discussion of class, race, and sexual relations in seventeenth-century Virginia. See also Mills, "Miscegenation and the Free Negro in Alabama," 32. His findings on miscegenation in Alabama call into question earlier historical conclusions about the general intolerance of interracial unions in the Lower South during the antebellum period. Mills distinguishes between the political ideology of the elite and the day-to-day behavior of the general populace, free Black and white. Too often, he argues, historians conflate planter ideology with that of the general populace. He writes that "nothing has emerged so far to support the theory that whites in Alabama hated or feared free blacks.... Instead it was the vague and theoretical mass of black freedmen that troubled them—the one popularized by political demagogues who built careers by swaying the emotions of voters." Perhaps the electoral analysis is too simple, but the wider implications of his data for southern historiography cannot be ignored.
23. *Douglas Register*, 348.
24. Ibid., 347.
25. David Granthum's will, G.D.B. 19:64, October 17, 1801, recorded June 18, 1804.
26. *Douglas Register*, 348.
27. See, for example, the List of Mulattoes and Free Negroes, 1803-12, LVA. This document lists husbands, wives, and grown children living together in a household, along with their occupations, and is referred to in the text as the "occupations list." Some of these free Blacks resided in the county before 1782, such as Jacob and Aggy Cooper, Nathan and Charlott Freeman, Harry and Molly Cochran, and James and Nanny Scott.

28. On the participation of Goochland residents in Protestant revivals, see Morgan Edwards, *Materials towards a History of the Baptists*, ed. Eve B. Weeks and Mary Bondurant Warren, 12 vols. (Danielsville, GA: Heritage Papers, 1984), 2:43, 54, 61–63, 71, 74; Reuben E. Alley, *A History of Baptists in Virginia* (Richmond: Virginia Baptist General Board, 1973), 39–40; and Robert B. Semple, *A History of the Rise and Progress of the Baptists in Virginia* (Richmond, VA: Pitt and Dickinson, 1894), 26, 140. On the founding of the Baptist church in Goochland in 1771 and the involvement of Blacks, Semple wrote that "a remarkable stir . . . took place among the black people in the year 1806. More than one hundred of them were baptized" (140). On the activity of Presbyterians in Goochland, see Morgan, "Slave Life in Piedmont Virginia."

29. Hening, *Statutes*, 4:129.

30. Ibid.; Samuel Shepherd, *Statutes at Large of Virginia, 1792–[1807]*, 3 vols. (Richmond: S. Shepherd, 1835–36), 2:77.

31. For laws pertaining to juvenile apprenticeship before 1782, see Hening, *Statutes*, 1:274–75, 337; 2:298; 3:87, 375–76, 453; 4:212, 482; 6:32, 558; 8:134–35, 876; 10:335.

32. See Tithes of Anne Scott, Daniel Banks, William Banks, 1746; Tithes of Walter Leake, 1748, Lists of Tithables.

33. Tithes of Colonel Phillip Lightfoot, 1746, 1749; Tithes of John Christian 1746, 1748, 1755; Tithes of William Douglas, 1755, Lists of Tithables.

34. Tithes of William Pledge, 1755, Lists of Tithables. Pledge's inventory may be found in G.D.B. 13:220–21, July 16, 1782.

35. County Levy for 1756, G.O.B. 7:584, January 20, 1756; 7:636, November 9, 1756; County Levy for 1759 and 1760, G.O.B. 8:178, January 16, 1759; 8:278, January 15, 1760, recorded payments to Pledge for his work at the courthouse as jailer and caretaker.

36. *Charles Bates v. John Cousins*, G.O.B. 7:512–13, March 18, 1755.

37. Hening, *Statutes*, 3:459.

38. The proceedings were first recorded as an "Examination of Frank Cousens Charged with the Felonious intent of Poisoning Obadiah Smith," G.O.B. 7:381, April 3, 1754; 7:383, May 21, 1754; 7:489, December 18, 1754. A separate trial in the court of oyer and terminer for Squire, Myrtilla, and Murrocker also charged in the attempted poisonings appeared in G.O.B. 7:380–81 April 1, 1754.

39. G.O.B. 7:381, April 3, 1754.

40. For a lengthy discussion of the cultural role of and societal response to "poisoning," see Phillip J. Schwarz, *Twice Condemned: Slaves and Criminal*

Law in Virginia, 1705-1865 (Baton Rouge: Louisiana State University Press, 1988), 100-125.

41. G.O.B. 7:381, April 3, 1754; 7:383, May 21, 1754; 7:489, December 18, 1754.
42. In 1733, slaves Champion and Valentine were hanged, quartered, and burned when found guilty of murdering Robert Allen, a white man. Lucy, a supposed accomplice, received twenty-one lashes. G.O.B. 3:199-200, June 5, 1733.

2. MANUMISSION AND PLANTER RESPONSE

1. On the debates surrounding passage of the 1782 act, see Fredrika Teute Schmidt and Barbara Ripel Wilhelm, eds., "Early Proslavery Petitions in Virginia," *William and Mary Quarterly*, 3rd series, 30 (1973): 133-46; Theodore S. Babcock, "Manumission in Virginia, 1782-1806" (M.A. thesis, University of Virginia, 1973); Duncan J. MacLeod, *Slavery, Race, and the American Revolution* (New York: Cambridge University Press, 1974); David Brion Davis, *The Problem of Slavery in the Age of Revolution, 1770-1823* (Ithaca, NY: Cornell University Press, 1975), esp. 255-343; Russell, *Free Negro in Virginia*; and Albert, "The Protean Institution," 210-65.
2. See Russell, *Free Negro in Virginia*, 63-65, for similar petitions from Henrico, Hanover, Mecklenberg, Amelia, Pittsylvania, Halifax, Brunswick, and Lunenburg Counties.
3. On regional voting patterns, including that of Goochland County representatives, see Albert, "The Protean Institution," 244-54.
4. Ibid., 256-60; Berlin, *Slaves without Masters*, 79-107; Jordan, *White over Black*, 406-14.
5. Shepherd, *Statutes*, 1:239; 3:252. The registration law stated in part that it was the duty of the commissioners of the revenue to annually return a complete list of all the free Blacks who lived within their districts, with their names, places of abode, and trades, a "copy to be placed on the door of the courthouse." See also Donald Sweig, ed., *"Registration of Free Negroes Commencing September Court 1822, Book No. 2" and "Register of Free Blacks 1835, Book 3": Being the Full Text of the Two Extant Volumes, 1822-1861, of Registrations of Free Blacks Now in the County Courthouse, Fairfax, Virginia* (Fairfax, VA: Office of Comprehensive Planning, 1977).
6. Shepherd, *Statutes*, 3:252.
7. A comprehensive discussion of secular and religious antislavery ideology may be found in Albert, "The Protean Institution," 159-209, 116-59.

8. Evidence of these manumissions in Goochland County comes from two main sources. Planters recorded testamentary manumissions and deeds with the local county clerk. These appeared in the county court deed and order books. They permit the most accurate identification of manumitters and the slaves they freed.
9. Thomas Massie emancipation of James Barrett, G.D.B. 16:287, April 21, 1794.
10. Albert, "The Protean Institution," 270–71, notes, for example, that "the manumissions to be found in local court records do not comprise all the private emancipations which occurred in a given community."
11. Putting these aside, however, in at least twenty-five of the remaining cases, a corresponding deed of manumission or will could not be found in the court records for individuals clearly identifiable as having been freed in the county.
12. To illustrate that the registration rules were often ignored, Berlin, *Slaves without Masters*, 328, notes that "in Amelia County, for example, a consecutively numbered Register of Free Negroes kept between 1800 and 1865 listed about 150 freemen. In 1860, however, almost 200 resided in the county and many more had been born, had been manumitted, and had migrated into and out of the area during those years."
13. Sam, G.O.B. 20:350, September 19, 1796; Robin, emancipated by Samuel Couch, G.O.B. 23:92, December 21, 1801; Eliza and children emancipated by William Morris, G.O.B. 30:335, May 17, 1824.
14. Berlin, *Slaves without Masters*, 38.
15. The examination of Frank Brown, G.O.B. 31:193, October 15, 1827.
16. Ibid.
17. Ibid.
18. Berlin, *Slaves without Masters*, 95, writes that in Virginia the law directed that free Blacks could be hanged for a second offense of misusing a free register. See Shepherd, *Statutes*, 2:177. See also Hening, *Statutes*, 11:365, and Russell, *Free Negro in Virginia*, 64.
19. For laws governing runaways, see Hening, *Statutes*, 6:364–66. See also Mullin, *Flight and Rebellion*.
20. Berlin, *Slaves without Masters*, 41.
21. Ibid.
22. RV: Duplicate registrations for Diana Cooper, G.O.B. 30:282, August 18, 1823; G.O.B. 30:399, March 21, 1825.
23. Requests for duplicates certificates appeared in the Goochland County Order Books: John Copeland, G.O.B. 30:245, December 16, 1822; Bartlett

Hooker, G.O.B. 30:266, May 19, 1823; Diana Cooper, G.O.B. 30:282, August 18, 1823; Diana Cooper, G.O.B. 30:399, March 21, 1825; Isaac Fuzmore, G.O.B. 31:63, July 17, 1826; Betsy Lawson, G.O.B. 31:70, August 21, 1826; William Cooper, G.O.B. 31:185, September 17, 1827; Frank S. Moss, G.O.B. 31:186, September 17, 1827; Maria Cousins, G.O.B. 31:187, September 17, 1827; Lewis Scott, G.O.B. 31:246, May 19, 1828; Woodson Granthum, G.O.B. 31:362, June 15, 1829; Pleasant Smith, G.O.B. 32:10, March 22, 1831; Allen Cooper, G.O.B. 32:153, September 17, 1832; John Redd, G.O.B. 32:180, December 17, 1832. On forged certificates of freedom in Virginia, see Russell, *Free Negro in Virginia*, 64, 101, 107. RV: "Virginia Untold: The African American Narrative," https://lva.primo.exlibrisgroup.com/discovery/search?vid=01LVA_INST:VU&lang=en, has images of the replacement certificates for Diana Cooper (stolen in Richmond) and Woodson Granthum (destroyed with his clothes in a house fire).

24. James Curtis Ballagh, *A History of Slavery in Virginia* (Baltimore: Johns Hopkins University Press, 1902), 124, makes the argument that written registers provided free Blacks with some means of protection against re-enslavement while offering the slaveholder insurance against "unjust suits for freedom." Yet in what amounts to an apology for this means of social control, he fails to explain why so many legally freed Blacks avoided the registration laws.

25. Manumitters who immediately responded to the law included John Hunnicutt, G.D.B. 13:257, October 21, 1782; Benjamin Watkins, G.D.B. 13:250–51, October 21, 1782; Mary Pleasants, G.D.B. 13:254, July 4, 1781; 13:255–56, October 19, 1782; 13:260–61, October 21, 1782; Thomas Pleasants, G.D.B. 13:246–48, October 21, 1782; Mary Younghusband, G.D.B. 13:248–49, October 21, 1782; 13:258–59, October 21, 1782; and Strangeman Hutchins, G.D.B. 13:259–60, October 21, 1782, all recorded on October 21, 1782. My estimates of the total number of slaves freed and of the patterning of this manumission activity come principally from the recorded wills and deeds, unless otherwise specified. Even this evidence is not without problems. In some instances, deeds and wills of manumission did not indicate the exact numbers of slaves being manumitted. In two instances, slaveholders simply indicated they were manumitting "all" their slaves.

26. U.S. Census, 1810, 1820, 1830.

27. For similar regional patterns, see Albert, "The Protean Institution," 282, 286, 290.

28. Ibid., 288; Hening, *Statutes*, 11:39–40.

29. Ceasar emancipated by Thomas Fleming, G.D.B. 17:157–58, June 25, 1797.
30. Hannah emancipated by William Webber, G.D.B. 17:140, September 18, 1797.
31. Strangeman Hutchins, deed of manumission, G.D.B. 13:259–60, October 21, 1782; Ursula Mosby, deed of manumission, G.D.B. 16:288, June 12, 1794.
32. Mary Pleasants, deeds regarding slaves, G.D.B. 13:254, July 4, 1781; 13:255–56, October 19, 1782; 13:260–61, October 21, 1782.
33. RV: Will of Thomas Pleasants, Henrico County Records 1744–48:9–12, November 19, 1743.
34. Mary Pleasants, deeds regarding slaves, G.D.B. 13:254, July 4, 1781; 13:255–56, October 19, 1782; 13:260–61, October 21, 1782; Lists of Tithables, 1746.
35. Hening, *Statutes*, 11:39–40.
36. Also see Hunnicut's deed, G.D.B. 13:257, October 21, 1782.
37. See G.D.B. 13:285–86, October 24, 1782, for the transfer of Pleasants's slaves to his mother.
38. G.D.B. 13:257, October 21, 1782.
39. Binding orders also document the Pleasantses' and Hunnicutts' continued authority over their provisionally emancipated juvenile slaves. See chapter 4.
40. See Stanley L. Engerman and Robert William Fogel, "Philanthropy at Bargain Prices: Notes on the Economics of Gradual Emancipation," *Journal of Legal Studies* 3 (1974): 377–400, for a discussion of the economic advantages for northern planters of having provisionally emancipated slaves on their plantations.
41. Albert, "The Protean Institution," 782.
42. Ibid., 286.
43. G.D.B. 28:126, 1829 (?), will of John Webber. RV: This source was not found during a search of the archives in 2024.
44. G.D.B. 27:307–8, September 19, 1825, recorded October 15, 1827.
45. On petitions to remain in the county, see Berlin, *Slaves without Masters*, 146–47; Ballagh, *A History of Slavery in Virginia*, 125; and Johnston, *Race Relations in Virginia*, 17–18.
46. G.D.B. 13:246, October 21, 1782. On Quaker participation in antislavery thought and practice, see Albert, "The Protean Institution," 165–78, 116–59. See also Stephen B. Weeks, *Southern Quakers and Slavery: A Study in Institutional History* (Baltimore: Johns Hopkins University Press, 1896), chap. 10.

47. Mary Younghusband, G.D.B. 13:248–49, October 21, 1782; John Hunnicutt, G.D.B. 13:257, October 21, 1782.
48. Archibald Cary Randolph's manumission of Juba and Nanny, G.D.B. 17:101–2, November 1796.
49. John Curd's manumission of John Pierce, G.D.B. 22:292–93, November 20, 1816.
50. See annual county levies from 1803–27, for example, "To Wm Miller for John Pierce for his keeping the Ct House, jail and furnishing the stove with fuel &c," in G.O.B. 28:405, June 15, 1812. John Pierce's deed of manumission may be found in G.D.B. 22:292–93, November 20, 1816.
51. Will of Gideon Cawthon, G.D.B. 17:515–16, July 17, 1797.
52. Babcock, "Manumission in Virginia," finds that manumitters tended to be slaveholders with no children or immediate inheritors. His work is a multivariate analysis of the factors that influenced manumission decisions.
53. Holman to Granthum, 20 acres, G.D.B. 18:429–30, April 28, 1802.
54. Will of Gideon Cawthon, G.D.B. 17:515–16, July 17, 1797.
55. Catherine Granthum's last name is variously spelled in the records, appearing as Grantham and Grantum. Manumitted by will of Gideon Cawthon in 1797, G.D.B. 17:515–16, recorded November 18, 1799, she then purchased and freed Woodson, G.D.B. 17:553, February 17, 1800, and then her husband, Phil, G.D.B. 18:428–29, April 28, 1802. The deed of loan in which she transferred her property to him with restrictions appeared in G.D.B. 18:357, June 15, 1802. Her will may be found in G.D.B. 20:53–54, June 15, 1802, recorded February 15, 1808.
56. Nancy and Tempy emancipated by Thomas Gray, G.D.B. 21:705–6, February 17, 1815.
57. Ibid.
58. See G.O.B. 31:164, July 16, 1827, for Tempy's description, which was not transcribed into the Goochland County Register of Free Negroes.
59. G.D.B. 21:705–6, February 17, 1815.
60. Ibid.
61. Goochland County Citizens, Petition to the Legislative Assembly, December 15, 1831, LVA; List of Personal Property Taxes, 1821.
62. Robert McColley, *Slavery and Jeffersonian Virginia* (Urbana: University of Illinois Press, 1964), 110–13. See also Jordan, *White over Black*, 378–87, 391–92, and Berlin, *Slaves without Masters*, 89, 95, 115, 124.
63. For the involvement of slaves from Goochland, see James H. Johnston, "The Participation of White Men in Virginia Negro Insurrections," *Journal of Negro History* 16 (1931): 161.

64. Mullin, *Flight and Rebellion*, 156; Schwarz, *Twice Condemned*.
65. For a full description of the participation of slaves from the county, and specifically of Arthur and Lewis, see Lewis's confession located in the Executive Papers, LVA.
66. Ibid.
67. See John Brown's deed of manumission for Jack, G.D.B. 18:720, January 16, 1804.
68. Free Black slaveholders would have a different concern—for example, separation of family members.
69. These individuals included provisions in response to the 1806 law: Sally Coley, G.D.B. 20:201–3, March 9, 1807; Thomas Gray, G.D.B. 21:705–6, February 17, 1815; Joseph Cross, G.D.B. 21:598–99, November 4, 1813; Martha Peers, G.D.B. 28:166–68, April 22, 1829; Martha Symes, G.D.B. 26:12–14, June 12, 1820; Judith Shoemaker, G.D.B. 27:307–8, September 19, 1825; Sally Taurman, G.D.B. 26:197–98, September 13, 1825; and John Tinsley, G.D.B. 21:511–13, October 1, 1811.
70. Will of Sally Coley, G.D.B. 20:201–3, March 9, 1807, recorded September 19, 1808.
71. Ibid.
72. The registrations for Lucy and her children are in the Goochland County Register of Free Negroes, 29–31, February 20, 1809.
73. Will of Martha Peers, G.D.B. 28:166–67, April 22, 1829, recorded August 17, 1829.
74. Sweig, "Registration of Free Negroes" 1–6, discusses similar inconsistencies in the registration system in Fairfax, Virginia.
75. Berlin, *Slaves without Masters*, 144. Slaves were liable to be sold if their master or mistress died intestate.
76. Will of Joseph Cross, G.D.B. 21:598–99, November 4, 1813; Petition to the Legislative Assembly, December 18, 1822, LVA.
77. Ibid.
78. Albert, "The Protean Institution."

3. SECURING FREEDOM

1. Historians have noted that petitions were mere formalities as free Blacks were rarely denied exemptions from the removal law. It is difficult to assess the validity of such claims without a systematic examination of the nature and patterning of petitions in Virginia or for the South in general.
2. Albert, "The Protean Institution," 45; Berlin, *Slaves without Masters*, 147.

3. G.O.B. 31:129, March 21, 1827. For Sampson's deed of manumission, see G.D.B. 20:621–23, May 10, 1810.
4. Berlin, *Slaves without Masters*, 147. See also Jackson, *Free Negro Labor and Property Holding in Virginia*, 29, 81, 130, 131n, and Russell, *Free Negro in Virginia*, 149n.
5. For documentation of Sampson's economic and familial activities, see G.D.B. 25:369–70, June 16, 1823; 26:94–95, January 31, 1825; 28:98–99, December 13, 1828; 29:451–52, November 2, 1832; 30:512–13, November 13, 1835; 32:294–95, February 1, 1840; 32:295–96, December 10, 1838; 41:566–67, September 1, 1854; U.S. Census, 1830; and List of Personal Property Taxes, 1830.
6. John Pierce petition to remain in state, G.O.B. 29:550, January 20, 1817.
7. For Moses Cross's manumission, see G.D.B. 21:598–99, November 4, 1813; Petition to Goochland County Court, G.O.B. 30:206–7, May 20, 1822; and Petition to the Legislative Assembly, December 18, 1822, LVA.
8. Cross, Petition to the Legislative Assembly.
9. Ibid.
10. The List of Personal Property Taxes, 1801, indicates that Judith Peers owned seven slaves.
11. Cross, Petition to the Legislative Assembly.
12. Ibid.
13. Ibid.
14. See Thomas Peers's addendum, Cross, Petition to the Legislative Assembly.
15. Cross, Petition to the Legislative Assembly.
16. See Jane Purcell Guild, *Black Laws of Virginia. A Summary of the Legislative Acts of Virginia Concerning Negroes of Earliest Times to the Present* (New York: Negro Universities Press, 1969), 106.
17. John S. Fleming, Petition to the Legislative Assembly, December 9, 1824, LVA.
18. Ibid.
19. Ibid.
20. Will of Martha Symes, G.D.B. 26:12–14, June 12, 1820, recorded October 18, 1824.
21. Fleming, Petition to the Legislative Assembly.
22. Ibid.; accompanying signed petition, December 21, 1824, LVA.
23. Goochland County Citizens, Petition to the Legislative Assembly, December 15, 1831, LVA.
24. Ibid.

25. On the colonization movement in Virginia, see MacLeod, *Slavery, Race, and the American Revolution*, 83, 85, 104, passim; Jordan, *White over Black*, 546–69; and Berlin, *Slaves without Masters*, 103–8, 202–7.
26. See Albert, "The Protean Institution," 143–45.
27. MacLeod, *Slavery, Race, and the American Revolution*, 110.
28. Ibid.
29. Berlin, *Slaves without Masters*, 83.
30. See Shepherd, *Statutes*, 1:363–65; 2:77–78; 3:251–52, for limitations on slaves' right to institute freedom suits and the exclusion of Quakers from participation in such suits.
31. John Fleming's account is located in MSS 5:3 F6294, Virginia Historical Society, Richmond. Russell's motion to bring suit for freedom appears in G.O.B. 8:175, January 16, 1759. RV: See "Courthouse Custom as an Archival Filter," 174–75, for discussion of *Russell v. Drumwright's Ext'rs*.
32. *Miles v. Smith*, G.O.B. 22:362, July 21, 1800; 22:456–58, November 18, 1800. RV: See *Miles v. Smith* in Goochland Judgments, box 78, barcode 1141397, LVA.
33. Ibid.
34. List of Personal Property Taxes, 1801.
35. For an excellent examination of the tensions between questions of property rights and freedom in postrevolutionary Virginia, see MacLeod, *Slavery, Race, and the American Revolution*, 124: "Lawyers would be unwilling strongly to prosecute a freedom suit for fear of offending slaveholders," but "despite the evidence of popular hostility to the efforts of Negroes and their friends to gain freedom through court action, it is nonetheless true that juries frequently found in favor of freedom."
36. *Miles v. Smith*, G.O.B. 22:362, July 21, 1800; 22:456–58, November 18, 1800.
37. *Hannah and Her Children v. McRae*, G.O.B. 22:287, April 21, 1800; 22:465–66, November 19, 1800. RV: See: *Hannah and Her Children v. McRae* in Goochland Judgments, November 1800, box 78, barcode 1141397, LVA.
38. RV: Will of Charles Moorman, Louisa County Will Book 2:432–34, September 2, 1778, recorded October 12, 1778.
39. Hening, *Statutes*, 12:613–16, for the decisions of the assembly bearing on the Moorman estate. See also Russell, *Free Negro in Virginia*, 56–58.
40. Hening, *Statutes*, 12:613–16.
41. *Hannah and Her Children v. McRae*, G.O.B. 22:466, November 19, 1800.
42. Ibid.

43. Goochland County Register of Free Negroes, 63, August 16, 1813, for Hannah Moorman; 107, November 16, 1818, for Charles Moorman; 153, November 17, 1823, for Thomas Moorman; 106, October 19, 1818, for Wilson Moorman.
44. RV: Also see *John McCrae v. Robert Moorman,* Louisa Chancery Case, 1819–20, LVA, from which we learn that McCrae received the loan of Hannah in return for serving as a substitute for Thomas during the Revolution. According to Robert Moorman, his grandfather's emancipation of his slaves would have been known by McCrae, he "living within a mile or two" of Charles Moorman, because "this fact was a subject of conversation and Public notoriety."
45. John Baker emancipates wife Aggy, G.D.B. 18:255–56, September 21, 1801.
46. Catherine Granthum, G.D.B. 17:553, February 17, 1800; 18:356–57, June 15, 1802; Roger Cooper, G.D.B. 16:147, February 12, 1793; Titus Freeman, G.D.B. 18:155, June 12, 1800; Jack Baker, G.D.B. 19:22, April 16, 1804; 18:255, September 21, 1801; Francis Cousins, G.D.B. 22:191, March 18, 1816; Jacob Sampson, G.D.B. 29:6, February 15, 1831.
47. See Jacob Sampson, Petition to the Legislative Assembly, December 17, 1830, LVA; Sampson manumission of wife and children, G.D.B. 29:6, February 15, 1831; will of Daniel Wade, G.D.B. 28:98–99, December 13, 1828; and will of Jacob Sampson, G.D.B. 41:566–67, September 1, 1854 (Daniel Wade's will allowing Sampson to purchase his son Robert). See also Guild, *Black Laws of Virginia,* 106.
48. For the statute legalizing the sale of free Blacks for the violation of the 1806 law, see Guild, *Black Laws of Virginia,* 106.
49. See Schwarz, "Emancipators, Protectors, and Anomalies," 327.
50. Carter G. Woodson, "Free Negro Owners of Slaves in the United States in 1830," *Journal of Negro History* 9 (1924): 6–35; R. Halliburton Jr., "Free Negro Owners of Slaves: A Reappraisal of the Woodson Thesis," *South Carolina Historical Magazine* 76 (1976): 129–42; Larry Koger, *Black Slaveowners: Free Black Slave Masters in South Carolina, 1790–1860* (Jefferson, NC: McFarland, 1985); Jackson, *Free Negro Labor and Property Holding in Virginia.*
51. Schwarz, "Emancipators, Protectors, and Anomalies," 329, 321.

4. YOUTH AND BOUND LABOR

1. W. J. Rorabaugh, *The Craft Apprentice: From Franklin to the Machine Age in America* (New York: Oxford University Press, 1986), vii.

2. Apprenticeship orders appeared in the Goochland County Order Books for the year in which the child was apprenticed. Hannah, G.O.B. 2:13, July 1730; Tom, G.O.B. 2:179, August 3, 1731; Moll and Eleanor Griffin, G.O.B. 3:16, November 16, 1731.
3. David Galenson, *White Servitude in Colonial America: An Economic Analysis* (New York: Cambridge University Press, 1981), 7.
4. For discussion of the history of apprenticeship in England and colonial Virginia, see Grace Abbott, *The Child and the State: Legal Status in the Family Apprenticeship and Child Labor, Select Documents*, 2 vols. (Chicago: University of Chicago Press, 1938), 1:79–90, 1:189–213. For the history of English apprenticeship, see Reginald A. Bray, *Boy Labour and Apprenticeship* (London: Constable, 1911); Robert Francis Seybolt, *Apprenticeship and Apprenticeship Education in Colonial New England and New York* (New York: Arno Press, 1969); Margaret Gay Davies, *The Enforcement of English Apprenticeship: A Study in Applied Mercantilism, 1563–1642* (Cambridge, MA: Harvard University Press, 1956); and O. Jocelyn Dunlop and Richard D. Denman, *English Apprenticeship and Child Labor: A History* (London: T. F. Unwin, 1912).
5. Abbott, *The Child and the State*, 1:195–98.
6. Hening, *Statutes*, vols. 1–2; Robert C. Johnson, "The Transportation of Vagrant Children from London to Virginia, 1618–1622," in *Early Stuart Studies: Essays in Honor of David Harris Willson*, ed. Howard S. Reinmuth Jr. (Minneapolis: University of Minnesota Press, 1970), 137–51.
7. Virginia Bernhard, "Poverty and the Social Order in Seventeenth-Century Virginia," *Virginia Magazine of History and Biography* 85 (1977): 141–55.
8. Hening, *Statutes*, 1:336, October 1646.
9. Morgan, *American Slavery, American Freedom*, 154–57, 334.
10. Apparently, the situation did arise in which indentured mixed-race children received training and education as if they were in an apprentice role. In 1716, the church wardens bound a two-year-old mixed-race boy, George Petsworth, to Ralph Beavis. Beavis was ordered to provide the youth three years' schooling and to carefully "instruct him afterwards that he may read well any part of the bible." Churchill G. Chamberlayne, ed., *Vestry Book of Petsworth Parish, Gloucester, County, 1697–1793* (Richmond: Virginia State Library, 1979). See also the case of Ann Leaver, a mixed-race woman. In 1725, the church wardens bound Ann, described as the "base daughter of Mary Leaver," a white woman, deceased, in James City County. Churchill G. Chamberlayne, ed., *The Vestry Book of Blisland Parish, New Kent and James City Counties, 1721–1786* (Richmond, VA: Division of

Purchase and Printing, 1935). Ann's mother must have died in childbirth for there was confusion as to the race of the child. Racial identification would have determined the nature of her indenture. The churchwardens bound her out with the intention to make a further determination when her racial characteristics became visible. In 1756, Ann, identified as a mixed-race woman, petitioned the county court and received freedom dues. I am grateful to John Hemphill for bringing these two cases to my attention.

11. For reduced years of servitude, see Hening, *Statutes*, 8:134–35; on education of indentured free Black children, see Shepherd, *Statutes*, 3:124.
12. Hening, *Statutes*, 5:11. Free Black apprentices and their parents seemed aware of a clause that first appeared in 1705 and was renewed in subsequent rewritings of statutes. A 1785 version stated that "the court of every county, city or borough, shall at all times receive the complaints of apprentices or hired servants, being citizens of the confederated states of America, who reside within the jurisdiction of such court, against their masters or mistresses, alleging undeserved or immoderate correction, in-sufficient allowance of food, raiment, or lodging, or want of instruction, and may hear and determine such cases in a summary way . . . removing the apprentices, and binding them to other masters and mistresses, when it shall seem necessary."
13. See, for example, Hening, *Statutes*, 12:198, 1785.
14. Jordan, *White over Black*, 52.
15. Rorabaugh, *The Craft Apprentice*, 8, 188.
16. Franklin, *The Free Negro in North Carolina*.
17. Pleasants's undated letter to the court is to be found in Goochland County Miscellaneous Court Papers, 1728–40, box 294, 10, LVA. RV: Butler's citation is for a past filing of this document at LVA. See "Courthouse Custom as an Archival Filter," page 170, for discussion of Philip Pleasants's letter and current citation.
18. Hunnicutt deed, G.D.B. 13:257, October 21, 1782. For apprenticeship orders, see G.O.B. 20:259, April 18, 1796; G.O.B. 26:323, May 16, 1808. For Watkins's deed of manumission, see G.D.B. 13:250–51, October 21, 1782. For a contemporary opinion that Quakers used free Blacks as a semi-enslaved labor force, see Babcock, "Manumission in Virginia," 34–35. Babcock cites a letter from Jefferson to Dr. Edward Bancroft in which he passed on the information that "many Quakers in Virginia seated slaves on their land as tenants. They were distant from me, and therefore I cannot be particular in the details, because I never had very particular

information. I cannot say whether they were to pay rent money, or share of the produce; but I remember that the landlord was obliged during every season & according to the weather to watch them daily & almost constantly to make them work, even to whip them." Obviously, Jefferson was not a neutral observer. Babcock points out that such Quakers were likely in the minority. But in any event, manumitters may well have used juvenile apprenticeship as one means of guaranteeing a somewhat stable free Black labor force.

19. Names were culled from the List of Personal Property Taxes, and the Lists of Tithables.
20. William Bolling is on the List of Personal Property Taxes, 1820.
21. Roger, Tarlton, and Halley Barnett, children of Franky Barnett, were apprenticed to David Ross in 1795; see G.O.B. 20:132, July 20, 1795. The List of Mulattoes and Free Negroes provides information on residency. Between 1806 and 1809, at least five free Black heads of household lived on David Ross's lands: Jesse Wood, 1806, 1809, 1811; Richard Tyler, 1806, 1809; Phil Tyler, 1806, 1809; David Banks, 1806, 1809; Thomas Lynch, 1806. Joseph Scott in 1806, 1809, 1811, and 1813, and Daniel Cooper in 1811 and 1813 were listed as living on land owned by William Bolling.
22. Berlin, *Slaves without Masters*, 226.
23. See G.O.B. 22:690, June 15, 1801, and Helen Tunnicliff Catterall, ed., *Judicial Cases Concerning American Slavery and the Negro*, 5 vols. (Washington, DC: Carnegie Institution, 1926–37), 1:114.
24. Lucy Lynch, G.O.B. 30:73, March 22, 1820.
25. Daniel Cooper, G.O.B. 29:551, January 20, 1817; Nutley Sanders, G.O.B. 12:458, April 17, 1775; Elisha Symes, G.O.B. 28:406, June 15, 1812; William Profitt, G.O.B. 22:113, October 21, 1799.
26. Complaint of David and Daniel Cooper by Rachel Cooper, G.O.B. 14:173, April 22, 1783.
27. In 1764, for example, Mary Cousins was summoned to show cause why her two children, Nan and Sam, should not be bound. She failed to respond, and the court subsequently ordered that the children were to be bound to Richard Daves Hines. G.O.B. 9:320, May 15, 1764.
28. See also G.O.B. 30:180, November 22, 1821, in which relatives seem to have taken on family members as apprentices and "all the children of Emily Copland" were apprenticed to Rich'd Copland. Free Black apprentices also filed complaints on their own behalf. In 1790, Jane Cousins appealed to the Overseers of the Poor when her master Edward Redford refused to release her from her indenture. She had been apprenticed to Redford

eighteen years earlier in 1772. Similarly, John Woodson was summoned to court in 1791 to "show cause why he kept Shepard Cousins beyond full age." Both of these apprentices were later released from their indentures. Elizabeth Mealy, who brought such a complaint against William O'Barrett in 1827, was similarly successful, but only temporarily. On first hearing her case, the court ruled that she was to be released from her indenture of eleven years. A month later, however, it reversed its initial decision, ordering that she was to be rebound to O'Barrett for another year. For Jane Cousins's original binding order, see G.O.B. 12:115, March 16, 1772; her complaint was recorded in G.O.B. 1:162, April 21, 1789, and dismissed G.O.B. 18:173, May 18, 1789. See G.O.B. 18:162, April 21, 1789, for Woodson's summons, which was also dismissed G.O.B. 18:202, July 20, 1789; for Elizabeth Mealy's complaint and reapprenticeship, see G.O.B. 31:117, February 19, 1827; G.O.B. 31:121, March 19, 1827. RV: Charlotte Freeman was emancipated by Joseph Pleasants in 1788 when she was eight years old; see G.D.B. 15:263, December 8, 1788. See Goochland County Miscellaneous Papers, March 25, 1797, barcode 1176172, LVA, for the apprenticeship indentures of Charlotte Scott's oldest children, Cary Scott and Judy Scott, to Joseph Pleasants. When Pleasants died in 1814, Cary was bound to Joseph's widow, Molly Pleasants. Charlotte appears in the List of Mulattoes and Free Negroes between 1802 and 1813 as the wife of Nathan Freeman. They separated around 1814, and her children with Nathan were subsequently bound out. See G.O.B. 29:464, July 15, 1816, for the order to bind Nancy Freeman and Hanna Freeman to Judith Scott; Goochland County Miscellaneous Papers, barcode 1176172, LVA, June 15, 1818, for a writ to bind out Phebe Freeman; and G.O.B. 30:47, September 27, 1819, for the order to bind out Nathan Freeman (age 15), Peyton Freeman (10), Charlotte Freeman (8), John Scott (6), and Joshua Scott (3). The Scott surname for John and Joshua suggests they were born after her separation from Nathan Freeman.

29. For the Daniel Cooper case, see David Cooper bound to William Bolling, G.O.B. 31:461, March 18, 1830; John Cooper bound to William Bolling, G.O.B. 31:120, March 19, 1827; William Bolling administration of Daniel Cooper estate and Burwell Cooper bound to William Bolling, G.O.B. 29:551, January 20, 1817; inventory and appraisal of estate of Daniel Cooper deceased, G.D.B. 22:354–55, March 12, 1817.

30. See order to bind out Austin, Martin, Peyton, and Wilson Isaacs, children of Mary Isaacs, G.O.B. 24:251, August 22, 1804; indenture for Peyton and Austin Isaacs to William Clarke, Goochland County

Miscellaneous Court Papers, box 2-286, LVA. RV: Now see Goochland County Miscellaneous Papers, barcode 1176172, LVA. The October 22, 1804, indenture also includes Wilson Isaacs whose name was struck out with the notation "dead."

31. In July 1820, for example, Mary Alvis was summoned to "shew cause why her children should not be bound out to learn a trade." She appeared in court one month later to "shew why her children should not be bound," and the summons was dismissed. G.O.B. 30:88, July 17, 1820; 94, August 21, 1820. Parental consent as a factor emerged when "by consent of Rachel Cooper" her son was bound to Thomas Eldridge, G.O.B. 14:152, October 21, 1782. Although apprenticeship contributed to a fracturing of family and kin bonds, parents nearly always maintained connections with their apprenticed children, who normally lived in the same vicinity. When Daniel Moss, a free Black boatman, decided to resettle in Ohio in 1827 and to take along his apprentice, William, he had to get the formal approval of Betsy Scott, the boy's mother. Nor could a master legally place his apprentice under the authority of another without going through the court. In 1827, when William Guerrant wished to transfer the indenture of Betsy Cousins to a relative, John Guerrant (probably William's brother), William had first to notify and receive the consent of the court. So too did Philip Pleasants, who in 1830 transferred the indenture of sixteen-year-old Ned Moss to Joseph Pleasants, his son. G.O.B. 31:193, October 15, 1827; 31, 196, November 19, 1827; 31:536, December 20, 1830.

32. Seven original contracts of indenture for free Black children were found in the Goochland County Miscellaneous Court Papers, box 2-286, LVA. They are Peyton and Austin Isaacs to William Clarke, October 22, 1804; Jerdin to Thomas Eldridge, November 18, 1806; Kitty Banks to Joseph Payne, November 18, 1806; Milly James to Rebecca Hunnicutt, August 17, 1798; Charlott, Jack, Betsy, Jordan Scott, and Rebecca Moss to Joseph Pleasants, March 25, 1797; and James, "a poor boy," to John Hunnicutt, August 17, 1798. RV: Twenty-four additional contracts of indenture are in Goochland County Miscellaneous Papers, barcode 1176172, LVA, and another thirty-four in Goochland County Apprentice Indentures, barcode 1176518, LVA.

33. James's indenture to John Hunnicutt, ibid.

34. Hening, *Statutes*, 12:197, 1785.

5. WORK AND FREEDOM

1. Shepherd, *Statutes*, 2:301. The 1804 statute required the county commissioner to record the names, sex, places of residence, and occupations of all free Blacks living in their jurisdictions.
2. List of Mulattoes and Free Negroes, 1811. For Granville Smith's account, see G.D.B. 27:352–53, October 29, 1827. According to the tax list of 1821, Smith owned five slaves.
3. Russell, *Free Negro in Virginia*.
4. Shepherd, *Statutes*, 1:238; 2:301. If the sources are to be considered in some way as part of the story, it is essential to describe and place them in context. The records used in this chapter are roughly divided into three categories. Those that were collected for purposes of identification and social control include residency, occupational, and registration lists. In the late eighteenth and early nineteenth centuries, Virginia's legislature responded to an increasing free Black population and slave unrest by passing a series of laws intended to monitor and restrict local populations of free Blacks. Instruments of measurement and supervision, these lists required rural county commissioners to, first, keep a yearly register of the occupations and residence of all free Black adults and, second, maintain a bound copy of free Black registrants, to be updated every three years, with descriptions of physical characteristics, ages, dates of manumission, and the nature of the individual's free status.
5. The second category of sources, including property and land tax lists, court levies, and the U.S. Census from 1790 to 1830, were general administrative and fiscal records collected according to schedules and conventions established by the state and federal governments. A more diverse group of records make up the final category. These are the estate accounts, inventories, and criminal court cases, records of transactions involving free Blacks that were not regulated by any administrative powers but created in response to the idiosyncratic and chance interactions of the county's residents. If the first two categories of documents provide an "official," almost regimented view of free Blacks, then this final group of documents may be said to provide, given the unavailability of strictly subjective material, insight into the ordinary routines of free Black workers.
6. Data on the occupation and residency of free Black individuals were taken from the List of Mulattoes and Free Negroes.
7. The Tuckahoe and Licking Hole Creeks were navigable in the county's lower district. A petition by Goochland and Henrico residents from the early 1800s requested that the assembly permit them to convert the

Tuckahoe into a "highway" for the transportation of coal, wheat, corn, and other products to the James River and hence to Richmond. See Petitions to the Assembly, D5–6052, LVA. (RV: Now see Legislative Petitions of the General Assembly, 1776–1865, accession number 36121, box 90, folder 77, May 20, 1812, LVA.) Also in this regard, in 1803, Josiah Leake requested the county court's permission, "according to an act of Assembly, Dec. 21st, 1792," to clear obstructions to allow passage of boats from the mouth of the Licking Hole up to Leake's mill. G.O.B. 23:556, July 18, 1803. For further references to the James River and canal traffic, see G.O.B. 31:23, March 18, 1826; 31:65, July 17, 1826.

8. Richard Adams's economic activities in the county emerged in account books, in licenses for his boat, and in the occupation and tax lists. See, for example, List of Personal Property Taxes, 1804–30. Adams paid taxes on slaves, livestock, and horses. For land ownership, see Land Taxes, 1822–28, LVA. His involvement as a wagoner and boatmen is documented in James Carter's accounts: G.D.B. 25:397, February 8, 1821; Thomas Miller, G.D.B. 26:225, August 16, 1820; William Mullins, G.D.B. 25:293, January 1807; 25:295, April 3, 1815; Robert Lewis, G.D.B. 20:156, March 29, 1805; Richard Adams boat ownership, G.O.B. 31:263, July 21, 1828.

9. See Mullin, *Flight and Rebellion*, 156, on the movement and independence of boatmen, wagoners, and other Blacks involved in the transportation of goods from Richmond to western counties. For John Lynch, see G.D.B. 28:358–59, August 15, 1828. For a description of regional roadways, see Nathaniel Mason Pawlett and Howard Newlon, *The Route of the Three Notch'd Road: A Preliminary Report* (Charlottesville: Virginia Highway and Transportation Research Council, 1976).

10. Wayland Fuller Dunaway, *History of the James River and Kanawha Canal Company* (1922; New York: Columbia University Studies in History, Economics, and Public Law, 1969); George William Bagby, *Canal Reminiscences: Recollections of Travel in the Old Days on the James River and Kanawha Canal* (Richmond, VA: West, Johnston, 1879); List of Mulattoes and Free Negroes, 1803–12.

11. Account of Francis Harris, G.D.B. 26:153, December 23, 1824.

12. *Commonwealth v. Nathaniel Banks and Jacob Banks*, in Goochland Superior Court Order Book, 22:292, 299, 327, 352, 389, 395, 417, 449, 476, running from April 5, 1819, to February 14, 1822.

13. On Sampson's operation of the tavern and other enterprises, see G.O.B. 31:474, May 17, 1830; 32:22, May 16, 1831. At the same time that Sampson received a license to operate a tavern, the similar request of a white

resident (John P. Cosby) was denied; see G.O.B. 31:149, May 15, 1826. But in 1844, the court, for reasons that are not specified, revoked Sampson's license. In spite of repeated petitions to the assembly, Sampson was unable to regain a license to operate his business; see G.O.B. 1844–52:8, May 20, 1844. See also Jackson, *Free Negro Labor and Property Holding in Virginia*, 29, and Schwarz, "Emancipators, Protectors, and Anomalies," 317–38.
14. Charges against Peyton, David Cousins, and Tarlton Barnett, G.M.B. 1811–18:403, October 20, 1817; trials of Peyton, David Cousins, and Tarlton Barnett, G.M.B. 1811–18:406, October 21, 1817.
15. According to a 1797 statute it was illegal for free Blacks and slaves to retail goods to one another; see Shepherd, *Statutes*, 2:94.
16. Henry and David Cousins posted fifty dollars each for David Cousins; see G.M.B. 1811–18:403, October 20, 1817.
17. On the shift to mixed-grain agriculture, see John C. Robert, *The Tobacco Kingdom: Plantation Market and Factory in Virginia and North Carolina, 1800–1860* (Durham, NC: Duke University Press, 1938); Kulikoff, *Tobacco and Slaves*; Lewis C. Gray, *History of Agriculture in the Southern United States to 1860*, 2 vols. (Washington, D.C.: Carnegie Institution, 1933); Morgan, "Slave Life in Piedmont Virginia"; Dunn, "Black Society in the Chesapeake"; and Ronald L. Lewis, "'The Darkest Abode of Man': Black Mines in the First Southern Coal Field, 1780–1865," *Virginia Magazine of History and Biography* 87 (1979): 190–202.
18. U.S. Census, 1810, 1820, 1830.
19. This data was compiled from the LVA tax lists of 1782, 1791, 1801, 1811, 1821, and 1831.
20. Data compiled from planters' accounts in which payments were made to free Blacks from 1782 to 1832, G.D.B. 13–29.
21. Argyle's account, G.D.B. 25:489, September 13, 1811, for unnamed boatman; February 14, 1814, for John Pierce.
22. For Pierce's boat registration, see G.O.B. 28:69, April 15, 1811.
23. G.D.B. 25:489–91, December 15, 1823.
24. List of Personal Property Taxes, 1821. For Harris's account, see G.D.B. 26:152–55, February 19, 1825; 28:374–76, April 19, 1830. For Cowig's apprenticeship as a shoemaker, see G.O.B. 29:201, December 19, 1814.
25. G.D.B. 26:153–54, May 17, 1825; G.D.B. 28:375, August 18, 1829. RV: Also see G.D.B. 24:331, November 1, 1825, for Probst's purchase of a lot adjacent to the canal. Henry Probst (1789–1849) was a Richmond grocer whose store was on the James River Canal in the 1820s; he also owned canal boats.

26. For a joint payment to James Tyler and Frank Coley, see G.D.B. 26:152–53, June 18, 1824; for two payments to Frank Coley, see G.D.B. 26:152–53, July 3 and December 23, 1824.
27. For one payment to Nancy Jennings, see G.D.B. 26:152–53, May 21, 1823; for two payments to Lucy Crouch, see G.D.B. 26:152–53, November 13, 1823, and April 15, 1824; for three payments to Lucy Crouch, see G.D.B. 28:374–75, July 19, 1828, September 1, 1829, and November 21, 1829.
28. List of Personal Property Taxes, 1813; Harris's accounts, G.D.B. 26:152–55, February 19, 1825; 28:374–76, April 19, 1830. See also List of Personal Property Taxes, 1830, for an estimate of Harris's estate value.
29. Tax and occupational lists indicate the patterns of residency in both the lower and upper districts of the county.
30. Francis Harris's accounts, G.D.B. 26:152–55, February 19, 1825; 28:374–76, April 19, 1830; Lewis, "'The Darkest Abode of Man.'" On John Martin, see G.D.B. 27:58, May 1, 1826.
31. U.S. Census, 1850, Occupational Schedule; Lewis, "'The Darkest Abode of Man.'"
32. List of Mulattoes and Free Negroes.
33. See Berlin, *Slaves without Masters*, 234–40.
34. Ibid., 236.
35. Appraisal of Robert Lewis estate, G.D.B. 20:153–59, May 28, August 14, 1802.
36. To Bartlett Isaacs for making a coffin, G.D.B. 29:166, January 1, 1830. For Isaacs's apprenticeship, see G.O.B. 24:65, 77, January 16, February 20, 1804, and William Shelton's account, G.D.B. 26:362–64, January 15, 1826; 27:506, August 3, 1826.
37. William Howell in William Shelton's accounts, G.D.B. 27:506, March 17, August 7, 1826; April 3, May 2, August 27, October 28, 1827; Henrietta Gray in William Shelton's accounts, G.D.B. 26:362–63, May 28, October 6, 1824; February 14, June 4, 1825.
38. Samuel Cocke and Woodson Cocke in Granville Smith accounts, G.D.B. 27:352–53, February 23, November 14, 1828; William McRae and Kenneth McRae in William George accounts, G.D.B. 28:224, February 23, November 14, 1828; Jessee Fuzmore in William Mullins accounts, G.D.B. 25:294, January 7, 1814. For other free Black blacksmiths, see John Cousins, G.O.B. 32:164, October 15, 1832, apprenticed as a carriagemaker and blacksmith to James Clarke, and David and Daniel Cooper apprenticed to William Bolling, G.O.B. 29:551, January 20, 1817; G.O.B. 31:461, March 18, 1830.
39. List of Mulattoes and Free Negroes, 1811, 1817.

40. U.S. Census, 1850, Occupational Schedule. Moses Cross was not listed as a miller in the List of Mulattoes and Free Negroes. He learned his craft while a slave of Joel Cross, a miller. In his petition to the assembly, Moses Cross described his experience in the production and sale of milled grain; see Legislative Petitions of the General Assembly, December 18, 1822. For other free Black millers, see G.O.B. 28:225, October 21, 1811, in which Ben, a juvenile, was apprenticed to Isaac Webster to learn the trade of a miller, and Noel Smith, a free Black miller in the upper district. For barbers and tailors, see John Pierce and Charles Henley, List of Mulattoes and Free Negroes.
41. G.D.B. 28:225, 1826, 1827, September 3, 1829; 28:358–59, August 15, 1828, 1829; John Lynch in Thomas Matthews account, G.D.B. 27:59, May 23, 1825.
42. G.D.B. 25:104, March 2, 1822; 21:624–25, January 28, 1814. For Isaacs's apprenticeship, see G.O.B. 22:113, October 21, 1799; 24:65, 77, January 16, February 20, 1804.
43. G.D.B. 25:104, March 2, 1822; 21:624–25, January 28, 1814.
44. Ibid.
45. For transaction receipts documenting the multistranded participation of free Blacks in the marketing and exchange activities between Goochland and bordering counties, see Loose Papers at Cabell Library (no online index), Goochland County Historical Society, Goochland, VA.
46. Insolvent list for 1826, G.D.B. 27:202, May 22, 1827; List of Personal Property Taxes, 1830.
47. G.O.B. 29:120, June 26, 1814.
48. G.O.B. 30:64, February 21, 1820.
49. Hening, *Statutes*, 11:40. For the statute imposing an additional poll tax on free Blacks, see Guild, *Black Laws of Virginia*, 137, and Russell, *Free Negro in Virginia*, 112–16.

6. KIN, NEIGHBORS, AND COMMUNITY CONSOLIDATION

1. Tithes of Walter Leake for 1746, 1755, Lists of Tithables. Leake died in 1758; his will transferred slaves, land, and household goods to his wife and children; see G.D.B. 7:279–80, October 31, 1757, recorded May 16, 1758.
2. Tithes of Walter Leake, 1746, Lists of Tithables.
3. Gideon Banks was probably Mary's son, although the order to bind him to Walter Leake does not mention Mary; see G.O.B. 4:132, October 19, 1742. Jane's apprenticeship order may be found in G.O.B. 5:490, September 18, 1744, and Louisa's in G.O.B. 6:561, November 21, 1749; John, Judith, Jacob, and Agnes, children of Mary Banks, were apprenticed in 1757

to Walter Leake, G.O.B. 7:646, May 17, 1757, and following his death to Judith Leake, G.O.B. 8:180, February 20, 1759.
4. Following Walter Leake's death, Jane and Louisa were reapprenticed in 1760 to Judith Leake, G.O.B. 8:365, September 16, 1760.
5. Jane's suit for freedom dues and release from her indenture appeared in G.O.B. 9:208, July 19, 1763. RV: Jane's suit was among the unprocessed Goochland County manuscripts when Butler conducted his research. It is available in Goochland Judgments (Freedom Suits), 1763, box 32, barcode 7635206; July 1763, box 32, barcode 1138413, LVA.
6. For Jacob's complaint against Elisha Leake and his reapprenticeship, see G.O.B. 12:263, December 21, 1772.
7. *Douglas Register,* 347, August 29, 1775.
8. Jackson, *Virginia Negro Soldiers and Seamen in the Revolutionary War,* 29. RV: For digital sources for pension applications unavailable during Butler's research, see C. Leon Harris, "Pension Application of Jacob Banks S8056," Southern Campaigns Revolutionary War Pension Statements and Rosters, 2014, https://revwarapps.org/s8056.pdf, and for John Banks, C. Leon Harris, "Pension Application of John Banks W5763," Southern Campaigns Revolutionary War Pension Statements and Rosters, 2015, https://revwarapps.org/w5763.pdf.
9. List of Personal Property Taxes, 1782; List of Mulattoes and Freed Negroes, 1806.
10. Jacob claimed a pension as a Revolutionary War veteran in 1832. He would have been in his eighties. See G.O.B. 32:152, 1832. RV: John reported that Jacob died on January 5, 1835, and John died on November 24, 1842, at age ninety-four. See their pension applications previously cited and *Ledgers of Payments, 1818–1872, to U.S. Pensioners, under Acts of 1818 through 1858, from Records of the Office of the Third Auditor of the Treasury* (Washington, DC: Department of the Treasury, 1962), 349.
11. See List of Personal Property Taxes, 1811, 1813. An 1808 deed between Archibald Bryce, a white planter, and John Banks documented Banks's purchase of household furniture and livestock, including "a steer, one heifer, one sow and pigs, one bed and furniture, together with all my [Bryce's] household and kitchen furniture and plantation tools and utensils, also a quantity of tobacco on hand supposed to contain 1000 or 1800 weight." G.D.B. 20:72–73, March 3, 1808.
12. The two brothers and their children appeared on the List of Personal Property Taxes, 1782–1824. See also U.S. Censuses, 1810, 1820, and 1830, for the Bankses' households.

13. Elisha and John Banks were listed as renters in 1811. See List of Mulattoes and Free Negroes, 1811.
14. Records of the Bankses' family marriages before 1815 may be found in Williams, *Marriages of Goochland County*. After that date, marriages were documented in Hughes and Standefer, *Goochland County Virginia Marriage Bonds*.
15. Marriage of John Banks Jr and Polly Randolph, in Hughes and Standefer, *Goochland County Virginia Marriage Bonds*, 6, April 7, 1819.
16. Marriage of John Tiler and Polly Banks, in Williams, *Marriages of Goochland County*, 98, December 23, 1797; marriage of Dick Adams and Jane Banks, in ibid., 1, December 5, 1803; marriage of Elijah Day and Judith Banks, in ibid., 23, December 28, 1815.
17. Marriage of Drury Farrar and Elizabeth Banks, in ibid., 28, December 2, 1801; marriage of John Banks and Biddy Anne Tyler, in Hughes and Standefer, *Goochland County Virginia Marriage Bonds*, 6, March 14, 1823.
18. Berlin, *Slaves without Masters*, 340.
19. For the names of his children, see Walter Leake's will, G.D.B. 7:279, October 31, 1757. For Mary Banks and Henry Isaacs's marriage, see Williams, *Marriages of Goochland County*, 45, November 4, 1787. RV: Henry Isaacs was formerly enslaved in Fluvanna County. The lack of familial support for this marriage follows the pattern of the Richard Adams marriage Butler describes.
20. For the marriage of Richard Adams and Jane Banks, see Williams, *Marriages of Goochland County*, 1, December 5, 1803.
21. Richard Adams's self-purchase from James Holman is recorded in G.D.B. 18:671–72, July 21, 1803. See List of Personal Property Taxes, 1801, for Josiah Leake's slaveholdings.
22. John Banks's suit for breach of the peace against Richard Adams, G.O.B. 24:56, December 19, 1803.
23. On Richard Adams, see chap. 5, note 8, above. The later chapter was never written. See Joshua D. Rothman, "Introduction," above.
24. *Commonwealth v. Nathaniel Banks and Jacob Banks*, in Goochland Superior Court Order Book 1809–22:292, 299, 327, 352, 389, 395, 417, 449, 476, running from April 5, 1819, to February 14, 1822.
25. For John Banks's trial, see G.O.B. 30:170, October 15, 1821; 30:176–77, November 20–21, 1821.
26. Thomas Ford registration, Number 82, Goochland County Register of Free Negroes, 40, December 24, 1810.
27. Thomas Ford's will, G.D.B. 22:193, November 22, 1813.

28. Ibid.
29. Ibid.
30. Charles Bates's inventory lists nineteen slaves, including a girl, Judy; a boy, Squire; and a girl and boy at the bottom of a damaged page. G.D.B. 20:653–54, September 20, 1808.
31. List of Personal Property Taxes, 1809.
32. See Frank Cousins in Goochland County Register of Free Negroes, 137, December 18, 1822, which states that he was emancipated by virtue of the wills of John and Jonathan Pleasants. The chancery court approved the Pleasants will in which slaves were to be freed if private manumission became legal. See *Pleasants v. Pleasants,* in Catterall, *Judicial Cases Concerning American Slavery,* 1:105.
33. For Frank Cousins's purchase and manumission of Ridley and her children, see G.D.B. 22:191, March 18, 1816. For Ridley's marriage to John Copeland, see Hughes and Standefer, *Goochland County Virginia Marriage Bonds,* 22, August 12, 1824.
34. Thomas Ford's will, G.D.B. 22:193, November 22, 1813; Squire Caesar's will, G.D.B. 23:1–2, May 28, 1817; Titus Freeman's will, G.D.B. 18:155, June 12, 1800; Samuel Cooper's will, G.D.B. 31:411, June 20, 1838; Catherine Granthum's will, G.D.B. 20:53–54, June 15, 1802; David Granthum's will, G.D.B. 19:64, October 17, 1801.
35. Free Blacks regularly stood security for each other in criminal procedures. Riley Scott and Grief Scott were securities for Joel Scott, who was convicted of breach of the peace against William Martin; see G.O.B. 29:307, July 17, 1815.
36. List of Personal Property Taxes, 1811, 1813; U.S. Census, 1810.
37. In addition to purchasing her family members, Catherine purchased at least two tracts of land, one totaling two hundred acres; see G.D.B. 18:374–75, March 13, 1802; the other, twenty acres, G.D.B. 18:429–30, April 8, 1802.
38. Catherine Granthum's last name is variously spelled in the records, appearing as Grantham and Grantum. Manumitted by will of Gideon Cawthon in 1797, G.D.B. 17:515–16, July 17, 1797, she then purchased and freed her son Woodson, G.D.B. 17:552–53, February 17, 1800, and also purchased her husband, Phil, G.D.B. 18:428–29, June 21, 1802, and freed him, G.D.B. 18:356–57, June 15, 1802. The deed of loan in which she transferred her property to him with restrictions appeared in G.D.B. 18:357, June 15, 1802. Her will may be found in G.D.B. 20:53–54, June 15, 1802. An inventory of her estate by James Holman and others was valued at £12.5.9,

G.D.B. 20:334–35, March 25, 1808, and a settlement of accounts by Josiah Leake was recorded in 1822, G.D.B. 25:172–73, July 15, 1822. RV: Richard Bates and John Herndon refused to serve as executors and Josiah Leake agreed to settle the estate, but it apparently wasted under Leake's administration, in spite of the appointment of James Carter as guardian in 1811.

39. See Deed of Loan to Phil Granthum from Catherine Granthum, G.D.B. 18:356, June 15, 1802.
40. Lebsock, *The Free Women of Petersburg*, 23–26.
41. List of Personal Property Taxes. John Herndon owned four and Thomas Bates ten slaves in 1801.
42. See annual county levies from 1803 to 1827, usually recorded in May in Goochland Order Books. John Pierce's deed of manumission may be found in G.D.B. 22:292–93, November 20, 1816. Exemption from removal law granted in G.O.B. 29:550, January 20, 1817.
43. See annual levy, G.O.B. 26:82–83, September 21, 1807. On the centrality of court day, and of social networks see Isaac, *Transformation of Virginia, 1740–1790*, 88–94. The power of the information gained during involvement in the frequent court days must not have escaped Goochland County's authorities. In 1837, they attempted to limit free Blacks' and slaves' participation in or observation of trials and courthouse activities. The local justices ordered the sheriff to "keep all slaves and free negroes out of the courthouse while the court is sitting unless they have business before the court." G.O.B. 1836–44:50, August 21, 1837.
44. Milly Pierce appeared on the List of Mulattoes and Free Negroes, 1804, 1806, 1811, and 1817, when John was first listed. See also U.S. Census, 1820, 1830. For taxes paid on land, see Land Tax List for 1806, 1818, LVA. For land purchases, see G.D.B. 21:682, April 21, 1814.
45. Transactions between the Pierces and John Fleming appeared in G.D.B. 26:168, 1825. They had earlier entered into a similar agreement with Benjamin Anderson, G.D.B. 24:355, July 20, 1820.
46. Addendum providing life tenure for children, G.D.B. 26:168–69, May 5, 1825.

COURTHOUSE CUSTOM AS AN ARCHIVAL FILTER

1. Butler, *Evolution*, 1.
2. For an example of this concept, see Joanne M. Braxton, "Symbolic Geography and Psychic Landscapes: A Conversation with Maya Angelo," in Braxton, ed., *Maya Angelou's I Know Why the Caged Bird Sings: A Casebook* (New York: Oxford University Press, 1999), 1–20.

3. Butler, *Evolution*, 3.
4. Bridgett Cooper's inquisition, G.O.B. 19:432–34, January 15, 1794.
5. A notable exception to this generalization is that civil and criminal cases in Albemarle County were separated and Albemarle has a record series called "Judgments" for civil cases and another for "Commonwealth Causes," filed as "Criminal Records." The series for Albemarle Criminal Records was microfilmed by the LVA and consists of 104 reels that span 1749 to 1922. Images of Albemarle Criminal Records from 1749 to 1826 are now available online in the Reginald D. Butler Local History Archive, https://community.village.virginia.edu/cvhr/universalviewer/scans. As of 2023, Goochland Judgments are only available as manuscripts at the LVA.
6. The LVA probably retains an inventory for Goochland papers with information that date when Goochland records were moved from the courthouse to Richmond. When Albemarle's loose papers were transferred in February 1984 an unindexed inventory of over 160 pages was created.
7. *Commonwealth v. Cooper*, Goochland Judgments, January 1794, box 65, barcode 1138445, LVA.
8. Ibid.
9. James Richmond, "Lost Goochland—The Forest," Goochland History Society, https://goochlandhistory.wordpress.com/2012/05/12/the-forest/. Also see G.D.B. 11:97–99, February 15, 1776.
10. G.D.B. 19:40–42, December 13, 1803, and recorded June 18, 1804.
11. G.D.B. 20:147–49, March 8, 1808. The plats are located between pages 160 and 161 of G.D.B. 20. Copies of the "Charlie Forest" and "Beaverdam" plats were also included in an 1825 chancery suit: *Pleasants' Adm'r v. Pleasants, etc.*, Goochland County (Va.) Chancery Causes 1825-001, LVA.
12. Goochland County, "Free Negro and Slave Records," oversize box 2, barcode 1149995, LVA. Lists are available for the upper and lower districts of Goochland for most years between 1802 and 1817, except 1808 when no taxes were collected in Virginia. See "Virginia Untold" for transcriptions and images of lists.
13. Bridgett was ten years old when she was emancipated in 1782. G.D.B. 13:246–47, October 21, 1782.
14. William H. Pleasants was married about a year after the death of Bridgett's child, on October 3, 1795, to Mary Ladd. See Hinshaw, *Encyclopedia of American Quaker Genealogy*, 6:194, 208.
15. *Commonwealth v. Cooper*, Goochland Judgments.
16. Butler, *Evolution*, 7.

17. See the LVA list of Goochland County records available on microfilm. The only significant record book missing is the County Surveyor's Book. FamilySearch.org has a useful inventory of books, county records, and manuscripts available for Goochland County.
18. *Douglas Register.*
19. See Birth and Baptismal Record Book, Louisa County, VA, Tennessee Virtual Archive, https://cdm15138.contentdm.oclc.org/digital/collection/p15138coll14/id/56, for what appears to be a register for Trinity Parish in Louisa County.
20. See FamilySearch.org for more information on Hanover records. The LVA maintains a "Lost Records Localities Digital Collection" with images of Hanover manuscripts.
21. Burned Jurisdiction Database, LVA, https://www.lva.virginia.gov/public/guides/burned_juris/index.htm.
22. See the important work of Jack D. Forbes, *Africans and Native Americans: The Language of Race and the Evolution of Red-Black Peoples,* 2nd ed. (Urbana: University of Illinois Press, 1993), 103.
23. This freedom suit is an example of archival filtering. It was formerly available as *Kinney v. Johnson,* Albemarle Chancery, 1798–017, LVA. When chancery suits were scanned it was recatalogued as *Kinney, Wilson: Freedom Suit* (1798), Albemarle County (Va.) Judgments (Freedom Suits), 1782–1832, and is available through "Virginia Untold." Also see *Kenney, Joney: Freedom Suit,* Albemarle County (Va.) Judgments (Freedom Suits), 1798, LVA. It was filed in Louisa County and references a suit in the "District Court of Richmond between Jno Kenney one of the descendants of Joan Kenney in the maternal line and John Hicks."
24. "List of the Free Negros and Mulattoes in the District of Peter Crawford (Green Springs) about 1860." The date given for this list is incorrect. Peter Crawford was a commissioner of the revenue in Louisa County between 1801 and 1807. A careful comparison of the names in his list with names in the personal property tax indicates that this list was made in 1803.
25. See C. Leon Harris, "Pension Application of Zachariah Bowles S39201," Southern Campaigns Revolutionary War Pension Statements and Rosters, 2017, https://revwarapps.org/s39201.pdf. According to the Pension Roll of 1835, he resided in Hanover County and died February 1, 1829. Secretary of War, "Statement, &c. of Hanover County, Virginia," in *Report from the Secretary of War in Relation to the Pension Establishment of the United States,* 3 vols. (Washington, DC: Duff Green, 1835), 2:67. See the

will of Zachariah Bowles, son of Amy Bowles, Albemarle County Will Book 12:95–96, December 1834 and recorded June 1, 1835, AC (microfilm copy at LVA). He was born in 1769 in Albemarle County, according to the 1833 Albemarle list of free people of color. See Free Black Records, 1833–63, Virginia Auditor of Public Accounts (1776–1928), accession APA 757, LVA. An inventory of the estate of a third Zachariah Bowles was taken in Goochland County; see G.D.B. 8:170, June 9, 1761.

26. Catherine Foster's purchase of 2⅛ acres for $450 from John Winn is recorded in Albemarle County Deed Book 31:208–9, December 13, 1833, AC (microfilm copy at LVA).

27. Joshua Rothman, *Notorious in the Neighborhood: Sex and Families across the Color Line in Virginia, 1787–1861* (Chapel Hill: University of North Carolina Press, 2003), 204–5.

28. Tipton Ray Snavely, *The Taxation of Negroes in Virginia* (Charlottesville, VA: Michie, 1916), 12. Snavely cites *Acts Passed at a General Assembly of the Commonwealth of Virginia* (Richmond, VA: Samuel Pleasants, 1813), 6–8, which specifies that "all free negroes and mulattoes above the age of sixteen years shall be subject to a poll tax of one dollar and fifty cents." The act was modified in 1814 limiting the tax to "all male free negroes and mulattoes." It also required "the several commissioners of the revenue . . . to make out correct lists and set the same down in a separate column . . . of all male free negroes and mulattoes . . . who are subject to the tax."

29. Virginia personal property tax records are available on microfilm at the LVA.

30. Goochland County, "Free Negro and Slave Records."

31. Shepherd, *Statutes*, 2:301.

32. Powhatan County (Va.), "Free Negro and Slave Records," 1780–1866, "Virginia Untold."

33. "Fluvanna County Lists of Free People of Color," located in the archives of the Fluvanna County Historical Society, on file at Maggie's House, Palmyra, Virginia (adjacent to the courthouse).

34. "List of People of Color and Free Negroes," A.O.B. 1801–3:428, October 4, 1802. A thorough search at the LVA of many bundles of unprocessed loose county papers returned in 1802 for Albemarle County has not produced a copy of this list.

35. Although Butler does not cover the distinction between "at" and "on" in his manuscript, the topic was a point for lively discussion in our private conversations. Luther Porter Jackson, "The Virginia Free Negro Farmer

and Property Owner, 1830–1860," *Journal of Negro History* 24 (1939): 390–439, at 400.

36. Very little is known about Aaron Barbour aside from his identity as an "Indian," his occupation, and the fact that he lived in Albemarle, Goochland, and Fluvanna Counties between 1807 and 1816. Also see Albemarle Criminal Records, reel 241, frames 238–43, 271–75.
37. List of Personal Property Taxes, 1810, 1811.
38. *Journal of the House of Delegates* (Richmond, VA: Thomas Ritchie, 1832), December 3, 1832.
39. *Acts Passed at a General Assembly of the Commonwealth of Virginia* (Richmond, VA: Thomas Ritchie, 1832): 14–15, March 4, 1833.
40. A.M.B. 1832–34:223, June 3, 1833.
41. For these lists and the material in the previous two paragraphs, see Free Black Records, 1833–63.
42. Albemarle County Book of Orphan's Indentures, 1817–87, 51, July 3, 1826; 67, July 5, 1830, barcode 1110444, State Records Center, LVA.
43. Butler, *Evolution*, 46.
44. "Cooper, Davy (M): Free Negro Affidavit," 1831, "Virginia Untold." Also see Butler, *Evolution*, 100, for his account of Daniel and David Cooper, sons of Rachel Cooper, who were "ill treated" during their apprenticeship to Japheth Towler.
45. David Cooper Registration, no. 483, Goochland County Register of Free Negroes, 238, December 19, 1831.
46. Searches on some counties did not return any document images. That may be because they are burned counties (Buckingham and Hanover) or because manuscripts have not been processed. Searches by county do not list registrations that were presented in other counties. For example, a copy of William Isaacs's 1818 Nelson County registration can be found among Albemarle registrations, but cannot be found in a search of Nelson County registrations.
47. Goochland County Register of Free Negroes, 142–43, January 20, 1823, for Darkas Brown; 144, January 1823, for Abram Porter; 146, April 5, 1823, for Henry Cousins; 251–52, June 27, 1833, for Lavinia Johnson.
48. Butler, *Evolution*, 47.
49. My classification of the 468 documents for Albemarle County in "Virginia Untold" mostly followed the website's metadata categories.
50. West Gardner registration, A.M.B. 1854–56:292, July 7, 1856. A transcription of the order book entry was filed at the courthouse with Gardner's replacement register.

51. A.M.B. 1854–56:306, August 5, 1856.
52. Reverend Edgar Woods, *Albemarle County in Virginia* (Charlottesville, VA: Michie, 1901), 232.
53. West Gardner registration, A.O.B. 1842–44:216, August 7, 1843.
54. The Virginia Open Data Portal hosts a website for "Free Registrations" that contains over 7,500 entries derived from "Free Negro and Slave Records" for many counties at the LVA. See https://data.virginia.gov/group/education. A CSV file is available for download. Some of the analysis of primary sources presented here is used to supplement information from "Virginia Untold"; "Free Negro Registers" for Goochland, Fluvanna, and Louisa Counties; and the entries for registrations in the Albemarle County order books.
55. See, for example, Registrations of James James Jr., available in "Virginia Untold."
56. Free Registers (indexing), "Virginia Untold."
57. Butler, *Evolution*, 127.
58. Ibid., 126–28, 132–34.
59. Gideon Banks, G.O.B. 5:132, October 19, 1742; Jane Banks, G.O.B. 5:490, September 18, 1744; Louisa Banks, G.O.B. 6:561, November 21, 1749; Agnes, Jacob, John, Judy Banks, G.O.B. 7:646, May 17, 1757; Agnes, Jacob, John, and Judy Banks, G.O.B. 8:180, February 10, 1759; Jane and Louisa Banks, G.O.B. 8:365, September 16, 1760; Jane Banks [petition for freedom and dues], G.O.B. 9:63, June 15, 1762; Jane Banks [petition for freedom and dues], G.O.B. 9:208, July 19, 1763; Jacob Banks [petition to remove from Elisha Leake], G.O.B. 12:263, December 21, 1772.
60. *Banks v. Leak*, Goochland Judgments, July 1763, box 32, barcode 1138413, LVA. For court decree, see G.O.B. 9:208, July 19, 1763. Also see Gloria Whittico, "The Rule of Law and the Genesis of Freedom: Survey of Selected Virginia County Court Freedom Suits (1723–1800)," *Alabama Civil Rights and Civil Liberties Law Review* 9 (2018): 445–46.
61. Benjamin Via indenture, FPVB, 1742–87:64, 1755 [no day or month].
62. P.D.B. 4 (1774–78):144, May 19, 1775; Pittsylvania County Order Book 3 (1772–75):431, May 25, 1775, PC (microfilm copy at LVA).
63. See Louisa County Deed Book B (1754–59):210–12, August 19, 1757, Louisa County Clerk's Office, Louisa, VA (microfilm copy at LVA).
64. See Hening, *Statutes*, 8:134–35.
65. P.D.B. 4 (1774–78):144, May 19, 1775.
66. Butler, *Evolution*, 93.

67. Bathsheba Holloway indenture, FPVB, 38, June 27, 1749; Janey Brown indenture, FPVB, 124–25, August 11, 1763; Lucy Hagar indenture, FPVB, 125–26, November 21, 1763.
68. See Hening, *Statutes,* 8:134–35.
69. Ibid., 12:274.
70. "List of Overseers of the Poor of the First District of the County of Goochland," Goochland County Apprenticeship Indentures, 1817–87, Overseers of the Poor, folder 1, barcode 1176518, LVA. Some of the children in this list were bound out in 1806; see G.O.B. 25:220, July 21, 1806, and "A Return of Orphins in the North East District," January 11, 1787, Albemarle County Unprocessed Court Records, 1800–1820, barcode 1176182, LVA.
71. See Butler, *Evolution,* 96, and "Philip Pleasants' Letter to Court," n.d., Goochland County Apprenticeship Indentures.
72. As of November 2024, images for 1,901 indentures of apprenticeship dating from 1726 to 1893 were available at "Virginia Untold." In addition, a spreadsheet containing abstracted data from 2,383 indentures of apprenticeship is available for download at the Virginia Open Data Portal. Images available from "Virginia Untold" for central Virginia counties include sixty-four from Goochland, eighty-three from Powhatan, fifty-six from Fluvanna, thirty-eight from Cumberland, thirty-three from Louisa, and forty-two from Albemarle. Between 1808 and 1820, at least thirty-four apprenticeship indentures were recorded in Nelson County Deed Books. Also see the Reginald D. Butler Local History Archive for images of apprenticeship indentures and court orders to bind out children from Albemarle, Fluvanna, Goochland, and Louisa Counties.
73. Apprenticeship indentures were not recorded in the vestry book of St. Ann's Parish in Albemarle County (1772–85), the vestry book of St. James Northam Parish in Goochland County (1744–1850), or the vestry book of King William Parish in Henrico and Goochland Counties (1707–50).
74. See, for example, "Petition of Jane Matthews," n.d. but c. early 1800s, Albemarle County Unprocessed Court Records, barcode 1176192, LVA.
75. See, for example, Charles Sprouse in Louisa County Order Book 1772–74:32, June 8, 1772; 69, December 12, 1772; and 74, January 11, 1773, Louisa County Clerk's Office, Louisa, VA (microfilm copy at LVA).
76. Louisa County Overseers of the Poor Records, Indentures, 1778–1900, and Minutes, 1772–1830, barcode 1153165, LVA. For Mary Thacker, see Louisa County Commonwealth and Ended Causes, April 10, 1786, box 1, 1786 folder, barcode 1153136, LVA.

77. George and William Booth, A.O.B. 1798-1800:136, October 3, 1798.
78. Catharine Martin petition, G.O.B. 8:125-26, February 21, 1758. The manuscript petition can be found in Goochland County Apprenticeship Indentures.
79. Butler, *Evolution*, 173.
80. Hening, *Statutes*, 4:213; 3:452. For a detailed discussion of laws relating to illegitimate children in Virginia, see Dominik Lasok, "Virginia Bastardy Laws: A Burdensome Heritage," *William and Mary Law Review* 9, no. 2 (December 1967): 402-29.
81. See Rothman, "Introduction," xxiii-xxiv.
82. For an example, see the indentures of "Joseph Going & Sarah Going two Bastard Children of Agness Going," which gives their dates of birth in FPVB, 92-93, November 28, 1759.
83. Joseph Welch and Hannah Welch, A.O.B. 1744-48:62, September 26, 1745. No other Welches appear in this order book.
84. John Russell, G.O.B. 8:175, January 16, 1759.
85. See Butler, *Evolution*, 81, for his discussion of the Hoosling and Russell freedom suits. I did not encounter a case for Hoosling in a review of Goochland Judgments, 1755-57, box 27, barcode 1138407, and box 28, barcode 1138408, LVA.
86. The manuscripts for this case are now filed in *Russell v. Drumwright's Ext'rs.*, Goochland Judgments, June 1762, box 31, barcode 1138412, LVA. Also see Minor Tompkins Weisiger, "Depositions Relating to Residents, King and Queen County, 1759-1761," *Tidewater Virginia Families: A Magazine of History and Genealogy* 10 (2001): 98-103.
87. G.O.B. 7:36, September 19, 1750.
88. *Hatcher v. Parish's Adm'x*, Goochland County Chancery Records, 1754-001, LVA.
89. Peter Wallenstein, "Indian Foremothers: Race, Sex, Slavery and Freedom in Early Virginia," in *The Devil's Lane: Sex and Race in the Early South*, ed. Catherine Clinton and Michele Gillespie (New York: Oxford University Press, 1997), 57-73; Thomas Jefferson, "Robin et al. v. Hardaway et al.," in *Reports of Cases Determined in the General Court of Virginia, from 1730, to 1740 and from 1768, to 1772* (Charlottesville, VA: F. Carr, 1829), 114. This case was cited in Catterall, *Judicial Cases Concerning American Slavery*, 1:91-92. For a more detailed account of legal precedents for natural rights in *Robin v. Hardaway*, see Honor Sachs, "Freedom by a Judgment: The Legal History of an Afro-Indian Family," *Law and History Review* 30 (2012): 186-90. Also see Gregory Ablavsky, "Making Indians 'White':

The Judicial Abolition of Native Slavery in Revolutionary Virginia and Its Racial Legacy," *University of Pennsylvania Law Review* 159 (2011): 1457–1531.

90. Sachs, "Freedom by a Judgment," 186.
91. Depositions of Robert Napier and John McQuarry, in *Hatcher v. Parish's Adm'x*, Goochland County Chancery Records.
92. See Ablavsky, "Making Indians 'White,'" 1481–84, for a discussion of the interpretations of the 1682, 1691, and 1705 laws relating to the distinctions between African and Indian slavery. The act of 1705 was not interpreted as repealing Indian slavery until the decision of the General Court in 1772 with the case of *Robin v. Hardaway*.
93. John McQuarry or Mackquery was born about 1690 and had presumably served his eight-year indenture to John Aldridge prior to the birth of his daughter Mary in May 1716. John Aldridge died on April 16, 1720. See *The Parish Register of Saint Peter's, New Kent County, Virginia 1680–1787* (1904; Baltimore: Genealogical Publishing, 1966), 92, 53.
94. G.O.B. 7:436, July 16, 1754; 7:594, February 17, 1756.
95. G.O.B. 7:623, June 15, 1756. The quotation is from *Battersby v. Napier* in Goochland Judgments, June 1756, folder A–F, box 28, barcode 1136409, LVA.
96. Butler, *Evolution*, 80.
97. The word "Indian" only appears twice in Butler's manuscript: in the title of a publication he cites and when he uses it in a quote of the provisions of the 1705 statute. Ibid., 229n18, 40.
98. See particularly Forbes, *Africans and Native Americans*. See also Wallenstein, "Indian Foremothers," and W. Stitt Robinson Jr., "The Legal Status of the Indian in Colonial Virginia," *Virginia Magazine of History and Biography* 61 (1953): 247–59.
99. The other is *Rezin Porter v. Nathaniel Watkins*, Albemarle County Judgments, box 14, *Porter v. Watkins*, August 1786, barcode 1175989, Local Government Records Collection, Albemarle Court Records, LVA.
100. The papers for *William Scott, assee. v. James Quigg* are available on "Virginia Untold."
101. Formerly filed as Goochland County Miscellaneous Papers, barcode 1176172, Local Government Records Collection, Goochland Court Records, LVA. Refiled as *Scott, William v. Quigg, James*, Judgment, 1805, "Virginia Untold," LVA.
102. The original indenture is from Goochland County Apprenticeship Indentures, bundle 2. It states that "the apprentice is 16 years old 23rd July 1795. Service expires 16th July 1800."

103. See Butler, *Evolution*, 94, which cites Hening, *Statutes*, 12:198.
104. Deposition of Samuel Cosby, in *Scott, William v. Quigg, James*, Judgment. Also see G.O.B. 23:222, May 20, 1802, and G.O.B. 23:453, March 24, 1803, for Cosby as a witness for Scott.
105. Hening, *Statutes*, 12:545. Over the years this rule on evidence appears several times in Hening.
106. Deposition of Robert Smith, in "Scott, William v. Quigg, James: Judgment," Goochland Judgments.
107. The court ordered payments to Connerly Mullins and Wright Moreland for giving evidence for William Scott, but copies of their testimony were not found among the case papers. See G.O.B. 23:222, May 20, 1802; 23:453, March 24, 1803; 23:598, 599, August 18, 1803.
108. Receipt for medications, in "Scott, William v. Quigg, James: Judgment," Goochland Judgments.
109. See Butler, *Evolution*, 91.
110. G.O.B. 20:16. This order was issued on March 17, 1795, and the indenture of apprenticeship was drafted the next day.
111. "A List of Insolvents in the Upper District of Goochland County for the County Levy in the year 1798," Insolvents, Tithable and Personal Property Lists, box 4, possibly barcode 1114762 and 1114760 (photocopied prior to barcoding and listed as 11/C/09/05/04), Local Government Records Collection, Goochland Court Records, LVA.
112. G.O.B. 24:531, July 15, 1805.
113. On Luther Porter Jackson's distinction between "at" and "on," see note 35 of this essay, above.
114. G.D.B. 19:185, April 15, 1805.
115. No indenture of apprenticeship or order to bind out has been found for Joshua. Johnson Hodges does not appear in the 1815 Goochland Land Tax because he sold his 82.5 acres of land to Martin Key in September 1810. G.D.B. 20:626–27. Key's land is recorded as being ten miles northwest.
116. Goochland County, "Free Negro and Slave Records."
117. William Scott, Goochland County Register of Free Negroes, 5, October 12, 1805; Joshua Scott, Goochland County Register of Free Negroes, 8, March 12, 1806.
118. Compare the Deposition of Michael Ailstock and "Kinney v. Johnson," both Albemarle Chancery, 1798-017, LVA.
119. Hughes and Standefer, *Goochland County Virginia Marriage Bonds*, 91
120. List of Mulattoes and Free Negroes, Upper District, 1809.

121. See Butler, *Evolution*, 183. The other names were Banks, Cochran, Cooper, Cousins, Granthum, Howel, and Mealy.
122. French, "A 'Forceful and Effective' Leader," 202, 205–6.
123. The concept of liminality was developed by Arnold van Gennep in *Rites of Passage*, trans. Monika B. Vizedom and Gabrielle L. Caffe (1909; Chicago: University of Chicago Press, 1960), and more recently used by anthropologist Victor W. Turner in *The Ritual Process: Structure and Anti-Structure* (Chicago: Aldine, 1969) and other works.
124. V. W. Turner, *Schism and Continuity in an African Society: A Study of Ndembu Village Life* (Manchester, UK: Manchester University Press, 1957).
125. Clifford Geertz, "Thick Description: Towards an Interpretative Theory of Culture," in *The Interpretation of Cultures: Selected Essays* (New York: Basic Books, 1973), 3–30.
126. See Butler, *Evolution*, 143–45.
127. See ibid., 22–23.
128. R. G. Collingwood, *The Idea of History* (Oxford: Oxford University Press, 1956), 10.

A "FORCEFUL AND EFFECTIVE" LEADER

1. Reginald D. Butler, "Evolution of a Rural Free Black Community: Goochland County, Virginia, 1728–1832" (PhD diss., Johns Hopkins University, 1989), v.
2. Ford Foundation Fellowship Programs, National Academy of Sciences, https://sites.nationalacademies.org/PGA/FordFellowships/index.htm.
3. Zak M. Salih, "Scholars Remember Armstead Robinson's Intellectual Legacy," University of Virginia School of Law, April 17, 2006, https://www.law.virginia.edu/news/200604/scholars-remember-armstead-robinsons-intellectual-legacy. For a full history of UVa's African American Studies program, particularly its origins under the leadership of Vivian V. Gordon, see Claudrena N. Harold, "'Of the Wings of Atalanta': The Struggle for African American Studies at the University of Virginia, 1969–1995," *Journal of African American Studies* 16 (2012): 41–69.
4. For biographical details, see Armstead L. Robinson Papers, Albert and Shirley Small Special Collections Library Repository, Manuscript and Archival Materials, University of Virginia Library, https://archives.lib.virginia.edu/repositories/uva-sc/resources/armstead_l_robinson_papers.

5. "Rethinking African-American and African Studies: New Approaches to Teaching and Research in the 21st Century," Ford Foundation Grant Proposal, Reginald D. Butler, P.I., June 1999, copy in author's possession.
6. For a list of Woodson Fellows by year (1981–2021), see the Carter G. Woodson Institute, People/Fellowship Alumni, https://woodson.as.virginia.edu/woodson-fellows.
7. "Rethinking African-American and African Studies." Butler based his critique, in part, on a 1995 report by a committee of external reviewers, discussed below on pp. 199–200.
8. "Graves Offer Clues to Lost Way of Life; Construction Halted as UVa Excavates to Learn More of 19th-Century Black Family," Charlottesville *Daily Progress*, June 5, 1993.
9. For a summary of archaeological findings and other pertinent site details, see "The Foster Site," National Register of Historic Places Registration Form, May 16, 2016, Virginia Department of Historic Resources, https://www.dhr.virginia.gov/VLR_to_transfer/PDFNoms/104-5140_FosterSite_2016_NRHP_FINAL.pdf.
10. Venable Lane Burial Site Task Force Meeting, minutes, June 24, 1993, Foster-Canada Portal Resources/Venable Lane Task Force/Minutes, UVa Collab (access restricted).
11. His book, *Bitter Fruits of Bondage: The Demise of Slavery and the Collapse of the Confederacy, 1861–1865*, was published posthumously by the University of Virginia Press in 2004.
12. "Armstead L. Robinson, Historian," *Washington Post*, September 3, 1995; "Scholars Remember Armstead Robinson's Intellectual Legacy," University of Virginia School of Law, April 17, 2006, https://www.law.virginia.edu/news/200604/scholars-remember-armstead-robinson%E2%80%99s-intellectual-legacy.
13. See *Inclusive Scholarship: Developing Black Studies in the United States, a 25th Anniversary Retrospective of Ford Foundation Grant-Making, 1982–2007* (New York: Ford Foundation, 2007), 208: "In 1995, when the Institute's director, Armstead Robinson, died at age 49, the faculty reported their concern about the status and survival of the Institute."
14. Minutes of the Venable Lane Task Force meeting held on September 28, 1995, discussed plans to honor Robinson and the future of the taskforce. Reference was made to UVa Provost Leonard Sandridge's "sentiment that the Task Force has done its job and that the research work should henceforth be turned over to the Provost." Jeffrey Hantman—the lone faculty member present—suggested "that perhaps the Task Force should make some

suggestions regarding the ideas brought up so far and then should perhaps disband," adding that "whoever wants to remain involved in the project can."
15. Lucia (Cinder) Stanton to Robert Vernon, December 27, 2000; quoted with permission.
16. *Inclusive Scholarship*, 208.
17. Reginald D. Butler, Letter of Recommendation for Scot French, December 30, 2009, copy in author's possession.
18. Final Narrative, "The Holsinger Studio Photograph Exhibit: History, Race, and the Value of Place in Central Virginia, 1900–1925," VFH Grant no. 5-29324-98-11, copy in author's possession.
19. Ibid.
20. Reginald D. Butler to Alison R. Bernstein, Vice President, Education, Media, Arts, and Culture Program, Ford Foundation, March 13, 1998, copy in author's possession.
21. "Building Digital Communities" was funded by an $110,000 grant, c. 1999–2003, from the NEH Education Development and Demonstration Program "to support the development of a digital archive on the African American community of Charlottesville, Virginia, during the period of racial segregation." The grant funded the design and development of "Race and Place—An African American Community in the Jim Crow South: Charlottesville, Va.," Virginia Center for Digital History, http://www2.vcdh.virginia.edu/afam/raceandplace/.
22. "NEH Grant Will Help U.Va. Work with Historically Black Colleges to Develop African-American History Projects on the Web," University of Virginia News, October 27, 1999, https://web.archive.org/web/20000823030614/http://www.virginia.edu/topnews/releases/nehgrant-oct-27-1999.html.
23. "Rethinking African-American and African Studies."
24. "Race and Place: An African American Community in the Jim Crow South."
25. Butler to Bernstein, March 13, 1998, copy in author's possession.
26. "UVA Gets Grant to Revamp Black Studies," *Diverse Issues in Higher Education*, May 24, 2000, https://www.diverseeducation.com/demographics/african-american/article/15076941/uva-gets-grant-to-revamp-black-studies.
27. Reginald D. Butler, P.I., "Mapping Monticello's Diaspora: The Center for the Study of Local Knowledge in the Construction of Race, Gender, and Nation at the Carter G. Woodson Institute for African-American and African Studies," Ford Foundation Grant, Annual Report for Grant Year Ending April 30, 2005, and Request for a Two-Year, No-Cost Extension, copy

in author's possession; "Annual Report for Grant Year Ending April 30, 2005," Ford Foundation Grant no. 1020–0963, "Mapping Monticello's Diaspora," copy in author's possession.

28. "Mapping Monticello's Diaspora: The Center for the Study of Local Knowledge in the Construction of Race, Gender, and Nation at the Carter G. Woodson Institute for African-American and African Studies," executive summary, Ford Foundation Grant Proposal, March 2002, copy in author's possession.

29. For speakers and events on the fall 2022–spring 2023 schedule, see the web-archived CSLK Calendar, http://web.archive.org/web/20030814035608/http://www.virginia.edu/cslk/calendar.html.

30. Butler, "Mapping Monticello's Diaspora," Ford Foundation Grant, Annual Report for Grant Year Ending April 30, 2005.

31. For an overview of the Vinegar Hill project, see "Virtual Vinegar Hill: Preserving an African American Memoryscape—A Collaborative Research Initiative of the Carter G. Woodson Institute's Center for the Study of Local Knowledge and the Virginia Center for Digital History," Virginia Center for Digital History, 2008, http://www.vcdh.virginia.edu/cslk/vinegarhill/.

32. In 2006, after completing my term as interim director of the Woodson Institute, I was appointed by then-College of Arts and Sciences Dean Edward Ayers to become director of the Virginia Center for Digital History and continued my codirectorship of CSLK in that role. I hired Bill Ferster, a recent PhD from the Curry School of Education, as director of technology the following year. Together, we secured a 2008 NEH Digital Humanities Startup Grant ("Jefferson's Travels") to support development of VisualEyes. Unfortunately, the Vinegar Hill Memoryscape project is no longer web-accessible, as it requires the use of the now-defunct Adobe Flash Player. Only the Vinegar Hill historic photo archive, stored on Flickr, and a twenty-minute documentary, *That World Is Gone: Race and Displacement in a Southern Town* (Field Studio, 2010), remain publicly accessible.

33. "Rethinking African-American and African Studies II: Race, Ethnicity, and Identity in Africa and the African Diaspora," Ford Foundation Supplemental Grant Proposal, Reginald D. Butler, P.I., September 30, 2003, copy in author's possession.

34. "UVA's Carter G. Woodson Institute Celebrating Its 25th Anniversary," *UVA Today*, April 19, 2007, https://news.virginia.edu/content/uva%3Fs-carter-g-woodson-institute-celebrating-its-25th-anniversary: "Participants include Paul Gaston, professor emeritus of history, who worked with the founding director, the late Armstead Robinson, to get the institute

established; William Jackson, professor emeritus of German, who served as the first associate director; and Norfolk State University history professor Cassandra Newby-Alexander, a U.Va. alumna who was active in the late 1970s pushing for more emphasis on black studies." Butler, who had recently stepped down as director, is not mentioned in the news story or official program.

35. *Inclusive Scholarship*, part 4, "A Changing Political Context," featured a review of AAS programs prepared by Dianne M. Pinderhughes (University of Illinois at Urbana-Champaign) and literary scholar Richard Yarborough (University of California at Los Angeles).
36. Ibid., 211. For concerns about the institute's survival, see p. 208: "In 1995, when the Institute's director, Armstead Robinson, died at age 49, the faculty reported their concern about the status and survival of the Institute. Paula McClain, former Chair of the Department of Government and Foreign Affairs, chaired the search committee for Robinson's replacement and, along with her committee, nominated Reginald Butler as Director. She reported that faculty had been quite concerned about the status of the Institute."
37. Ibid., 206–10; emphasis added.
38. "The Difference a Department Makes: Woodson Institute Determines Its Destiny," *UVA Today*, October 9, 2017, https://news.virginia.edu/content/difference-department-makes-woodson-institute-determines-its-destiny.
39. "In Memoriam: Historian Reginald D. Butler, Former African American Studies Director," *UVA Today*, July 22, 2019, https://news.virginia.edu/content/memoriam-historian-reginald-butler-former-african-american-studies-director.
40. Butler, "Evolution of a Rural Free Black Community," v.
41. Virginia General Assembly, Legislative Information System, 2020 session, House Joint Resolution no. 415, https://lis.virginia.gov/cgi-bin/legp604.exe?201+ful+HJ415ER.

· INDEX ·

abolition, 43, 57, 80, 175
Academical Village (UVa), 197
Adams, Richard ("Dick"), 107, 132–33
affidavit, marriage, 13; in lieu of registration, 163, 164
Africa, 24, 29, 79, 161, 207, 211
African American and African Studies (AAAS), 190, 194, 199, 205, 211
African American community life, photographs, 201–2. *See also* Rufus W. Holsinger Studio Collection and Digital Image Database
African diaspora, 207, 208, 211
Afro-American Studies (AAS), 193–95, 199, 207, 210, 213
agency, free Black, 15
Aggy, 52
Albemarle Charlottesville Historical Society, 209
Albemarle County, 24, 157, 171, 173, 216; colonization, 160–62; court order books, 159, 164, 166, 174; free Blacks in, xxv, 184; migration, emigration, 166–67; records, 153, 154, 158, 159–62, 170, 173–74, 258n5; register, 164–65
Albemarle County Real Estate Office, 185
Albemarle Mapping Project, 185
Albert, Peter J., 51, 54–55
Aldridge, John, 176

Alexander, Adele Logan, xxi
Alkalimat, Abdul, 203
All God's Dangers: The Life of Nate Shaw (Rosengarten), xiii
Alsup, Mary, 127
Altman, Ida, xi
Amelia County, free people of color reject colonization, 161
American Anthropological Association, 184
American Negro Slavery (Phillips), 13
American Revolution, 42, 66, 80, 154, 157
American Slavery, American Freedom (Morgan), xviii
Anderson, Benjamin, 112
anthropology, Butler's interest in, 184, 186
antislavery sentiment, 54, 57, 66. *See also* Quakers
apprentices, juvenile, xxiii, 30, 37, 38, 53, 64, 83, 90–104, 126–27, 129, 162; gender ratio, 95–96; indigent, 92; mixed race, 169, 244n10; numbers, 94, 263n72; orphans, 170–73. *See also* masters, of apprentices
apprenticeship indentures, 30, 83, 90–104, 126–27, 156, 167–74, 178–80; books, 172; children of common-law marriages, 173; children of enslaved

274   INDEX

apprenticeship indentures (*continued*)
  fathers, 173; contractual rights, 93–94, 167, 178–80, 186; court process, 171–74; English antecedents, 91; legislation, 91–93; parental interest, 173, 248n31; suits concerning, 178–80; terms, 83, 84, 94, 96–98, 102–4, 128, 167, 178, 186
ArcGIS Online, Albemarle maps, 185
archival filters, 152–54
archives, xiii
Argyle, Frederick, 112–13
"arrabbers," xii
Arthur (conspirator in insurrection plot), 57
Arthur (emancipated by Mary Pleasants Younghusband), 65
artisans. *See* crafts, skilled
Asafo military company shrine, 212
Atlantic Ocean, xi
attorney, Commonwealth, 109
attorneys, hired by free Blacks, xv, 72, 81–82, 83, 85, 128, 164
autonomy, individual, 18, 58, 105, 122, 135, 145
Ayers, Edward L., 206

Bahia, Brazil, 211–12, 215
bail, 134
Baker, Hannah, 86
Baker, Jack, 86, 88
Baker, John, 86
Balogh, Brian, 202
Baltimore, xi
Banks, Agnes, 126, 167
Banks, Betsy Ann Howell, 130
Banks, Elisha, 129, 130, 132
Banks, Eliza, 131, 132
Banks, Gideon, 168
Banks, Jacob, 35, 109, 126, 127–28, 128–29, 132, 133–34, 168
Banks, Jane, 12, 127, 130, 132, 133, 168
Banks, John, 126, 128–29, 130, 132, 167

Banks, John, Jr., 109, 130, 133–34
Banks (Day), Judith, 35, 126, 130, 132, 168
Banks, Louisa, 126, 168
Banks, Martin, 129, 130
Banks, Mary, 35, 38, 125–27, 132
Banks, Nancy Lynch, 130
Banks, Nathaniel, 109, 133–34
Banks (Tyler), Polly, 130
Banks, Sally, 129
Banks, Susannah Jones, 129
Banks, William, 38
Banks family, 28, 125–35; and Leake family, 126–28, 132–34
Baptism, baptismal records, 29, 31–32, 36
Baptists, 36, 234n28. *See also* Dover Baptist Church; Lickinghole Baptist Church; Maniken Baptist Church
barber, 119
Barbour, Aaron, 160, 162
Barnett, Franky, and sons, 98
Barnett, Tarlton, 110–11
Barrett, James, 45–46
basketball, 219
bastards, 169, 173–74; bastardy bonds, 173–74, 178. *See also* children, illegitimate
Bates, Charles, 40, 138–39
Bates, Richard, 142
Bates, Thomas, 102, 143
Bates, Thomas F., 178–80, 183
Baucom, Dean Ian, on Woodson Institute, 214
Bearinger, David, 203
Beaverdam estate (home of Philip Lightfoot), 39; free Blacks residing at, 150; home of Thomas and James Pleasants, 149–50
Beeman, Richard R., xxi
Bellingham, Washington, 219
Ben, 52
Bennett, Amey, 182
Bennett, Herman, 203

INDEX

Berlin, Ira, xx–xxi, xxii, 10, 19, 34, 80, 203; on enslaved passing as free, 47; on free Black community, 14–15; on identifying enslaved, 48–49; on informal manumissions, 68–69; on market for Black apprentices, 98; on racially stigmatized work, 116–17; on white participation in marriages, 131–32, 203
Bernhard, Virginia, on apprenticeship, 92
Betty, 175–76
Beyond Slavery's Shadow (Milteer), xxv
Black Atlantic, 207, 215
Black historians, xix–xx, 13–14
Black identity, and Indigenous ancestry, 177. *See also* free Blacks: consciousness; race
Black Masters (Roark and Johnson), 16
Blackness, xix
Black Power, 219
blacksmiths, 65, 108, 112, 116, 117, 118, 119, 122, 178, 180
Black Studies, 193, 212–13, 220
Black Studies in the University: A Symposium (Robinson), 193
Blue Ridge Mountains, 23, 152
blues, 221
Bluestone, Daniel, 209
boatmen, 65, 74, 107–8, 110, 111, 112, 113–14, 121, 163; difference from watermen, 107
Bob, Dr., 117
Bolling, William, 98, 101–2
Booth, George, 173
Booth, William, 173
Boston, 218
Bowles family, Black and white branches, 157
Brazil, 211–12
Breen, T. H., xviii, 19–20
Bridgett, 52
Brown, Ann, 169
Brown, Darkas, 163

Brown, Flora Bryant, 204
Brown, Frank, 47–48, 49
Brown, Janey, 169
Brown, John, 20, 65
Brown, Lucy, 169
Buckingham County, 24; and Gabriel's Rebellion, 65; migration from, 167
Burdette, Gervas, 39
Burton, 67
Burton, Orville Vernon, xxi
Butler, Alfred, 216
Butler, Geri, 216
Butler, Howard, 216
Butler, Ishmael, 216
Butler, Maya, 217
Butler, Omar, 216
Butler, Reginald D.: Central Virginia Social History Project cofounder, xvii, 197–98; collaboration with Robert Vernon, 161, 177, 184; collaboration with Scot A. French, 190, 198–99, 209, 210; at Colonial Williamsburg, 217; and digital technology, 214, 216; Emerging Scholars Program cofounder, 202–3; family, xiii–xiv, 22, 178–84, 216; family tree, 181; and historiography, xv–xxvii, 184–88; homeplace, 215; legacy, 212–16; life of, xi–xiv, xxii, 22–23, 190–92; memorial service for, 214–15; on Monticello's Advisory Committee on African American Interpretation, 216; Museum of American History fellow, 217; plans for this book, 184–88; research, 147–49, 170, 175, 183, 185; retirement, 212; travels, 211–12, 215; and Venable Lane Task Force, 196–97. *See also* Carter G. Woodson Institute for African-American and African Studies; Scott, William: family

Cachoeira, Brazil, 211
Caledonia district, 125
California, xi

calomel, 180
camphor, 180
"Canada" (Charlottesville neighborhood), 196
Cape Coast, Ghana, 190, 211–12, 215
Caribbean, 207; mixed-raced peoples in, 10
carpenters, 2, 4, 86, 101, 107, 113, 115, 116, 118–19, 120–21, 128, 129, 182
Carter, Ann W., 209
Carter, Dr., 112, 117
Carter G. Woodson Institute for African-American and African Studies, vii–ix, xvii, 153, 186, 189–90, 193–216; Building Digital Communities, 205–6; Butler and, xvii, 189–216; Center for the Study of Local Knowledge (CSLK), 208–10; "Changing Cultures of Race in the Modern World" (Race Seminar), 200–201; Chesapeake Regional Scholars Summer Seminar, 203–4; community engagement, 201–2; fellowship program, 192, 193, 194–95, 199, 207, 213; "History, Race, and the Value of Place in Central Virginia," exhibit, 201–2; program review, 199–200; "Rethinking African-American and African Studies," 206–7, 210–12; rethinking core curriculum, 207–8; Vinegar Hill Project, 209–10
cattle, 40, 123, 189–221
Cawthon, Gideon, 59–60, 143; estate, 59
Ceasar, 51
Census, U.S., 101; 1790, 111; 1830, 95; 1850, 116, 119
Center for the Study of Local Knowledge (CSLK), 208–10, 214
Central Virginia History Repository, 154. *See also* Reginald D. Butler Local History Archive
Central Virginia Social History Project (Free Black Forum), xvii, 187, 195, 197–99, 214, 216

certificates of freedom, 21, 47, 48, 49, 164, 165, 166, 176; duplicates, 49. *See also* registers of free Blacks
Chancellor, Robert Washington, 47
Chancery court, 139, 177
"Changing Cultures of Race in the Modern World" (Race Seminar), 200–201
Charles City County, 39; migration to, 167
"Charlie Forest" (land tract), 149
Charlottesville, 108, 153, 162, 164, 209; African American neighborhoods, 197, 209–10. *See also* Race and Place: An African American Community in the Jim Crow South
Charlottesville Area Community Foundation, 210
Charlottesville Redevelopment and Housing Authority, 209
Chesapeake region: settlement, 33–34; slavery in, 19–20
Chesapeake Regional Scholars Summer Seminar: "Building an African-American Digital History Archive: A Workshop for Principal Investigators and Project Teams," 203; "Finding Funding Sources/Writing Winning Grant Proposals," 203–4, 214, 216
Chief Imam ("Zongo"), 212
childbirth, 113; and family and neighbors, 5; women's central role, 7–8
children, illegitimate, 98–99, 169, 173–74; indigent, 96; among manumitted, 50–53; mixed-race, 28, 30–32, 33, 93, 244–45n10. *See also* apprentices, juvenile
Chiles, Washington, 165
Christian, John, 39
Christian, Thomas, 119
church wardens, 30, 126; apprentice children, 96; St. James Northam Parish, 128, 173

civil rights movement, xxi, 177, 193, 207, 219
Clarke, William, 102
coal diggers, 116
Cobb, Ned (Nate), xiii
Cochran, 28
Cocke, James, 30
Cocke, Samuel, 118
Cocke, Woodson, 118
coffin-makers, 118–19
Cohen, David, xi
Coley, Frank, 109, 114
Coley, Sally, 67–68; estate, 67–68
College of William and Mary, 204, 208
Collingwood, R. G., 188
Colonial Williamsburg Foundation, Research Department, 217
colonization, 64, 67–68, 79–80; act promoting (1833), 159; resistance to, 160–61
color: and free Black community, 22, 40, 130, 135, 151; and racial identity, 158
Columbia University, 11
common law, and marriage, 143
community, free Black, viii, xiii, xvi, xx, 18, 25, 27, 41, 70, 79, 90, 95, 123–46; absence before 1782, 27; achieves economic stability, 95; and family, 35–36
Connecticut, 218
Continental Army, U.S., 128, 134
contracts, 109, 112, 113, 114–18, 121. *See also* apprenticeship indentures
Conway, Thomas, 114
Cooper, Aggy, 170; children, 96
Cooper, Becca, 2–3, 6, 148
Cooper, Betsy, 96
Cooper, Billy, 99
Cooper, Bridgett, 2–3, 4–8, 147–51, 154
Cooper, Burwell, 101
Cooper, Chloe, 6–7, 149, 150
Cooper, Clarissa, 6–8, 86
Cooper, Daniel, 38, 100, 101–2; estate, 102

Cooper, David, 100
Cooper, Davy, 163
Cooper, Diana, 49
Cooper, James, 2, 4, 5–8
Cooper, Jesse, 99
Cooper, Nancy, 101–2
Cooper, Polly, 5–6
Cooper, Rachel, 99, 100
Cooper, Sall, 57
Cooper, Sally, 96
Cooper, William, 49; as overseer, 32
Cooper family, xiii, xiv, 28; and Pleasants family, 6–7
coopers, 35, 96, 107, 116, 132, 133, 160
corn, 40, 111
coroner's inquisition, 149, 150
Cosby, Samuel, dialogue with William Scott, 179
cotton, xiii, 118
Couch, Samuel, 47, 99
court days, 257n43
Cousins, Chloe, 35, 139, 140, 141
Cousins, David, 110–11
Cousins, Francis, 35, 86
Cousins, Frank, 40–41; and Thomas Ford, 139, 141
Cousins, Frank William, 140
Cousins, John, 39–40, 140
Cousins, Lucy Ann, 140
Cousins, Maria, 49
Cousins, Ridley, and children, 86, 139–40
Cousins family, 139–41
Cowig, James, 113, 115
Craddock, Lilly Anne, 2, 3–4, 5–8
crafts, skilled, 116–19. *See also* occupations, lists/registers; work
Crawford, Peter, 157
Cross, Franky, 86
Cross, Joel, 69
Cross, Joseph, 69
Cross, Moses, 69, 78, 86; appeals removal from Virginia, xv–xvii, 73–77
Crouch, Lucy, 114

Cuba, 211
Cumberland County, 24
Cupid, 52
Curd, John, 58, 112
Curry, Leonard P., 9
Curtin, Philip, xi

Daily Progress (Charlottesville), 196
Danville, 210
Day, Judith Banks, 130
Deal, Joseph Douglas, 19–20, 34
Delaware, free Blacks in, 18
Delaware State University, 204
demography, 34, 60; free Blacks in South, xx, 18–19; in Tidewater and Piedmont, 25–26
digitization, 153–55, 165, 185–86, 189–90, 200–201; building digital communities, 205–6; digital history courses, "Race and Place," 202; digital humanities, 203–4; Vinegar Hill Project, 209–10
Dinah, 57
Dinwiddie County, 65
ditchers, 108–9, 115, 118, 138
Diverse Issues in Higher Education, 207
Doll, 30
Douglas, Reverend William, 31, 32, 35–36; *Douglas Register*, 151
Dover Baptist Church, 36
Dover coal pits, 116
Dover Episcopal Church, 31, 35, 36
Dover estate (Philip Lightfoot), 39
Dover Mills district, 125
Dover Parish, 35
Drigus, Emanuel, 26
Drigus, Frances, 26
Drumwright, Thomas, 174
Drumwright, William, executors, 81
Du Bois, W. E. B., 218
Duke of Gloucester Street, Williamsburg, 217

Duke University, 208
Dunn, Richard S., 25–26

East Carolina University, 204
Eastern Shore, xxii, 26
Ecole des Hautes Etudes en Sciences Social, Paris, 208–9
Edgefield, South Carolina, xxi
Edmonds, Allen, xii
Edmunds, Emma, 210
Elinor (orphan), 30
Eliza, 47
Elizabeth Stuart James Grant Trust, 210
Ellison, William, 16–17
Ely, Melvin Patrick, xxiv–xxv
emancipation, mass, 45. *See also* manumission; self-emancipation
Emerging Scholars Program (ESP), 202–3, 205; alumni, 203
Engerman, Stanley L., 193, 199
enslaved people: insurrection, 65; owned by family members, 123; owned by free Blacks, 72, 85–89, 123; population in Goochland, 111; as property, 45, 111–12, 180; and race-mixing, 33
equity, 80, 85
Erie Canal, xii
Esprit, Schuyler, 209
estate accounts, 106, 112–19

Faded Colors project, 185
family, vii, xiv, 123–45; and childbirth, 5; consolidation, 125; extended, 125, 129; importance for community, 35–36, 155; names, 28–30; networks, 101, 183, 187; and property, 123–25; size of, 125, 129. *See also* genealogy; naming practices
FamilySearch.org, 154
Fanny, 52
Ferguson, James, 175
Farmer, Fanny, 6
Farmer, Thomas, 6

farmers, 107, 108; indenture for, 103
Farrar family, 131; Black and white branches, 157
Farrish, Richard, 65
Farrow, Amy (Bowles), 157
fathers: enslaved children, 136–37; as heads of household, 105, 106, 162, 172
Federal University of Bahia, Center for the Study of Afro-Orientals, 211
females, as heads of household, 162
Ferguson, James, 47–49
Ferrar, Drury, 35
Ferrar, Joseph, 35
Ferrar, Molly, 35
Ferster, Bill, 210
Festa da Boa Morta (Feast of the Good Dead), 211–12
Fields, Barbara Jeanne, xxi; on presence of free Blacks in slave societies, 19
Fife district, 125
fishtrap maker, 119
Fitchett, E. Horace, xix, 13
Fleming, John, 81, 134, 144
Fleming, John S., 77–79
Fleming, Thomas, 51
Fluvanna County, 24, 157; records, 156, 159, 160
Ford, Gabriel, 136
Ford, Judy, 136, 138
Ford, Moses, 136
Ford, Squire, 136
Ford, Susannah, 31, 32
Ford, Thomas, 135–41; Charles Bates inventory, 138–39; Charles Cousins, executor, 139–41; enslaved children, 136–38; may have owned enslaved wife, 138; parental authority, 137–38; transferred property by will, 136–38, 140
Ford Foundation, 190, 193, 198; Fellowships for Minorities (Diversity Fellowships), 192; grant proposal, 205; grants, 204, 206–7, 208, 210–11; *Inclusive Scholarship*, 212–13

Forest, the (home of William H. Pleasants), 149–50; free Blacks residing at, 150; misidentified, 2–3
fornication, legal definition, 6
Foster, Catherine (Kitty), 158; descendants, 197; homesite, family burial ground, 195–96
Fowler, Alexander, 115
Frank (emancipated by Francis Cousins), 86
Frank (enslaved by Granville Smith estate), 118
Frankey, 67–68
Franklin, John Hope, xix, 13, 15; on apprentice gender ratio, 96
Fraser, Gertrude F., 184, 203; essay by, xi–xiv
Fredericksville Parish, Albemarle, 152, 157, 160, 161, 162, 168; vestry book, 172, 174
Free Black Forum. *See* Central Virginia Social History Project
free Blacks: access to courts, 80, 99, 103–4; in Albemarle County, xxv; character, 56, 58, 71, 74–79, 106; comparative studies, 19; consciousness (identity), 17–18, 28–29, 130–31, 134–35, 140; early history in Goochland, 27–42; in Goochland County, xxii, 50–51, 111; lists, 49–50, 158–61; population, xix, 18–19, 26–28, 78; in Prince Edward County, xxiv; relations with enslaved people, 17, 18, 36–38, 48, 75, 105, 110, 135; relations with whites, 38–42, 74–79, 156, 167; slave ownership, 72, 85–89; in upper South, xxiv. *See also* mixed-race people
freedom, meaning of, xxvii
freedom dues, 127, 168, 169, 171, 179
freedom suits, 71, 79–85, 157, 174–77
Freedom Summer (1964), 219
Freeman, Charlotte, 101
Freeman, Molly, 86

Freeman, Nathan, 101
Freeman, Robert, 84–85
Freeman, Titus, 86
Free Negro Heads of Families in the United States in 1830 (Woodson), xix
Free Negro in North Carolina, 1790–1860, The (Franklin), xix, 13
Free Negro in Virginia, 1619–1865, The (Russell), xix, 12
Free Negro Labor and Property Holding in Virginia, 1830–1860 (Jackson), xix, 13
free people of color. *See* free Blacks
French, Scot A., 184; at Butler memorial service, 214–15; collaboration with Butler, xvii; essay by, viii–ix; at Woodson Institute, 190, 198–99, 209, 210
French, William, 173
French West Indies, 211
Fuzmore, James, 119

Gabbin, Peter, 118
Gabriel's rebellion, 44, 64; involvement of Goochland slaves, 65
Galenson, David, on apprenticeship, 91
Galt, Dr., 112
Gamble, Kenny, xii
gang labor, free Blacks and, 115–16
Gantlet, Molly, 35
Gardner, West, 164, 165
Gaspar, Barry David, 202
Gaston, Paul, on Armstead Robinson, 193
Gaunt, Kyra, 203
Geertz, Clifford, 209
genealogy, 22, 155, 176, 178–84. *See* Butler, Reginald D.: family
General Assembly. *See* Virginia General Assembly
General Court (Virginia), xix
Genovese, Eugene D., 193
George, William, 118, 119
Georgia, 11
Ghana, 190, 211–12, 215
Gideon, 58–59

Gillespie, Andra, 203
Goen, John, 162
Goen, Mary, 162
Goochland County: boundaries, 9, 23–24, 152; early history of free Blacks, 27–42; history, xxii, 23–26
Goochland County, courts: apprenticeship indentures, 27–42, 71–105, 127–28; county court, xv; court of chancery, 139; court of oyer and terminer, 48; criminal cases, freedom suits, 82–85; district court, 79; infanticide cases, 1–8; insolvency, 122; inventories, 149; manumissions, 43–70, 73; Orphan's Court, 172; racial conflict, 41–42; registration of free Blacks, 155–56, 158, 162–67
Goochland County, grand jury, 109; presentments, 133, 173
Goochland County, records, 147–88, 230n1; bonds, security, 130–32, 140, 182; book, 46; chancery records, 177; county court, binding orders, 94, 99, 101, 103; deeds, xvi, xxiii, 45–46, 50, 51, 52, 53, 56, 84, 86, 156; extending service, 54–55; familial connections, 58–60; letter recorded in lieu of will, 60–63; lists, 158, 249n4; "loose papers," 148, 152, 164; marriage records, 22, 28, 31, 34–36, 94, 131, 140, 151–52, 182; order books, xxiii, 61, 103, 148, 148–49, 151, 153–54, 164, 165; orders, 61, 101, 161, 168, 169, 173, 174, 177, 180, 181; parish registers, 151; registers of free Blacks, xxiii, 20–21, 46–49, 85, 155, 165; welfare of freed people, 55–56, 67–70, 77–79; white participation in wills, 140; wills, 46, 47, 54–70, 84, 88, 152, 156; wills and deeds compared, 53–55. *See also* apprenticeship indentures; manumission; taxes

INDEX   281

Goochland County clerk's office, xiii, 22–23, 68, 112, 136, 153, 191; order on Blacks' presence (1836), 23, 191
Goochland County Courthouse, xxiv, 21, 24, 73, 147, 152, 182
grain, mixed, 108, 110, 111, 119. *See also* corn; wheat
Granthum, Betty, 183
Granthum, Catherine (Kate), xxvi–xxvii, 59–60, 86, 142–43; deed of loan, 142; marriage, 142–43; will, 142
Granthum, David, 35, 39; as overseer, 39
Granthum, Gideon, xxvi, 142
Granthum, Phil (Phillip), xxvi, 60, 142–43
Granthum, Sam, 39
Granthum, Will, 39
Granthum, Woodson, 59–60, 142
Granthum family, xxvi–xxvii, 8, 28, 35, 142–43; alternative spellings of family name (Grantham, Grantum), 239n55, 256n38
gravedigger, 118
Graves, Rice, 182
Gray, Henrietta, 118
Gray, Lucy, 62
Gray, Thomas, 60–63; estate, 61–62; on growth of free Back population, 61
Gray, William, 61–63
Greenbriar County, free Blacks reject colonization, 161
Greene, Jack P., xi, xviii
Griffen, Elizabeth (servant), 31
Guinn, Jenny, 105–6
Guinn, Ned, 105–6
Gumsprings district, 125

Haitian Revolution, 44, 64
Halevi, Rabbi Kohain, 212
Halley, Kathleen, recollection of Butler, 219–21
Halst, Henry, 113

Hannah (emancipated by William Webber), 51
Hannah (orphan), 30
Hanover County, 157; records, 152, 154
Hantman, Jeffrey, 198
harness-makers, 116
Harris, Alexnder, 113
Harris, Edward, 113
Harris, Francis, 109, 113–14; estate, 113–14, 115
Harris, Jordan, 136
Harris, Mrs., 113
Harris, Sarah, 113
Harrison, 67–68
Harry, 77–79
Harvey, John, 113
Hatcher, Edward, 176
Hatcher, Jack ("Indian Jack"), 175–76, 177
Hatcher v. Parish's Adm'x (1754), 177
Hawaii, xi
Hawkins, Joseph, 173
HBCUs (historically Black colleges and universities), 204, 205–6
Hemings, Sally, xii
Henrico County, 23, 57, 151; records, 154
Herndon, John, 142, 143
Hickman, Edwin, 174
Hicks, John, 182
historiography: on free Blacks, xv–xxvii, 9–26; on free Black slave ownership, 87–88; on Indian slavery, 177; on race, 200. *See* Butler, Reginald D.
"History, Race, and the Value of Place in Central Virginia," exhibit, 201–2
Hodges, Johnson, 182
Holloway, Bathsheba, 169
Holman, James, 41, 59–60, 132–33, 143
Hoosling, James, freedom suit, 81, 174
Hopkins, Charles, 99
horses, 40, 48, 49, 55, 62, 67, 114, 115, 121, 122, 123
hostler, 108
Houchin, Charles, 118

household heads, 88, 105, 106, 155, 172; death, 172; female, 126; gender ratio, 125; male, 105, 106, 162, 172
households, 16, 92, 95, 99, 123–45; of enslaved, 25; formation, 14; separate, 124; taxable, 95; white, 91, 95, 97
House of Burgesses, xix, 30
houseworkers, 105
Howel, Charles, 35
Howel, Judah, 29
Howel, Lucy, 29
Howel family, 28
Howell (Banks), Betsy Ann, 130
Howell, Charles, 113, 131
Howell, Isaac, 35, 130
Howell, Judith, 130; description, 21
Huff, Leon, xii
Hughes, Brandi, 203
Huguenot settlement, 35
Humber, 120–21
Hunnicutt, James, 50, 53, 103
Hunnicutt, John, 102
Hutchins, Strangeman, 50, 51

Idea of History, The (Collingwood), 188
identity, free Black. *See* free Blacks: consciousness
Ile Aiye Dance and Drumming Class, 211
Imam, Chief ("Zongo"), 212
Inclusive Scholarship: Developing Black Studies in the United States, a 25th Anniversary Retrospective of Ford Foundation Grant-Making, 1982–2007 (Ford Foundation), 212–13
"Indian Jack." *See* Hatcher, Jack
"Indian Mary," 175
Indians. *See* Indigenous people
Indigenous people, 40, 156, 157, 163, 174–77; Butler's neglect of, 177; and freedom suits, 175–77; identity, 177; indentured servants, 176–77
indigent children. *See* paupers, apprenticed

individualism, economic, 15–16
infanticide, xviii, 1–8, 186; cases in Goochland, 226–27n1
in forma pauperis (plea), 79, 81, 82
Innes, Stephen, xviii, 19–20
insolvency, 121–23; lists, 121, 124, 170, 181
insurrection, 44, 75; of 1802, 65; fear of, 37, 44. *See also* Gabriel's rebellion; Haitian Revolution
Irtenkauf, Erik, 185
Isaac, Rhys, xviii, 5
Isaacman, Allen, 199
Isaacs, Austin, 102, 118, 120–21
Isaacs, Bartlett, 118
Isaacs, Henry, 132
Isaacs, Peyton, 102
Israel Hill (free Black community), xxiv
Ivy Depot, Virginia, 210

Jack, 65
Jackson, Luther Porter, xix, 15, 88; "at" and "on" distinction, 159–60, 182; on free Black prosperity, 13–14
Jackson, Samuel, 99–100
Jackson, Samuel, wife of, 99–100
Jackson, William, interim director, Woodson Institute, 197
jail, 1, 40, 41, 58, 83, 134, 144, 160
jalap, 180
James (emancipated by Sally Coley), 67
James (enslaved laborer sold by Francis Harris estate), 114
James, Edy, 50
James, Frank, 103
James, Lettis, 50
James River, 23–24, 35, 107, 108
James River Canal, 107
jazz, 221
Jefferson, Thomas, 196, 216
Jefferson Park Avenue, 196
Jenkins, Anthony, 112
Jennings, Nancy, 114
John, 55

Johns, John, 108
Johns Hopkins University, vii, xviii, 11, 184, 189, 191, 192, 216; Atlantic History and Culture Program, xi
Johnson, Anthony, 26
Johnson, James, 35
Johnson, Michael P., xxi; on William Ellison's racial identity, 16–17; on free Black "freedom," 10
Johnson Springs district, 125
Jones (Banks), Susannah, 35, 128
Jordan, Winthrop D., on rights of apprentices, 94
Journal of Negro History, x
Juba, 58
Judith, 52

Kate. *See* Granthum, Catherine
Kenzer, Robert C., xxi
Kinney family, freedom suits, 157
Kulikoff, Allan, on fear of free Blacks, 11

labor, free Black, xxiii; market for, 112–20. *See also specific trades;* work
land ownership, free Black, xxiii, 103, 181–82, 185, 190, 196; and economic independence, 120–21, 123, 145. *See also* property, free Black
Lansford, Elizabeth, 36
Lansford, Milly, 36
Lansford, William, 35, 36
Latin America, mixed-raced peoples in, 10
law, and free Blacks, 12, 18, 80, 99, 111; in South Carolina, 18. *See also* Goochland County, courts; statutes
Lawson, Elizabeth, 148
Lawson, Phillip, 149
Leake, Elisha, 127–28, 168
Leake, Josiah, 132
Leake, Judith, 126, 168
Leake, Walter, 38, 126, 132, 133, 168; estate, 38

Leake family, and Banks family, 126–28, 132–34
Lebsock, Suzanne, xxi
Lewis, 65, 67
Lewis, Robert, Jr., 117; estate, 117
Lewis, Ronald, on coal diggers, 116
Lewis, Warner, 110
Lexington Street, Baltimore, xii
Liberia, emigration to, 159, 160
Library of Virginia, xxiv, 147–49, 152–54, 166–67, 170, 175, 177, 178, 185; "Burned Jurisdiction Database," 154; "Free Negro and Slave Records," 165, 166–67, 170, 185; judgments, 148–49, 150, 153, 168, 170, 175; Overseers of the Poor, 154, 170, 178; "Virginia Untold: The African American Narrative" (digital collection), 154, 163–66, 178
Lickinghole Baptist Church, 36
Lickinghole Creek, 107, 181
Lightfoot, Colonel Phillip, 39
liminality, 21, 148, 186, 197
liquor, sale without license, 109, 133
Liverpool, docks, xii
livestock, 123, 129
local history, importance for Butler, 185, 189, 214
"local knowledge," xiv, 208–9
London, 91
Longshoremen strike (Seattle), xi
Louisa County, 24, 84, 157, 171; courthouse, 49; court order books, 173, 174; and Gabriel's Rebellion, 65; parish registers, 151–52; records, 152, 153, 154, 156, 158, 169
Low Country, South Carolina, 17
Loyola College (Maryland), 204
Lucas, Ann, 198
Lucy, 67–68
Lucy Ann, 86
Lunenberg County, xxi
Lynch, Henry, 121–22
Lynch, John, 99–100, 108, 119

284   INDEX

Lynch, Lucy, 99–100
Lynch (Banks), Nancy, 130
Lynch, Nanny, 31
Lynch, Polly, 131
Lynch, Robert, 131
Lynchburg, migration to, 167
Lynchburg College, 204

MacLeod, Duncan J., on freedom suits, 80
Maddox, Polly Younghusband, 6, 7, 151
Madison, Barbara, 220
Madison, James, 204
Maniken Baptist Church, 36
Maniken Town, 35
manumission, xix, 12, 43–70; age distribution, 50–52; documentation, 45–50; familial bonds, 56, 58–63; in family groups, 51–52; gender ratio, 50; individual choice, 66; informal, 46–47; motivations for, 55–63; numbers over time, changing attitudes toward, 63–70; opposition to, 44; private, 43–45, 47; reward for service, 58; service until majority, 52–53. *See also* Goochland County, courts; Goochland County, records; self-emancipation; statutes
Manumission Act (1782). *See* statutes
Maria, 52
marriage, 2, 6, 27, 31, 34–36, 56, 100, 129–32, 134, 141–42, 182, 185; common-law, 100, 142, 173; with enslaved, 131, 141–42, 237n25; and race, 93, 130–31; records, 22, 28, 31, 34–36, 94, 131, 140, 151–52, 182, 191; security (bonds), 130–32, 140, 182; witnessed by whites, 131–32
Martha, 67–68
Martha Emmalina, 47
Martin, Catharine, 173
Martin, Francis, 173
Martin, John, 115

Martin, Mary, 35
Mary (emancipated by Sally Coley), 67
Mary (petitioned to stay in county), 77
Maryland, 11; free Blacks in, 18
Mason, Thomson, on natural rights of Indigenous people, 175
masons, 108, 116
Massie, Thomas, 45–46
masters, of apprentices: artisans, 97–98; family members, 99–101, 246–47n28; planters, 97–98; Quakers, 97
Mathews, Bristol, 31
Mathews, Elizabeth, 29, 31
Mathews, James, 31, 32
Mathews, Richardson, 31, 32
Mathews, Ruth, 29, 31
Mathews family, 31
Matthews, Thomas, 119
McClain, Paula, 198
McColley, Robert, on 1806 act and suppression of free Blacks, 64
McCrae (Moorman), Hannah, and children, freedom suit, 83–85, 174; chose name, 85
McCrae, John, 83–85
McDowell, Deborah, 203, 212, 214
McKinney, Alexander, 176
McQuarry, John, 175–76
McRae, Kenneth, 118
McRae, William, 118–19
Mealy, Elizabeth, 35
Mealy, Frankey Scott, 182, 183
Mealy, James, 35, 182; as overseer, 39
Mealy, Jennie, 35
Mealy family, xiii, xiv, 28
medications, 180
Michaux, Paul, 41
Microsoft Access, 185
Middlesex County, xxi
midwives, 105, 113
Mignolo, Walter, 208
migration, 24, 126, 155, 160, 166–67, 187, 200; local patterns, 166

INDEX   285

Miles, Hagar, 81
Miles, Samuel, freedom suit, 81, 85, 174
Miles, Soloman, 81
Miller, Peter N., on academic administration, 189
Miller, Thomas, 107
Miller, William, 136
millers, 74, 119
Mills, Gary B., xxi
Milteer, Warren Eugene, Jr., on free Blacks in South, xxv
Milton Chronicle (Caswell County, North Carolina), 164
Mimes, David, 174
Mingo, 113–14
miscegenation. *See* mixed-race people
Mississippi, 11, 215, 219
mixed-race people, 10, 119, 126, 130, 197; attitudes toward, 6; children, 28, 30–32, 33, 93, 244–45n10; couples, 34–36; distinguished from free Blacks, 93; historians on, 32–34, 233n22; laws, 30; servants, 93; white mothers, 93, 157. *See also* mulattoes
mobility, 59, 94, 115, 160
Monroe, James, 196
Monticello, plantation, 208; Advisory Committee on African American Interpretation, 216
Montpelier, 204
Moorman, Charles, 84–85; estate, 84
Moorman, Thomas (elder), 84–85
Moorman, Thomas (younger), 84–85
moral economy, 110
Moreland, Wright, 180
Morgan, Edmund S., xviii; on race-mixing in early Virginia, 34
Morgan, Philip D., 25–26; on free Blacks in "twilight zone," 10
Morgan State University, 204
Mosby, Ursula, 51
Moss, Frank, 49
Moss, Saniel, 121

mothers, single: and custody of children, 100–101, 103, 127; as guardians of apprentices, 100, 103
mulattoes, 27, 30, 31, 35, 40, 62, 81, 93, 121–22, 132, 156–57, 159, 168, 169, 174, 178, 179, 183; lists, 149–50, 159, 160, 161. *See also* mixed-race people
Mullins, 81–83
Mullins, Connerly, 180
Mullins, William, 118
Murrocker, 40–41
Museum of American History, Smithsonian Institution, 217
"Myne Owne Ground" (Breen and Innes), xviii, 19–20
Myrtilla, 40–41

naming practices, 28–30, 231n6; absence of African names, 29; counterfeit, 134; diminutives, 29, 133; first names, 29; and free Black consciousness, 28–29; surnames, 28, 141, 142, 183
Nancy, 61–62, 118
Nanny, 58
Napier, Robert, 175–76
National Archives, College Park, Maryland, 204
National Endowment for the Humanities (NEH), 198; grant, 205
natural rights, 57; and freedom suits, 175
neighborhood, importance of, 4–5, 48, 197
Nelson, Dean Ray, 198, 201
Nelson County, 118
New Kent County, 176
New York City, 218
Nicholls, Michael L., xxi
Norfolk State University, 204
Norrell, Robert J., 199
Norris, Jesse, 110
Northam Parish, 31, 128, 173
North Carolina, 11, 218
North Carolina State University, 204

Northern Neck, 69
Nothing but a Man (film), 218
Nutshell (data base), 184

occupations, lists/registers, 101, 105, 106, 108, 109, 119, 129. *See also specific trades;* work
Ohio, 220
Old Salem Inc., 204
Orange County, North Carolina, xxi
Ore, Joseph, 173
orphans, xiii, 30, 64, 98, 101–2, 156; books, 172; English, 156; guardians, 53, 63, 85, 100, 101, 172; illegitimate children, 98, 173–74; lists, 170
Orphan's Court, 172
overseers: free Black, 32, 38–40; white, 39
Overseers of the Poor, apprentice children, 93–104, 113, 149, 154, 170–73, 178; acting *in loco parentis,* 187
Ovid, 53, 57

Pacific Northwest, xi
Pan African Festival of Arts and Culture, 212
parents, authority of, 99–101, 143, 172–73; over enslaved children, 141. *See* fathers; mothers, single
Paris, xii
Parish, Humphrey, 102
Parish, John, 175
Parish, Judith, 176
Parrish, Peter, 6
Parrish, Sophia, 3–4, 6–7
Parrot, 57
passes, 65, 163. *See also* registers of free Blacks
"passing," 177
paternalism, 132; historiography, 232n17
patronage relations, white-black, xxvi, 7, 32, 41, 71, 102, 117–18, 140, 151, 186

Patt, 40
Patten, Drake, 198
Patterson, Caleb Perry, 9
paupers, apprenticed, 91, 127, 172
Payne, Archer, 47–48
Payne, Fleming, 82
Peers, Judith, 74–75; estate, 74
Peers, Martha, 68
Peers, Sally, 68
Peers, Thomas, xv–xvi, 68, 74–75
Peers family, 75
Pennsylvania, 24
Peter, 47–49, 164
Petersburg, 26, 47, 65, 119
petitions, 71–89; to County Court, for exemptions to 1806 act, 71–73; for exemptions to 1806 act, 56, 71–79; to General Assembly, against Manumission Act, 44; on indentures, 127
Peyton, 110
Philadelphia, xi, 81, 83, 217
Phillips, Ulrich B., 11, 14; on slavery as benevolent institution, 13
Phillips Academy, Institute for the Recruitment of Teachers, 202
Phillis, 40
Phoebe, 69
physicians, 112, 117; free Black, 117; papers of, 155
Piedmont, Virginia, xxii, 28, 38, 65, 69; compared with Tidewater, 25–26; demography, 25; planters, 38; settlement of, 24–25, 28
Pierce, John, 58, 73, 87, 112, 143–44, 186; and courthouse, 144–45
Pierce, Milly (Mildred), 112, 144, 186; land purchase, 144–45
Pierce family, 143–45
Pinderhughes, Dianne M., on Butler and Woodson Institute, 213
Pittsylvania County, deed book, 169
plantation manager, free Black, 74

planters, property rights, 12, 45, 47, 52–53, 58, 59, 67, 80, 82, 84, 115, 139. *See also* manumission
Pleasants, Debra, 5–7, 151
Pleasants, John, manumissions by, 47; legatees, 139
Pleasants, Mary, 50, 52, 53
Pleasants, Philip, 96, 170
Pleasants, Thomas, 96; apprentices, 96; and the Forest, 149–50; manumissions by, 7, 50, 52–53, 57
Pleasants, Thomas, Sr., 52
Pleasants, William H., 149–51; possible paternity of Bridgett Cooper's child, 150–51
Pleasants family, 52, 57, 97; estate, 149–50; manumissions, 52
Pledge, William, 39–40; estate, 40
poisoning, 40–41
Pollock, Peter, 128, 168
Pope, William, 81, 83, 85
population. *See* demography
Powhatan County, 24, 57, 109, 113, 114, 136, 139, 160, 163, 167; records, 159, 160, 163
Prince Edward County, xxiv; migration to, 167
Prince William County, free people of color reject colonization, 161
property, free Black, xx, 12, 13, 14, 15–16, 26, 35, 55, 134, 141–43; in family members, 88; horses, 48, 115; inherited by enslaved children, 137
Public Housing Association of Residents (Charlottesville), 209

Quakers (Society of Friends), xix, 6, 47; and apprentices, 96–97, 245–46n18; by deeds, 54, 58; and freedom suits, 80, 84–85, 178; manumissions, 47, 50, 51, 54, 56–58, 63, 94; Pleasants family and Coopers, 6–7
Quigg, James, 178–80, 181–82

race: boundaries, 10, 22, 23, 25, 87; exclusion, 120, 124; hierarchy (order), vii, ix, xvi, xxii, xxv, 17, 120; history of, viii; illegitimate children, 173–74; racism, 10–11, 12–13, 18, 90, 147, 219, 221; reciprocal relations, xvi, 7, 11, 103, 120, 143; scholarship on, 200–201; structural, xx, xxiii, xxiv, xxv, 7, 9, 21, 34, 39, 138; tax lists, 157–58; and work, 117–20. *See also* mixed-race people
"Race and Class in Colonial Virginia" (Deal), 19–20
Race and Place: An African American Community in the Jim Crow South (website focused on Charlottesville), 206, 214
Randolph, Archibald Cary, 58
Randolph, William, 40
Ray, Andrew (father), 168–69
Ray, Andrew (son), 169
Reginald D. Butler Local History Archive, 154
registers of free Blacks (registration papers), xxiii, 20–21, 46–49, 85, 155–56, 158, 162–67; book, 46; lists, 158, 249n4; lost and replaced, 164; nonregistration, 162–63
registration act (1793). *See* statutes
religion, and manumission, 56, 58, 61. *See also* Quakers
removal law (1806). *See* statutes
renters, 124, 132, 140, 182, 183. *See also* tenants
residence, 159–60; patterns, 124–25, 129–30, 181–82. *See also* migration
"Rethinking African-American and African Studies: New Approaches to Teaching and Research in the 21st Century" (grant), 206–7
"Rethinking African American Studies in the Digital Age" (grants), 190, 214

Richmond, 22, 26, 47, 65, 73, 85, 99, 108, 112, 113, 119, 128, 133, 153, 157, 218; district court, 85, 148; falls at, 107; fire, 148, 152, 154; jail, 164; police records, 158

rights, 128; contractual, of apprentices, 94, 99, 102–4; property, 12. *See also* natural rights

rites of passage, 130, 186

Rivanna district, 185

Rivanna River, 169

Roark, James L., xxi; on William Ellison's racial identity, 16–17; on free Black "freedom," 10

Robin, 46–47

Robinson, Armstead L. (founding director of Woodson Institute), 193, 196–99, 212, 213; death, 197, 213; on Foster homesite, 196

Robinson, Samuel, 181–82

Robin v. Hardaway (1772), 175

Rochelle salts, 180

Rollins, Sonny, 221

Rorabaugh, W. J., on craft apprenticeship, 90, 95

Rosengarten, Theodore, xiii

Ross, David, 98

Rothman, Joshua D.: essay by, vii–viii, xv–xxvii; on "new social history," xxi, 187; on racial categories, 158

Rotunda Dome Room, University of Virginia, 208

Rufus W. Holsinger Studio Collection and Digital Image Database, 201–2

Russell, John, freedom suit, 81, 174, 175

Russell, John H., xxi, 78; on legal framework of free Black life, 12; pioneering scholarship, xix

Russell, Nann, 175

Rutman, Anita H., xxi

Rutman, Darrett B., xxi

Sachs, Honor, on *Robin v. Hardaway* (1772), 175

Saint Augustine's University, 204

Saint-Domingue, revolution in, 44, 64

Saint James Northam Parish, 31, 128, 173

Salvador da Bahia, Brazil, 190, 211

Sam, 46–47

Sampson, Franky Cross, 86

Sampson, Jacob, 72–73, 86–87, 109, 144–45

Sarah (emancipated by Mary Pleasants Younghusband), 57

Sarah (mother of Jack Hatcher), 175

Saunders, Robert, 99

schools for free Blacks, 64, 179–80

Schwarz, Phillip J., on free Black slave ownership, 88–89

Schweninger, Loren, on free Black property, 15–16

Scot, Abbie, 35

Scott, Christopher, 182, 183

Scott, Eliza (Betty), 183

Scott, Elizabeth, 35

Scott (Mealy), Frankey, 182

Scott, James, 181

Scott, John (Freeman), 101

Scott, Joshua, 182, 183

Scott, Josiah (Freeman), 101

Scott, Judith, 101

Scott, Judith (mother or sister-in-law of Judith Scott), 101

Scott, Peggy, 182

Scott, Robert (father), 180–81, 183

Scott, Robert (son), 181

Scott, Stephen, 35

Scott, William: apprenticeship, 178–81; dialogue with Samuel Cosby, 179; family, 178–84; health, 180; native identity, 182; registered, 182; schooling, 179–80; as security, 182; suit, 178–81, 183, 186–87

Scott family, 28, 51

Scruggs, Finch, 163

Seattle, xii
security (surety), standing for, 1, 40, 111, 121, 131–32, 137, 140, 173, 182; and marriage, 130–32, 140, 182
segregation, culture of, 190
self-emancipation, 85–87
servants, white, 30; distinguished from apprentices, 93; female, and race-mixing, 33, 93
Shelton, William, 118; estate, 118
sheriff, 22, 23, 122, 133, 191
Shoemaker, Holman, 114
Shoemaker, Judith, estate, 55
shoemakers, 106, 112, 113, 116, 117, 163
Shore, Melissa, 210
Sims, Patsy, 182
slaveowners, free Black, 16–17, 72
Slaves without Masters: The Free Negro in the Antebellum South (Berlin), xx–xxi, 14–15
slave trade: British, 212; domestic, xxvi; Portuguese, 21; trans-Atlantic, 207
Small, Clara, 204
Smith, Granville, 106, 118
Smith, Mary, 40–41
Smith, Noel, 182
Smith, Obadiah, 40–41
Smith, Robert, 180
Smith, William, 5–6, 81–82
Smithsonian Institution. *See* Museum of American History, Smithsonian Institution
Sobel, Mechal, xviii; on planter "inconsistencies," 32; on white-Black interactions, 4
social history, xiii, xxi, xxiv, 12, 19, 21–22, 184–88
soldiers, 128. *See also* Continental Army, U.S.
Sophia, 57
Souls of Black Folk, The (Du Bois), 218
South, American, viii, xvii, xix, xxv, xxvi, 11, 14, 15, 18, 19, 88, 116, 211

Southampton Rebellion (1832), xxvi, 13, 160
South Carolina, xxi, 16, 18, 88
South Lawn project (UVa), 196
Southside, 69
space, domestic, 4
spinners. *See* weavers
Sprouse, Charles, 173
St. Ann's Parish, Albemarle, 157, 161, 162
Stanton, Lucia (Cinder) (co-founder of Central Virginia Social History Project), 197–98
Starke, Willmouth, 175
Stateburg, South Carolina, 16–17
status of free Blacks, xix, xxv, xxvi, 9, 17–18; boundaries, 47; legal and customary, 20–22
statutes: on apprenticeship, 91–92, 93, 103; colonization of free people of color, 159, 160–61; on free Blacks, 37, 87, 159; on freedom suits, 80; legalizing Indian slavery, 176; local court jurisdiction over exemptions to 1806 act, 73; on manumission, 27–28, 37, 42, 43–45, 50, 51, 52, 53, 55, 84, 94, 135; manumission restricted, xv, 45, 56, 61–70, 71–72, 77–79, 88; overseers to compile lists of orphans, 170; on race-mixing, 30, 93; reduced terms for servants, except mixed-race, 93; registration act, 20–21, 44, 46; slave code (1705), 30, 31, 40, 176
Stepney, Little, 118
Steve Biko Cultural Institute, 211
Student Non-Violent Coordinating Committee, 215
Sublett, Peter, 113, 135
sulfur, 180
superior court (Virginia), 48, 79
Symes, Martha, 77–79

tailor, 119
Tamer, 38, 126

tavern: license, 109; owners, 72, 86–87, 124, 144–45
taxes, 115, 121–22, 123; on enslaved property, 138; higher on free Blacks, 158, 260n28; on horses, 115; insolvency, 122–23, 132; land (1815), 181; lists, xxiii, 97, 101, 106, 122, 129, 138, 152, 155, 156–58, 159, 160, 182, 249n5; personal property, 158; records, xxiii, 95, 97, 106, 114
Tempy, 61–63
tenants, 107, 115, 123–24n132, 160; bridge to land ownership, 123
Tennessee, free Blacks in, 9
Tete-Katchan, Samuel, 212
Texas, 11
Thacker, Mary, 173
"thick description," 186
Thomas, William G., III, 203
Thomas Jefferson Foundation (Monticello), 198, 204
Thompson, Steve, 175
Three Chopt Road, 86
Tidewater, xxii, 28, 69; compared with Piedmont, 24–26; planters from, 38
tithes, 38, 39, 126, 155, 156, 185; lists, 39, 97, 135, 152, 155, 156
tobacco cultivation, 24, 25, 40, 108, 109, 111, 112, 160, 173
Tom (emancipated by Joseph Cross), 69
Tom (son of Doll), 30
Towler, Japheth, 100
Trouillot, Rolphe-Michelle, xi
Tuckahoe Creek, 23, 107
Turner, Nat, and Southampton Rebellion, xxvi, 13, 160, 190
Turner, Thomas, 175
Turner, Victor, 186
Tyler, Biddy Ann, 130
Tyler, Francis, 131
Tyler, George, 4, 134
Tyler, James, 114

Tyler, Polly Banks, 130
Tyler family, 131

Underwood, Sheriff John, 123
Union Mills, 160
University of Iowa, 213
University of Rochester, 193
University of Virginia (UVa), vii–ix, 158; African American and African Studies (AAAS), 190, 194, 199, 205, 211; Afro-American (Black) Studies (AAS), 193–95, 199, 207, 210, 213; Board of Visitors, 193; College of Arts and Sciences Faculty, 193; digital resources, 200–201; Emerging Scholars Program, 202–3; History Department, 193, 194, 202–3, 216; Holsinger Exhibit, 201–2; Institute for Advanced Technology in the Humanities, 154; relations with Black community, 196; Venable Lane Task Force, 196; Virginia Center for Digital History (VCDH), 205–6; and Woodson Institute, 213–14. *See also* Carter G. Woodson Institute for African-American and African Studies
"Unknown No Longer" project (Virginia Museum), 154
Utley, Daniel, 113, 115
UVA Today (Charlottesville), 214

"Valley of the Shadow, The: Two Communities in the American Civil War" (Ayers), 206
Vancouver, British Columbia, 219
Vaughn, Dr., 112, 117
Venable Lane, Charlottesville, 195
Venable Lane Task Force (1993–95), 195–97
Vernon, Robert, 214; and Central Virginia Social History Project, 198; essay by, viii, 147–88; work with Butler, xvii
vestry, and apprentices, 171, 173, 178; records, 168, 174

Via, Benjamin, indentures, 168–69
Via, Mary, 168
Vinegar Hill Project, 209–10; digitization of records, 209–10; "Vinegar Hill Memoryscape," 210
Virginia Center for Digital History (VCDH), 205–6; building networks of scholars at HBCUs, 205–6; Vinegar Hill Project, 210
Virginia Company of London, 91
Virginia Foundation for the Humanities (VFH), 201
Virginia General Assembly, xv, xix, 9, 20, 56, 71, 85, 105, 179; resolution honoring Butler (2020), 215–16; ruling on Moses Cross property (1831), 86. *See also* petitions; statutes
Virginia General Court, records, 154
Virginia Historical Society, 192
Virginia House of Delegates, 160, 216. *See* statutes
Virginia Museum of History and Culture, "Unknown No Longer" project, 154
Virginia Open Data Portal, 166, 167
Virginia State Library. *See* Library of Virginia
Virginia Union University, 204
"Virginia Untold: The African American Narrative" (Library of Virginia), 154, 163–66, 178
VisualEyes, 210
von Daacke, Kirt, ix, xxv; on Butler's achievement at Woodson Institute, 214
Voting Rights Act (1965), 219

Wade, Dabney, 129
wagoners, 65, 108, 133, 137, 163
Walker, Corey D. B., 208–9, 210
Walker, Emanuel, 83
washerwoman, 162
Washington (state), 215
Washington Park, Charlottesville, 202
Washington Post, 197

watermen, 98, 107, 108; difference from boatmen, 107
Watkins, Benjamin, 50
weavers, 96, 98, 105–6, 114, 117, 118, 129, 144
Webber, John, 55
Webber, Martha, 55
Webber, William, 51
Weil, François, 208–9
Welch, Eleanor, 174
Welch, George, 174
Welch, Hannah, 174
Welch, Joseph, 174
well-diggers, 116
Western Washington University (State College), 193, 215, 219, 220
West Philadelphia, 215
wheat, 40, 110–11, 112, 113, 114
wheelwrights, 108, 116, 160
whiskey, and labor, 115–16
Whitehurst, Arthur, 162
white mothers of mixed-race children, 28
whiteness, 10
whites, relations with free Blacks, 3, 4, 9–10, 12, 16, 18, 22, 27, 32, 37–39, 40–42, 48–49, 56, 69, 71, 73, 76, 80, 105, 111, 115–17, 119–20, 131–32, 134, 140–44, 149, 156, 167, 191
William, 86
Williams, Luann, 209
Williams, William, 121
Williamsburg, 218
William Scott, assee. v. James Quigg (1801), 178
Williamson, Joel: on free Blacks as "new people," 10; on miscegenation, 34
wills. *See* Goochland County, records
Woodly, Deva, 202
Woodson, Carter G., xix, 207; on benevolent Black slave ownership, 87–88
Woodson Institute. *See* Carter G. Woodson Institute for African-American and African Studies

work, 105–22; and community interactions, 106; competition between white and Black labor, 119–20; gendered, 129; racially stigmatized, 116–17, 119; and registration, 163; remuneration for whites and Blacks, 117–20; for women, 105–6

World They Made Together, The (Sobel), xviii

Yale University, Black Studies, 193
Younghusband, Mary Pleasants, 50

Zwelling, Shomer, recollection of Butler, 217–19

Recent books in the
CARTER G. WOODSON INSTITUTE SERIES

Roses in December: Black Life in Hanover County from Civil War to Civil Rights
Jody Lynn Allen

The Struggle for Change: Race and the Politics of Reconciliation in Modern Richmond
Marvin T. Chiles

A Little Child Shall Lead Them: A Documentary Account of the Struggle for School Desegregation in Prince Edward County, Virginia
Brian J. Daugherity and Brian Grogan, editors

We Face the Dawn: Oliver Hill, Spottswood Robinson, and the Legal Team That Dismantled Jim Crow
Margaret Edds

Keep On Keeping On: The NAACP and the Implementation of Brown v. Board of Education *in Virginia*
Brian J. Daugherity

Schooling Jim Crow: The Fight for Atlanta's Booker T. Washington High School and the Roots of Black Protest Politics
Jay Winston Driskell Jr.

The Punitive Turn: New Approaches to Race and Incarceration
Deborah E. McDowell, Claudrena N. Harold, and Juan Battle, editors

Freedom Has a Face: Race, Identity, and Community in Jefferson's Virginia
Kirt von Daacke

Gabriel's Conspiracy: A Documentary History
Philip J. Schwarz, editor

www.ingramcontent.com/pod-product-compliance
Lightning Source LLC
Chambersburg PA
CBHW021648230426
43668CB00008B/555